# THE CONSUMPTION OF JUSTICE

# THE CONSUMPTION OF JUSTICE

EMOTIONS, PUBLICITY,

AND LEGAL CULTURE

IN MARSEILLE,

1264–1423

DANIEL LORD SMAIL

*Cornell University Press*

*Ithaca and London*

First published 2003 by Cornell University Press

Printed in the United States of America

Library of Congress Cataloging-in-Publication Data

Smail, Daniel Lord.
  The consumption of justice : emotions, publicity, and legal culture in Marseille, 1264–1423 / Daniel Lord Smail.
      p. cm. — (Conjunctions of religion & power in the medieval past)
Includes bibliographical references and index.
  ISBN 0-8014-4105-6 (cloth : alk. paper)
1. Justice, Administration of—France—Marseille—History. 2. Marseille (France)—Social life and customs. I. Title. II. Series.
  KJW7693.37.S525 2003
  340.5'6'0944912—dc21
                    2003010112

Cornell University Press strives to use environmentally responsible suppliers and materials to the fullest extent possible in the publishing of its books. Such materials include vegetable-based, low-VOC inks and acid-free papers that are recycled, totally chlorine-free, or partly composed of nonwood fibers. For further information, visit our website at www.cornellpress.cornell.edu.

Cloth printing          10 9 8 7 6 5 4 3 2 1

# CONTENTS

# TABLES

# ACKNOWLEDGMENTS

Lawsuits are much the same the world over: underneath the tedious procedures, masked by the legal form demanded by the law, lie enmity, spite, aggravation, and the desire to avenge. Reading lawsuits leaves one with a rather jaundiced view of humankind. This opportunity to acknowledge all the assistance that made this book possible, therefore, is a happy occasion to reflect on the fact that the law and its emotions represents just a small part of what we are and what we do. Certainly scholarship would not be possible without the generosity of family, friends, colleagues, and institutions.

Fellowships awarded by the American Council of Learned Societies and the National Endowment for the Humanities made research for this book possible in more ways than one. It is important to have sabbaticals and salary support, but even more gratifying to know that others are interested in one's work and want to see the results. It is a pleasure to convey my enormous appreciation to both institutions. I am likewise indebted to Fordham University and to the Ames Fund of the Graduate School of Arts and Sciences for fellowships, grants, and leaves of absences and gratefully acknowledge the support of the deans and of my colleagues in the Department of History. In France, it has always been a pleasure to return to the Archives Départementales des Bouches-du-Rhône and the Archives Municipales de la Ville de Marseille, and I thank the staff of both of these archives for their assistance during a decade of research. Laure Verdon of the Université de Provence has provided much assistance on this and other projects, and I would also like to thank her colleagues Anne Mailloux and Jean-Paul Boyer for their invitation to a conference that helped crystallize some of the arguments in this book. M. Noël Coulet has been a constant presence to those of us who work on the history of Provence, and it was his encouragement that got me started on the little-used archival series on which this book is based. The invitation from Mme Claude Gauvard to present some of the early stages of this research to her seminar and her continuing patronage have had a profound impact on this book, and her intellectual contributions will be evident throughout. Chris Wickham was and remains a source of great inspiration and has provided much helpful criticism on elements of the larger project of which this book is a part. An invitation from Isabel Alfonso gave me a chance to develop an initial version of the arguments that appear in chapter 5, and I thank her and her colleagues at the Consejo Superior de Investigaciones Científicas in Madrid for a truly memorable visit. Peter Schuster and Professor Neithard Bulst invited me to a conference in Biele-feld, Germany, that was instrumental in shaping several key arguments. I also gratefully acknowledge the advice and suggestions give me over the years by, among others, Steven Bednarski, Howard Brown, Charles Bur-roughs, John Drendel, Samantha Kelly, Maryanne Kowaleski, Christian Maurel, Bill Miller, Josée Murat, and Susanne Pohl.

Elements of the larger research project to which this book belongs have been published as articles and book chapters. Certain portions of chapter 2 of this book originally appeared in "Hatred as a Social Institution in Late-Medieval Society," *Speculum: A Journal of Medieval Studies* 76 (2001): 90–126. Portions of chapter 5 were published as "Los archivos de conocimiento y la cultura legal de la publicidad en la Marsella medieval," *Hispania: Revista Es-pañola de Historia* 57 (1997): 1049–77. This article was an element of a *Sección Monográfica* entitled "Desarrollo legal, prácticas judiciales y acción política en la Europa medieval," coordinated by Isabel Alfonso. I gratefully ac-knowledge permission to republish material from both these articles. Among the many who contributed thoughts and advice on my earlier publi-cations I would like to single out Tom Kuehn, who, perhaps more than any-one, has shown why social history needs legal history (and vice versa). Tom Green, likewise, deserves a special note of thanks for getting me started on the path of legal history and for commenting on early research proposals.

Susan Reynolds read and provided immensely helpful criticisms on the first half of the book as well as the appendix. In responding to her comments I found myself reworking a number of key passages, and although faults un-doubtedly remain the book is much better for having passed under her gaze. Barbara Rosenwein, as series editor and tireless reader, has made a profound difference on this book both intellectually and stylistically, and I have much to thank her for. Stephen D. White also read the entire manuscript and, with characteristic acuity, pointed out failings and logical flaws that I subse-quently wrestled with while revising the manuscript. All three have made this a better book. It has always been a pleasure to share ideas with John Ackerman of Cornell University Press and his encouragement over the years has meant a great deal to me.

Laura L. Smail knows just how much she has contributed to the style and usage of this book, both as a mother and as an editor; beyond that, it is a joy to know someone who is always interested in just about everything. This goes for Kathleen as well, as it does for our children, Benedict, Irene, and Gregory, all three of whom have talents and interests that continually amaze and delight their parents. They readily forgave my absences while researching and writing this book, and always seemed to enjoy having me back. It is a wonderful family to come back to.

# ABBREVIATIONS

| | |
|---|---|
| ADBR | Archives Départementales des Bouches-du-Rhône |
| AM | Archives Municipales de la Ville de Marseille |
| Durand, *Speculum iudicale* | Guillaume Durand, *Speculum iudicale*, 2 vols. Basel, 1574; reprint ed., Aalen, Germany: Scientia Verlag, 1975. |
| Mabilly, *Inventaire* | Département des Bouches-du-Rhône. Ville de Marseille. *Inventaire Sommaire des Archives Communales Antérieures à 1790*. Série BB. Vol. 1. Marseille, 1909. |
| Pernoud, *Statuts* | Régine Pernoud, ed. *Les statuts municipaux de Marseille*. Monaco: Imprimerie de Monaco, 1949. |
| Tancred, *Ordo* | Tancred, *Ordo iudiciarius*. In *Pilii, Tancredi, Gratiae, Libri de iudiciorum ordine*, ed. Friedrich Christian Bergmann. Gottingen, 1842. |

# A NOTE ON USAGE

The vernacular language of late medieval Marseille was a form of Provençal that incorporated a number of loan words from Latin and French. Latin was the most common language of record, though notaries of the court sometimes chose to leave insults and certain phrases in witness testimony in the vernacular. Wherever possible, I have translated names from Latin into their Provençal equivalent. Thus, a man known as *Johannes* in Latin records and as *Jean* in modern French was known as *Johan* in Marseille, the form I have used throughout this book. Surnames are more diverse than forenames, and there are some surnames for which I have been unable to find a Provençal equivalent; these I have left in Latin. Married women normally took their husbands' surnames though in a feminized form, and I have followed this convention in naming women. To take an example, a woman named Johana who was married to a man with the surname Robaut will appear as Johana Robauda in this book.

All dates in this book are given in the new style, with the new year beginning on 1 January rather than 25 March. Thus, a case whose date is given in this book as "20 March 1343" will be dated "20 March 1342" in the record.

For reasons discussed in the appendix, judicial registers were rarely paginated, and the material nature of the record makes it difficult to note the folio of a quotation or passage with much accuracy. The notaries' habit of sewing elements of the record into the register, often sheets or quires of paper with very different trim sizes, means that there can be no modern consensus about the foliation of a given register. Dates are not particularly helpful either, for although registers consist of a series of cases usually ordered by the date of initiation, the cases themselves internally proceed in rough (though not exact) chronological order. As a result, references to a given date will occur at various intervals throughout a given register. Dates are especially unhelpful in appellate cases, for the record of a given appeal includes transcripts of prior cases and therefore jumps around in time a great deal. For these reasons, the citation style consists of the foliation and date on which a given case was initiated along with the folio on which the specific reference appears. Thus, to find folio 118r in the following reference—ADBR 3B 861, fol. 118r, case opened 5 May 1408 on fol. 69r—one should flip through register 3B 861 until one finds a case initiated on 5 May 1408 that is on or near fol. 69r. Counting approximately forty-nine more folios will then get the reader in the vicinity of what I call folio 118r. The problem arising from the almost inevitable divergence in opinion about foliation is somewhat lessened by counting folios from the beginning of the trial itself.

In early fourteenth-century Marseille, the standard unit of currency was the royal pound, at twenty shillings per pound and twelve pennies per shilling (see Henri Rolland, *Monnaies des comtes de Provence, XIIe–XVe s. Histoire monétaire, économique, corporative. Description raisonnée* [Paris, 1956]). Most sums were expressed in this currency, though the florin was infiltrating the local economy by the mid to late fourteenth century. The value of the florin was nominally fixed at thirty-two shillings though notarial records note that the exchange rate fluctuated considerably over the course of the century. In the places where I have made arguments based on the cost of litigation I have not tried to adjust either for this fluctuating exchange rate or for inflation: references in the sources themselves are generally too spotty and uncertain to warrant such care. Other coins, such as silver marks, were also in circulation.

# THE CONSUMPTION OF JUSTICE

# INTRODUCTION

Come to terms with thy opponent quickly while thou art with him on the way; lest thy opponent deliver thee to the judge, and the judge to the officer, and thou be cast into prison. Amen I say to thee, thou wilt not come out from it until thou hast paid the last penny.

—Matt. 5:25–26

Lawsuits are types of enmities.

—Leon Battista Alberti, *De iciarchia*

Troubles began for the shoemaker Antoni d'Ays in the early 1330s when his wife, Douselina, left him and left Marseille too.[1] Several years after her departure, at Antoni's prompting, the judge of the palace court wrote a stern letter ordering her to return to her husband. She, or someone writing on her behalf, impertinently scribbled a refusal on the back of the letter and returned it to the judge, declaring that she wished to have nothing further to do with that man. With his wife gone, Antoni's possibly sexual relationship with his maid, Dousa, developed into a cozy domestic one. The situation was not wholly irregular: as the shoemaker would later argue, it was normal for any man without a wife to keep a maid or concubine to do his work. He called on several witnesses to corroborate this claim—they seemed surprised that it was necessary to do so. Surely Antoni was not the only single man employing the services of a maid in mid-fourteenth-century Marseille. But trouble was brewing nonetheless, for Dousa, the maid, was not well liked by her neighbors. She was said to be quarrelsome, equally loose in

---

[1] For the case of Antoni d'Ays see ADBR 3B 41, fols. 164r–187v, case opened 16 Aug. 1340. The epigraph is taken from Leon Battista Alberti, *De iciarchia*, in *Opere volgari*, ed. Cecil Grayson (Bari, 1966), 2:254, cited in Thomas Kuehn, *Law, Family, and Women: Toward a Legal Anthropology of Renaissance Italy* (Chicago, 1991), 71.

tongue and body. People whispered behind her back. She had, in short, developed bad *fama*.

Antoni d'Ays was a relatively inconspicuous artisan who lived on Negrel street, at the heart of the largest of Marseille's four shoemaker districts, in the decades before the Black Death. He appears only once in notarial contracts from the mid-fourteenth century, a sign of his relative lack of community standing. For all that, he was relatively skilled at law and, when it came time to assemble a group of supportive witnesses, proved himself to be well connected to shoemakers and other artisans in the leather trades. Even so, we would know little about his life and travails were it not for the noisy lawsuit lodged against him in August 1340. The suit was initiated by a respectable married man named Guilhem de Podio, also a shoemaker, also a resident of Negrel street, also skilled at law, willing to spend a great deal of money in an effort to purge the neighborhood of those he considered a threat to its morals and good name. Joining Guilhem were his sons Raolet and Huguet and, with them, a neighbor named Gilet Alfans, all shoemakers. The suit was the culminating episode in a messy dispute that spread out over at least five years, roiled the shoemaker community, and drew the attention of several courts and officials, eventually making its way to the seneschal of Provence. Though the dispute generated a good deal of paperwork in its various official incarnations, only the record of the 1340 lawsuit has survived. By virtue of its rich set of arguments and witness depositions, this record contains a more or less complete history of the affair, an affair that in turn provides insights into how and why people used the courts in late medieval Europe.

Court actions began around 1335, a year or two after Douselina's departure, when Paul Fabri, a resident of Negrel street and a jurist (*iurisperitus*), went to the episcopal court and accused Antoni or perhaps Dousa of some unspecified delict. The accusation was probably one of selling Dousa's sexual favors to friends and colleagues: at one point in the later trial Antoni was called a pimp and Dousa a prostitute. The good folk of Negrel street were especially thin-skinned when it came to illicit sex, for the imagined boundaries of the quarter to which the city's prostitutes were nominally confined, located just a block or two north of Negrel street, often proved to be quite porous. Whatever the accusation, Antoni managed to beat back the charge. But the animosity was there and grew over the next several years. Guilhem de Podio took up the case: in 1339, he went before the city's leading officials, namely the *viguier*, Rostahn Gautelm, direct representative of the Angevin crown in the city of Marseille, and the palace judge, Peire Dalmas, and acquired an eviction notice. Antoni was not one to take things lying down, and in a series of careful moves he laid the groundwork for his subsequent defense. Matters came to a head in August 1340, when Antoni went before

Bulgarin de Tiboldis, the new palace judge in a position that rotated yearly, and asked, once again, that the court force Douselina to return to him. That the court was powerless to enforce such an order, whatever its will in the matter, was beside the point: by proving his bona fides, Antoni hoped to illustrate that Dousa was a stop-gap measure in his domestic arrangements. Guilhem de Podio and his allies immediately lodged a suit against Dousa on the grounds that she was cohabiting illicitly with Antoni: at one point they cited the statute titled "On Woman's Lust" (*De libidine mulieris*). What they sought was her eviction from the "good street" (*bona carreria*) of Negrel. During the course of the trial, a group of witnesses testified in flowery and repetitive detail to Dousa's misdeeds. Antoni then mounted a spirited defense: Douselina had left him and refused to return; every man is allowed to keep a maid or concubine as long as he doesn't prostitute her, and he certainly never did *that*; all the neighbors used to accept Dousa, and even accorded her the respectful salutation *domina Dousa*, "mistress Dousa," and shared fruit with her in a friendly way; they have launched this suit now only to pursue a budding enmity against Antoni; they have illicitly solicited contributions from members of the shoemaker confraternity to defray the costs of litigation; all this is commonly known among the neighbors of Negrel street; and so on. All in vain. As the trial dragged into its second month, Antoni's opponents went behind the judge's back and acquired a letter from the seneschal of Provence ordering the judge to uphold prior eviction notices issued by the viguier. It was a dramatic moment: the palace judge declared himself incompetent to overrule a higher authority, and the trial came to an abrupt end. Antoni immediately appealed, but the appeal, if pursued, has not survived. In 1341, Antoni made his only appearance as a witness to a notarial contract and then disappeared for good from the historical record. Dousa, his maid, vanished without a trace, having never even made an appearance at court. Guilhem de Podio, a rather more substantial figure, was before the court once again in 1344, this time suing a creditor-adversary, the merchant Isnart de Montesecuro, on the grounds that he unjustly ordered the seizure of Guilhem's goods to repay a small overdue debt.[2] His litigating career, however, had drawn to a close by 1348, for he was dead by the time of his daughter's remarriage in April.[3] It is just possible that Antoni was around to see his old adversary die a victim of the Black Death.

Marseille in the fourteenth and fifteenth centuries was a commercial center of international significance and a prize possession of the Angevin kings

[2] ADBR 3B 45, fol. 226r–v, case opened 1 June 1344.
[3] The dowry act for Ugueta de Podio, AM 1 II 61, fol. 12r–v, 14 Apr. 1348, identifies her father as deceased.

and queens of Naples. The leading port on the Provençal coastline east of the Rhone, the city, along with its periurban enclaves, was home to some twenty-five thousand men, women, and children around 1300. Marseille's modern-day archives are among the richest in France: the case of Antoni d'Ays is but one of several thousand cases of civil litigation and judicial appeal extant from the fourteenth and fifteenth centuries. In the course of my research for this book I have read about a thousand of these. To judge by the quantity of sealing wax that crumbled off as I turned the pages, many of the registers containing these cases have not been consulted for 650 years. Not all, admittedly, are as lively or as long as the case of Antoni d'Ays, though many come close and several surpass it. About one in six contain the depositions of witnesses, those extraordinary moments when the dry facts of a case are suddenly transformed and one feels, if only for a moment, the bizarre sensation of seeing the world through the eyes of someone long dead. Reading cases such as these, one is forcefully reminded why the history of justice in late medieval Europe cannot be written from the perspective of procedural manuals, juristic commentaries, anecdotal observations, or even case summaries alone. Case records are punishing sources: often fragmentary, difficult to get at, hard to read. But cases complement the learned sources nicely, for they offer the perspective not of those who designed the courts but of those who used them, the consumers of the law who invested both financially and emotionally in the procedural apparatus of late medieval justice.

It is easy to understand why kings, princes, and communes chose to invest in courts of law—this was a key element of the state-building process. But our histories of law and justice in medieval Europe, written largely from the perspective of rulers, rarely pause to consider why individuals such as Guilhem de Podio chose to invest in courts of law or what they hoped to get out of litigation. The amount of money spent annually on litigation was immense, far outstripping the annual revenues generated for the Angevin crown by the operations of Marseille's civil and criminal courts. This casts doubt on the assumption that rulers alone were responsible for the rise of law in late medieval Europe. Though the costs of litigation varied wildly from case to case, Guilhem de Podio and his allies may have spent as much as forty pounds in their efforts to evict Dousa from Negrel street. Theirs was but one of some one hundred and thirty to two hundred suits generated per year, not to mention the roughly eight hundred simple requests to enforce a debt that creditors requested on an annual basis. Forty royal pounds was a lot of money, roughly equivalent to the cost of a modest dowry or a house, about twice the annual wages of a baker's assistant or an agricultural laborer. From another perspective, forty pounds was roughly equivalent to the fine that Guilhem could expect to pay to the crown had he chosen to kill either Antoni or Dousa—though peacemaking efforts with their kin, a strict necessity if he wished to avoid retribution, would have cost an additional sum.

So why did ordinary people such as Guilhem and his allies choose to invest in law courts? This question, curiously, has rarely been addressed at length in histories of law in medieval Europe, most of which focus instead on the interests and desires of kings, princes, and jurists. Given this focus, arguments about consumer interest do not often surface as forcefully argued positions. They circulate instead in the form of unstated assumptions and, for that reason, resist easy analysis. Three assumptions, as I see it, are particularly influential, and at the risk of oversimplification I will characterize them in the following way. First, centralized criminal courts with the means and procedures for prosecuting crime offered more personal security in a world of unpredictable violence. Ordinary people were only too happy to exchange a little freedom of action for the prospect of peace, and thus willingly participated in the criminal law system through raising the hue and cry, denouncing criminals to the court, and so on. Second, users of the courts were attracted by the superior rationality offered by the new law and its experts and appreciated a system that worked according to logical and predictable rules. Finally, the state's growing monopoly on violence was, by the later middle ages, slowly encouraging people such as Guilhem to abandon violence in favor of law. Levelheaded people learned to pursue their disputes decorously in courts, and only the hotheads clung to violence.

All three arguments have points in their favor. But do they really help explain why individuals such as Guilhem de Podio invested as much as they did in the law?

The argument that citizens tend to prefer the safety offered by muscular criminal courts and security agents has a long pedigree in Western political thought.[4] Though undoubtedly true on some level, the formula masks a good deal of complexity. Historians of crime and repression in early modern France, for example, have argued that village communities in many regions preferred to regulate themselves and kept agents of the state at arm's length.[5] Members of criminal juries in later medieval England showed themselves surprisingly unwilling to punish homicide capitally, despite the

[4] See Paul Hyams's discussion of this subject in "Due Process versus the Maintenance of Order in European Law: The Contribution of the *Ius Commune*," in *The Moral World of the Law*, ed. Peter Coss (Cambridge, 2000), 62–90, here 76–78.

[5] An argument associated with Nicole Castan, *Justice et répression en Languedoc à l'époque des Lumières* (Paris, 1980), and others. The literature is summarized in Howard G. Brown, "From Organic Society to Security State: The War on Brigandage in France, 1797–1802," *Journal of Modern History* 69 (1997): 661–95, here 662–64.

strictures of the English common law.[6] In a similar vein, the behavior of men and women in later medieval Marseille reveals a real ambivalence toward the local constabulary and its supposed monopoly on legitimate violence. Those present at the scene of violent altercations often did not wait for the arrival of the police but intervened personally to stop the fight. As the police drew near, bystanders helped assailants flee to sanctuary in local churches, encouraging their efforts to evade arrest and imprisonment. Interpreting such behavior, my inclination is to believe that communities in the later middle ages stood solidly behind the criminal courts when it came to prosecuting vagabonds or other enemies of the peace but were often uneasy about the potentially dangerous consequences of prosecuting respectable citizens. People were all too aware of the problems that could arise when someone made use of the criminal court to denounce an enemy for less than legitimate reasons.

Arguments to the effect that users of the courts in the twelfth century preferred the superior rationality of Roman-canon procedural law have figured prominently in some histories of medieval justice.[7] "The evolution of judicial procedure in the eleventh and twelfth centuries can be described as the replacement of irrational methods of proof by rational procedures," remarked Kenneth Pennington in 1993, though he immediately qualified the stark character of this observation.[8] Raoul Van Caenegem explicitly links the rationalization of justice to choice on the part of the users of the courts:

> Other sections of society were likewise turning their backs on the old modes of evidence, even before the theologians did. Townspeople had shown their aversion by obtaining privileges of exemption, and rulers had made declarations and issued charters and decrees that left their

---

[6] Thomas A. Green, *Verdict according to Conscience: Perspectives on the English Criminal Trial Jury, 1200–1800* (Chicago, 1985). John Hudson speaks of "resistance" to the extension of royal criminal justice; see *The Formation of the English Common Law: Law and Society in England from the Norman Conquest to Magna Carta* (London, 1996), 181–82.

[7] The literature on the rise of Roman law in western Europe is dauntingly large. Useful overviews include Brian Tierney, "Medieval Canon Law and Western Constitutionalism," *Catholic Historical Review* 52 (1966): 1–17; Stephen Kuttner, "The Revival of Jurisprudence," in *Renaissance and Renewal in the Twelfth Century*, ed. R. L. Benson and Giles Constable (Cambridge, Mass., 1982), 299–323; Harold Joseph Berman, *Law and Revolution: The Formation of the Western Legal Tradition* (Cambridge, Mass., 1983); Charles M. Radding, *The Origins of Medieval Jurisprudence: Pavia and Bologna, 850–1150* (New Haven, 1988); Manlio Bellomo, *The Common Legal Past of Europe, 1000–1800*, trans. Lydia G. Cochrane (Washington, D.C., 1995).

[8] Kenneth Pennington, *The Prince and the Law, 1200–1600: Sovereignty and Rights in the Western Legal Tradition* (Berkeley, 1993), 132.

distrust of the old methods of inquiry, and preference for more reliable ones, in no doubt.[9]

Prior forms of justice are characterized as having the potential to be "capricious and serendipitous," "arbitrary, even irresponsible," "the haphazard way of doing justice," in comparison with the *ordo iudiciarius* or the procedures developed in the English common law.[10]

This argument is very dubious from a late medieval perspective. By the fourteenth century, complaints about the patent unfairness of the now-established legal process had become commonplace, at least from those who counted themselves among its victims.[11] Roman-canon procedural law empowered Roman-canon lawyers, whose ability to undermine simple equity drew complaints even in the twelfth century. But the argument has been challenged on its own turf by a number of early medieval historians using case evidence. Anglo-Saxon, Carolingian, and early medieval Italian courts of law normally favored witness testimony, relied heavily on written instruments in adjudicating property disputes, and followed a defined set of formal procedures.[12] What all this work shows is that users of the law in early medieval Europe had a satisfactory and rational judicial system before the twelfth century, throwing into doubt Pennington's admittedly subtle and nuanced defense of the idea that some users of twelfth-century courts (he

[9] R. C. Van Caenegem, "Law and Power in Twelfth-Century Flanders," in *Cultures of Power: Lordship, Status, and Process in Twelfth-Century Europe*, ed. Thomas N. Bisson (Philadelphia, 1995), 149–71, here 157. This article reprises arguments first made in the author's important 1965 synthesis, "La preuve dans le droit du Moyen Âge Occidental," in *La preuve*, part 2, *Moyen Âge et temps modernes*, vol. 17 in Recueils de la Société Jean Bodin pour l'histoire comparative des institutions (Brussels, 1965), 691–753, trans. in idem, *Legal History: A European Perspective* (London, 1991), 71–113. See also Pennington, *Prince and the Law*, 135: "Hyams believes, rightly I think, that laymen . . . were largely unhappy with the ordeal as a procedure long before the Lateran Council. He would argue that laymen voted against the ordeal with their feet." Pennington, here, is referring to Paul R. Hyams, "Feud in Medieval England," *Haskins Society Journal: Studies in Medieval History* 3 (1991): 1–21.

[10] Pennington, *Prince and the Law*, 140; Van Caenegem, *Legal History*, 63.

[11] The storm of protest accompanying the introduction of Roman law into Germany in the sixteenth century provides a case in point; see Gerald Strauss, *Law, Resistance, and the State: The Opposition to Roman Law in Reformation Germany* (Princeton, 1986).

[12] Wendy Davies and Paul Fouracre, eds., *The Settlement of Disputes in Early Medieval Europe* (Cambridge, 1986); Patrick Wormald, *The Making of English Law: King Alfred to the Twelfth Century*, vol. 1, *Legislation and Its Limits* (Oxford, 1999); François Bougard, *La justice dans le royaume d'Italie: de la fin du VIIIe siècle au début du XIe siècle* (Rome, 1995). See also Maurizio Lupoi, *The Origins of the European Legal Order*, trans. Adrian Belton (Cambridge, 2000), 204–5.

refs exclusively to cases involving ecclesiastical corporations or individuals) preferred the *ordo iudiciarius*.[13]

But even if we assume that the justice meted out in the new law courts *was* rationally superior to older legal habits, does this really explain why Guilhem went to court? From a purely psychological perspective, the argument that men and women preferred rational justice is hardly creditable. It is the rare disputant in a heated civil trial who can be said to be motivated by such a desire. Most want to win, or, better yet, use the court as a lever to force an equitable compromise, and will employ every means at their disposal to do so, rational or otherwise.

Third and last, Guilhem's choices were not so constrained by the growing coercive power of the state as we might imagine. Killing Antoni or Dousa was a very real option, for the culture of vengeance and violent retribution was in flourishing condition in mid-fourteenth-century Marseille. At the political summit, the city was riven by a great enmity pitting members of the Vivaut faction and their allies, the Martin, against a party named after the de Jerusalem family. Members of both parties sat on the city council and held important posts in municipal government.[14] This axis of hatred in turn polarized the many enmities of less prominent families or groups and resulted in numerous assaults and vengeance killings. Many more altercations fell outside the umbrella of the great Vivaut/de Jerusalem enmity. Most were transacted in nonviolent ways, but bloodings and limbings were not infrequent and any one of these could result in the victim's death, given the state of medical care in the fourteenth century. Women like Dousa were not exempt from this system: there are numerous records of women assaulted and even killed by men who were not their husbands, like Adalays Rogerie, wife of the baker Jacme Rogier, whose insulting, harsh, and contumelious words toward Antoni Bort in 1353 earned her the sword-blow to the head from which she died.[15]

Such killings persisted, in Marseille and elsewhere, despite the fact that by 1340, homicide had been nominally outlawed in most if not all western European jurisdictions and was commonly subject to the death penalty—at least in principle. Legal norms, however, never bear a tidy relationship to social practice. Studies have shown that the punishment for homicide in many regions of late medieval Europe was normally a fine rather than exe-

[13] Pennington, *Prince and the Law*, 132–64. Pennington, of course, is aware of this literature.

[14] Daniel Lord Smail, "Telling Tales in Angevin Courts," *French Historical Studies* 20 (1997): 183–215.

[15] ADBR 381E 79, fols. 67v–68r, 9 June 1353.

cution. To get oneself executed by the court, one had to be unlucky or inept at law, or conspicuously infamous, or perhaps too grossly violent for anyone to stomach. This is certainly the case in Marseille, where executions were rare. Homicides and serious woundings almost invariably resulted in contumacy fines, peacemaking procedures, and the relatively rapid repatriation of the killer. Guilhem, surely, was perfectly aware of this.

As this suggests, late medieval states did not have the monopoly on violence that is sometimes imagined in the literature. The persistence of vengeance killings in many core regions of Europe throughout the fourteenth and fifteenth centuries shows that medieval states, with the possible exception of England, had at best a tenuous control of coercive force.[16] In many areas, the power of families and other groups remained strong and, apart from certain rhetorical or propagandistic stances, largely uncontested by the state. More to the point, as Giorgio Chittolini and others have recently argued, regional states were thoroughly imbued with the coercive power of families and private interests.[17] The Austrian historian Otto Brun-

[16] An argument established in the older literature and subsequently confirmed by many studies: see Charles Petit-Dutaillis, *Documents nouveaux sur les moeurs populaires et le droit de vengeance dans les Pays-Bas au XVe siècle* (Paris, 1908), which includes commentary and a brief orientation to the large contemporary bibliography (39–40); Gabriel Maugain, *Moeurs italiennes de la Renaissance: la vengeance* (Paris, 1935). For some of the more recent literature see Daniel Waley, *The Italian City-Republics*, 3rd ed. (London, 1988 [1969]), 118–31; Lauro Martines, ed., *Violence and Civil Disorder in Italian Cities, 1200–1500* (Berkeley, 1972); Jacques Heers, *Family Clans in the Middle Ages: A Study of Political and Social Structures in Urban Areas*, trans. Barry Herbert (Amsterdam, 1977); Carol Lansing, *The Florentine Magnates: Lineage and Faction in a Medieval Commune* (Princeton, 1991); David Nicholas, *The Van Arteveldes of Ghent: The Varieties of Vendetta and the Hero in History* (Ithaca, 1988); Hyams, "Feud in Medieval England." Claude Gauvard has calculated that roughly a third of the crimes described in letters of remission resulted from vengeance; in the case of homicides, the figure is more than 80 percent. See *"De grace especial": crime, état, et société à la fin du Moyen Âge*, 2 vols. (Paris, 1991), 2:755. Some of the more important early modern studies include Jenny Wormald, "Bloodfeud, Kindred, and Government in Early Modern Scotland," *Past and Present* 87 (1980): 54–97; Keith M. Brown, *Bloodfeud in Scotland, 1573–1625: Violence, Justice, and Politics in an Early Modern Society* (Edinburgh, 1986); Stephen Wilson, *Feuding, Conflict, and Banditry in Nineteenth-Century Corsica* (Cambridge, 1988); Osvaldo Raggio, *Faide e parentele: lo stato genovese visto dalla Fontanabuona* (Turin, 1990); Edward Muir, *Mad Blood Stirring: Vendetta and Factions in Friuli during the Renaissance* (Baltimore, 1993); Susanne Pohl, "Negotiating Honor and State Authority: The Prosecution and Punishment of Manslaughter in Zurich and Southwest Germany, 1350–1600," Ph.D. diss., University of Michigan, 1997. See also John Bossy, *Peace in the Post-Reformation* (Cambridge, 1998).

[17] Giorgio Chittolini, "Il 'privato,' il 'pubblico,' lo stato," in *Origini dello stato: processi di formazione statale in Italia fra medioevo ed età moderna*, ed. Giorgio Chittolini, Anthony Molho, and P. Schiera (Bologna, 1994), 554–64, trans. by Daniel Bornstein in *The Origins of the State in Italy, 1300–1600*, ed. Julius Kirshner (Chicago, 1995), 34–61.

ner pointed out more than six decades ago that the bloodfeud was not necessarily antithetical either to medieval kingship or to medieval notions of
justice.[18]

Guilhem and his allies were not coerced into using the courts by a sovereign state possessing a monopoly on legitimate violence. Their options were
numerous, including violence or insult, denunciation to the episcopal or
criminal court, private arbitration, or simply lumping it.[19] So why did they
opt for litigation? And what resulted from their decision to use the courts?

In line with two of the positions described above, one response may be
that they were looking to the officials of the court to help them police the
morals and security of their street, and, as rational beings, shunned recourse
to private violence. Antoni had a different idea:

> The said Guilhem de Podio and the others persecuting Antoni and
> Dousa without any reasonable prior cause are willful and capital ene-
> mies of Antoni and Dousa, and pursue Antoni and Dousa more out of
> pure and simple malice and iniquity and envy than for a legitimate and
> just preexisting cause.

His witnesses agreed:

> He said that it seems to him that Guilhem de Podio and the others per-
> secuting Antoni and Dousa were hostile and ill-disposed toward them
> since they persecuted him more from pure malice and iniquity than
> from reasonable cause. (testimony of Johan de Trets, fol. 176r)

> He said that he had seen and heard, and indeed it was the *fama* on Ne-
> grel street, that the said de Podio and the said Gilet were great enemies
> of Antoni and Dousa, although he did not know why they persecuted
> him now. (testimony of Paulet Fabri, fol. 177v)

> He said that Guilhem de Podio and the others persecuting Antoni and
> Dousa were willful enemies of Antoni and Dousa. Asked how he knew
> this, he said because six days or so ago, as he was standing in the plaza of
> the Palace of Marseille, he saw and heard the shield-bearer of Andrieu

---

[18] Otto Brunner, *Land and Lordship: Structures of Governance in Medieval Austria*, trans.
Howard Kaminsky and James Van Horn Melton (Philadelphia, 1992 [4th rev. ed. 1959]),
1–94. The first edition was published in 1939.

[19] That options are available to disputants is a central tenet of legal anthropology. For
a twelfth-century perspective on this question, see Chris Wickham, *Legge, pratiche e conflitti: tribunali e risoluzione delle dispute nella Toscana del XII secolo* (Rome, 2000), 26.

THE CONSUMPTION OF JUSTICE

Bonvin, Johan Augier the notary, and a certain tanner whose name he does not remember, so he says, together in the said plaza with the late Johan Martin, with a son of Guilhem Martin, and with a tall youth, all shoemakers, whose names he does not recall. The shield-bearer of Andrieu Bonvin then said to the shoemakers that they were doing wrongly in persecuting Antoni d'Ays and Dousa in causing them to be eaten up [faciebant eos consumari]. The shoemakers, and especially Johan Martin, answered in turn that if they did not get justice on these matters that they are pleading, or could not obtain it against Antoni and Dousa in the palace court, then they would appeal it to the first appellate court, then to the judge of the Towers, then to the lord Seneschal of Provence, then to our lord the King, and he would sooner be wholly eaten up if he did not win his case. (testimony of Antoni Beromes, fols. 180v–181r)

According to Antoni and his witnesses, Guilhem and his allies chose to invest in civil litigation because it offered them a convenient way to pursue a neighborhood enmity. Those, like Antoni, who were "eaten up" by legal actions in late medieval Marseille were intensely aware of how the courts could be used to pursue grudges and gain emotional satisfaction. This is often how, throughout history, courts were, and still are, put to use.[20] Andrea Zorzi has called this the "publicization" of the vendetta, the process whereby the vendetta was taken up by the public competency of the official judicial apparatus.[21] David Cohen has argued vigorously that litigation in ancient Athens was used to pursue enmities and advance private interests.[22] Richard Kagan notes that "a lawsuit in the sixteenth century was a good sign that other, more amicable methods of reconciliation and compromise had failed. It signaled the end of friendship, and for many it was a precursor of violence."[23] Further:

[20] On "conflict theory," as it is known, see Timothy Curtis, "Explaining Crime in Early Modern England," *Criminal Justice History: An International Annual* 1 (1980): 117–37, and Terry S. Chapman, "Crime in Eighteenth-Century England: E. P. Thompson and the Conflict Theory of Crime," *Criminal Justice History: An International Annual* 1 (1980): 139–55. Both are cited in Sarah Rubin Blanshei, "Crime and Law Enforcement in Medieval Bologna," *Journal of Social History* 16 (1982): 121–38, here 138.

[21] Andrea Zorzi, "The Judicial System in Florence in the Fourteenth and Fifteenth Centuries," in *Crime, Society, and the Law in Renaissance Italy*, ed. Trevor Dean and K. J. P. Lowe (Cambridge, 1994), 40–58, here 53. See also Kuehn, *Law, Family*, 80–81.

[22] David Cohen, *Law, Violence, and Community in Classical Athens* (Cambridge, 1995), 87–118; see also Matthew R. Christ, *The Litigious Athenian* (Baltimore, 1998), esp. 161–63.

[23] Richard L. Kagan, *Lawsuits and Litigants in Castile, 1500–1700* (Chapel Hill, 1981), 91; see also 18–20 and esp. 136: "A lawsuit was an excellent means of settling scores, exacting revenge, and getting what one had hoped to achieve through other, more amicable means."

Going to court in the sixteenth century was not a "civilized" act. For many contemporaries, it closely resembled feuding except that it took place in a new arena where the contestants armed themselves not with arquebuses and rapiers but with a brace of lawyers and a torrent of legal briefs . . . The winner, moreover, had the satisfaction of seeing his opponent defeated, dishonored, and humiliated before the public's eye.[24]

Civil litigation could also be used in the pursuit of local precedence. As Martin Ingram has put it, speaking of early modern England, "Some gentry and sub-gentry families were for years locked into conflict and rivalry with their neighbours, constantly jockeying for the power and precedence that conferred local influence and prestige. Certain slander suits emerge on investigation of the context as symptoms of such continuing status struggles, mutual demands for and denials of social recognition."[25] Bruce Frier is even more blunt about the nonlegal dimension of legal pursuits: "At Rome it was . . . a sign of status to have sued or been sued."[26]

In light of these arguments, Guilhem de Podio was not especially interested in the rationality offered by the courts of law; he was looking to the courts not so much for protection as revenge. To this extent, he and his colleagues were surely goaded by their wives and daughters—Biatris de Podio, Ugueta de Podio, Elis Alfanta, and others. Though Antoni's clever defense deflected attention onto himself, testimony repeatedly showed that tensions between the women accounted for a good deal of the animosity in this trial. These women never showed up at court—uncharacteristically, since the women of Marseille were hardly bashful about litigating or testifying. Their nonappearance has an easy explanation. Defendants were not allowed to cross-examine witnesses, but they could challenge the legal standing of those witnesses by exposing their enmities and challenging their moral fitness. Nothing would have pleased Antoni more than to use the ins and outs of procedural law to have a crack at his enemies' wives.

It is perhaps easy to exaggerate the vengeful nature of litigation and simpleminded to assume that animosity was always present. At one extreme, some cases of litigation from late medieval Marseille were clearly contrived set pieces. Others, such as inheritance disputes between kin, may have involved a great deal of animus without being vengeful per se. The expression "mortal enmity" rarely appears in such cases. Finally, the very concepts of

[24] Ibid., 161.

[25] Martin Ingram, "Law, Litigants, and the Construction of 'Honour': Slander Suits in Early Modern England," in *Moral World*, ed. Coss, 134–60, here 145.

[26] Bruce W. Frier, *The Rise of the Roman Jurists: Studies in Cicero's* Pro Caecina (Princeton, 1985), 276.

vengeance and justice were closely paired in medieval society, as Otto Brunner argued. This remained the case throughout the fourteenth and fifteenth centuries, despite the existence of procedural norms that sought to uncouple the two. For us to acknowledge the presence of anger and see this emotion as illegitimate is to adopt, uncritically, the defendant's perspective. Guilhem de Podio surely thought he was pursuing justice. Going to law was his natural right. If his actions were motivated by a little anger . . . so what? Anger can be righteous and just. It was Antoni who characterized Guilhem's righteous anger as hateful and envious.

The results of litigation, moreover, were not invariably nasty. It is true that the law has the capacity to exacerbate antagonism.[27] Paradoxically, this capacity allows a judicial initiation to be used as a last resort, as a dramatic gambit that, if successful, helps promote a relatively peaceful resolution. Stephen D. White has argued that the ordeal was not used primarily as a mode of proof in twelfth-century France: instead, ordeals were proposed so as to raise the temperature of a legal dispute, threatening an all-or-nothing resolution, and therefore encouraging arbitration.[28] Or Thomas Kuehn: "Lawsuits had the effect frequently, by design or not, of pushing parties to mediated or arbitrated settlements."[29] Such resolutions were preferred by many. Court actions, in this model, promoted the amicable resolution of disputes by virtue of being so potentially destabilizing as to transform the emotions of the disputants. It was the very power of the court to exacerbate rather than soothe emotional heat that made it so useful as a lever. Vengeance entered the picture only when the lever failed.

The argument that courts were used to lever recalcitrant opponents represents one of the few concerted attempts by historians to explain both how and why ordinary men and women used the courts. The power of the argument comes in part from the willingness of historians to bring emotions

[27] An argument closely associated with Max Gluckman: see the discussion in William Ian Miller, *Bloodtaking and Peacemaking: Feud, Law, and Society in Saga Iceland* (Chicago, 1990), 275. See also Stephen D. White, "'Pactum . . . Legem Vincit et Amor Judicium': The Settlement of Disputes by Compromise in Eleventh-Century Western France," *American Journal of Legal History* 22 (1978): 281–308; Barbara A. Hanawalt, *Crime and Conflict in English Communities, 1300–1348* (Cambridge, Mass., 1979), 267; Michael T. Clanchy, "Law and Love in the Middle Ages," in *Disputes and Settlements: Law and Human Relations in the West*, ed. John Bossy (Cambridge, 1983), 47–67.

[28] Stephen D. White, "Proposing the Ordeal and Avoiding It: Strategy and Power in Western French Litigation, 1050–1110," in *Cultures of Power*, ed. Bisson, 89–123.

[29] Kuehn, *Law, Family*, 22; see also, for the early modern period, Kagan, *Lawsuits and Litigants*, 83: "Residents of the Montes generally used the lawsuit as part of a larger strategy designed to force an out-of-court settlement in an ongoing, often protracted dispute." See also Massimo Vallerani, "Pace et processo nel sistema giudiziario del comune di Perugia," *Quaderni Storici* 101 (1999): 315–53.

back into the study of law.[30] The emotions were always there. In their legal narratives, Antoni and other defendants from late medieval Marseille refer freely and unselfconsciously to hatred, spite, envy, and fear. Talk about love and friendship also crops up from time to time; and emotions or moral sentiments such as humiliation, honor, and shame, though not often present as words, lurk just below the surface of texts. Medieval judges and jurists, as creatures of their own culture, intimately understood the role of emotions in the disputing process.[31] But emotions were written out of the histories of law that developed in later centuries. More accurately, by the early twentieth century intense emotions had come to be seen as primitive or bestial, characteristic of the Hobbesian state of nature, and therefore possessing no legitimate role in civilized society.[32] The imposition of centralized law courts became synonymous with the civilizing process whereby excessive emotions were restrained. Bringing emotions back into the picture is a crucial element in any effort to understand how men and women use the law in any society, medieval or modern.

Doing so, however, is not easy. Consider for a moment the hatred and envy that Antoni d'Ays imputed to Guilhem de Podio. Did Guilhem really hate Antoni—physiologically, chemically, somatically—or did he just adopt the social script of hatred expected of any adversary? Was the imputation of hatred simply a legal ploy adopted by Antoni on the advice of his lawyer, who knew that proof of hatred could invalidate Guilhem's legal standing? The answers one chooses to give to these questions result in very different perspectives on the history of law and emotions.

If Guilhem really did hate Antoni in a way that would satisfy a modern physiological definition of the emotion, then the law can be seen as one of the many forces operating in civilized societies that allow people such as Guilhem to act on their hatred in a civilized, nonviolent way. Depending on one's theory of mind, one can make the historical argument that personal hatred, over time, gradually withered away, or that hatred persists but is

[30] The large and growing field on emotions in history is ably surveyed by Barbara H. Rosenwein, "Worrying about Emotions in History," *American Historical Review* 107 (2002): 821–45.

[31] For discussions of certain emotions such as enmity and anger in juristic sources see Richard M. Fraher, "Conviction according to Conscience: The Medieval Jurists' Debate concerning Judicial Discretion and the Law of Proof," *Law and History Review* 7 (1989): 23–88, and Robert Bartlett, "'Mortal Enmities': The Legal Aspect of Hostility in the Middle Ages," T. Jones Pierce Lecture, University of Wales (Aberystwyth, 1998).

[32] For historiographical reflections on the disappearance of enmity as a legitimate legal category see Brunner, *Land and Lordship*, 23; see also William Ian Miller, "In Defense of Revenge," in *Medieval Crime and Social Control*, ed. Barbara A. Hanawalt and David Wallace (Minneapolis, 1999), 70–89, here 73–74.

now largely mediated through civilized institutions—though, bottled up, it may occasionally explode. In either case, law, as a historical force, contributed to the growth of self-restraint, the virtue upon which modern civilization is built.[33] In this basically hydraulic model, aggressive tendencies should be periodically vented through a variety of institutions and practices. Exercise, sport, and recreational sex evolved in modern civil society for just this reason.[34]

The alternative perspective holds that it doesn't really matter whether Guilhem de Podio was physiologically full of hate. First, physiology is morally neutral. What was at stake in this case was the right to define the moral contours of Guilhem's hatred, to define it as righteous anger or envious wrath. Antoni, I think, was winning this battle before the intervention of the seneschal. Second, disputants can't choose how they engage in disputes. Instead, local culture provides them with a limited number of scripts that they, as actors, must follow. In medieval Marseille, mutual enmity was the most basic script, though it could be colored by other emotions and moral sentiments such as shame, frustration, humiliation, or envy. Following this line of reasoning, Guilhem naturally conformed to the script of enmity while disputing with Antoni. In my own view, it is likely that his physiological states roughly approximated his political needs. Just as relevant is the fact that observers of Guilhem's behavior, naturally prone to see any dispute through the lens of hatred, were fully prepared to accept any argument

[33] For some perspectives on this see Paul R. Hyams, "What Did Henry III of England Think in Bed and in French about Kingship and Anger?" in *Anger's Past: The Social Uses of an Emotion in the Middle Ages*, ed. Barbara H. Rosenwein (Ithaca, 1998), 92–124. The standard work is Norbert Elias, *The Civilizing Process: The History of Manners and State Formation and Civilization*, trans. Edmund Jephcott, 2 vols. (Oxford, 1994 [1939]). See also Johan Huizinga, *The Autumn of the Middle Ages*, trans. Rodney J. Payton and Ulrich Mammitzsch (Chicago, 1996 [1919]), 2; Marc Bloch, *Feudal Society*, 2 vols., trans. L. A. Manyon (Chicago, 1961), 1:128–30. A useful survey is found in James Given, *Society and Homicide in Thirteenth-Century England* (Stanford, 1977), 33–35. See also C. Stephen Jaeger, *The Origins of Courtliness: Civilizing Trends and the Formation of Courtly Ideals, 939–1210* (Philadelphia, 1985); Marvin B. Becker, *Civility and Society in Western Europe, 1300–1600* (Bloomington, Ind., 1988); Aldo Scaglione, *Knights at Court: Courtliness, Chivalry, and Courtesy from Ottonian Germany to the Italian Renaissance* (Berkeley, 1991). For a useful survey of the literature in evolutionary psychology that argues for a basically universal and unchanging set of emotions see Stephen Pinker, *How the Mind Works* (New York, 1997), 406, 413–14, and 496–97; also valuable are the works of Martin Daly and Margo Wilson, including *Homicide* (Hawthorne, N.Y., 1988). Note how Pieter Spierenburg adopts the perspective of Elias without accepting the conclusions of evolutionary psychologists; see Spierenburg, ed., *Men and Violence: Gender, Honor, and Rituals in Modern Europe and America* (Columbus, Ohio, 1998), 2.

[34] See Eric Dunning, *Sport Matters: Sociological Studies of Sport, Violence, and Civilization* (London, 1999).

to the effect that Guilhem was full of hate.[35] The script of hatred could take several different plots. The rise of law is simply the result of a large-scale rewriting of the basic plot line: over time, violent self-help gave way to litigation and other forms of emplotting hostility and competition.

In keeping with both these positions I will be arguing throughout this book that the emotions and moral sentiments that informed violent methods of self-help in early medieval society did not subsequently disappear. Litigation, denunciation, and other forms of "legal" vengeance in late medieval society were often influenced by hatred, spite, envy, and the desire to humiliate or ostracize. In the arguments that follow I tend to follow the script-based model of the emotions. In the tradition of Bourdieuan sociology, this book focuses on the users of the courts, and therefore tends to see them as agents in pursuit of political goals, though agents constrained by the available cultural scripts.[36] It wouldn't make sense to see them as passive victims of their own emotional states. All the same, I recognize that my arguments could be reinterpreted to fit a model rooted in certain strands of thinking in evolutionary psychology: aggression endures despite changes in the institutional forms of dispute processing. This book is not the best venue for resolving this large, and I suspect illegitimate, theoretical dispute.

To focus on people like Guilhem and Antoni is to see them as agents whose decisions to purchase the services of the court had a bearing on the development of judicial apparatus in late medieval Marseille. The growing investment in the courts of law had an unintended by-product, for it gave states a sound basis for developing their own monopoly over legitimate violence. This is an important feature of the political argument developed in this book: the state slowly developed a monopoly on legitimate violence partly as officials were *invited* into disputes by individual men and women seeking the best way to get back at their enemies. Choice is the key. Though the state's growing role in the practice of violence surely created some constraints on the market in retribution, it is too simplistic to argue that the investment in litigation was coerced by the growing security apparatus of the state.[37] This is not to say that either states or legal professionals were reluc-

---

[35] This perspective probably represents the predominant view in recent writings about emotions in medieval Europe. The position, and the anthropological literature on which it based, is outlined by Stephen D. White in "The Politics of Anger," in *Anger's Past*, ed. Rosenwein, 127–52.

[36] Kagan uses similar language in *Lawsuits and Litigants*, 89: "Shrewd, calculating individuals, well acquainted with the use of the courts." Note the concerns raised by John L. Comaroff and Simon Roberts in *Rules and Processes: The Cultural Logic of Dispute in an African Context* (Chicago, 1981), 16.

[37] This is the situation presumed by Brunner, *Land and Lordship*, 29–30; see also Bartlett, "'Mortal Enmities'," 15.

tant to take up their growing monopoly on the methods for transacting enmity. Quite the contrary: the interests of users and states probably harmonized on this point. State sovereignty was promoted by a court system that could be used to exacerbate antagonism and encourage more litigation in law courts—a very Machiavellian idea that, as David Cohen notes, was not lost on Machiavelli.[38] But the basic argument holds even without Machiavelli, even if we assume that kings were honest in their disapproval of enmity and that judges did not like to see their courts tarnished by the pursuit of enmity. Writing about contemporary legal practice in the United States, Sally Engle Merry has argued that working-class users of the courts—neighbors, friends, lovers, spouses—will push for legal solutions to certain disputes against the wishes of the mediation-minded courts. Her conclusions are telling: "Recourse to the courts for family and neighborhood problems has paradoxical consequences. It empowers plaintiffs with relation to neighbors and relatives, but at the same time it subjects them to the control of the court. People who take personal problems to court become more dependent on the state to manage their private lives."[39] Use of the courts creates dependence on the part of the users independently of the motives and desires of the state. However apt for the contemporary United States, this argument resonates even more powerfully in the historical context of late medieval Europe.

A fundamental premise of this book is that centralized courts of law in late medieval Europe would not have developed so rapidly without the monetary and emotional investment of ordinary users of the law.[40] This is not a new argument: it is fully in keeping with the positions taken by Pennington, Van Caenegem, Paul Hyams, and others. Charles Duggan puts it nicely in the case of appeals to the Roman curia: "The extraordinary popularity of the appeals procedure is proof of its relevance to the needs of the period. The process was activated from the periphery, not from the center, by litigants not by judges."[41] I would insist only that the pursuit of grudges, rather than a reasoned preference for rationality or a desire to achieve an outcome, was the chief motive for the investment.

Much the same is true even for the criminal courts of late medieval Eu-

[38] Cohen, *Law, Violence*, 87.

[39] Sally Engle Merry, *Getting Justice and Getting Even: Legal Consciousness among Working-Class Americans* (Chicago, 1990), 2.

[40] On this see also Cohen, *Law, Violence*, 23: Athenian legal institutions "provided the framework for, and were *constituted and transformed* by, the competitive efforts of groups and individuals." Italics in the original.

[41] Charles Duggan, "Papal Judges Delegate and the 'New Law'," in *Cultures of Power*, ed. Bisson, 172–99, here 195.

rope, often seen as the quintessence of royal or communal investment in the new law. As Alfred Soman has put it, "inquisitorial procedure, rapidly adopted almost everywhere in the thirteenth century, could not have been fastened down upon an unwilling populace . . . There was virtually no police force to carry out the job of detecting and apprehending criminals; and the courts had only very limited funds to finance criminal prosecutions." Policing, as a result, was not possible without "voluntary consent in the relations that obtained between the criminal courts and the community at large."[42] The point has also been emphasized by Sally Falk Moore:

> There is [a] . . . conception of Western law in which police and public prosecutors are conceived to move on their own against violations of law, like impersonal angels of justice, punishing wrongdoers on behalf of "society." In fact, in industrialized societies, even in criminal prosecutions, officials are frequently set in motion by citizens who have suffered some damage or injury and have complained.[43]

Surely some people in Marseille and elsewhere denounced others out of simple public-spiritedness. But many denunciations, on close inspection, turn out to be moves in the game of retaliation. This is precisely why many third parties in Marseille were very uneasy about the operations of the criminal court. Failure to acknowledge the motives of the users of the courts results in histories that see courts as self-executing agents of the state, dispassionately controlling the misbehaviors that threaten local harmony. The argument is as psychologically implausible as it is institutionally impossible. No medieval or early modern European state had the omnipotence or the omniscience imagined by this model. All courts must rely on their users. And people do not denounce or sue an offending party because they wish to preserve social harmony. If they profess a belief in social harmony at all, it is often because this ideology provides a convenient excuse for ostracizing or penalizing an adversary.

To speak of "investments" and the "market in retribution," to refer to "monopolies" on "the transaction of enmity," is to propose a wholly new metaphor for the understanding of judicial change, that of consumerism. Histories of law and justice, especially criminal justice, are as metaphorically bound as any history. Authors often prefer one of two metaphors, either agonistic/military ("the battle against crime") or psychological ("the

[42] Alfred Soman, "Deviance and Criminal Justice in Western Europe, 1300–1800: An Essay in Structure," *Criminal Justice History* 1 (1980): 3–28, reprinted in idem, *Sorcellerie et justice criminelle (16e–18e siècles)* (Hampshire, Great Britain, 1992).

[43] Sally Falk Moore, *Law as Process: An Anthropological Approach* (London, 1978), 105.

desire to repress vengeance"). Both are rooted in the perspectives of princes and states. Neither is particularly useful for explaining why Guilhem and Antoni chose to invest in civil court actions. They were certainly not battling against crime, and their emotions were enabled, not repressed, by legal actions.

So why consumerism and consumption? Though the "use of justice" would serve reasonably well to describe this book's dominant metaphor, I prefer the "consumption of justice" for several reasons. The idea of consumption acknowledges that users invested time, money, and emotion in the actions they pursued in courts of law. It suggests that the investment was not coerced; instead, consumers of the courts had a variety of options and, in some cases, deliberately chose litigation because, like a fashion item, it made a statement. In adopting a consumerist perspective I have been influenced by recent studies on consumers and consumption in the early modern and modern world that show that consumerism has had a fundamental influence on the development of economic and status systems.[44] Economic development in early modern Europe was not simply a product of new manufacturing technologies or mercantilist policies; it was also driven by taste and fashion. Suitably adapted, this is the argument I wish to bring to bear on the subject of justice.

A consumerist model cannot be applied without modifications to the practice of justice in late medieval Europe. The "product," for example, consisted of the services of officials and legal professionals rather than material goods. These were acquired in the pursuit of a named adversary rather than indefinite social prestige. Conspicuous consumption of judicial services did not necessarily lead to greater social prestige; often, quite the contrary. In other respects, however, a consumerist model fits the evolution of late medieval justice quite well, and often in a more than metaphorical way. In the case of both judicial and economic development, an emerging class of specialists—judges, lawyers, and other court officials on the one hand, merchants and artisans on the other—were attempting to shift consumer practice away from self-help or self-sufficiency by fostering a dependency on the products of specialists or professionals. In both cases, the service or product was marketed in spaces controlled or regulated by a prince or other sovereign who, eager to enhance both sovereign authority and the sovereign's

[44] Works I consulted include Chandra Mukerji, *From Graven Images: Patterns of Modern Materialism* (New York, 1983); Pierre Bourdieu, *Distinction: A Social Critique of the Judgement of Taste*, trans. Richard Nice (Cambridge, Mass., 1984); Arjun Appadurai, ed., *The Social Life of Things: Commodities in Cultural Perspective* (Cambridge, 1986); Leora Auslander, *Taste and Power: Furnishing Modern France* (Berkeley, 1996); John Brewer and Roy Porter, *Consumption and the World of Goods* (London, 1993).

treasury, found ways to shut down or criminalize competing marketplaces for the transaction of goods and enmity. Artisans and retailers as well as officials of the court had an interest in promoting the state, since state regulations contributed to their own growing monopolies. The investment in both cases consumed a great deal of disposable income that was knowingly and deliberately invested in the pursuit of some long-term goal.

Finally—the most challenging and admittedly the most speculative hypothesis of this book—conflict and consumerism are historically linked as competing forms of status negotiation and communication. The growing range of material goods and luxury items available on the markets of eighteenth-century Europe led to declining investments in litigation, insults, and street violence, for there was little need to defend honor and moral standing in the streets or courts once the advertisement of taste through the purchase of commodities came to serve this role.[45] In Colin Campbell's words, "fashion-conscious conduct" can be seen "as an effort to protect one's 'good name'."[46] This is exactly why people in late medieval Marseille pursued grudges and vendettas: to protect their good names. The much-criticized model of Thorstein Veblen and his latter-day interpreters—conspicuous consumption as a form of social competition—probably fits the argument best.[47] But using the language of Mary Douglas and Baron Isherwood, one could also argue that vengeance and litigation, as ritual forms, provided critical "marking services" insofar as they contributed to a "classifying project" that helped in "drawing the lines of social relationships."[48] Challenging the Veblenesque argument, Douglas and Isherwood prefer to emphasize the more positive role of goods as communicators that serve to integrate social groups: goods "make and maintain social relationships."[49] It is difficult to deny the competitive dimensions of the dispute between Guilhem de Podio and Antoni d'Ays, and it is curious that Douglas and Isherwood chose not to discuss the fact that societies with a limited

[45] On the use of courts to protect honor in western Europe see Thomas V. and Elizabeth S. Cohen, *Words and Deeds in Renaissance Rome: Trials before the Papal Magistrates* (Toronto, 1993); Kagan, *Lawsuits and Litigants*, 90–91; for sixteenth-century Russian society see Nancy Shields Kollmann, *By Honor Bound: State and Society in Early Modern Russia* (Ithaca, 1999).

[46] Colin Campbell, "Understanding Traditional and Modern Patterns of Consumption in Eighteenth-Century England: A Character-Action Approach," in *Consumption and the World of Goods*, ed. Brewer and Porter, 40–57, here 49.

[47] See Thorstein Veblen, *The Theory of the Leisure Class: An Economic Study in the Evolution of Institutions* (New York, 1899); also relevant is Werner Sombart, *Luxury and Capitalism*, trans. W. R. Dittmar (Ann Arbor, 1967 [1913]), 58–112.

[48] Mary Douglas and Baron Isherwood, *The World of Goods: Towards an Anthropology of Consumption*, 2nd ed. (London, 1996 [1979]).

[49] Ibid., 39.

array of material goods are often those that most often engage in competitive feuds. (The Nuer of the Sudan, who define social processes and relationships using just a single material good [cattle], are a case in point.) But in light of their arguments it is important to bear in mind that civil litigation demanded the support of kinfolk, friends, and neighbors and helped to define and redefine social groupings.[50]

To take a consumer's perspective is not to imply that judicial development was driven by consumer desire alone. The practice of justice in later medieval Europe was a product of the converging interests of consumers, kings and princes, and the growing body of legal professionals with specialized knowledge of expert law. But we already know why medieval princes and sovereigns chose to invest in law courts. Numerous studies have made it clear that medieval kings, princes, popes, and bishops were quite conscious of their responsibilities as the bringers of justice and understood the symbolic, political, and financial benefits that would accrue.[51] There is no need to add to these histories.

The study of medieval legal officialdom—judges, expert pleaders, lawyers—is a different matter, since the field is still very much in its infancy and deserves much more attention.[52] In his general arguments regarding the rise of professional law in the ancient and medieval world, Alan Watson has emphasized the initiatives and interests of lawyers and jurists, whose intellectual admiration for Roman law is a sufficient explanation for its adoption, regardless of whether the law fit the society.[53] Susan Reynolds is similarly inclined to emphasize the motives of the developing class of legal experts in twelfth-century Europe.[54] Bruce Frier suggests that the rise of the Roman jurists in the late Republic was propelled by a rising tide of litigation, itself the result of demographic and political factors. With the jurists came a sys-

---

[50] Litigation could also be analyzed in terms of its periodicity—it was an infrequent, high-expense event that, insofar as it typically engaged men and women in the prime of life, often served as a life-cycle marker. See ibid., 82–92.

[51] A particular rich statement of the royal duty to keep peace can be found in the "Prooemium" to *The Liber Augustalis; or Constitutions of Melfi, Promulgated by the Emperor Frederick II for the Kingdom of Sicily in 1231*, trans. James M. Powell (Syracuse, 1971), 4.

[52] See Bernard Guenée, *Tribunaux et gens de justice dans le bailliage de Senlis à la fin du Moyen Âge* (Paris, 1963); Joseph R. Strayer, *Les gens de justice du Languedoc sous Philippe le Bel* (Toulouse, 1970); David S. Chambers and Trevor Dean, *Clean Hands and Rough Justice: An Investigating Magistrate in Renaissance Italy* (Ann Arbor, 1997); Paul Brand, "Inside the Courtroom: Lawyers, Litigants, and Justices in England in the Later Middle Ages," in *Moral World of the Law*, ed. Coss, 91–112.

[53] Alan Watson, *The Evolution of Law* (Baltimore, 1985), 117–18.

[54] Susan Reynolds, "The Emergence of Professional Law in the Long Twelfth Century," unpublished paper delivered at the American Society for Legal History conference, Chicago, 2001.

tem of procedural rules that served to justify the pronouncements of these "external specialists" as authoritative.[55] This argument fits the conditions of twelfth- and thirteenth-century Europe very closely.

The sources extant from late medieval Marseille, unfortunately, are not particularly helpful for this sort of study. In case records, lawyers and judges are often shadowy figures whose motives and interests are subsumed under those of their clients and paymasters. We get little sense of the secret economy that surely filled their pockets with gifts and bribes. The records of legal proceedings from late medieval Marseille are best equipped to tell us about how and why litigants used the courts.

A key to understanding how the courts could be used for the transaction of status and honor and for the purposes of providing marking services lies in the "principle of publicity," to use Frier's apt expression.[56] Justice in most societies is, to some degree, a public affair: word of the events invariably leaks out in some form or other. Rituals of judicial punishment and atonement were public spectacles in medieval and early modern Europe.[57] But justice in Marseille was public in another way, for the secular courts assigned to Marseille's lower city, the major jurisdiction within the urban agglomeration, convened outdoors throughout the thirteenth and fourteenth centuries—bizarrely enough, in market stalls belonging to candle-makers. In addition, the process of summoning an adversary required that a messenger of the court (*nuncius*) carry the summons to the adversary's house and deliver it in person—an event, as we can see in witness testimony, that was much commented on by neighbors. In particularly nasty lawsuits, adversaries took advantage of the power to summon in order to harass their opponents continuously. Certain rulings of the court had to be announced at key locations throughout the city. Those suspected of insolvency had their names proclaimed at markets, plazas, and gates, thus warning potential creditors of the impending bankruptcy. The names of debtors whose goods had been forcibly distrained were publicly announced at the auction. All

---

55 Frier, *Rise of the Roman Jurists*, 277.

56 Ibid., 241.

57 Esther Cohen, *The Crossroads of Justice: Law and Culture in Late Medieval France* (Leiden, 1993); idem, "To Die a Criminal for the Public Good: The Execution Ritual in Late Medieval Paris," in *Law, Custom, and the Social Fabric in Medieval Europe: Essays in Honor of Bryce Lyon*, ed. Bernard S. Bachrach and David Nicholas (Kalamazoo, Mich., 1990), 280–304; Claude Gauvard and Robert Jacob, eds., *Les rites de la justice: gestes et rituels au Parlement au Moyen Âge occidental* (Paris, 2000). For arguments regarding the ritualistic nature of procedural law, see Andrée Courtemanche, "The Judge, the Doctor, and the Poisoner: Medieval Expertise in Manosquin Judicial Rituals at the End of the Fourteenth Century," in *Medieval and Early Modern Ritual: Formalized Behavior in Europe, China, and Japan*, ed. Joëlle Rollo-Koster (Leiden, 2002), 105–23, here 105–7.

these actions were punitive, and formed an element of the litigation strategies of the consumers of the law.

The public nature of judicial activity in late medieval Marseille had certain consequences for how the courts were used. The public shaming or humiliation of enemies and wrongdoers; the defense of honor; the display of social connectedness and social rank; the effort to inscribe all this information in memory and gossip: all these functions flowed from the publicity of justice. Behind these observations lies a very basic point that forms one of the major arguments of this book: users of the court did not necessarily assume that a favorable decision was the only worthwhile goal of litigation. The social drama, the game, was just as significant.[58]

Consider, once again, the case of Antoni d'Ays, who by his own reckoning spent twenty-five pounds in a losing effort to prevent the eviction of a maid. Maids and prostitutes were a dime a dozen in medieval Marseille, so far more was at stake than simple access to Dousa's labor or her sexual favors. Clearly, Antoni's defense was at once a highly public defense of his standing among the shoemakers of Negrel street and a defense of his right to employ a maid and have sex with her in the continuing absence of his wife. One assumes that Antoni was also fond of Dousa. Antoni, though, was not moved by emotion alone to spend twenty-five pounds in his defense. He was also moved by a sensible calculation of the risks involved with *not* rising to the challenge. In this regard, he may have won even though he lost. To judge by the list of witnesses who testified on his behalf—Bernat Gavot; the notary Ugo Giraut; Paulet Fabri, grandson of a jurist; the notary Johan Augier; the leather-worker Antoni Beromes: the list goes on—he was able to generate ample sympathy and support among not only leather-workers and other artisans but also members of the legal profession.

What all this suggests is that histories of law that focus on the nature of evidence and the changing forms of proof have missed a fundamental point, namely that evidence and proof were often incidental to what users of the courts hoped to gain through litigation. Antoni's travails neatly illustrate the point, for the testimony offered against Dousa had little to say about woman's lust, *de libidine mulieris*—there were no eyewitnesses to corroborate this charge—and a great deal to say about her bad *fama*.[59]

He saw and knew that Dousa was a garrulous, quarrelsome woman, overflowing with great wickedness and garrulousness. During the time

---

[58] A point emphasized by recent historians of classical Athenian law. S. C. Todd provides a convenient summary of the literature in his "The Language of Law in Classical Athens," in *Moral World*, ed. Coss, 17–36, here 24–25.

[59] For these examples see ADBR 3B 41, fols. 166r–168v.

that Dousa lived on the street inside the house of Antoni d'Ays, Dousa incessantly brought forth many taunts and insults and defamations and affronts against the ladies and wives of certain good men of Negrel street. Interrogated about the words Dousa said to the ladies, he said [words bringing] dishonor to them; he said he did not remember them at present. (testimony of Bernat de Baro, shoemaker, fol. 166r)

The witness also said that he thought her a woman vile of body, in that Dousa lived for a long time with Antoni as his concubine, garrulous and also quarrelsome, overflowing with violence, wickedness, and garrulousness for the reasons expressed above. He added that Dousa was not worthy to live in Negrel street nor in any other good or wholesome street on account of the fights that she continually had with the ladies and other people of the street, and even on account of the danger to the men living on the street because she truly stood out in her carnality. Asked what words Dousa had with the ladies, he said that at present he did not recall, so he said. (testimony of Peire Raos, shoemaker, fol. 167v)

He also said that on various days and at various times he had heard Dousa quarreling with the good and honest ladies of Negrel street, with defamatory and insulting words, to which ladies, Dousa, in the audacity of her boldness, kept saying, to the dishonor of the ladies, various vituperative, insulting, and defamatory words with many and various people of the street listening. Asked with which people and ladies Dousa had these insulting words, he said that with Elis Alfanta, wife of Gilet Alfans, with Biatris de Podio, with the wife of Andrieu de Sancto Marcello, and also with the wife of Bertomieu de Seyna, shoemaker, and with various other ladies and people of the street. Asked what sort of verbal battles and fights Dousa had with the ladies, he said that he does not remember at present, so he said. (testimony of Peire de Trets, shoemaker, fol. 168v)

And so on. Here, Guilhem de Podio and his allies were using legal procedures to deliver insults that could have been prosecuted as slander if they had been issued on the street.[60] The facts were incidental to the desire to calumniate.

But the facts were incidental in a different way, for even if these stylized

---

[60] Insults were one of the chief elements of criminal prosecutions in Marseille. For legal and social historical studies of insult and defamation in medieval Europe, see Richard H. Helmholz, *Select Cases on Defamation to 1600* (London, 1985); Daniel Lesnick, "Insults and Threats in Medieval Todi," *Journal of Medieval History* 17 (1991): 71–89;

insults had amounted to proof of a woman's lust, Antoni would have had no difficulty deflecting them. Most of the witnesses arrayed against him, like the principals, could probably have been shown to be in a state of formal enmity with him. Proven capital enmity negated the probative value of witness testimony. As I will illustrate throughout this book, challenges to the standing of witnesses, called "exceptions," were more common than many histories of Roman-canon legal procedure seem to acknowledge.[61] Moreover, they were usually successful in Marseille's secular courts. Facts, at least in Marseille, did not possess a stand-alone value: they depended in part on the public character of the witness and on the state of relations between witness and defendant. Reputations and relations, admittedly, are facts. So significant were they as facts that they often turn out to be the facts on which judges adjudicated. But these are not the facts that figure most prominently in the volumes of writing that have been devoted to the system of proof in the Roman-canon legal system.

The starting point of 1264 for this study of Marseille is imposed by the extant records: little, apart from isolated charters, survives from earlier centuries. Only in the early fourteenth century do registers of cases survive in abundant numbers. The early fifteenth century is a little more arbitrary as a terminus, though judicial records become less numerous after the 1410s. The great sack of Marseille by the Aragonese took place in 1423; afterward, the courts abandoned the candlers' booths and retreated indoors. The period covered in this book, 1264–1423, embraces the richest series of extant judicial registers and the time period during which justice was manifestly public.

The study is centered on the mid-fourteenth century. Apart from the Black Death of 1348, an event that sets many legal processes into sharp relief, there is nothing particularly significant about the quarter century between 1337 and 1362, but it is the period on which my previous work has focused and therefore the period I know best. The courts of law did not operate in a vacuum, and to appreciate fully how they were used one ought to examine not only the court records themselves but also all other available documentation, notably the vast notarial archives for which Marseille is deservedly well known, as well as rent records and other less common types of sources

<hr>

Lawrence R. Poos, "Sex, Lies, and the Church Courts of Pre-Reformation England," *Journal of Interdisciplinary History* 25 (1995): 585–607.

[61] Though note the important article by Bernard Schnapper, "*Testes inhabiles*, les témoins reprochables dans l'ancien droit pénal," *Tijdschrift voor Rechtsgeschiedenis/Revue d'histoire du droit* 33 (1965): 575–616. See also James A. Brundage, *Medieval Canon Law* (London, 1995), 131.

such as monastic cartularies, records of ecclesiastical or pious foundations such as hospitals and confraternities, tax records, council deliberations, financial and other records pertaining to the Angevin crown, and so on.

From this central location in the mid-fourteenth century I have worked both earlier and later. The archival holdings for the city of Marseille, like those of many other similarly sized late medieval Mediterranean jurisdictions, are inconveniently large, and I could never have completed the research if I conscientiously examined every available document between the late thirteenth and the early fifteenth centuries. I have read most of the extant records of civil suits between 1264 and 1362 and have balanced this with a careful study of the judicial records between 1400 and 1412 and a rather more haphazard survey of the remaining material, focusing on certain outstanding documents such as the sole surviving record of the court of inquest, from the year 1380. The period between 1400 and 1412 is particularly richly documented. A number of letters emanating from the Angevin royal administration in the late fourteenth and early fifteenth centuries show that plans for judicial reform were in the air, and sometimes implemented, in this period. One result may have been a conscientious record keeping of criminal sentences that for the most part were left out of earlier records. The most far-reaching judicial reforms in Marseille took place around the middle of the fifteenth century, during the reign of King René of Anjou, and lie outside the framework of this work.[62]

The first chapter, "Using the Courts," serves as a necessary introduction to a source that has rarely been used in serial fashion by historians of law and justice in late medieval or Renaissance continental Europe, namely the registers of secular courts of civil law.[63] By virtue of describing the institutional setting and providing profiles of caseloads, the chapter serves as an important introduction to many of the themes developed at greater length in ensuing chapters, and illustrates how the procedural delays and challenges available in Roman-canon law were generated by, and in return generated, strong emotions. Important for the consumerist themes of this book are the arguments regarding the costs of litigation, for the civil courts in Marseille consumed a good deal more money than did the criminal courts. But explaining this investment is a problem, for the civil courts were conspicuously ineffective at producing favorable sentences. The key to understanding the investment lies in seeing the initiation of a suit as an inimical

[62] For general overviews see Raoul Busquet, "L'organisation de la justice à Marseille au Moyen Âge," *Provincia* 2 (1922): 1–15; Raymond Teisseire, *Histoire des juridictions et des palais de justice de Marseille depuis leur origine jusqu'à nos jours* (Paris, 1931).

[63] By contrast, proceedings roughly equivalent to late medieval civil suits are the staple of early medieval legal history; see Wickham, *Legge*, 39.

gesture, an increasingly fashionable way to transact an enmity, regardless of the eventual outcome.

Focusing on numerous examples of procedural exceptions and other emotion-bearing elements of civil court proceedings, the next chapter, "Structures of Hatred," provides a close reading of the emotions that informed many civil suits. The social emotions, notably love and hatred, were emotions performed in the public eye that served to notify observers about the state of relations between individuals or parties. Given the hostile nature of civil suits, hatred, anger, and malevolence tend to outweigh affection and love. The chapter sets up one of the most basic arguments of this book: not only did civil courts serve as an important venue for the pursuit of enmity, but contemporary observers were also intensely aware of this function. In a culture where the publicization of emotions was a significant element in building and displaying social networks, the courts served an important advertising function. The obvious exception to this might be debt litigation, a seemingly emotion-free type of lawsuit that was one of the most prominent forces driving the use of late medieval civil law courts. But even here, I will argue in chapter 3, "The Pursuit of Debt," that debts and credits were intimately related to community standing, and that debt litigation was therefore routinely interpreted as a move detrimental to the community standing of the debtor and therefore worth resisting.

Chapter 4, "Body and *Bona*," takes up a key issue alluded to in many of the arguments above, namely the nature of coercive force in late medieval Marseille. Force was not monopolized by the officials of the Angevin crown, for although a constabulary had been in existence since at least the early fourteenth century its activities were embedded in a much larger matrix of family- and group-based force, whose legitimate exercise of force underpinned many of the operations of the criminal and civil courts. Perhaps the most significant element in the system of sanction, in turn, was that respectable men and women, for all intents and purposes, could not suffer bodily punishment at the hands of the court. The body was eminently sanctionable, but only through acts of customary vengeance. Instead, men and women were penalized in their *bona*—in their goods, possessions, and inheritances. This sanction was not trivial, for it was systematically publicized and deeply humiliating, unlike an honorable wound received in battle with an enemy.

The fifth and final chapter, "The Public Archive," takes up the elements of publicity and performance intrinsic to using the law in late medieval Marseille. Building on arguments raised in previous chapters, a major theme is that many facts relevant to Roman-canon procedural law were constructed and construed through public performances. This chapter is deliberately designed to challenge the long-standing assumption that Roman-canon procedural law was more fact-based than earlier systems of procedural law. The performative nature of late medieval justice also means that publicity was a key goal for many users of the civil and criminal courts. Use of the courts allowed disputes, and their underpinning emotions, to be advertised on a grand scale.

In writing this sort of history there is always the risk of taking too seriously documents that are by their nature imperfect. The record, though rich in anecdote, resists quantitative methods. The anecdotes, in turn, surely reveal only part of the story. Anthropologists never tire of reminding historians that those who work with archives can only guess at the larger disputes and social contexts that inform actions at law. Procedure is an enormously constraining force: it requires litigants to frame a wrong according to one of a limited number of categories, warping and twisting the narrative of the dispute in the process. For these reasons, I have chosen not to build this study around conventional categories of social-legal historical analysis, such as the types of civil disputes, the social status of users of the courts, crime rates, and the institutional framework. Elements of this type of analysis appear in chapter 1 but historians looking for this kind of information will, for the most part, be disappointed. Instead, this study takes a cognitive or intellectual approach, focusing on the nature of argumentation and guessing at motives wherever clues allow. To this end I have dealt seriously and at length with procedural law, since this was the "language" that constrained the evidence available for historical research. Though my conclusions will depart from those drawn by some legal historians, we nonetheless share the conviction that one must grapple with the procedures if one is to make sense of the sources. To the procedures, then, we now turn.

# CHAPTER ONE
# USING THE COURTS

Until 1348, Marseille consisted of three politically distinct jurisdictions, namely the upper or episcopal city, the small jurisdiction known as the Praepositura that surrounded the cathedral of La Major, and the lower or viscountal city. In the late twelfth century, the lower city began to emancipate itself from the control of the viscounts of Marseille, a process more or less complete by 1220. In the course of its political elaboration the commune almost certainly incorporated elements of Roman law.[1] Although no statutes survive from this period, and charters are few and far between, Italian communes such as Pisa had been experimenting with Roman law since the 1150s, Provençal communes from at least the 1160s, and it would have been unusual had Marseille not followed the general trend.[2] By the thirteenth century the evidence is clear, thanks to the existence of a dozen or so charters confiscated from the merchant Johan de Manduel, accused of

[1] In general, see Victor-L. Bourrilly, *Essai sur l'histoire politique de Marseille des origines à 1264* (Aix-en-Provence, 1925); Régine Pernoud, *Essai sur l'histoire du port de Marseille des origines à la fin du XIIIème siècle* (Marseille, 1935); Georges Lesage, *Marseille angevine: recherches sur son évolution administrative, économique et urbaine de la victoire de Charles d'Anjou à l'arrivée de Jeanne 1re (1264–1348)* (Paris, 1950); Édouard Baratier, *Histoire de Marseille* (Toulouse, 1973); Raoul Busquet, *Histoire de Marseille*, ed. Pierre Guiral (Paris, 1977).

[2] According to Wickham, the adoption of Roman procedural law in twelfth-century Tuscany was a piecemeal affair: Pisan courts transformed themselves swiftly, whereas Roman law was for a long time only superficially adopted in Genoa and Siena. In Lucca, in turn, the influence was very small. See Chris Wickham, *Legge, pratiche e conflitti: tribunali e risoluzione delle dispute nella Toscana del XII secolo* (Rome, 2000), 25–26. For the Provençal consulates, see Jean-Marie Carbasse, *Introduction historique au droit pénal* (Paris, 1990), 96–97.

and executed for treason in 1263.[3] These charters, the earliest of which is from the year 1230, record the outcome of court decisions that were favorable to Johan or his brother Bernat. All the business of the Manduel brothers was heard before the communal court of the lower city (*curia comunis*) or the secular court of the bishop (*curia episcopalis Massilie*), lord of the upper city. In these charters one encounters all the conventional apparatus of Roman-canon law courts: judges, lawyers, litigants, witnesses, legal guardians, procurators, suits (*lites, controversiae, causae*), libels, judicial orders (*mandamenta*), sentences (*sentenciae* and *summae*), notarial instruments, public summons and proclamations (*preconisationes*), and so on. As these charters show, both the communal and the episcopal courts were using Roman-canon procedural law fluently by at least the 1230s.

The city's legal and political institutions underwent a significant change in the middle of the thirteenth century, in conjunction with the conquests of Charles of Anjou. The lower city's quest for independence had met with resistance on the part of the counts of Provence, and in 1246 Charles of Anjou, the ambitious younger brother of Louis IX of France and future king of Naples, became count of Provence by virtue of his marriage to Beatrice, sole heir of the previous count.[4] Shortly after his accession to the countship, Charles undertook the military conquest of Marseille and other Provençal cities. In 1251, manifest resistance had ended, and in 1252 a treaty was drawn up that defined the constitutional relationship between the lower city of Marseille and its new sovereign. In 1253, a set of statutes was compiled, incorporating both older statutes dating back to at least the 1210s as well as elements deriving from the 1252 treaty.[5] A rebellion in 1257 had the effect of narrowing somewhat the privileges of the city of Marseille, resulting in a new treaty, the Chapters of the Peace, which remained the basic constitutional definition of Angevin sovereignty in Marseille. The city was rocked by a further revolt in 1261 and the unsuccessful coup led by Johan de Manduel and others in 1263, but by 1264 all resistance had ended and the Angevin order was in place. In the meantime Charles had purchased the lordship of the upper city of Marseille from the bishop, thus extending his authority over the entire city. His accession to the throne of Naples in 1247 meant that Marseille, and all of Provence, was absorbed into the Angevin kingdom of Naples, a realm that lasted until 1382. At the request of the citizens of Marseille, the upper and lower cities were formally unified by the queen of Naples, Jeanne, in 1348, though the administrative distinction be-

[3] See ADBR B 1501–1504.
[4] Jean Dunbabin, *Charles I of Anjou: Power, Kingship, and State-Making in Thirteenth-Century Europe* (London, 1998).
[5] Pernoud, *Statuts*, viii.

tween the two cities persisted for some decades. After the death of Jeanne in 1382, the now unified city of Marseille, along with the rest of the county of Provence (with the exception of Nice), fell under the dominion of the second house of Anjou, a dynasty with grand pretensions, including suzerainty over the fictive kingdoms of Sicily and Jerusalem, but little territory apart from Provence itself.

Angevin reforms, as we have seen, did not include the introduction of Roman-canon legal procedure; this had been in place for several decades. The Chapters of the Peace of 1257 instead outlined the structure of royal administration and gave definition to a new set of law courts, a move wholly in keeping with Charles's reputation as a lawgiver in the spirit of his predecessor, Frederick II.[6] The lower city's existing communal court was replaced by a comital court, eventually called the palace court. Two lower tribunals were also attached to the palace court to handle some of the civil caseloads. The judge assigned to each of these courts was called the "judge of the other court,"[7] but since "other courts" is ambiguous I will call these the two "lesser courts." By the fourteenth century, when cases survive in sufficient quantity to get a sense of caseload, we find that there was little difference in the sort of cases brought to the two lesser courts and the palace court, save that more serious affairs tended to gravitate to the palace court.[8] The secular court of the upper city, hitherto acting in the name of the bishop, was likewise absorbed into the Angevin administrative structure and renamed the court of the upper city or, in some records, the court of the City of Towers. The Chapters of the Peace also allowed for the creation of two appellate courts, a concession that ensured that no citizen of Marseille would have to appeal decisions to the distant count of Provence.[9] Following the formal union of the cities in 1348 the secular court of the upper city ceased to exist as an independent entity.

Marseille's secular judicial system from 1257 onward was headed by an Angevin representative called the *viguier*, the chief Angevin official in the city. The viguiers of Marseille were always knights, often lords of towns or encastellated villages, and never graduates of law schools. Fourteenth-century sources occasionally speak of a "tribunal of the viguier" and apparently meant by that the palace court but for the most part the viguier did not meddle directly in the operations of the courts. One of the viguier's most

[6] Dunbabin, *Charles I of Anjou*, 19–20.

[7] *Judex alterius curie*, sometimes simply *judex alterius*.

[8] The formal division of jurisdiction between the palace court and the two lesser courts is described in Bourrilly, *Essai sur l'histoire politique*, 197–98.

[9] Mireille Zarb, *Histoire d'une autonomie communale: les privilèges de la ville de Marseille du Xe siècle à la Révolution* (Paris, 1961), 167–71.

important public responsibilities was his duty to announce criminal sentences in six annual *parlements* held in the plaza of the Palace. As direct representative of the king, however, the viguier could, if he wished, make rulings in his own name. In 1385, for example, a nobleman named Bertomieu Vivaut appealed a decision involving water rights made by the viguier, a knight named Peire Guitard. The original case was not heard in the palace court, and the acts and testimony introduced during the case make it clear that the viguier, responding to a plea lodged by Bertomieu's opponent, had traveled to the rural site in question to hear testimony and delivered his sentence in situ.[10]

On a day-to-day basis, the civil, criminal, and appellate courts were usually run by seasoned, professional judges, the norm throughout the Angevin realms.[11] Records from fourteenth-century Marseille show that these judges always held law degrees of one sort or another.[12] Their salaries stood at sixty pounds per year in the early fourteenth century, which was not a large sum, about twice the annual income of an agricultural laborer.[13] Additional income probably came in the form of gifts presented by litigants and lawyers, although these were never recorded. More significantly, when judges rotated off the bench they stood to make considerable profits as lawyers and expert pleaders, known as "procurators." As was customary in many Mediterranean jurisdictions, the judges in Marseille were rotated every year, taking office in the fall, anywhere between August and November, along with other Angevin officials and members of the city council. Later in the fourteenth century, judges began taking office in February. A notary was also appointed to each court to serve a yearlong term; he received twenty pounds per year in salary, not including the fees charged to litigants for the cost of drawing up instruments, and was assisted by several associate notaries. Other members of the court included messengers (*nuncii*) who carried summons and other notices and made public announcements on street corners and public squares.[14] When faced with recalcitrant debtors, messengers occasionally engaged in strong-arm tactics.

---

[10] ADBR 3B 837, fols. 64r–163v, case opened 15 May 1386.

[11] On Angevin judges, see Jean-Luc Bonnaud, "Les agents locaux de l'administration royale en Provence au XIVe siècle: catalogue et étude des carrières" (Thèse [Ph.D.], Université de Montréal, 1999). Elsewhere in Mediterranean Europe degrees were not the norm; see Lauro Martines, *Lawyers and Statecraft in Renaissance Florence* (Princeton, 1968), 34, 222. My thanks to Susan Reynolds for bringing this matter to my attention.

[12] The degrees or titles include *legum doctor*, *licentiatus in legibus*, *bacallarius in legibus*, and *jurisperitus*.

[13] Salaries of officials are given in ADBR B 1936 and B 1937.

[14] For details on the summoning procedure, at least as it was exercised in contemporary Italy, see Peter Raymond Pazzaglini, *The Criminal Ban of the Sienese Commune*,

The apparatus of secular justice in Marseille was therefore part and parcel of the apparatus of the Angevin state. Angevin administrators, however, did not determine how people would use this resource. This chapter will survey, in three sections, the civil, criminal, and appellate courts as seen through the eyes of the consumers of the law. Many of the points, such as the prominence of debt litigation, the participation of women and Jews, and the role of emotions, will lay the groundwork for subsequent chapters. As the chapter develops, however, two themes become especially important, namely the public nature of justice and the oppressive weight of procedures. The public nature of justice derives from the public emplacement of the law courts. From at least 1290 onward, the courts of law convened at market stalls (*tabulae*) located in front of a house belonging to a candler named Pons Durant and his heirs and successors.[15] However odd, it was a convenient location, situated at the very heart of the city, before the lower doors of the great parish church of Notre Dame des Accoules, at the conjunction of two major streets that fed pedestrian traffic into the great market of Accoules and the nearby artisanal neighborhoods where drapers, goldsmiths, and butchers sold their products. Negrel street, where the dispute between Antoni d'Ays and Guilhem de Podio played itself out, was located just a few blocks to the north. By 1338, Pons Durant was dead, and notaries of the palace court identified the house as belonging to his heirs.[16] In 1348, in the midst of the Black Death, a notary saw fit to remark that the terrible stench

*1225–1310* (Milan, 1979), 23–33. On the Provençal *criée* or proclamation, see Michel Hébert, "*Voce Preconia*: note sur les criées publiques en Provence à la fin du moyen âge," in *Milieux naturels, espaces sociaux: études offertes à Robert Delort*, ed. Élisabeth Mornet and Franco Morenzoni (Paris, 1997), 689–701.

[15] In an otherwise insignificant appeal arising from a tangled inheritance, we learn of an earlier decision reached by the judge, a knight and doctor of laws named Guilhem Raymond of Marlana, who had delivered his sentence while "sitting as tribune before the gates of the lower church of the Blessed Mary of Accoules, where judges are accustomed to sit out of reverence for honest women." ADBR 3B 802, fol. 29v, case opened 13 Kalendas of Jan. 1290 on fol. 26v: "sedens pro tribunali ante valvas ecclesie inferioris Beate Marie de Acuis ubi judices sedere consueverunt ob reverenciam honestarum mulierum." A few folios later the notary recording the decision reached by the appellate court identified the location in the following way: "This sentence was delivered in Marseille at the doorway of the house [*ostium domus*] of Pons Durant, candler, that is to say before the lower gates of the Blessed Mary of Accoules."

[16] ADBR 3B 37, fols. 49r–51r, case opened 12 Dec. 1338. There are several relevant expressions in this case: "sedente ante domum heredum Poncii Duranti condam ubi judices ius redere consueverunt ob mulierum reverenciam honestarum"; later in the case, "existens in presencia nobilis viri domini Petri Dalmacii iudicis reginali curie palacii Massilie pro tribunali sedenti supra quandam tabulam domum heredum Marquesii Duranti condam ante valvas inferioris Ecclesie Beate Marie de Acuis ubi interdum domini judices sedere iusque reddere consueverunt ob dominarum reverenciam honestarum."

of the bodies of the dead lying in the nearby cemetery of Accoules temporarily forced the palace court to shift a few blocks south, to the Change.[17] An act from the 1350s confirms that the two lesser courts also convened before the lower doors of Notre Dame des Accoules, though the location was identified in a slightly different way: "above the stone drain of the apothecary, Guilhem Bonet."[18] All three courts, the palace court and the two lesser courts, were still in the same location in 1408, although the house had fallen out of the patrimony of the heirs of Pons Durant and now belonged to a candler named Felip Colrat.[19] Various clauses in subsequent acts and contracts show that all the secular courts of law—the two lesser courts, the palace court, the two appellate courts, and the criminal court of inquest—met in this outdoor space throughout the fourteenth and into the fifteenth century. Only in the 1420s, after the city was sacked by the Aragonese fleet in 1423, did the courts leave the candlers' stall. A document from 1424 shows that the courts were now convening within the courtyard of the hospital of St. Esprit, a move that mirrors, in microcosm, the global historical shift in judicial space from open air courts to enclosed spaces and rooms.[20]

Publicity is crucial to the practice of justice. The sophisticated and often entertaining stories told by litigants and defendants alike, for example, make most sense as stories designed for public circulation, not unlike the orations delivered to ancient Greek and Roman jurors. The process of recruiting witnesses, in turn, was shaped not only by the facts they knew but also by the spectacle of upstanding citizens attesting to the authenticity of a litigant's claims and, necessarily, giving the lie to the claims of the adversary. Finally, there is influence. A resolution adopted by the Marseille city council at a meeting in February 1351 enjoining that no person should come before the court on behalf of the defendant apart from lawyers, procurators, and kinfolk seems to hint at the large crowds that could forgather at the court space in the hopes of swaying the proceedings.[21] I would not want to insist too much on the relationship between the publicity of justice and the outdoor placement of the law courts. Clearly participants in court can interact with the public in a variety of ways even without an immediate audience. The outdoor nature of justice in Marseille simply makes it easy to appreciate a function that surely was, and is, typical of courts in all but the most closed societies.

---

[17] ADBR 355E 285, fol. 20r.

[18] ADBR 3B 58, fol. 60v, case opened 30 Apr. 1354: "supra egredotam lapideam Guillelmi Boneti apothecarii."

[19] ADBR 3B 861, fol. 118r, case opened 5 May 1408 on fol. 69r.

[20] Numerous clauses to this effect can be found in ADBR 3B 157 (1424).

[21] Mabilly, *Inventaire*, 63.

THE CONSUMPTION OF JUSTICE

This chapter also addresses, at length, the nature and role of legal procedures. From the early thirteenth century onward, the lineaments of Roman-
canon procedural law were developed and subsequently refined by jurists
and other legal scholars trained in the schools. Their procedural manuals
and commentaries and the statutes they influenced have formed the basis of
modern reconstructions of Roman-canon procedural law, both civil and
criminal. Some understanding of procedural law is necessary if one wants to
make sense of the records of practice, and because criminal procedures are
fairly well known I have paid much more attention, in this chapter, to civil
procedures. Several interrelated points emerge when we look at procedural
law from the perspective of the user. To begin with, the average length of
the records of legal proceedings grows remarkably over the fourteenth and
fifteenth centuries, a process driven largely by the increasingly prominent
role of procedural ploys. These ploys were used largely in suits involving
bitter or intractable emotional disputes; hence, there is a close relationship
between the use of procedures and the pursuit of emotional satisfaction or
vengeance. The growing length of cases, in turn, is naturally associated with
growing court costs. Justice was expensive, costing roughly one royal pound
per litigant per page of recorded proceedings. In a very real way, the mea-
surable consumer investment in procedural ploys was an investment in
emotional satisfaction. The public nature of justice, in turn, ensured that
these emotional gambits would reach a large and gossiping audience. Finally, as argued below, procedural ploys used by defendants often brought
about the failure of the plaintiff's case. People did not, could not, enter litigation with high hopes of recovering the property or the sum of money
under dispute. This being so, it becomes difficult to explain the investment
in civil litigation as a rational calculation of economic benefit.

## THE SECULAR COURTS OF CIVIL LAW

### Jurisdiction and Caseload

Though a great deal of fragmentary evidence attests to the activity of
courts of law in thirteenth-century continental Europe, as a rule of thumb
few registers of cases are still extant, though the number of surviving registers may be greater than we once thought.[22] Marseille certainly conforms to

[22] Extant registers are surveyed in Gero Dolezalek, "Une nouvelle source pour l'étude
de la pratique judiciaire au XIII siècle: les livres d'imbreviatures des notaires de cour," in
*Confluence des droits savants et des pratiques juridiques: actes du colloque de Montpellier* (Milan,
1979), 225–41.

this rule. The few judicial registers extant from the thirteenth century—two registers of sentences of the first appellate court from the years 1264 and 1290, one register of the palace court from 1289 to 1291, and one register of the court of the upper city from 1286—are too sporadic and unsystematic to provide much evidence about the workings of the civil and appellate courts in the early decades of Angevin administration, and the courts of inquest and ecclesiastical courts are scarcely documented at all. The thirteenth-century registers, moreover, are an indiscriminate mixture of all the business transacted in the court. The first surviving appellate court record, for example, contains the records of twenty-four sentences issued by the appellate judge between February and September of 1264 but also includes a number of wholly unrelated notarial acts, as does the appellate register from 1290. The only extant palace court register from the thirteenth century is an equally indiscriminate collection of suits, mandaments, and other judicial orders.

The surviving series of court records becomes less sporadic after 1300 and by the 1320s the extant records are relatively dense. This is the local reflection of a Europeanwide phenomenon, namely the vast increase in extant judicial records after 1300, something Claude Gauvard has labeled "a frenzy of registers."[23] In Marseille, it is likely that the business of the secular courts was increasing significantly at more or less the same time. The economic depression that set in after 1289, for example, caused a considerable number of bankruptcies that eventually made their way into the civil courts. Francine Michaud's study of the growing number of women's claims for the recovery of dowries from insolvent husbands between 1280 and 1320 has revealed the straitened financial circumstances of Marseille's citizens in those decades and indirectly shows how economic downturns can promote the use of the courts.[24] The great famine of 1316–22 generated a great deal of litigation, not only inheritance disputes but also attempts to recover the debts owed to or by the deceased. Financial problems also cropped up later in the fourteenth century: John Drendel has argued for the existence of a fiscal crisis throughout Provence, beginning in the early 1340s, that caused indebtedness in rural areas.[25] Notarial records from the 1340s contain numerous

[23] "Une folie de registres." Claude Gauvard, oral remarks delivered at "Pratiques sociales et politiques judiciaires dans les villes de l'Occident européen à la fin du Moyen Âge," Avignon, France, 30 Nov.–2 Dec. 2001. Italian judicial series become rich at an earlier date; see, among others, Jean-Claude Maire Vigueur, "Justice et politique dans l'Italie communale de la second moitié du XIIIe siècle: l'exemple de Pérouse," *Comptes rendus de l'Académie des inscriptions et belles-lettres* 2 (1986): 312–28, here 313.

[24] Francine Michaud, *Un signe des temps: accroissement des crises familiales autour du patrimoine à Marseille à la fin du XIIIe siècle* (Toronto, 1994).

[25] John Drendel, personal communication, March 2001.

acts suggesting that Marseille's citizens were also feeling the pinch, as does a 1345 comital inquiry into the decrease in revenues from the port of Marseille.[26] The problems associated with tangled estates became endemic during the cycles of plague that set in after 1348, and lawsuits flourished as a result. The civil courts, in short, were sensitive to economic and demographic changes, and use of the courts was inversely proportional to the demographic and economic health of European society.

As seen in these records, the judges of the civil courts spent most of their time handling very ordinary business, notably the recovery of simple debts, rather than lawsuits. One register kept by the notary of one of the lesser courts over the space of eleven months in the years 1358 to 1359, for example, consists solely of ninety-three judicial orders requiring debtors to satisfy their creditors, and related orders to messengers to go and seize items from the houses of debtors to hold in security for the debt.[27] Between February and May of 1340 the notary of the palace court recorded 201 debt-related orders.[28] Simple extrapolation from these figures suggests that the three civil courts together processed eight hundred or more such requests per year. Other registers sporadically preserved from the fourteenth century show judges assigning legal guardians (*curatores* or *tutores*) for orphans, managing intestate succession, conducting inventories, supervising bankruptcies, and so on.[29] All this activity generated a huge number of acts recorded either in court registers or, in some cases, in notarial casebooks, most of which have not survived.[30]

In sheer volume of extant documentation, though, civil suits (*causae*) easily dominate the record. Roughly two-thirds of the 250 civil court records extant from the later thirteenth to the early fifteenth centuries are registers of civil suits, and these are typically larger than registers devoted exclusively to business other than litigation. The registers containing civil suits, moreover, are usually written in a better hand with wider margins, suggesting that officials valued their contents more highly.

Given the gaps in the record it is difficult to estimate the annual number of cases brought before the courts. One register that corresponds exactly to the normal yearly tenure of a judge, from 9 December 1336 to 21 November

26 See Lesage, *Marseille Angevine.*

27 AM FF 536.

28 ADBR 3B 39. There are two distinct registers under this shelf number. The orders are recorded in a register thirty-five folios in length.

29 Examples from the mid-fourteenth century are ADBR 3B 32–33, 35, 40, 44, 46–47, 49, 51, 55–56, and 59.

30 The series ADBR 381E 368–385 consists of the records of judicial proceedings kept in ordinary notarial casebooks rather than in court registers.

1337, shows that Peire de Furno heard forty-two cases during his tenure.[31] There is no guarantee, however, that his notary kept only a single register. One of his immediate predecessors, Guilhem Calladier, kept at least two concurrent registers, one of which started on 20 April 1334 and the other on 24 May 1334. Both ran until October of that year.[32] Records from the tenures of two other judges, Peire Dalmas (three registers extant from 1338 and 1339) and Simon de Girona (three registers extant from 1353 and 1354), seem to be reasonably complete, and show that Peire heard seventy-two cases and Simon ninety-seven over the course of a year.[33] Judges of the two lesser courts on the whole heard fewer cases than did palace court judges, between thirty and fifty per year. Using these and other figures as a basis, one can estimate that in the fourteenth century the judges of the palace court and the two lesser courts of the lower city were hearing between one hundred and thirty and two hundred lawsuits per year. Note that this is in addition to the roughly eight hundred orders to repay debt issued annually at the simple request of creditors.

The types of suits brought before the civil courts are not easy to categorize. For one thing, notaries and judges made no effort at categorization, and most plaintiffs or their advocates never justified their suit through reference to a particular law or statute. Beyond that, many cases are complex enough as to defy simple categorization. A suit over an unpaid legacy might, from the defendant's point of view, turn out to be a case of fraud. Even simple debt cases reveal, at times, complex motives. A case in point is a suit from 1362 in which the plaintiffs were seeking the recovery of thirty-six florins from a laborer named Laurens Vital. As it develops, the suit reveals that Laurens, along with several other men, had been captured and held for ransom by some bandits identified only as "inimical Spaniards running about Provence" (*yspanos innimicos discurrentes per Provinciam*).[34] Laurens was elected by the others to return to Marseille and collect ransom money on their behalf, which he did, going to all their wives to collect thirty florins of ransom money and six florins for his personal expenses. He promptly absconded with the money, thereby exposing the other hostages to great peril—or so they claimed, in lodging the suit to recover the lost money. As can well be imagined, the money, though a not insignificant sum, was not the point of the suit. It is crucial to bear in mind, as the anthropologist

---

[31] ADBR 3B 31.
[32] ADBR 3B 28 and 29.
[33] ADBR 3B 36–38 and 52–54.
[34] ADBR 3B 66, fol. 14r, case opened 24 Mar. 1362 on the same folio.

Simon Roberts has noted, that the external form of a given dispute often has little to do with what was "really" going on.[35]

Disputes most commonly appear, in their external form, as instances of debt litigation. To a certain extent this is a trivial observation. Like the suit against Laurens Vital, almost all suits centered on a debt or obligation of some sort rather than an injury. Even injuries such as insults were assessed at a going rate and expressed in the form of currency. Dissolving the category of debt even further, Trevor Dean has remarked on the tight association that existed between the Florentine vendetta mentality and the Florentine habit of using household cartularies (*ricordanze*) to keep a minute accounting of credit and debt relationships.[36] Yet even if we severely limit the debt category to efforts to recover loans, simple sale credits, and other unpaid monetary debts, the pursuit of debt still outstrips all other categories of suits heard before the courts, and, coupled with related suits involving mercantile or complex commercial transactions, constitute about 41 percent of the caseload of the palace court (table 1.1). By way of comparison, the percentage of cases of debt litigation in comital courts in Castellane (Provence) between 1030 and 1316, according to Rodrigue Lavoie, was 58 percent; elsewhere in Provence, Lavoie cites figures ranging from 40 percent to 70 percent.[37]

Family-related suits, including disputes over inheritances, dowries, and the guardianship of minors, constitute the next largest category. As these show, and as work done on the rich records of the secular criminal court of fourteenth-century Manosque corroborates, the jurisdiction of Provençal secular courts, both civil and criminal, extended deep into familial or moral arenas.[38] Dowry suits were especially common in Marseille. Some came about because the husband was verging on insolvency. In other cases, the husband had died and his heirs were unwilling or unable to repay the widow's dowry, thus forcing her into the courts. Several dowry claims include accusations of spousal abuse, such as a case from 1424 concerning an abusive husband who had imprisoned his wife for two days on bread and water. She was finally rescued by officials who had to beat down

[35] Simon Roberts, "Introduction," in *Disputes and Settlements: Law and Human Relations in the West*, ed. John Bossy (Cambridge, 1983), 22.

[36] Trevor Dean, "Marriage and Mutilation: Vendetta in Late Medieval Italy," *Past and Present* 157 (1997): 3–36, here 34–35.

[37] See Rodrigue Lavoie, "Endettement et pauvreté en Provence d'aprés les listes de la justice comtale, XIVe et XVe siècles," *Provence historique* 23 (1973): 201–16, here 202–3.

[38] See Andrée Courtemanche, *La richesse des femmes: patrimoines et gestion à Manosque au XIVe siècle* (Montréal, 1993); Steven Bednarski, "Crime, justice et régulation sociale à Manosque, 1340–1403" (Thèse [Ph.D.], Université de Montréal, 2002).

**Table 1.1 Types of Civil Suits in Selected Palace Court Records, 1323–1416**

| Category | N | % |
|---|---|---|
| Money and Commerce | | |
| Loan, sale credit, other unpaid debt | 246 | |
| Commenda contract, other dispute among merchants | 64 | |
| Bankruptcy | 17 | |
| Subtotal | 327 | 41 |
| Family Matters | | |
| Inheritance dispute | 102 | |
| Dowry | 87 | |
| Estate administration | 35 | |
| Contested seizure of inheritance or legacy | 22 | |
| Alimony | 6 | |
| Marital separation | 3 | |
| Subtotal | 255 | 32 |
| Property | | |
| Ownership of real estate | 58 | |
| Rent or lease | 35 | |
| Decaying infrastructure, vandalism | 10 | |
| Subtotal | 103 | 13 |
| Miscellaneous | | |
| Appeal from arbitration and lower courts | 41 | |
| Labor | 14 | |
| Other miscellaneous | 19 | |
| Subtotal | 74 | 9 |
| Injuries | | |
| Private distraint, theft | 9 | |
| Insult or threat | 8 | |
| Abuse of animal | 6 | |
| Piracy | 3 | |
| Other injuries | 11 | |
| Subtotal | 37 | 5 |
| Total | 796 | 100 |

*Sources:* ADBR 3B 16, 19, 24, 25, 26, 27, 28, 29, 30, 31, 33, 34, 35, 36, 37, 38, 39, 41, 42, 43, 44, 45, 50, 51, 52, 53, 54, 57, 58, 60, 61, 62, 63, 64, 65, 66, 94, 95, 132, 136, 138, 141, 143, 147, 151, 152.
*Note:* This table identifies only the suits where the chief cause of litigation is readily apparent. Another hundred suits are too ambiguous or too short to determine the cause of litigation.

the door to save her.[39] A few cases that may have also been motivated by spousal abuse turn on a woman's refusal to cohabit with her husband. A tantalizing fragment of a case from September 1359, actually a suit for alimony, involves a woman named Biatris de Jerusalem, a member of one of Marseille's great families, who refused to live with her husband Peire, lord of the encastellated village of Lambesc, and demanded alimony from

---

[39] ADBR 3B 157, fols. 1r–29r, case opened 14 Aug. 1424. Another case that led to a marital separation on the grounds of spousal abuse and fornication with prostitutes is ADBR 3B 57, fols. 96r–104r, case opened 26 Jan. 1355.

him.[40] The case ended after two folios with no resolution. A much better documented case is that of Antoni d'Ays, who, as seen in the introduction, recruited the court in his efforts to force his wife Douselina to return to him. Secular judges in Marseille were not at all reluctant to assist husbands with their marital problems. This is worth emphasizing. A recent survey of medieval canon law asserts that church courts had "exclusive competence" to deal with marriage, family, and sexual behavior.[41] As a blanket assertion this is not quite accurate, though it may be true enough for England.[42] A brief series of ecclesiastical court registers from 1398 to 1405 shows that although Marseille's ecclesiastical court did handle inheritance disputes and family-related issues from time to time, it was primarily concerned with clerics, particularly criminous clerics.[43]

Suits related to property and delicts of various kinds round out the list. Several types of dispute, particularly disputes relating to urban infrastructure (including drainage and crumbling walls), trespass, boundary disputes, and right-of-way, were often initiated before certain subcommittees of the city council, though litigants were free to appeal to the civil courts if necessary.[44] The city council, though nominally under the authority of the viguier and the count of Provence, was a quasi-autonomous body that represented the city and its interests before the count of Provence and also had local responsibilities ranging from the supervision of craft regulations to taxation. Each year about forty-five subcommittees composed of several members of the council were formed to take up each of the responsibilities. All of these subcommittees had some supervisory power or legal authority, and many of them may have had some sort of adjudicating function, but only three left surviving records of their activities. These were the mason-assessors (*extimatores peyreriorum*), responsible for the upkeep of walls and houses within the city walls; the governors of the ban (*districtores bannorum*), who handled disputes regarding trespass outside the walls, particularly damage caused to agricultural lands by trespassing herds of animals; and the boundary assessors (*aterminatores*), who heard disputes over boundaries, water rights, and right-of-way. The men who filled these offices had no formal legal training but their hearings followed the basic procedural norms of Roman-canon law. All three bodies left records that

[40] ADBR 3B 62, fols. 21r–22r, case opened 30 Sept. 1359. For a similar case of spousal abuse and dotal recovery see ADBR 3B 31, fols. 7r–18r, case opened 14 Dec. 1336 (discussed below).

[41] James A. Brundage, *Medieval Canon Law* (London, 1995), 72.

[42] Though noting the theoretical existence of jurisdictional boundaries, Martines observes that Florence "paid little attention to some of these boundaries"; see *Lawyers and Statecraft*, 93.

[43] See ADBR 5G 771–776, covering the years 1398–1405.

[44] These were called "cases of reversion" (*causae recurssus*).

are now scattered throughout the notarial and judicial archives. The mason-assessors, who were always masons, produced acts called "rulings of the mason-assessors" (*cognitiones extimatorum peyreriorum*) that recorded their decisions in cases involving neighborly squabbles over drains, walls, and boundaries. Several of these can be found in the casebooks of public notaries who were paid to record the results of their rulings,[45] and a few were appealed by losing parties to the palace court and show up there as "cases of reversion" (*causae recurssus*).[46] Similar decisions made by the governors of the ban and the boundary assessors were appealed by losing defendants and hence show up in the palace court records.[47] Two registers of the decisions of the governors of the ban have survived, the first from 1288 and the second from 1376. The "court of the ban" (*curia banni*), as it was called in the records, followed an inquisitorial mode, receiving denunciations and inquiring ex officio. Most cases involved damage done to fields and vines by herds of animals, though a civil suit from 1402 speaks of an inquest made by the court of the ban into a case involving the theft of some blocks of stone and the destruction of a wall in the countryside.[48] In several cases the accused made a defense and called witnesses.[49] The fines assessed against those found guilty of trespass were usually minor, between five and twenty shillings, and the accused typically paid up quickly. In the case of the vandalized wall, one of the guilty parties, a laborer named Antoni Raynaut, was fined the large sum of fifty pounds.

### Procedures

Like most courts of law in Mediterranean Europe in the later middle ages, Marseille's civil courts followed Roman-canon procedural law.[50] This is true of all adjudicating bodies, including the subcommittees of the city

[45] Nine of these *cognitiones extimatorum peyreriorum* can be found in the casebooks of the notary Peire Aycart, active in the 1350s and 1360s; see ADBR 355E 34–36. The body of men were described as "master masons elected to take care of walls and drains"; see ADBR 3B 34, fol. 1r. This kind of dispute has been discussed by Peter Schneider, "Honor and Conflict in a Sicilian Town," *Anthropological Quarterly* 42 (1969): 130–54.

[46] An example of the latter can be found in ADBR 3B 138, fols. 55r–124v, case opened 28 Apr. 1402.

[47] See, for example, ADBR 3B 818, fols. 87r–122r, case opened 19 Sept. 1355; ibid., fols. 136r–176r, case opened 7 Mar. 1356. Other cases can be found in 3B 38, 43, 52, 53, 57, 58, and 60. A particularly long and embittered case involving the boundary assessors is an appeal found in ADBR 3B 837, fols. 64r–163v, case opened 15 May 1385.

[48] ADBR 3B 138, fol. 25r, case opened 15 Mar. 1402 on fol. 24r.

[49] For these registers see AM FF 892 and 893.

[50] Useful introductions to the procedures of civil law in southern France and more generally in medieval Europe include Arthur Engelmann et al., *A History of Continental Civil Procedure*, vol. 7 of *The Continental Legal History Series* (Boston, 1927); Brundage, *Medieval Canon Law*, 120–53.

council, which were headed by ordinary citizens who had no law degrees. The procedures, evidently, were thought to belong to everyone, not just to legal experts. In a very important way, Roman-canon procedural law, *grosso modo*, was just customary procedure and as such was relatively well known to most property-owning or suit-worthy citizens of Marseille.

A civil case was initiated when a party showed up before a judge and presented a libel (*libellum*), the word from which the modern English "libel" is derived. (It is illustrative of some of the arguments of this book, such as the emotion-driven nature of suits, that a Latin word used to designate a suit-initiating plea has come to mean a type of slander in modern English.) Many or most of these appear to have been drafted with the aid of the plaintiff's advocate or even by the advocate himself, although by the early fifteenth century public opinion of lawyers was low enough that one procurator, hoping to avoid lawyerly quibbling, noted that a list of arguments had been drawn up "by the principal person and without the advice of any advocate."[51] The libel described a complaint or injury and asked for redress. A copy was immediately sent by messenger to the defendant along with a summons to respond to the libel within ten days. Not all pleas lodged before judges of the civil courts were libels that were intended to initiate a case. As mentioned earlier, most of those who appeared before a judge were creditors asking for a judicial mandament ordering the debtor to repay a modest debt. Some of these judicial orders could evolve into suits—often a suit initiated by the aggrieved debtor resisting a wrongful claim by the creditor— but the immediate result of a simple petition like this, if well founded, was the issuance of a judicial order to repay a debt, not a civil suit.

The principal parties in cases heard before the civil courts included practically the entire spectrum of the population with the major exception of household servants (who show up rarely in civil cases), prostitutes, and slaves.[52] Jews were represented roughly proportionally to the size of the Jewish population in Marseille, though it is a curious and interesting fact that cases pitting Jews against Christians are typically shorter than cases whose principal parties are exclusively Christian or exclusively Jewish. Though men predominated, women were involved in roughly 27 percent of all cases, either singly, in groups of women (typically sisters), or in complex groups involving both men and women (table 1.2). Litigation over dowries and alimony naturally involved women's concerns, though the fact that women had to litigate shows that men did not necessarily acknowledge these rights willingly. Beyond this, Marseille's women, at least in the four-

[51] ADBR 3B 143, fol. 131r (foliated in the original).
[52] Engelmann, *History*, 459–61.

**Table 1.2 Sex of Principal Parties in Selected Palace Court Cases, 1323–1416**

| Sex of the Member(s) of the Principal Parties | Plaintiff's Party (N) | Defendant's Party (N) | Total (N) | % |
|---|---|---|---|---|
| One or more men | 659 | 683 | 1,342 | 73 |
| One or more women | 229 | 169 | 398 | 22 |
| Married couples or groups of both sexes | 44 | 52 | 96 | 5 |
| Total | 932 | 904 | 1,836 | 100 |

*Sources:* as for Table 1.1.
*Note:* The numbers of litigants and defendants in the total line are different because records are often incomplete and, in some cases, notaries failed to include even the names of the defendants.

teenth century, were noticeably active and visible in public life: as retailers, lenders, borrowers, agricultural laborers, businesswomen, and so on. Women were also notable as proprietors: at least 24 percent of all intramural real estate in mid-fourteenth-century Marseille was owned by women, and the figure of female ownership is even higher for rural property, at 30 percent.[53] It is not a coincidence that the percentage of female litigants was roughly the same as the percentage of female proprietors.

A short case from 1335 pitting two female principal parties amply illustrates the degree to which these rights and activities naturally encouraged women to engage in litigation.[54] The case sprang from the attempt of Esteva de Poriers to force Alazays Buena to cease pursuing her for 26s. owed from the sale of two barrels of tuna. Though Alazays eventually hired a man to act as her procurator, the trial began with both women speaking on their own behalf, and at one point the notary expressly noted that Alazays was present and listening when Esteva's witnesses came to give testimony. Numerous civil suits reveal situations in which a female principal party appeared at court, revoked her procurator, and spoke in her own name. A wine-merchant (*mercatrix*) named Ricarda Borgella, sued by her step-children in 1323 for having privately distrained some jars of wine from the house of her late husband, represented herself throughout a trial that lasted a year.[55] Women often relied on procurators and other parties to plead their cases at court, but this was a question of convenience, not a question of reticence to appear in public.

Litigation was difficult and not especially pleasant work, and in many cases both women and men preferred to get others to plead their cases. A man in his capacity as paterfamilias could appear at court to represent the interests of his wife or children, even grown children; wives, by the same token, could represent husbands, though this was less common; and occa-

[53] See my "Démanteler le patrimoine: les femmes et les biens dans la Marseille médievale," *Annales: histoire, sciences sociales* 52 (1997): 343–68, here 358.
[54] ADBR 3B 30, fols. 37r–47v, case opened 7 July 1335.
[55] ADBR 3B 16, fols. 60r–82v, case opened 16 Mar. 1323.

sionally someone appeared as an "attached person" (*coniuncta persona*) for a sibling or other relative. But most litigants and defendants in civil as well as criminal cases relied heavily on the services of procurators, individuals officially delegated to plead a case in the name of the principal party. The longer or more complex the case, the more likely it was that a procurator would be hired along the way. There are many reasons for this practice, not the least of which is that with a procurator one needn't always be at the beck and call of one's adversary. The continual state of uncertainty was both humiliating and, for traveling merchants who were often absent from the city, inconvenient. Procurators, by contrast, always hung around the court and were therefore always there to answer a summons. Paul Brand has suggested that use of legal representation in late medieval England served another useful purpose: serjeants at the bar were "clinically detached from the raw emotions which might be motivating their clients."[56] All procurators had to show proof of their legal right to appear in the name of the principal party, and hence whenever a procurator made a first appearance at court he would present a notarial instrument of procuration. This was sometimes copied into the record. Such instruments of procuration are exceedingly common in notarial casebooks from the period.

Like the orators of classical Roman law, procurators did not have to be lawyers or jurists; principals sometimes chose relatives or friends.[57] Choice of a relative was encouraged by the fact that the procurator, in one's absence, had complete power to speak in one's name. Other choices were possible. In November 1353 a Christian noblewoman named Jacma Grifena chose as her procurator a Jewish man named Boniuse Mosse. She did so probably because Christian property lords sometimes used Jews to serve as family procurators, collecting rents and so on, and Boniuse would have been well situated to handle her legal affairs in court.[58] Already by the 1320s, however, the role of procurator was considerably professionalized—certain men with legal training show up repeatedly as procurators. In the 1350s, important cases frequently set a lawyer named Primar Mirapeis against another lawyer named Guilhem Bayssan. This was an especially interesting situation because the two men belonged to the rival factions of the Vivaut and the de Jerusalem: their verbal sparring at court mirrored the armed street battles they were sometimes involved in. Both men frequently represented mem-

---

[56] Paul Brand, "Inside the Courtroom: Lawyers, Litigants, and Justices in England in the Later Middle Ages," in *The Moral World of the Law*, ed. Peter Coss (Cambridge, 2000), 91–112, here 96.

[57] Andrew D. E. Lewis, "The Autonomy of Roman Law," in *Moral World*, ed. Coss, 37–47, here 41–2.

[58] ADBR 3B 53, fols. 170r–172v, case opened 28 Nov. 1353.

bers of their respective factions at court, and they may well have recruited new faction members from their hitherto neutral clients. Legal representatives, in other words, did not necessarily operate in a hermetically sealed emotional universe. In the early fifteenth century, most cases of any gravity were being argued by just three procurators, namely Johan de Ysia, Guilhem de Mellomonte, and Bertran Gombert. One fifteenth-century appellate case even identifies an appellant, Pons Autras, as a "procurator," as if procuration had become a status or profession on a par with "notary," "merchant," "goldsmith," and so on.[59] Most of these professional procurators had legal degrees such as licentiate-in-laws although a degree was not strictly necessary since most litigants and procurators consulted professional advocates and lawyers (*advocati* and *causidici*). Many procurators, including Primar Mirapeis and Guilhem Bayssan, were judges who were not currently in office either in Marseille or elsewhere in Provence. In one extraordinary case from 1407 Johan de Ysia even briefly served as a temporary replacement for an absent judge in a case in which he was also serving as procurator.[60] Situations like this, naturally enough, created conflicts of interest. Toward the end of a long and complex case that started in 1400 and lasted into 1403, one of the parties submitted a petition complaining about the problem of judges who were partial. Since the case had gone on for such a long time it spanned the tenure of several judges, and some of the current judges had previously served as advocates or procurators for the opposing party, thus rendering them suspect.[61]

The libel could be presented to the judge by the principal party, the procurator, or an attached person. A copy was sent by messenger to the adversary, who was simultaneously summoned to appear at court, and the libel itself was either copied out or stuck in the binding of the court register. Libels identify the principal parties to the case and usually provide a fairly good description of the circumstances that generated the dispute.[62] Sometimes a suit initiated before the palace court was a transferal of a case from the competency of the two lesser courts. Such a case was called a *causa suspicionis* ("case of suspicion"), and in most such cases the roles of plaintiff and defendant were reversed, so that the defendant in the lesser court became the plaintiff in the palace court. Despite the name, these cases of suspicion rarely suggest that the original defendant was actually concerned about judi-

---

[59] ADBR 3B 140, fol. 318r, case opened 10 Sept. 1403 on fol. 318r. Pons was not the sort of procurator who pleaded cases in court; instead, he collected debts and did similar business on behalf of his clients and indeed was accused of having defrauded one of them.

[60] ADBR 3B 147, fol. 24r, case opened 24 Feb. 1407 on fol. 21r.

[61] ADBR 3B 136, fol. 207r, case opened 27 June 1401 on fol. 151r.

[62] Engelmann, *History*, 461–63.

cial bias. Rather, it was used as a procedural ploy to change the venue and seize the initiative. The ploy was acceptable because the lesser courts were almost always staffed by judges drawn from Marseille—unlike the palace court, which was staffed by judges who were not citizens—and the judges of the lesser court might well have been friends or relatives of the opposing party. One could therefore hold these judges "suspect" (*in suspectam*) and thereby transfer jurisdiction to the palace court. The transfer was automatic: former defendants did not have to explain their reasons for so doing. What they did have to do was present a letter from the lesser court explaining that the judge was being held suspect, and in such cases this letter preceded the libel in the palace court register. Often, a transcript of the stages of the trial already heard before the lesser court was sent up as well, and this would sometimes be copied or even bound into the palace court register. Much the same was true for cases of reversion from the court of the ban and the other adjudicating bodies of the city council.

If the case was not abandoned shortly after the presentation of the libel— a not infrequent event—what typically follows the libel is a series of procedural notes, sometimes running on for several pages, that record the lengths to which the opposing party would go to avoid responding to the adversary's libel. Early in the fourteenth century adversaries often responded to the libel with little or no fuss, thereby allowing the evidence phase to begin. By the fifteenth century, however, it had become normal to exploit procedural delays to their fullest. Consider the suit lodged by a young apprentice named Johanet Salvayre against his employer, Jacme Niel, late in February 1407.[63] Jacme Niel was a merchant of some standing, affiliated to the house of his mother, Reseneta Cambale, a woman who had earned a considerable reputation among Marseille's merchants for the flourishing regional trading network she had built up over her lifetime. In January of that year, the apprentice Johanet had gone to Avignon to purchase some wax and cotton with forty florins given him by Jacme. Problems arose when the shipment of goods did not arrive in a timely fashion. A series of unfortunate events only widened the rift between master and apprentice, and the dispute eventually ended up in court.

Once Johanet's suit was formally lodged, Jacme and his procurator, Johan de Ysia, used several of the procedural ploys available if one wished to avoid responding to the libel. One of the strategies was a simple refusal to answer the summons in a timely fashion. Another more devious device was to challenge Johanet's legal status, which they did by suggesting both that he was a cleric and that he was still a young man in *patria potestas*. If either were true,

[63] ADBR 3B 147, fols. 21r–96v, case opened 24 Feb. 1407.

Johanet would have had no standing to sue in a secular civil court. Both charges, as it turns out, were spurious—Johanet called them "frivolous exceptions"—but note the consequences of the second accusation: Johanet was forced to write to his father, Guilhem Salvayre, in Nîmes, in order to receive written license to proceed with his suit, and had to pay to have the license entered into the current proceedings. Jacme then challenged the fitness of the license, though the judge declined to admit the challenge, and then denied the fitness of the libel. These initial challenges went on for two months and take up twenty pages in the record of the proceedings. Reluctance to respond to the libel presumably served a variety of purposes, not the least of which was jacking up Johanet's costs and irritating him. The procedural jockeying continued throughout the evidence phase and the trial itself lasted a year and a half, consuming 150 pages in the process. Jacme was almost too successful at staving off his adversary, for he died seven months into the trial, leaving it to his mother, the redoubtable Reseneta, to bring it to a victorious conclusion.

Once the truth of the libel was formally contested, Johanet's procurator, Guilhem de Mellomonte, was finally able to present his evidence.[64] Evidence in civil cases took the form of a list of positions, titles, or articles (*tenor positionum, tenor titulorum,* or *tenor articulorum*) that set out the facts the party hoped to prove by means of acts, witnesses, or public fame. Usually the articles of proof would be offered by the initiating parties, but sometimes the defendant, confident in his or her witnesses or documents, would seize the initiative. Constructing these articles of proof—creating a story, in effect—was something of an art form because establishing a basic context and chronology of events was in some cases as important as identifying the facts to be proven.[65] Johanet Salvayre's list of articles was somewhat narratival and ran like this.[66] In January, at the request of his master, Johanet had traveled to Avignon and purchased the goods required. Shipment was promised. He returned to Marseille and told Jacme, who in turn expressed his satisfaction. Between the eighth and tenth of February, however, Jacme began to complain about the nondelivery of the goods and accused Johanet of defrauding him. To avoid any hint of deception, Johanet made restitution by

---

[64] On the *litis contestatio,* see Engelmann, *History,* 465–67; on positions, ibid., 471–74.
[65] See Natalie Zemon Davis, *Fiction in the Archives: Pardon Tales and Their Tellers in Sixteenth-Century France* (Stanford, 1987); Kim Lane Scheppele, "Foreword: Telling Stories," *Michigan Law Review* 87 (1989): 2073–98; John M. Conley and William M. O'Barr, *Rules versus Relationships: The Ethnography of Legal Discourse* (Chicago, 1990); Peter Brooks and Paul Gewirtz, ed., *Law's Stories: Narrative and Rhetoric in the Law* (New Haven, 1996); Wickham, *Legge,* 496–98.
[66] ADBR 3B 147, fols. 30r–31r.

means of a privately written act (*apodixa*). Jacme openly and publicly (*palam et publice*) acknowledged receipt, both orally and in writing. The goods then arrived. Johan repeatedly asked Jacme to restore the reimbursement, but Jacme, unsatisfied with the quality of the goods purchased, refused.

Lists of articles in other lawsuits are even more story-like. Consider the following, told by a goatherd named Marin de Morlans in August 1339 in an attempt to evade a fine of ten pounds assessed when his goats strayed into another man's field and damaged the crops.[67] The enumeration exists in the original. I have eliminated certain formulaic expressions, including the routine denials made by the opposing party:

(1) One Saturday during the Lenten period just past, while in the mountains called Marseilleveyre with his herd of goats, Marin suffered a terrible pain in his abdomen; the pain then rose to his heart, taking away his speech and sight, and he fell to the ground as one half-dead, and lay there prostrate from the middle of terce up to the ninth hour. (2) Around the ninth hour, Marin arose from that ground and, looking around him, saw none of the animals of his herd. (3) Having thus arisen from the ground, Marin, still overcome with pain, began to make his way, and with the aid of a staff came as best he could to his house in Marseille. (4) On that same Saturday, from the hour of sunset to around dawn, he lay in bed inside his home, infirm, suffering from that pain, such that he could not go back in search of his flock. (5) The same evening on which he returned weakly from those mountains, Alexander Teyseyre, a citizen of Marseille, came to Marin, lying sick in bed owing to the pain, and said to Marin that he had found a herd of goats in the walled farm of Berengier Vivaut of Marseille and asked if he knew whose it was. Marin responded "What mark did they have?," and he answered him "a scar on the left foreleg." Marin answered that it [the herd] was his and he had lost it because of the sickness and pain that had come upon him in the Marseilleveyre. (6) After taking some food and feeling a little better he mounted one of his animals and went to search for his herd and to recover it from Berengier's walled farm, in which Alexander had penned it. (7) A herd of goats lost or escaped and going about without a keeper in the territory of the viscountal city of Marseille is not supposed to be liable to court action or held to pay a fine.

As a list of articles this is legally rather inept: the first two points were not witnessed by anyone and point five was not terribly relevant to Marin's guilt

---

[67] ADBR 3B 38, fol. 22v, case opened 4 Aug. 1339 on fol. 20r.

or innocence. Subsequent testimony shows that Marin's case centered on points three and four (witnesses did not discriminate between them) and point seven, the key to his case. As a story, however, the tale is quite compelling.

Other stories were less story-like but similarly designed to play on the sentiments of judges or members of the audience, such as the wrenchingly sad tale told in April 1340 by an impoverished and childless goldsmith, Guilhem Godofred, whose in-laws were trying to recover his late wife's dowry. The dowry included some real estate and a bed:

(1) First, Guilhem was solemnly married by words of present consent to the late Guilelma. (2) The marriage was consummated by carnal copulation and they had a son from the marriage who died. (3) Guilhem is a poor man and does not have the wherewithal to make his living unless he works manually as a goldsmith in exchange for a wage. And sometimes he goes in galleys to earn money, leasing his labor in sailing . . . from which labor he manages to get by. And this is widely known and understood by his neighbors in Marseille; and without this income he would not have the wherewithal to make his living. (4) Guilelma, his wife, gave in dowry unappraised vineyards and a field and a vineyard, which she left to him in her testament, as he has shown by means of written instruments. (5) He could hardly make a living working even with those things given to him in dowry along with his wife during the time that she, Guilelma, his late wife, was living. (6) Guilhem has only the said bed in which he lies and used to lie with his late wife, and he does not have any other bed in which he might lie, and this is widely known among the neighbors. (7) He has only those iron instruments and other things given him in dowry by his late wife for carrying on his goldsmithing, and without those things he will not be able to work at the craft by which he, Guilhem, lives. (8) Guilhem sold his late wife's clothing to pay for the funeral expenses and for burying her. (9) This is public talk and fame in Marseille.[68]

Most lists of articles were less melodramatic than those told by Marin and Guilhem. The least narratival lists of articles, curiously, often seem to have been made deliberately uninformative so as to hide problematic circumstances. A set of articles from a suit heard in January 1339 amounts to little more than the observation that a commercial loan of one hundred

[68] The entire case is ADBR 3B 39, fols. 33r–37r, case opened 26 Apr. 1340. These articles are copied from a loose cedula tucked into the binding around fol. 34.

florins was made and never repaid.[69] When the defendant got a chance to speak, however, he observed that the money was invested in a ship that sank, an eventuality which, according to the terms of the contract (or so he claimed), absolved him from the debt. As this shows, well-told stories were not always beneficial to a plaintiff's case. Sometimes it was best not to tell a story.

The civil court records from late medieval Marseille—or from any Mediterranean jurisdiction—contain stories in such profusion that they might well merit more extended analyses by literary scholars. But even from the legal perspective the existence of narratives has much to say about the practice of justice. For one thing, the stories fed off a presumption that they would be made public in some form or other. Beyond that, all legal stories are stories about good intentions or, as in the case of the goatherd Marin de Morlans, the absence of evil intentions. All are designed to show how a simple interpretation of the facts of a case, which may be damning on face value, overlooks mitigating states of mind and circumstances. The facts arrayed against Marin, after all, were undeniable: his herd of goats had strayed onto and damaged another's property. The rise of Roman-canon procedural law is often said to have placed a new emphasis on facts and fact-finding procedures. But Roman-canon procedural law, in practice, also prompted the ongoing development of good legal storytelling. That it did so in criminal contexts is already well known, thanks to the work of Claude Gauvard and Natalie Zemon Davis.

Both Johanet Salvayre's and Guilhem Godofred's lists of articles ended with a clause stating that the facts just outlined were "the public talk and fame in Marseille" (*publica vox et fama in Massilia*). This, a standard clause in most lists of articles, more or less means that everyone talked about these things and held them as true.[70] By the early fifteenth century the clause had transmuted into some variation on the following phrase: "All these things are true, notorious, and manifest, and the public talk and fame." It was recognized that in a city of twenty thousand to twenty-five thousand people the talk could only go so far, and a number of clauses qualify or limit the standard *fama* article in a variety of ways. In a typical example, a Jewish man named Salamonet Mordacayssii, suing his father-in-law to force the return of his absent wife, used his articles to prove the formal existence of the marriage. The articles closed with a clause stating that he "intends to prove that there is public talk and fame about all these things, each and every one, in

---

[69] ADBR 3B 37, fols. 59r–75v, case opened 18 Jan. 1339.

[70] It is not correct to translate *fama* with words such as "rumor" or "gossip," words that carry connotations of secrecy and deceit.

the city of Marseille, especially among Jews and acquaintances and neighbors and others who are aware of the foregoing."[71] Variations on the article observe that there is public talk and fame "especially among those knowing these things" (*maxime inter scientes predictae*). This was not a wholly tautologous observation. Fama was something different than merely being aware of a given set of facts. It was both knowing the facts and choosing to talk about them with others. The process of publicization gave the facts greater standing as knowable things.

In the same way that adversaries put off responding to the libel, so too did they avoid responding to the articles, often claiming that they were ineptly formed and unworthy of any response. In the case of Johanet Salvayre and the delayed shipment of goods from Avignon, his adversary's procurator "denied the story as told" (*negat narratus prout narratur*), a formulaic expression that occurs in many cases. Judges often had to compel a response to each of the articles. Once responses were extracted from reluctant defendants, the notary of the court typically flipped back through the record of the proceedings and annotated the list of articles with phrases such as "does not believe" (*non credit, dubitat*), "does not believe as phrased" (*non credit ut ponitur*), or, in some cases, "believes" (*credit*). In the case involving the wine-merchant Ricarda Borgella, her step-children's procurator responded to the fourth of her twelve points—that their father, her dead husband, had given her a large amount of wine so as to pay back an outstanding loan that he owed her—in the following way: "He does not believe this as phrased, and if it is proven he says that he has a legitimate defense."[72] This response and its variants can be found in a number of cases. Context shows that it was a polite way of saying, "What you say is true, but I'm going to make you go to the trouble and expense of proving it anyway and then will show that it is irrelevant."

Once adversaries had responded formally to the articles, plaintiffs had to prove the contested articles by means of documents or witness testimony or both. Documentary evidence, especially but not exclusively notarial instruments, was common enough, and litigants in these cases had no apparent difficulty assembling the testaments, dowry acts, property sales, sale credits, judicial sentences, and other documents they needed. Most individuals kept chests or pouches full of acts that confirmed their rights, duties, and obligations, and knew what each act said regardless of the fact that all were written in Latin, a language that could not easily be read by most citizens. Failing

---

71 ADBR 3B 94, fol. 62r, case opened 28 Apr. 1379 on fol. 59v.
72 ADBR 3B 16, fol. 68v, case opened 16 Mar. 1323 on fol. 60r. The remaining points are all annotated with the words "as above" (*ut supra*).

that, it was possible to ask a notary to extract an instrument from his original notes, though this was costly and inconvenient. On the whole, individuals took responsibility for keeping their own instruments and preferred to use those in court. Hundreds of thousands, perhaps millions, of these notarial instruments were produced and stashed away in late medieval Marseille alone. Very little of this archive has survived.

Few lists of articles relied exclusively on written evidence, although in some cases written evidence dominated the proceedings. In one such case, heard in May 1403, seven of the ten points were to be proven by means of documents. One of these was a thirty-three-year-old house sale; another, a sentence issued by one of the courts of law a few years before the case opened.[73] But the widespread belief that all notaries were potential swindlers contributed to a certain aura of suspicion that seems to have hung around private contracts, and no one relied exclusively on written evidence. Some of this suspicion was justified. Accusations of fraud against notaries are not uncommon in the record, and the fact that numerous notaries in the mid-fourteenth century were known to be members of the rival noble factions of the Vivaut and the de Jerusalem surely did not help matters much. In an effort to deter accusations of secrecy, notaries often wrote up contracts in the public eye, often on a public street or in the doorway to a house.

Public notaries were not the only source of written evidence. The courts generated important documents, notably rulings or sentences that might have an impact on future cases. Drawn up by notaries of the court, these were transmitted to the winning party for use in future cases. To judge by the cases in which litigants had recourse to published sentences, the courts were not responsible for searching through their own records to find past rulings. It was entirely up to the principal parties to prove the existence of a previous decision through instruments or even, in some cases, witness testimony.

Also common was a range of non-notarized documents, including household account books, roughly equivalent to the Italian *libri di ricordanze*, registers kept by merchants and retailers in which they noted day-to-day transactions, and handwritten receipts or acknowledgments (*apodixae*). In 1339, a shop owner named Mathendis Gaydona offered to show her household account book (*cartularium domus sue*) to prove that some wages had been paid to one of her workers.[74] In an appeal heard in 1408, several such cartularies were presented as evidence by a candler, an apothecary, a merchant, and

[73] ADBR 3B 141, fols. 59r–60v, case opened 5 May 1403 on fol. 53r.
[74] ADBR 3B 38, fol. 2r, case opened 10 Aug. 1339.

possibly even a manual laborer.[75] Early in the suit lodged by Johanet Salvayre, his procurator, Guilhem de Mellomonte, offered to the court a letter written in the vernacular by the Avignonese merchant with whom Johanet had done business, a letter that attested to the existence of the transaction and enumerated the goods sold.[76] A case from 1413 includes long extracts, in Provençal, from the book of accounts (*librum rationum*) of Laurens Ricau.[77] As one creditor noted in 1386, "all money-changers are accustomed to transfer large quantities of silver to goldsmiths for the purpose of making silver vases without an instrument apart from what they wrote in their shop cartularies."[78] The ability to transact would have been severely hampered if every transaction had to be notarized. Private writings may not have had quite the status of notarial instruments and were subject to the same accusations of fraud but nonetheless, as phrased so eloquently by a procurator in 1379, "it has always been the usage in this city to give credence to the shop cartulary and similar documents."[79]

Quite apart from its legal implications, the frequent use of private acts reveals the presumption that virtually all merchants and shopkeepers were literate. Clients as well: an interesting case from 1406 suggests that the debts recorded in shop cartularies were not to be given credence unless they were written in the hand of the debtor.[80] Court records from medieval Marseille suggest impressive rates of literacy.

Reading through the records from the fourteenth and early fifteenth centuries one gets the impression that written instruments, especially notarial instruments, were being used increasingly as evidence as the fourteenth century wore on. This is true in part. Particularly noticeable is the growing ability of litigants to track down and present notarized documents made many decades before. In contemporary Florence, men and women were learning how to use their household books to write down the names of no-

---

[75] See 3B 861, fols. 128r (candler), 128v (apothecary), 132r (possibly a laborer), 134r (merchant), case opened 5 May 1408 on fol. 69r.

[76] ADBR 3B 147, fol. 37v, case opened 24 Feb. 1407 on fol. 21r.

[77] ADBR 3B 151, fol. 183r, case opened 23 Oct. 1413 on fol. 181r.

[78] ADBR 3B 838, fol. 138r, plea of Antoni Bayle, case opened 14 Aug. 1386 on fol. 125r: "omnes campsores consueverunt tradere quantitates multas argenti aurifabris pro constructione vasorum argentorum absque instrumento sed illa scribant in cartulariis dictorum campsorum." Antoni offered witnesses to this effect: see the corroborating testimony of Johan Lenesa, a goldsmith, on fols. 138v–139v.

[79] ADBR 3B 94, fol. 85r, case opened 17 June on fol. 83r: "semper fuit usitatum dare fidem de cartulario dicti operatorii et similibus in dicta civitate." See also a similar expression in ADBR 3B 16, fol. 14v, case opened 21 Feb. 1323 on fol. 4r.

[80] ADBR 3B 857, fol. 394v, case opened 27 Oct. 1406 on fol. 392r: "Tum etiam cartularia antiqua nisi sint autentica nunquam faciunt fidem vel alias essent scripta manu debitoris sicut non est."

taries who had drawn up contracts for family members, and one can assume that citizens of Marseille were doing the same. This practice would have made easier the task of tracking down the registered version of a contract in cases where the instrument itself was lost. The practice of copying notarial instruments into the acts of the court was also becoming more common by the early fifteenth century and thus written instruments become more visible in the surviving record. Earlier in the fourteenth century, one only finds allusions to written instruments, or notes to the effect that they were shown to and read by the judge.

But even if written evidence was being used more by the early fifteenth century it is nonetheless clear that proof still relied to a very great extent on witness testimony. Some sense of the strategic or symbolic importance of having upstanding citizens take the time to support one publicly at court can be deduced from the curious fact that many litigants preferred to prove the existence of contracts by means of witnesses and not by means of the instrument itself. In a wholly typical and representative case from 1326 involving a disputed *commenda* contract, witnesses came to attest to the fact that a quittance had been drawn up by the notary Johan Locusta before the gates of Notre Dame des Accoules in the presence of many witnesses.[81] The quittance itself was not offered as evidence. There are also a surprising number of instances of notaries testifying to the existence of contracts they had written out, as in a case from 1330, in which a notary testified to the existence of a testament that he had drawn up and another notary mentioned that he had subsequently read the testament.[82] Even rulings or sentences of the court could be proven by witnesses who happened to be at court on the day. Lawyers and procurators were especially well placed to comment on rulings because they were so often at court. In 1339, a lawyer named Bernat Raymon testified that he had heard a judge absolve two litigants of each other's expenses.[83] A similar situation arose in 1336 in a case concerning a woman named Alazays who had separated herself from her husband, Jacme Guilhem, on the grounds of spousal abuse. Her son, Antoni, later sued Jacme to get his mother's dowry back. In his defense Jacme argued that a previous judge had ruled that Alazays had no right to leave her husband. The fact that Jacme had no instrument of this ruling did not matter: he got a lawyer named Serrutus de Gossolengo, who was present at court when the ruling was announced, to testify to its existence.[84]

---

[81] ADBR 3B 19, witness testimony on fols. 107r–116v, case opened 19 Feb. 1326 on fol. 95r.

[82] ADBR 3B 25, fol. 151r–v, case opened 21 Nov. 1330 on fol. 142r.

[83] ADBR 3B 38, fol. 52r, case opened 13 Oct. 1339 on fol. 47r.

[84] ADBR 3B 31, fols. 11v–12r, case opened 14 Dec. 1336 on fol. 7r.

The process by which witnesses were identified and selected by the plaintiff is at best murky, although it is clear that plaintiffs were constrained in their choices by legal rules and customs regarding eligible witnesses. Several categories of potential witnesses were formally debarred from offering testimony, including the plaintiff or plaintiffs. This sometimes led to complications if few apart from the plaintiffs had knowledge about a given matter. One strategy for getting around this rule was to have someone else initiate the suit so you yourself could testify. This practice, when spotted, generated a good deal of complaint from the opposing party. Jews, Muslims, and pagans were formally debarred from giving evidence in civil courts against Christians and virtually never did so. There is one exception. In 1413, a Christian nobleman named Laurens Ricau summoned a Jew named Salvet de Trets to give testimony against Laurens's Christian adversary. The judge expressed no objection. The notary was clearly caught off guard, for he wrote down that Salvet had been sworn in on "the holy gospels of God" and had to scratch out this phrase and replace it with "the holy law of Moses" (*sanctam legem Moysi*). It was Laurens's opponent, a tripe-maker named Johan Gaylet, who correctly pointed out later that Salvet's testimony could not be entered into the formal record of the proceedings.[85] Jews were allowed to testify against other Jews and the records of the criminal court provide several such examples.[86] I have found no instances of Jews testifying against other Jews in civil cases, though. There are some fifteen civil suits pitting two Jews against each other in the registers I have read but none of these got as far as the evidence phase. The testimony of close relatives, dependants, and enemies of the plaintiff was also viewed with some suspicion and the practice did in fact violate both statutory and procedural law, but such testimony was not uncommon and not systematically challenged by the defendant or discounted by the judge. Lepers were not debarred from testifying either by custom or law, though given their isolation in the leper hospital the occasions on which their testimony might prove useful were vanishingly rare, and there is only one such example among records I have consulted.[87]

Apart from restrictions on the testimony of Jews the most noteworthy feature of witness recruitment in the law courts of fourteenth-century Marseille is that there were no impediments whatsoever, either legal or customary, to the testimony of women. Women's testimony was fairly common. In

[85] ADBR 3B 151, fol. 182v (Salvet's testimony) and fol. 186r (Johan's exception), case opened 23 Oct. 1413 on fol. 181r.
[86] See, for example, ADBR 3B 96, fols. 75r–77r, case opened 15 Aug. 1380.
[87] ADBR 3B 151, fols. 141r–142r, case opened 25 Sept. 1413 on fol. 139r. Three lepers gave testimony in this case.

a sample of 945 suits initiated between 1323 and 1416, 147 contain the testimony of 912 witnesses, including 194 women (21 percent). This percentage is roughly equivalent to the percentage of cases involving women and the percentage of female property owners. In a number of cases, the evidence consists solely or in large part of women's testimony, often because women were in a better position than men to attest to certain facts. When the goatherd Marin de Morlans was stricken by his heart attack in the mountains of the Marseilleveyre he was nursed by several women of the neighborhood who subsequently gave convincing testimony to the effect that he was, in fact, in a very bad way.

Most plaintiffs and their lawyers and procurators were fully aware of these rules, customs, and strategies, and built groups of witnesses accordingly. The fact that notaries not infrequently recorded a witness's testimony by means of the simple expression "She (or he) knows nothing" (*nichil scit*) means that witness recruitment and selection was neither foolproof nor rigged, though in some instances a witness no doubt got cold feet when faced with the prospect of testifying against a powerful adversary and potential enemy. There is little question that defendants perceived hostile testimony as an inimical gesture: in 1307, according to one story, a man named Peire de Bellaygris had his eyes put out by members of one of Marseille's great factions, the de Jerusalem faction, almost certainly because he had testified against them.[88] At times, the written records of responses to interrogations prove to be remarkably, almost suspiciously, formulaic, as if they had been prearranged. In one case the defendant's procurator asked each witness not just whether he or she had been instructed as to what to say—a formula asked of all witnesses—but, more pointedly, whether she or he had been instructed by either of two particular men, the plaintiff and his procurator.[89] Clearly the coaching of witnesses was not unthinkable.

Witnesses were sworn in either on the Christian Bible or, in the case of Salvet de Trets and other Jews, the holy law of Moses, and subsequently interrogated either by the judge or a notary of the court. With rare exceptions, the interrogation took place in the vernacular and was translated into Latin by the notary, since Latin was the official language of record. The translation was probably done at a later time on the basis of notes taken during the interrogation, for transcripts of witness testimony are generally neat and orderly and rarely contain the erasures or insertions that one would expect from an on-the-spot translation. The adversary had a chance to guide the interrogation by providing the judge or the notary with a list of ques-

[88] ADBR 3B 820, fols. 77v and 78v, case opened 7 July 1356 on fol. 8r.
[89] ADBR 3B 94, e.g., fol. 298v, case opened 9 Dec. 1379 on fol. 193v.

tions. These questions were not routinely copied into the record—many exist as loose documents (*cedulae*) tucked into the binding, and many have been lost for this reason—but there are enough to provide a sense of the practice. Most were quite formulaic. All routinely asked witnesses to attest to very simple facts that seem ancillary to the facts of the case. In a case from 1407 involving a right-of-way on a recently purchased field and pasture, for example, people who were present when the plaintiff, Peire Mosson, bought the land were asked to identify the year, month, day, hour, the place where the contract was made, the locale within the place (*in quo loco* and *in qua parte loci*), and the names of those present. They were also asked whether the contract was notarized and an instrument made and, if so, who were the witnesses to the contract.[90] If witnesses should happen to disagree on these points then the defendant could seek to nullify all the testimony by objecting that "the depositions of the witnesses are varied and contradictory" (depositiones dictorum testium varii et contradictorii sunt).[91] All witnesses were asked to provide some information about their own status and competency as witnesses: Have you been instructed or suborned? Have you testified for lucre or out of fear, love, favor, or hatred? Are you related to the pleader by blood or affinity and in what grade? Where are you from? How old are you? How much do you possess in goods? Which party would you prefer to see victorious? and so on. In response to the fama clause, all were asked to explain how they knew the fama and just exactly what fama was. In the case of Peire Mosson, the rather snide list of interrogations posed by his adversary on this point ran like this: "On the last title, they are to be asked what is notoriety. Also what is truth. Also what is manifest. Also what is gossip and what is fama. Also what is the difference between them. Also who are the people who are aware of these things."[92] In this particular case these routine questions exposed certain flaws in the subsequent depositions that were later exploited by the defendant. Several witnesses, for example, provided contradictory dates; one of the witnesses was related to the pleader; and one of the witnesses, Antoni Vinsens, was in a state of excommunication and thus prohibited from taking an oath and giving testimony. He had been excommunicated at the request of Agneta Beroarde, a nun of the monastery of Syon. The irony here is that Agneta, as the direct lord over the land in question, participated in the trial as a principal member of the opposing party. Antoni was also accused of testifying against Agneta because of the

---

[90] ADBR 3B 147, fol. 155r, case opened 15 Mar. 1407 on fol. 136v.

[91] On this see also Durand, *Speculum iudicale*, I de teste § Quae possunt contra testes opponi 1.82 (1:300). The text states that witnesses may be impugned when they disagree over place, time, or the people involved.

[92] ADBR 3B 147, fol. 155v, case opened 15 Mar. 1407 on fol. 136v.

understandable hatred he held for the nun (quia habet odio dictam domi-nam monialem), and the testimony of his brother, Guilhem, was challenged on the same grounds of hatred.[93]

In addition to standard formulas, some questions asked during the inter-rogation also highlighted issues that the lawyer considered relevant to the case. In a trial that started in 1379, for example, a key set of arguments cen-tered on whether a young woman named Ricardona, dying, had acquitted her sister's husband, Johan Caprier, of all debts arising from his administra-tion of her paternal inheritance. In his articles, Johan argued that she had done so verbally. Moreover, he said, she had tried to call a notary to redact the quittance, but her husband, Antoni Bertran, had prevented the notary from coming. This was something of a problem for Antoni in his efforts to sue his brother-in-law. Johan's witnesses, at Antoni's request, were to be asked the following questions: At whose insistence or suggestion had Ricar-dona said the words found in the article? How did she say them? Who was the notary who was prohibited from coming? What was his name and fore-name? How did Antoni bring about this prohibition, whether by deed or by word, and by what deed or word?[94] All this was designed to find out whether the notary was a mere invention or whether a dying, muddled woman had been coerced into making the quittance. In Peire Mosson's right-of-way case, his adversary, faced with a set of articles in which Peire complained bitterly about the injustice of a previous decision, rather sarcastically in-sisted that the witnesses be asked "if they are jurists such that they might comprehend what is just and unjust."[95]

Testimony may have been given in the presence of the adversary, though this was not essential since adversaries always had access to the resulting transcript of the deposition.[96] Since the courts met outdoors, one must pre-sume that testimony likewise was taken outdoors, though perhaps screens were used to keep the curious at bay. Certainly there is nothing in the record to suggest that the judges retreated indoors to hear testimony. Testi-mony did not have to be taken in the presence of the judge. In cases involv-ing foreign merchants, for example, a judge elsewhere could record the tes-timony and send it to Marseille.[97] In the case of Johanet Salvayre, from

[93] For all these points see ibid., fol. 175r–v.

[94] ADBR 3B 94, fol. 267v, case opened 9 Dec. 1379 on fol. 193v.

[95] ADBR 3B 147, fol. 155v: "interrogentur dicti testes si sunt iuristi ut possint cognoscere quid est iustum vel iniustum."

[96] For an instance in which an adversary was clearly present see ADBR 3B 30, fols. 37r–47v, case opened 7 July 1335.

[97] See ADBR 3B 147, fols. 61–84, which includes a set of depositions taken in Avignon and bound directly into the register of the palace court. The case opened 24 Feb. 1407 on fol. 21r.

1407, the notary recorded the following about a proposed witness named Batrona, the wife of Antoni Dalmas:

> Although the wife of the said Antoni, summoned above as a witness, has also been summoned to give truthful testimony in the current trial, owing to her modesty [*honestatem*] it is not permitted that she come into the present court to take an oath. For this reason the notary of the case is ordered to go to the house of the said Antoni Dalmas to take his wife's oath in her own home and examine her.[98]

As this example shows, testimony did not have to be heard at the court. But even in instances where testimony was taken privately, procedural rules dictated that the names of witnesses had to be publicly announced when the attestations were published, and these rules appear to have been followed.[99] Incidentally, this particular circumstance—the sequestration of a married woman—was highly unusual and indeed unheard of as far as earlier fourteenth-century practice is concerned.

In the trial initiated by Johanet Salvayre, neither Batrona nor her husband Antoni were called to testify on the original set of titles, for by this point in the trial Johanet was onto his third set of articles. The additional sets of articles were added to counter exceptions that had been posed by his adversary. The exception (*exceptio*), in Roman-canon procedural law, was an objection made by adversaries to the veracity or legality of arguments or evidence offered by the plaintiff, and was used by defendants to halt a trial sequence.[100] If the exception was not dismissed peremptorily, the judge would have to take evidence and make a ruling on the legitimacy of the exception. At best, a key component of an adversary's suit might be quashed. At the very least, as James Brundage has noted, the posing of the exception, which invariably took time, gave an embattled defendant some breathing space.[101] Many exceptions centered on a procedural flaw such as a lack of standing. There are dozens upon dozens of absolutely gripping cases from fourteenth-century civil court records, and one of the most fascinating of these is a case from 1343, nominally a title dispute, in which the defendant, Gilet Alfans, successfully pleaded an exception to the plaintiff's libel by pointing out that the plaintiff, Ugo Gaydon, was in a state of excommunica-

[98] Ibid., fol. 59r.
[99] Durand, *Speculum iudicale*, I de teste § Qualiter sunt testes producendi 3.4 (1:307): "post publicationem attestationum testium nomina exprimi iubentur."
[100] Contemporary manuals of procedure drew a distinction between "peremptory" and "dilatory" exceptions (see Engelmann, *History*, 467–69). These expressions rarely surface in proceedings from Marseille's courts.
[101] Brundage, *Medieval Canon Law*, 131.

tion. Just a few years earlier, Gilet had been a member of the prosecuting team rounded up by Guilhem de Podio against Antoni d'Ays; now, he was involved in a land dispute. Gilet claimed that Ugo had been excommunicated for committing adultery with Ermessens, the wife of Peire Malian, in the vestibule of the altar of the church of St. Catherine and also for being a practitioner of the magical arts (*excerceus artem magicam*), because he had used magic and love potions to seduce Ermessens.[102] Ugo complained bitterly, claiming that exceptions based on sentences of excommunication were frequently used in malicious ways so as to avoid answering the real charges and to raise the expenses of the plaintiff, but the judge, perhaps out of his prurient interest, allowed Gilet to go ahead and prove his exceptions by means of witnesses—which he did, in lush detail.[103] Exceptions like this could be devastating to a plaintiff's arguments. Ugo almost certainly lost his case, and his community standing may have taken a beating as well, assuming that it could in fact go any lower.

It took Johanet Salvayre more than a year to escape the thicket of procedural delays and exceptions that his adversaries—first Jacme Niel and then, after Jacme's death, his mother, Reseneta Cambale—raised against his first two sets of articles. But shortly after the last of his utterly convincing witnesses in favor of the third round of articles left the court, Reseneta pleaded an exception in five articles to two of his witnesses, Antoni and Batrona Dalmas, for they were known to be Reseneta's mortal enemies and, as mortal enemies, were formally debarred from testifying against her.[104] Reseneta's own witnesses easily proved the existence of the hatred, and the judge then reached a sentence in her favor. Johanet had more than enough witnesses to his articles even without the testimony of Antoni and Batrona. His use of them, however, evidently suggested to the judge that Johanet was moved by hatred and bitterness—an entirely justifiable assumption, as the record makes plain.

The material record of a case shows that the Latin transcript of the witness depositions was often written out on a separate quire of paper and subsequently bound into the register. The practice is distinctly noticeable when the transcript was sent from afar, because foreign notaries used different size paper or even parchment, but is even evident in local cases. There are several reasons for this practice, not the least of which is the fact that testimony did not have to be taken at court. More significant, however, is that opposing parties did their best to prevent the admittance of the testimony, and

---

[102] ADBR 3B 45, fols. 170r–180v, case opened 15 Oct. 1343.
[103] Ibid., fol. 172v.
[104] See ADBR 3B 147, fols. 90r–95r, case opened 24 Feb. 1407 on fol. 21r.

until their objections could be overcome the testimony, which existed on paper, hung in a kind of legal limbo, presumably in the possession of the notary who took the transcription but officially unacknowledged by the court. Many cases show that witnesses were summoned and perhaps even sworn but their testimony never appears in the subsequent record.

This discussion of testimony and proof gives the impression that rulings and sentences were common. They were not.[105] Many cases brought before the palace court were exceedingly short and terminated abruptly after two or three pages, rarely lasting long enough to reach the evidence phase (table 1.3). In a sample of 849 palace court cases from 1323 to 1362 and 1400 to 1416, only 212 (25 percent) included articles of proof and only 136 (16 percent) included any witness testimony at all. Given the absence of anything that could be used as a basis for a sentence, actual sentences are therefore relatively uncommon. It is true that sentences (*summae*, *sententiae*) were not normally noted down in the proceedings, nor have the books of sentences survived. Even so, one can usually get a sense of whether a given case resulted in a sentence. The records of proceedings sometimes mention that a judge intends to issue a sentence—this was commonly noted in early fifteenth-century records—and other clues, such as an itemized list of expenses that includes an entry for the cost of writing the sentence, show that a sentence has been reached even if the notary did not mention it expressly.[106] A careful study of ten registers of lawsuits between 1323 and 1336 shows that just 10 percent of the cases (26 in 258) show obvious signs of having ended in a sentence (*summa*) or similarly definitive ruling. Eight registers from 1400 to 1416 yield a figure of about 14 percent (17 in 124).[107] Even if sentences were a little more common than the patchy records indicate it is nonetheless clear that most cases never ended in a sentence.

Historians who have used records of civil litigation often argue that many of the remaining cases ended in arbitration.[108] Marseille's records explicitly noted this outcome in a number of cases. To take one example, the notary recording a case heard in 1335 noted that the two parties had come to an

[105] For early modern parallels see Roberts, "Introduction," in *Disputes and Settlements*, ed. Bossy, 23.

[106] A very few cases include a sentence. Sentences can be readily identified because, following a brief synopsis of the case, they invariably begin with the expression "Therefore, we . . ." (*Tandem nos . . .* ). See, for example, ADBR 3B 147, fol. 96r, case opened 24 Feb. 1407 on fol. 21r. Examples of many sentences made by judges of the first appellate court can be found in ADBR 3B 801–804.

[107] ADBR 3B 16, 19, 24–31, 132, 136, 138, 141, 143, 147, 151–152.

[108] See Thomas Kuehn, *Law, Family, and Women: Toward a Legal Anthropology of Renaissance Italy* (Chicago, 1991). For a discussion of this practice in the canon law courts in England and a survey of the relevant literature, see Brundage, *Medieval Canon Law*, 134.

**Table 1.3 Length of Selected Palace Court Cases, 1323–1362 and 1400–1416**

| Page Length | Number of This Page Length | Percentage This Page Length or Less |
|---|---|---|
| 1 | 106 | 12 |
| 2 | 104 | 25 |
| 3 | 89 | 35 |
| 4–5 | 114 | 49 |
| 6–10 | 155 | 67 |
| 11–20 | 130 | 82 |
| 21–40 | 101 | 94 |
| 41–100 | 41 | 99 |
| 101–195 | 9 | 100 |
| Total | 849 | |

*Sources:* ADBR 3B 16, 19, 24, 25, 26, 27, 28, 29, 30, 31, 33, 34, 35, 36, 37, 38, 39, 41, 42, 43, 44, 45, 50, 51, 52, 53, 54, 57, 58, 60, 61, 62, 63, 64, 65, 66, 132, 136, 138, 141, 143, 147, 151, 152.

agreement, and did so to explain why a certain document wasn't written out in the cartulary.[109] A number of cases end with a note to the effect that "the judge has extended the trial in the hope of peace and concord" (*porrogavit sub spe pacis et concordie*), and this and similar expressions are common enough to show that the courts were very interested in recording this reasonably happy outcome to a dispute.

Evidence from mid-fourteenth-century notarial records shows that a number of notarized arbitrations started as palace court cases.[110] To judge by the 115 acts extant between 1337 and 1362, at least half of all arbitrations were enacted at court, and many of the remainder, enacted in various other locations such as the notary's house, the house of one of the arbitrators, or a church, may well have started in court. The evidence from Marseille, therefore, amply confirms the argument that individuals often used courts to promote amicable out-of-court settlements.

Yet it is important to note that a number of trials in medieval Marseille ended neither in a sentence or ruling nor in arbitration. Arbitrations are a relatively uncommon act in notarial casebooks from fourteenth-century Marseille: of the roughly sixty-six hundred notarial acts extant between 1337 and 1362, there are only 115 arbitrations, less than 2 percent of the total. Since extant acts account for about 10 to 15 percent of the original total of notarial acts in mid-fourteenth-century Marseille, the period 1337 to 1362 probably

[109] ADBR 3B 30, fol. 26r, case opened on 7 June 1335: "partes predicte inter se convenerunt et ideo cedula predicta posita in cartulario non fuit."

[110] Four such examples can be found in ADBR 351E 94, a casebook of the notary Guilhem Barban from the year 1395, beginning on fols. 5r, 27r, 41r, and 52v.

witnessed a total of between 770 and 1150 arbitrations, or thirty to forty-five per year. Even if *all* of these originally began as lawsuits, they would have accounted for somewhere between 15 and 33 percent of all suits initiated.

So what happened to the remaining lawsuits? In the absence of books of sentences it is difficult to know. In 1329, however, a conscientious notary created an index at the front of his register recording the names of the plaintiffs, the folio on which the case opened, and the outcome of each of the twenty-three trials. Eleven of these outcomes were identified as "finished" (*finita*) or "stilled" (*sopita*), and only four concluded in arbitration (*convenerunt*).[111] Eight were left blank, although the record of one shows that it eventually went to arbitration. Thus, only five out of twenty-three cases, or 22 percent, ended in arbitration, a proportion equivalent to that found in other registers and fully consonant with the figures suggested above that were based on extant arbitrations. One of the remaining eighteen cases ended when the plaintiff, a pregnant woman who had been recently widowed, abandoned her suit against her dead husband's heirs. She had been seeking a share of the inheritance on behalf of her unborn child but she suffered a miscarriage shortly after the suit was initiated.[112] Two cases were not contested by the defendant and ended in sentences. All the remaining fifteen cases, including those identified ambiguously as "stilled" or "finished," either terminated in a ruling or a sentence or simply fizzled out with no obvious conclusion: we cannot tell.[113] Given the notary's interest in recording cases of arbitration it is unlikely that many of these, if any, ended in arbitration. In most cases, it seems likely that plaintiffs dropped their suits, either because defendants left the city, or threw up significant procedural obstacles, or pushed the case to a point where the costs were becoming prohibitive.

The problem, of course, is that plaintiffs could not know in advance whether their suits would terminate rapidly in a settlement or favorable sentence, or, the worst scenario, drag out for months and even years. With some cases, like that of Antoni d'Ays, it comes as no surprise that neither party sought an arbitrated settlement. In the case of Johanet Salvayre, by contrast, relations between master and apprentice seem to have deteriorated with unusual rapidity, and it is somewhat surprising that the animosity persisted even after the death of one of the principal parties. In this case, surely the emotions themselves were transformed during the process of litigation, reaching the state of an implacable all-or-nothing hatred. It is not clear that

---

[111] ADBR 3B 24.

[112] Ibid., fols. 13r–15v, case opened 30 Dec. 1329.

[113] *Finita* and *sopita*, unfortunately, are ambiguous terms and cannot be taken to mean that these cases ended in a sentence.

we should necessarily blame the law for this development. All inimical gestures can result in this unpredictable feedback mechanism. The only point to stress here is that the procedural law, for all its vaunted orderliness, was readily reinterpreted by its users as a system of inimical gestures.

One should not exaggerate the absence of judgment in fourteenth-century Marseille. Judgments, it seems, were usually reached in criminal cases, even if the judgment was contumacy. At courts of first instance, a judge would sometimes arrive at a procedural ruling, a *cognitio* or an *interlocutoria*, that undermined a plaintiff's ability to continue a suit, thus encouraging abandonment. In such cases, a judge's intervention, even if less than a sentence, determined the outcome of a case. As this shows, however, the outcome of a case could be determined by rulings over procedures rather than rulings over facts.[114]

This is a point that is well worth stressing. Roman-canon procedural law, as I have already mentioned, is often associated with a new interest in facts and new methods for finding facts. Early medieval historians in recent years have objected strenuously to the idea that early medieval courts, indeed all primitive courts, were excessively ritualistic and hence irrational, an argument that is one of the historical legacies of Henry Sumner Maine.[115] But the casual assumption that there was progress toward greater emphasis on facts is flawed in another way. In reading through the records of cases from the law courts of fourteenth-century Marseille one finds facts and even arguments about facts, but far more visible than the facts, at least from the perspective of the user, is the oppressive weight of procedures, a burden that became ever more heavy by the early fifteenth century.

The point can be illustrated in a simple way: the growth in the average page length of cases across the fourteenth and early fifteenth centuries (table 1.4). I have grouped the data into four time periods with roughly the same number of cases, including twenty-five years before the Black Death (broken up into two time periods), fifteen years after the Black Death, and the first quarter of the fifteenth century. The increase in average page length is striking: the median almost doubles between the fourteenth and fifteenth centuries and the average more than doubles.[116] Much of the in-

---

[114] On the prevalence of interlocutory sentences in criminal trials, see Claude Gauvard, "Les juges jugent-ils? Les peines prononcées par le Parlement criminel, vers 1380–vers 1425," in *Penser le pouvoir au Moyen Âge: VIIIe–XVe siècle*, ed. Dominique Boutet and Jacques Verger (Paris, 2000), 69–87.

[115] See the discussion in Michael T. Clanchy, "Remembering the Past and the Good Old Law," *History* 55 (1970): 165–76, here 171.

[116] The large difference between the median and average page lengths reflects the fact that half the cases ended after five pages or fewer (see table 1.3 above).

**Table 1.4 Growth in Average Page Length of Selected Palace Court Cases between 1323 and 1416**

| Time Period | Number of Extant Cases | Median Length (In Pages) | Average Length (In Pages) |
| --- | --- | --- | --- |
| 1323–36 | 251 | 5 | 10.63 |
| 1337–47 | 207 | 4 | 11.48 |
| 1348–62 | 271 | 6 | 11.34 |
| 1400–1416 | 120 | 9.5 | 23.80 |
| Total | 849 | 6 | 12.92 |

*Sources:* as for Table 1.3.

creasing length of cases can be attributed to the growing use of procedural exceptions and delays, such as those used by Jacme Niel and then Reseneta Cambale to stymie the articles proposed by Johanet Salvayre.

Where did these procedures come from? The twelfth century saw a growing professionalization of the law and the reintroduction, or invention, of a set of procedural norms whose full details were known only to lawyers, jurists, and judges. These norms gradually worked their way into customary procedures as legal expertise began to suffuse throughout Mediterranean jurisdictions and legal classes implanted themselves in communities such as Marseille. Legal experts knew, or at least could learn, how to exploit procedural flaws and loopholes with the goal of frustrating the adversary. That they didn't do so systematically in the early fourteenth century is telling, for it shows that courts evolve according at least in part to usage, not rules alone. Principal parties in the thirteenth century may have thought it dishonorable or underhanded to exploit procedural flaws to their fullest. But as plaintiffs began to shift ever more resources into the courts—a shift of resources encouraged by a growing state investment in the apparatus of coercive force, notably a policing force and a system of debt recovery based on forcible distraint and imprisonment—the full scope of Roman-canon procedural law, including its obfuscatory powers, became ever more clear and more in demand. The use of procedural exceptions and delays, a use that depended on intimate lawyerly knowledge of Roman-canon procedural law, evolved as a result of this growing investment.

The investment was significant because these procedures cost a great deal of money, as both contemporary observers and modern historians have noted. The constant repetition of the phrase "he [or she] protests the expenses," a phrase seen constantly in the proceedings of Johanet Salvayre's suit, shows that court costs in late medieval Marseille could be burdensome. According to statute, procurators were to receive 2d. and lawyers 6d. for every royal pound implicated in the case. These fees amounted to 3.3 percent of the sum under litigation and were paid regardless of the length of the case, though some records note that lawyers occasionally charged additional sums.[117] Notaries and messengers charged fixed tariffs for their various services, and these fees mounted as the case wore on.[118] Below is a carefully itemized set of expenses presented by the victorious plaintiff, Guilhem Imbert, in a short case heard in 1331. The suit arose over an unpaid commenda contract of forty pounds:[119]

- salary of the two advocates, 1 florin each[120]
- salary of the procurator, 10 silver *robertos* (roughly 10s.)
- salary of the procurator who solicited the advocates, 10 silver robertos
- the scriptor who wrote the libel, 5 silver robertos
- the messenger who carried the libel to the opposing party, 2d.
- the notary who wrote the libel into the cartulary of the court, 2 silver robertos
- the scriptor who wrote out the titles, 2 silver robertos
- the notary who extracted a public instrument of the commenda, 10 silver robertos
- the messenger who carried it to the opposing party, 2d.
- the notary of the court who wrote the titles into the cartulary of the court, 2 silver robertos
- the notary of the court for a transcript of the mandament, 6d.
- the advocate who dictated the libel for the expenses, 10 silver robertos
- the advocate's notary or scriptor who wrote it out, 2 silver robertos
- the messenger who carried it to the defendant, 2d.
- the notary who wrote it out into the cartulary, 1 silver robertus
- the messenger who cited the defendant and the notary who wrote the citation, 6d.
- the procurator, Bernat Raymon, 2 *valodios* (roughly 2s.) and 5 silver robertos
- four more citations made to the heirs of the defendant, 12d.
- the notary of the court who wrote out two precepts, 4 valodios
- the notary who wrote out the decision of the arbitrators, 5 silver robertos
- the messenger of the court who collected a gage from the heirs, 4 valodios
- the messenger of the court for restoring the gage, 1 valodium

[117] In Florence in 1415, fees for judicial counsel were set according to a tariff that ranged from 1 to 8 percent, depending on the amount of money being litigated; see Martines, *Lawyers and Statecraft*, 100.

[118] The tariffs also surface from time to time in records of proceedings, as in a case from 1340 in which a lawyer sued his former client for nonpayment of his fee of 6d. per pound; see ADBR 3B 39, fols. 75r–76r, case opened 12 May 1340.

[119] ADBR 3B 27, loose sheet near folio 127r, case opened 6 Feb. 1332. I have paraphrased slightly and eliminated names to simplify things.

[120] According to the tariff, each advocate should have received 240d. or one pound, not one florin, which was nominally worth 32s. or 384d.

– the notary who wrote out the precept, 2 valodios
– for citing the defendant, 1 valodium
– for writing out a recommendation of his advocate, 6 valodios
– the messenger of the court who cited the heirs, 1 valodium
– for writing out citations, 2 valodios
– his lawyer, 30s.
– the notary of the court and the scriptors, 30s.

The total came to ten pounds, fifteen shillings, about a quarter of the sum being litigated. Other cases show other types of expenses. Toward the end of an unusually nasty 1334 trial that lasted a little over eight months and took up some forty-one folios of the court register, Bertran Vital presented expenses totaling twenty-five pounds, fifteen shillings.[121] The list includes not only the usual expenses—lawyer, procurator, notaries, and messengers—but also a bill of six pounds for sixty days lost labor (pro disturbio sexaginta dierum amissorum per eum). This figure was calculated at a rate of 2s. per day, a fairly standard wage for unskilled workers that shows up in other records. It is also likely that some palm greasing of judges was necessary, though no such payment is reflected in itemized expenses.

The full array of expenses associated with pursuing a civil suit is not easy to assess. Among other things, the sort of expense requested by Bertran for lost wages might have been more hopeful than realistic: perhaps the judge didn't allow it. Most cases that did not end with a sentence rarely include any itemization of expenses. Where cases went to arbitration, for example, there was no need for either party to itemize its expenses to the court, though arbitrators could and did include court costs in their final reckoning. Cases that fizzled out naturally include no reckoning of expenses. In the early fifteenth century, notaries did not record expenses with great care. There are no expenses listed, for example, in the case of Johanet Salvayre.

Despite these difficulties there are enough examples of expenses to provide a crude sense of the global costs associated with civil justice (table 1.5). Using the nominal exchange rate of thirty-two shillings per florin, the twenty examples given below show that victorious litigants spent a total of 22,299 shillings, or about 1,115 pounds, which comes to an average of roughly 56 pounds per case. Most cases did not cost this much: these examples, drawn from cases that ended in a sentence, are more than four times longer than the average case. It is more useful to note that the 924 pages used in these twenty cases cost, on average, about 1.2 pounds per page. This figure represents *only* the costs of the victorious party: we can safely assume that the losing party paid roughly the same amount. Assuming a conserva-

121  ADBR 3B 28, fol. 70r, case opened 12 July 1334 on fol. 29r.

## Table 1.5 Examples of Expenses in Palace Court Cases, 1323–1362

| Year | Length of Case (In Pages) | Expenses Requested by Victorious Litigant | |
| | | Original Sum (In Royal Pounds [li.] or Florins [fl.]) | Equivalent (In Shillings) |
|---|---|---|---|
| 1329 | 22 | 13 li. 10 s. | 270 |
| 1329 | 34 | 11 li. 11 s. | 231 |
| 1331 | 108 | 64 li. 1 s. | 1,281 |
| 1332 | 1 | 10 li. 15 s. | 215 |
| 1332 | 195 | 33 li. 3 s. 4 d. | 663 |
| 1334 | 84 | 25 li. 15 s. | 515 |
| 1334 | 7 | 4 li. 14 s. 9 d. | 95 |
| 1334 | 78 | 320 fl. | 10,240 |
| 1338 | 61 | 6 li. | 120 |
| 1338 | 26 | 10 li. 10 s. | 210 |
| 1338 | 54 | 28 fl. 12 li. | 1,136 |
| 1339 | 59 | 101 fl. | 3,232 |
| 1340 | 12 | 5 li. | 100 |
| 1341 | 36 | 41 li. 3 s. | 823 |
| 1353 | 8 | 9 fl. | 288 |
| 1353 | 36 | 15 li. | 300 |
| 1354 | 36 | 26 fl. | 832 |
| 1354 | 42 | 16 fl. 20 s. | 532 |
| 1354 | 9 | 19 fl. | 608 |
| 1362 | 16 | 19 fl. | 608 |
| Total | 924 | | 22,299 |

*Sources:* ADBR 3B 24, 27, 28, 29, 34, 38, 41, 42, 52, 53, 57, 58, 66.

tive cost of one royal pound per page per litigant, and given an average suit length of around eleven pages, the average civil lawsuit from fourteenth-century Marseille cost both parties a total of twenty-two pounds.

The estimates of twenty-two pounds per suit and one pound per page per litigant are very coarse figures. Costs are not closely correlated with the page length of a given suit, in part because transcripts of civil trials are not always complete, and in part because legal representatives were given a flat percentage of the sum under litigation. Ratios varied tremendously. The single page recording the proceedings of the case of Guilhem Imbert in 1331 cost the loser twenty pounds for Guilhem's expenses alone (admittedly an unusual example, since the notary failed to record most of the proceedings), whereas a sixty-one page case heard in 1338 cost the loser only six pounds for the winner's expenses, an average of only 2s. per page.

In the absence of any surer method for evaluating costs, however, let us proceed with the working assumption that the average civil case cost roughly twenty-two pounds per case. It is difficult to know what to make of this figure: was it unattainable or affordable for the average citizen? Looking at it from one perspective, Bertran Vital, who earned 2s. per day, could expect to work for 220 days to pay just the costs associated with losing a suit. Wages went up after 1348: a ruling of the city council set the maximum wage for male agricultural laborers at 4s. and, for female laborers, 2s. 6d.[122] Even so, unskilled workers would have had difficulty paying for the costs of civil justice. Yet the basic fallacy here is that Bertran, described as a *laborator* in the record, apparently had no difficulty coming up with the funds to defend himself over the course of a trial that lasted from July 1334 to March of the following year. Like most *laboratores* or urban peasants in Marseille at this time, Bertran may have worked for others but owned land on the side that could be used as a reserve fund. In addition, like Guilhem de Podio in the case of Antoni d'Ays, he was probably able to tap into the financial resources of sympathetic friends. Hundreds of self-described laboratores show up as plaintiffs and defendants in civil suits, and the courts were equally accessible to the entire spectrum of artisans, ranging from relatively modest shoemakers like Antoni d'Ays to wealthy drapers. Access to the courts was not a function of personal wealth alone—it also depended on social capital. To engage in litigation, one had to be enmeshed in a network of friends willing to extend credit. Reading through most cases of litigation from late medieval Marseille, one does not get the impression that the normal litigant was the prickly, isolated, antisocial figure sometimes envisioned by observers of modern litigation.

Using a figure of twenty-two pounds per case as a multiplier, we can arrive at a very crude estimate of the global costs associated with justice in fourteenth-century Marseille. As estimated earlier in this chapter, the palace court and the two lesser courts heard between one hundred and thirty and two hundred civil suits on an annual basis during the fourteenth century. Litigants, therefore, spent between 2,860 pounds and 4,400 pounds per year on civil litigation. These are absolute minimum figures for the costs associated with justice, for although the lesser courts were not as costly as the palace court the figures do not include the secular civil courts of the upper city, the appellate courts, or the episcopal court. Nor do the figures include the costs of requesting a simple judicial order to repay a debt, by far the most common type of case. In addition, the average page length of civil court cases was increasing dramatically over the course of the fourteenth century, reaching an average of 23.8 pages per case by the early fifteenth century and surely jacking up the costs of litigation. Finally, the secret economy of bribes inflated costs still further.

The crucial point to bear in mind here is that the state saw little of this money. The crown did collect fines (called *latae*) from the losers that consisted of 5 percent of the sum under dispute, but the infrequency of sentenc-

---

[122] Mabilly, *Inventaire*, 50. The wage maximums were reiterated after the plague of 1361–62; see 91–92.

ing means these fines were not, in fact, commonly assessed. Financial records of the crown show that total revenues from these fines were relatively small.[123] From a purely fiscal perspective, the state may have lost money on the civil courts, given the salaries paid to judges and other officials of the courts. Most of the money spent annually at court went directly into the pockets of the lawyers, procurators, notaries, and messengers who staffed the civil courts.

This being so, it is worth paying attention to the personnel of the court, and in particular the advocates or lawyers, a rather shadowy and ill-documented group of individuals. I have already mentioned how the role of the procurator was professionalized over the course of the fourteenth century. Much the same development can be seen in the case of advocates. Advocates are not very visible in records from the early fourteenth century. A few references, notably those found in lists of expenses, show that they were there, offering advice behind the scenes, though they often remained unnamed.[124] They come to be more obvious by the middle of the fourteenth century, working in tandem with procurators to build a legally defensible argument. By the early fifteenth century the presence of lawyers is inescapable, to the point where uneducated and illiterate litigants are requesting that lawyers be provided for them by the judge, where defendants like Jacme Niel plead for an extension because their lawyers are too busy to consult with them, and where plaintiffs challenge defendants to reply to articles of proof simply and without lawyerly obfuscation.[125] The increasing presence of lawyers is accompanied not only by the growth of the records but also growing frustration, a bitterness that sometimes seeps into the records of the longer cases. A case in point is a document presented by the procurator for Johanet Salvayre, Guilhem de Mellomonte, complaining about the frustrating series of exceptions and obstacles set up by the other party so as to evade any ruling.[126] In another case that opened in 1385, the plaintiff argued at one point deep in the trial that the defendant "has been maliciously

[123] In 1413, for example, the *clavaire* noted receipts from *latae* worth a total of 144 pounds 10s. 4d., probably little more than the salaries paid to the judge and the chief notary of the court. See ADBR B 1947, fol. 15r.

[124] Itemized lists of expenses typically include an entry for the advocate's fee. Some relatively early examples include ADBR 3B 24, loose sheet between fols. 23 and 24, case opened on 12 Dec. 1329 on fol. 18r; ADBR 3B 27, fol. 88r, case opened 16 Dec. 1331 on fol. 37r; ibid., loose sheet between fols. 127 and 128, case opened 6 Feb. 1332 on fol. 127r; ibid., fol. 181v, case opened 28 Jan. 1332 on fol. 143r.

[125] For the former example see ADBR 3B 141, fol. 129v, case opened 16 Oct. 1403 on fol. 128r. For Jacme Niel, see ADBR 3B 147, fol. 23v, case opened 24 Feb. 1407 on fol. 21r. For the latter example, see ibid., fol. 259r, case opened 14 June 1407 on fol. 257r.

[126] ADBR 3B 143, fol. 143a recto-verso, case opened 14 June 1404, foliation in the original.

and calumniously delaying this trial."[127] The growing presence of lawyers seems to have contributed to this change in emotional tenor.

But even if the growing significance of the procedural elements of Roman-canon law was driven in part by the economic motives of procurators and lawyers, these last two examples suggest how the process was also pushed along by enmity. The grudge had always been there and was exacerbated whenever a man used lawyerly tricks to avoid responding to a libel or a nun engineered the excommunication of an adversary so he couldn't testify against her party in court. In the early fourteenth century it was only just becoming clear to people that law courts were an effective way to pursue a grudge. Many other alternatives existed, including customary vengeance as well as a range of other behaviors that I will discuss in the next chapter. It took time to learn how to use the courts in pursuit of enmity. The growing significance of procurators and advocates and the procedural exceptions they made available to clients is only one sign of this learning process. That lawyers took all the blame is understandable, though in a sense unfair, given the underlying emotional context of the new legal habits. Lawyers were only doing what their clients asked them to do and were willing to pay for.

## THE CRIMINAL COURT

Before the advent of Angevin administration there is no evidence suggesting the existence of distinct criminal courts, or courts of inquest, using the characteristic elements of Roman-canon inquisitorial procedure, such as denunciation, ex officio proceedings, and judicial torture.[128] The Angevins themselves may not have taken to this innovation immediately. The earliest surviving record of the court of first appeals, from 1264, includes two ambiguous references to criminal activity and sentencing, both of which seem

[127] ADBR 3B 837, fol. 93v, case opened 15 May 1385 on fol. 64r: *maliciose et calumpniose retardet dictum processum*.

[128] On criminal procedure in Roman law, see, among others, Adhémar Esmein, *A History of Continental Criminal Procedure with Special Reference to France*, The Continental Legal History Series, vol. 5, trans. John Simpson (Boston, 1913); John Langbein, *Prosecuting Crime in the Renaissance: England, Germany, France* (Cambridge, Mass., 1974); Sarah Rubin Blanshei, "Crime and Law Enforcement in Medieval Bologna," *Journal of Social History* 16 (1982): 121–38; Laura Ikins Stern, *The Criminal Law System of Medieval and Renaissance Florence* (Baltimore, 1994), 20–46; John K. Brackett, *Criminal Justice and Crime in Late Renaissance Florence, 1537–1609* (Cambridge, 1992), 8–21, 57–77; Carbasse, *Introduction*.

to have been handled by the palace court rather than by a distinct criminal tribunal. In the first, a woman named Laudineta had denounced a certain Peire Rossa to the court for theft; Peire was fined fourteen pounds, which was subsequently assessed against his pledge, Bernat Gontart; and Bernat in turn appealed the decision. A second case speaks of a rape that was denounced to the court.[129] Technically, the word "denounce" would only be used in the context of a criminal court.[130] In neither case, however, do we find mention of a court of inquest (*curia inquisitionis*). The next surviving record of the court of first appeals from the year 1290 speaks explicitly of inquisitorial procedures (e.g., *inquisitionem factam ex officio curie*) and the procedures for dealing with criminal condemnations are much better defined.[131]

As the courts emerge from the shadows of the thirteenth century we learn that Marseille had two secular criminal courts, one in each of the upper and lower cities. This division of jurisdiction lasted until the union of 1348, at which time the court of inquest of the upper city ceased to function and the jurisdiction of the lower city's court of inquest was extended over the entire city. Though both courts kept systematic records of their proceedings, only three registers of criminal inquests are extant before the arrival of French royal administration late in the fifteenth century, and only one, covering the months from May 1380 to January 1381, is extant from the fourteenth and early fifteenth centuries.[132] This dismally poor rate of survival is slightly mitigated by the fact that records of appeals of criminal sentences from the mid-fourteenth century onward often include transcripts of the original proceedings of the court of inquest. These have the problem of surviving both sporadically and selectively, though some of the most compelling cases extant from fourteenth-century Marseille are criminal appeals found in the appellate court records. The best profile of the activity of the criminal court, though, can be gleaned not from records of the court of inquest directly but rather from five financial records of the crown extant before 1414. These record the fines paid by individuals or groups convicted by the court of inquest and also include a brief synopsis of each case. It is likely that these synopses constitute the text of the public notices of condemnation read out by the viguier at the public parlements. These records do not record the innocent verdicts, nor do they record cases involving people who either could

---

[129] ADBR 3B 801, fols. 22r and 30v.

[130] A person does not denounce an adversary to the civil court; instead, he or she submits a libel and asks that the adversary be summoned to respond. A denunciation, by contrast, would notify the court of some criminal delict, and if the judge agreed then the inquest would proceed ex officio.

[131] ADBR 3B 802, fols. 40v–41v, case opened May 1290 (date unreadable).

[132] ADBR 3B 96; see also ADBR 3B 170 and 172.

not pay (and suffered corporal punishment instead) or refused to pay, preferring to abandon the city. Even so, there is enough extant evidence to get a good sense of the activities and procedures of the court of inquest.

Given the sources at our disposal there are good reasons to believe that the caseloads of the two criminal courts were growing considerably from about the late thirteenth century onward. Among other things, criminal appeals, rare in 1264, dominate the three appellate court registers extant from the years 1290, 1308, and 1319, suggesting an increasingly active criminal court. Though the growth of criminal courts is natural enough in contexts of state building, in the case of the Angevin realms, including Marseille, the process was pushed along by the loss of Sicily in 1289, a devastating blow that turned the fiscal interests of the Angevin crown back onto its continental possessions in southern Italy and Provence. The incessant search for revenues encouraged the Angevin administration to extract as much profit as possible from the criminal courts.

The criminal court of the lower city, the best documented of the two secular criminal courts, was composed of three judges, namely the palace court judge and the judges of the two lesser courts. Although the criminal court, like the two lesser civil courts, was technically a branch of the palace court, it was institutionally distinct and had its own court notary and its own series of registers that were never mingled with those of the palace court. By the fourteenth century, notaries working within the court system were always careful to distinguish between what they called the palace court (*curia palacii*) and what they called the criminal court (*curia criminalis*) or the court of inquest (*curia inquisitionis*). Thirteenth-century records do not say whether the criminal court was assisted by a police force, although in theory it would have been difficult for a court of inquest to operate without the ability to capture and incarcerate suspects. By the early fourteenth century, however, there is ample evidence that the sub-viguier, assisted by his *familia*, was engaged in policing the city.

Like the civil courts, the criminal court met outdoors before the lower gates of Notre Dame des Accoules. Because all the courts met at this location, and because the criminal court was run by the judges of the three civil courts, the distinction between the civil and criminal courts was mental rather than spatial. On numerous occasions, however, personnel attached to the criminal court conducted hearings or did business in less public spaces. Witness depositions, for example, were not uncommonly heard in private homes, especially in cases where the victim of an assault was lying wounded in bed. In one case from July 1403, a smith named Jacme Albin was appealing a fine of four hundred pounds and a sentence of banishment for having

THE CONSUMPTION OF JUSTICE

ambushed and killed Johan Areat. Jacme argued, reasonably enough, that Johan was in a state of banishment for having killed Jacme's brother the previous year; as he pointed out, a person in such a condition, like a bandit or an outlaw, could be killed with impunity. The appeal includes a record of the original inquest, which reveals that Johan lived for a few days after the ambush. The court notary, Peire Calvin, had gone to Johan's house to take down his deposition; he recorded how he found Johan lying in bed, wounded in many places on his head and body.[133]

Assailants were occasionally captured by the sub-viguier, incarcerated, and interrogated. Many were not, because virtually all murderers and many others who had inflicted grievous wounds fled the scene of their crimes and sought sanctuary in one of the local churches. Officials of the court were therefore obliged to interrogate them in situ if they wanted a firsthand account of the battle. After the killing of Johan Areat, Jacme Albin made his way to St. Victor and was presumably interrogated there. In another case some forty years earlier, the notary Guilhem de Belavila, guilty of having assisted in the killing of Guilhem Tomas in 1365, immediately fled to the church of St. Antoine and eventually to the cathedral of La Major. Given the seriousness of this particular case—the two men were members of rival noble factions—the judge of the court of inquest, Leonardo da Siena, personally went to La Major to hear Guilhem's deposition.[134] It was more normal, though, for notaries to do the interrogation. In 1400, a cleric named Nicolau Jausap, having assaulted Bernat Berengier, fled immediately to La Major and scrambled up into the campanile. The notary of the ecclesiastical court, Guilhem Barban, laconically noted in the ensuing record how he and a priest climbed up the campanile to see whether Nicolau was indeed a cleric. They fingered his clothing and Nicolau obligingly raised his cap so they could see his tonsure.[135] Completing his rounds, Guilhem then made his way to Bernat's house and took the deposition of the dying man.

The most conspicuously indoor act of the criminal court, however, was torture. Instances of torture took place in a building known as the Palace, located just south of the court space, in a chamber located next to the jail. All three judges of the court of inquest as well as the notary were present at instances of torture, so once a decision had been made to apply torture the four men made their way down to the torture chamber where the defendant was strung up by the torturer. The only instrument of torture referred to in

<hr>

[133] ADBR 3B 140, fol. 245r–v, case opened 11 July 1403 on fol. 229r.
[134] ADBR 3B 825, fol. 71v, case opened 13 May 1365 on fol. 35r.
[135] ADBR 5G 772, fol. 25r–v, case opened 16 Dec. 1400 on fol. 24r.

the records was the *eculeum*, or horse, over which the accused was bent so that his or her arms could be bound behind the body and then raised up, wrenching the shoulders and causing excruciating pain.[136]

Judicial torture is one of the most obvious ways in which the procedures of the court of inquest differed from those of the civil courts. Inquests were formally initiated not by means of a libel but rather through a denunciation made by an official or a private citizen, or, in some cases where the rumor was loud enough, an ex officio proceeding initiated by the court itself. Responsibility for arguing the case then passed to the court, unlike a civil suit where it was up to the plaintiff to argue the case and assemble the evidence. In cases of homicide, the court of inquest allowed relatives of the victims to "make part" with the court and assist in prosecuting the case; this practice can be found in the case of Guilhem de Belavila and in other trials.[137] Most inquests involved what we would consider relatively minor issues, and in very simple cases a defendant might simply be summoned and admit guilt without any fuss. In two back-to-back cases heard on 6 July 1380, two prostitutes each denounced the other for slander. Summoned by the court, each admitted her guilt and returned to work.[138] The record in no way suggests that the two were dragged in by agents of the police, and why they chose to use the court in this way is unclear. Perhaps it was a way to drum up new business or to escape the tedium of the prostitutes' quarter to which they were nominally confined. Where the charge was contested the court of inquest evidently began by means of informal inquiries; these in hand, they then developed a basic narrative of the case and assembled a list of articles called *indicia*, similar in many respects to the articles of proof used in civil courts. In the case of the notary Guilhem de Belavila, accused of the murder of Guilhem Tomas, the indicia, which I have abbreviated and paraphrased, ran roughly as follows.[139] Each was identified carefully in the margin with the words *primum indicium, secundum*, and so on:

(1) First, before the death of Guilhem Tomas, Guilhem de Belavila was his capital enemy because Guilhem Tomas had had Guilhem de Belavila prosecuted in court for the crime of having written a false instrument. (2) Guilhem Tomas was struck with a sword belonging to Guilhem de Belavila [its measurements follow], and the sword is recog-

---

[136] Edward Peters, *Torture* (New York, 1985).

[137] ADBR 3B 825, fol. 60v, case opened 13 May 1365 on fol. 35r. A passage here reveals that a mason and prominent civil official named Restezin Johan "made part in this case" (*partem factus in hac causa*) and subsequently guided the interrogation of the witnesses.

[138] ADBR 3B 96, fols. 43r–44v, both cases opened 6 July 1380.

[139] ADBR 3B 825, fol. 60r–v, case opened 13 May 1365 on fol. 35r.

nized by many as belonging to Guilhem de Belavila. (3) Guilhem de Belavila and Fulco Robaut [a co-defendant] fled and took refuge in the church. (4) Guilhem de Belavila has also been inculpated of many crimes and was arrested last year. (5) All this is the public talk and fame.

Witnesses were then formally interrogated on each of these indicia. Defendants could subsequently present their own list of articles and call witnesses to their defense, though most seem to have preferred to reserve their defense for an appeal. But the possibility of a defense did exist. In 1380, a defendant named Raymon Berengier, seeking to defend himself and his faithful servant Johan de Cornet from charges arising from the stabbing of Bertomieu Jauseran, presented six positions, paraphrased and somewhat abbreviated below:[140]

(1) If it is found that he did have words with Bertomieu, then he will prove that Bertomieu was inimical to him before those words were spoken and was currently not speaking to him and hasn't spoken to him for some time, owing to a certain dispute that Raymon has with him arising from a pony that was damaged by Bertomieu. (2) That evening, Jacmeta Jauserane, the wife of Bertomieu, was having words with Mondina, the wife of Honorat Laydet, over money owing from the lease of a house. [Raymon intervened in their dispute. Bertomieu then came out into the street and threatened Raymon.] Bertomieu attacked him with the knife and would have skewered him had Johan his servant not intervened. (3) Bertomieu is quarrelsome. (4) Raymon is a good man. (5) If he drew his own knife, he did so in self-defense. (6) If it is found that Peire Mounier gave testimony as a witness against Raymon, he will show that for ten years and more, this man, along with his wife, has been his mortal enemy. Peire once lethally wounded the father of Raymon and hasn't spoken to him since [ipse est et fuit a decem annis citra et uxor sua inimicus mortalis ex eo quia semel vulneravit letaliter et ad mortem dominum patrem dicti domini Raymundi et ex post non locutus est sibi.]

This list of positions is in all respects characteristic of the exception procedure. As discussed in the next chapter, many such procedures evoked the emotions of hatred and anger. The refusal to converse with an enemy is also characteristic. But from the perspective of legal history the most significant element of this passage is that defendants caught up in the toils of Roman-canon inquisitorial procedure, at least in Marseille, *did* have an occasion to

---

[140] For the entire case see ADBR 3B 96, fols. 67r–72r, case opened 9 Aug. 1380.

challenge the testimony of hostile witnesses. Legal historians sometimes take it for granted that criminal courts using the Roman-canon inquisitorial procedure trampled on the rights of defendants. In this case, Raymon Berengier had full access to the depositions of hostile witnesses and was able to use the exception procedure to pose a challenge to the veracity of those witnesses. A fragmentary record of a criminal inquest into a street battle that took place around 1353 records a set of positions designed to undermine the criminal inquest (*ad tollendum vires inquisitionis*), positions that include exceptions to several of the witnesses arrayed against the defendants.[141] The practice is even more marked a feature of criminal appeals, as discussed in the next section below. It is worth pointing out that, in the former case, Raymon and his servant were both acquitted. The outcome of the latter case is not known.

One of the most striking features of several criminal inquests is the testimony provided by surgeons.[142] The appeal of Amiel Bonafos in 1356 includes a copy of the transcript of the inquest into the murder of Peire de Jerusalem, and the transcript includes a deposition provided by five surgeons:

> Immediately afterward, Johan de Beaulieu, Jaufres Homedei, Peire Jordan, Raymon de Montania, barber, and David, Jew and surgeon . . . said and attested that they had palpated and seen the body of the said Peire and probed the wounds according to the surgical art. They said that they had found twenty-two or twenty-three wounds on the body; of these, one to the head was mortal; another mortal wound was made with a crossbow quarrel on the right-hand ribs; another mortal wound was made with a blade on the right knee; another mortal wound was made on the right foot with an edged blade; and another mortal wound was made with an edged blade on the left arm near the elbow, and thus the said Peire de Jerusalem died owing to the above mentioned wounds.[143]

Jewish surgeons often show up among those summoned in this way.[144] Wounds on the body of Guilhem Tomas were carefully inspected by a Jew-

---

141 ADBR 3B 50, loose signature at back of register, fol. 4v, undated.

142 For a survey of the literature discussing the practice see Andrée Courtemanche, "The Judge, the Doctor, and the Poisoner: Medieval Expertise in Manosquin Judicial Rituals at the End of the Fourteenth Century," in *Medieval and Early Modern Ritual: Formalized Behavior in Europe, China, and Japan*, ed. Joëlle Rollo-Koster (Leiden, 2002), 105–23, here 114–15.

143 ADBR 3B 820, fol. 41v, case opened 7 July 1356 on fol. 8r.

144 On the role of Jewish surgeons in Manosquin trials see Joseph Shatzmiller, *Médecine et justice en Provence médiévale: documents de Manosque, 1262–1348* (Aix-en-Provence, 1989).

ish surgeon, Salves de Cortezono, and a Christian, Bertran Avensi. They found only one mortal wound, which was eventually attributed to Fulco Robaut.[145] This strict accounting is very similar to what is described in the Icelandic sagas and therefore not especially modern, though the role assigned to surgeons is a harbinger of the professionalization of scientific knowledge.

Criminal courts differed markedly from civil courts in one important respect: proceedings show that they moved along with far greater dispatch and were rarely stalled by procedural exceptions or delays. Lawyers are less evident in criminal procedures: the court did not need them and defendants were apparently not in a position to argue that the wording of the indicia was ineptly formed. The briskness of criminal cases also stems from the fact that the parties involved were usually immediately at hand, for the court ran its own prosecution and the defendant, often enough, was being held in the nearby jail. The major exception were those cases of serious violence in which the assailant had fled the city or sought sanctuary in a church, but even these moved along briskly because, following the three required summons, the defendant was invariably condemned for contumacy, declared guilty, and banished. The only question was the amount of the fine for contumacy. Procedural exceptions and other lawyerly tactics, perhaps by custom, were normally reserved for the appellate stage, though the case of Raymon Berengier shows that they could be used during the inquest as well.

Unlike their civil counterparts, criminal court registers show signs that judges actually read them. The margins of the single surviving record of the court of inquest from 1380 are littered with indexing devices by the notary to identify the testimony of witnesses and defendants. They also include even more interesting notations in the handwriting of the three judges as well as elegantly drawn hands with long index fingers indicating crucial passages of witness testimony. Marginal comments next to the testimony of the defendants include, "Guilty by virtue of his/her confession," "Not proven and therefore absolved," "This one is a cleric as shown by the letter below," "Guilty because he thrashed his daughter," "The penalty is mitigated because of his poverty," "Captured and interrogated," and so on. Judges wrote their initials next to their remarks, the chief judge, Johan Ysoart, going by the cheerful sobriquet "Joyso," the other two preferring more staid initials, namely "An" (for Antoni de Sarciano) and "G" (for Guilhem Lombart). In an involved appellate case that turned on the sequence of injuries and blows, one judge wrote "not after" (*non post*) in the margin next to a witness's re-

---

[145] ADBR 3B 825, fol. 59r, case opened 13 May 1365 on fol. 35r.

mark that a knife slash had preceded a hair-pulling.[146] Most depositions show similar signs of careful reading by judges in an effort to get the sequence of events correct. One finds marginal notations such as "This agrees with witness so-and-so below" or "This conflicts with what another witness said."

Of the eighty-one cases in the record that give a clear indication of the source of the accusation, fifty-one (63 percent) were initiated privately, four (5 percent) by public fame, and the remaining twenty-six (32 percent) by the sub-viguier, the viguier, or other officials of the court. Two-thirds of the inquests in this register, in other words, arose from the denunciation of private citizens or through public fame initiations resulting from gossip rather than the industry of officials.[147] The proportion of cases initiated by officials, moreover, is somewhat inflated, for three cases mention that although the sub-viguier had made the formal denunciation he had been prodded into doing so by a private citizen. In other cases it is likely that the formal denunciation by the sub-viguier masks private initiatives, for the sub-viguier and his servitors did not attempt to be a fully knowing police force with agents on every street corner and instead relied heavily on public willingness to make use of the coercion they offered.

As the high percentage of denunciation shows, agents of government in fourteenth-century Marseille were not the greatest users of the criminal court. The caseload of the criminal court, instead, was largely determined by the private citizens who chose to use it. As such, it is worth considering who the users were. The list of fifty-one private denouncers includes nineteen women, eight of whom were prostitutes; three Jews, two of whom denounced other Jews and one who denounced a Christian; at least two servants denouncing their employers; and a range of artisans, merchants, and tradesmen denouncing either on their own behalf or, in several cases, on behalf of children abused by parents or strangers. The list of denouncers includes no one identified as a noble or as distinguished (*nobilis*), apart from the officials of the court. Such elevated persons, it seems, preferred to pursue their differences through customary rather than judicial vengeance. In this regard, the possibility of denunciation to the criminal court can be seen as enabling less powerful, less wealthy individuals to pursue redress. Criminal courts democratized the access to vengeance.

The three judges often, though not always, noted the outcome of the cases they heard. Seven of the cases in this record were not canceled and

---

[146] ADBR 3B 808, fol. 191r, case opened 29 Oct. 1342 on fol. 184r.

[147] This figure is virtually identical to that found in early fifteenth-century Florence, where public fame (38 percent) and private accusation (28 percent) accounted for 66 percent of all initiations. See Stern, *Criminal Law System*, 204.

were therefore left hanging, and nine other cases, though canceled, do not reveal the outcome. The sentences would have been recorded elsewhere so it is perhaps not surprising that the judges and notary of the criminal court were not wholly consistent in marking this register. Fifty-four individuals or groups (79 percent), identified by means of the expressions *collectus* or *colligatus*, were found guilty. Fourteen of these fifty-four confessed voluntarily. In the remaining fourteen cases (21 percent) the defendants were absolved.

A successful inquest resulted in a sentence publicly read by the viguier during one of the annual parlements. The vast majority of sentences consisted of a fine, sometimes a modest amount, sometimes a rather heavier penalty. In cases of reprobates, foreigners, and defamed individuals, a sentence might consist of a bodily mutilation: the excision of a hand or foot, or, rarely, execution. I will discuss these practices at greater length in chapter 4. Here, it is worth stressing that financial penalties were by far the most common result of a successful inquest, as they were elsewhere in Europe at this time. But whatever the nature of the sentence, whether a fine or corporal punishment, the outcome of a successful inquest was a very public act of humiliation. Even in cases where a guilty verdict was not achieved we can assume that incarceration was shame enough and therefore partially satisfying to the denouncer. The emotional satisfaction available to denouncers helps explain why private citizens were willing to use the courts in this way, or, more to the point, why the outcome of a successful prosecution of one's enemy was deemed to be as emotionally satisfying as any other form of satisfaction.

The 1380 register of the criminal court, in addition to what it tells us about the practice of denunciation, provides good information about the nature of the accused parties as well as their crimes. A far better sense of the caseload of the criminal court, however, can be had from examining the lists of receipts paid to the crown arising from successful criminal inquests. The categories that stand out are assault and threat and the related charge of carrying prohibited weapons. Over the course of the century a growing number of individuals were successfully fined by the court of inquest for various infractions of craft regulations. Resistance to agents of the courts taking security for debt also occurs for the first time in the early fifteenth century, and accusations of fraud are also more common by the early fifteenth century.

The fines assessed by the court of inquest and collected by the crown were profitable, and profits increased dramatically from 1315 to 1413 (table 1.6), even though the number of fines paid remained steady, in the range of four hundred to five hundred per year. Clearly the average amount per fine was increasing steadily across the period. Possibly as a consequence of the

**Table 1.6 Criminal Fines Received by the Angevin Crown from Marseille, 1315–1471**

| Fiscal Year | Amount Received (Rounded to the Nearest Royal Pound) | Source (All ADBR) |
|---|---|---|
| 1315–16 | 223 | B 1517 |
| 1323 | 745 | B 1519 |
| 1330–31 | 654 | B 1940 |
| 1365–66 | 1,329 | B 1523 |
| 1407 | 5,313 | B 1943 |
| 1409 | 4,128 | B 1944 |
| 1410 | 5,835 | B 1945 |
| 1413 | 4,047 | B 1947 |
| 1438–39 | 466 | B 1948 |
| 1441 | 281 | B 1949 |
| 1442 | 447 | B 1949 |
| 1471 | 338 florins | B 1953 |

sack of Marseille in 1423 and the impoverishment of many citizens the fines collected by the crown from criminal inquests dropped just as dramatically after 1423.

One important feature about the fines collected by the criminal court early in the fourteenth century, as noted earlier, is that they amount to considerably less than the amount of money spent on proceedings in the civil courts, three to four thousand pounds or more per year around the middle of the century and perhaps double that by the early fifteenth century. The two sums cannot really be compared, since fines paid are quite different from the fees charged for registration, summoning, and so on. Even so, it seems likely that the criminal courts, as an economic engine, were less significant than the civil courts.


## THE APPELLATE COURTS


The two courts of first and second appeals, like the palace court, were staffed by judges who were not native to Marseille. Like the other courts, they convened outdoors. Records of the second appellate court are very sporadic. Those from the court of first appeals, by contrast, are extraordinarily rich and relatively dense from 1339 onward and are, in many respects, the crown jewel of Marseille's court records. The procedures of the two appellate courts were very similar to those of the civil courts: the appellant had to present a libel as well as a letter from the lower court, and most cases of any length consist of long periods of procedural jockeying. Appellants could appeal either sentences or simple rulings of the judges of the lower courts, and although the sentence or ruling was not usually given in full it was nonetheless described in the libel. Appellants complained routinely and at length about the injustice and iniquity of the sentence or ruling. If an appeal lasted any length of time the appellant had to present the judge with a complete transcript of the lower court's record. This is a curious practice in one sense, for the courts all met in the same location and, in theory, an appellate judge interested in consulting the transcript of a lower court case needed only to step over to the adjoining booth and consult the relevant register. The practice helps confirm the argument made above and also in the appendix that the courts did not consider themselves responsible for keeping archives and instead relied on private citizens to archive their own acts. Appellants were expected to request, and pay for, the transcript of their lower court cases before proceeding to the appeal; the transcript was then handed over to the notary who bound it into his register. By custom, all notaries of Marseille's courts used paper of the same trim size, so the transcripts are marked not by their differing size but rather by the discrete nature of their binding, the handwriting, and the wax seal typically found at the end of the transcript.

The percentage of criminal appeals relative to the percentage of civil appeals declined steadily from the thirteenth to the fifteenth century (table 1.7). The annual number of criminal appeals was probably also declining. The extant documents suggest a high figure of eight criminal appeals per year in the thirteenth and early fourteenth centuries declining to less than two in the early fifteenth century. Given the sporadic nature of preservation, it is impossible to be confident about absolute figures. Registers do not always include a complete year of appeals, and judges might well have kept multiple registers. For these reasons, the annual number of criminal appeals was almost certainly higher than the figures suggest. Even so, given the fact that the criminal courts were generating as many as five hundred successful inquests per year in the 1330s and around three hundred and fifty in the early 1400s it is clear that the vast majority of men and women sentenced by the criminal court never appealed their sentences and that criminal appeals were becoming increasingly uncommon.

In many cases it made economic sense simply to pay a fine and be quit, since the costs of an appeal, in most cases, would have far outstripped the amount of the fine. But appeals were also discouraged by statute: fines under 60s. could not be appealed. By the late fourteenth or early fifteenth centuries, judges of the criminal court had learned to keep fines below this threshold so as to minimize the number of appeals. Alternatively, and more

**Table 1.7 Declining Percentage of Criminal Appeals in Registers of the First Appellate Court, 1264–1409**

| Time Period | Extant Civil and Criminal Appeals | Criminal Appeals | |
|---|---|---|---|
| | | N | % |
| 1264–1342 | 118 | 59 | 50 |
| 1350–58 | 108 | 36 | 33 |
| 1365–86 | 48 | 8 | 17 |
| 1400–1409 | 115 | 12 | 10 |

*Sources:* ADBR 3B 801, 802, 803, 804, 805, 808, 810, 811, 812, 813, 815, 816, 817, 818, 819, 820, 821, 822, 824, 825, 835, 836, 837, 838, 839, 853, 854, 140, 855, 856, 857, 858, 859, 860, 861, 862.

*Note:* In Tables 1.7 and 1.8, for the period 1365–1386 I have analyzed a representative sample of registers from the years 1365, 1381, 1385, and 1386. For the other time periods I have analyzed most of the extant registers with the exception of several that are in very poor condition or not relevant.

fraudulently, judges figured out that they could divide a criminal prosecution under several different headings and ensure that each ensuing fine was less than sixty shillings.

Statutory law in Marseille, in short, conspired against the right of defendants to seek justice, at least defendants in the cases of petty violence and insult that dominated criminal court business. The legal situation of defendants, however, wasn't entirely bleak. Among other things, defendants in cases involving more than 60s. who chose to appeal had the right to view the proceedings of the inquests made against them, including the depositions of witnesses, and made free use of exceptions and other legal devices for overturning their fines. As discussed in the next chapter, for example, exceptions against the witnesses heard at the inquest were common in appellate cases. Witnesses could be excepted on several grounds, including the mortal hatred they bore for the defendant as well as a lack of moral or community standing. Defendants sometimes even sought to void a judge's ruling or sentence by arguing that he was in a state of excommunication at the time of the ruling. In 1356, a procurator arguing in an appeal on behalf of Amiel Bonafos noted that the palace judge, Bertran Tribolet, was in a state of excommunication when he issued a sentence of contumacy against Amiel.[148] Following a long and bitter 1352 civil suit pitting Isaac de Bonsenhor against another Jew, Benvenguda Mosse, Isaac appealed on the grounds that the palace judge, Johan Symeon, was in a state of excommunication for having willfully and knowingly imprisoned a cleric.[149] Compounding his error, he delivered his judgment, according to Isaac, "on the vigil of the Virgin Mary

---

[148] ADBR 3B 820, fol. 46r–v, case opened 7 July 1356 on fol. 8r.
[149] ADBR 3B 50, fols. 31v–32r, case opened 13 Oct. 1352 on fol. 27r.

which is celebrated by all Catholics and Christians," when judges ought not to render judgment out of reverence for the feast.

The first appellate court did not hesitate to accept arguments that seemed legitimate, and as a result, sentences of the court of inquest were occasionally overturned. In some thirty-seven appellate decisions reached between 1289 and 1319 where the original fines and sentences are clearly identified, five defendants were completely absolved, including one defendant whose sentence of execution was overturned because of a procedural flaw in the original inquest.[150] The most common practice of the court of appeals in this period, however, was simply to mitigate the penalty, the practice followed in twenty-nine cases. Fines were most commonly reduced by half. Reasons given by the appellate judges included not only the "just defenses" presented by the defendant but also, in several cases, extenuating circumstances such as excessive poverty and youth. In 1290, Guilhem Cozalongua, whose crime is unknown, was condemned by the court of inquest to pay twenty-five pounds or suffer the loss of his left hand. On appeal, this was reduced to fifteen pounds or amputation and exile. The judge cited both the defendant's excessive poverty as well as the loss of income resulting from his long incarceration.[151]

The growing infrequency of criminal appeals means that most cases heard before the first appellate court from the mid-fourteenth century onward were civil appeals. The annual number of civil appeals was relatively constant throughout the period 1264–1409, averaging about sixteen cases per year (table 1.8). This figure is at best approximate, given the patchy nature of the record, and is a minimum figure. It is surprisingly high. I argued earlier that only 10 to 15 percent of the one hundred and thirty to two hundred civil cases heard per year (thirteen to thirty cases) ever resulted in sentences that could be appealed. Even allowing for the fact that some appeals resulted from procedural rulings rather than sentences we are still faced with the probability that at least half of all civil cases that terminated in a sentence were pursued in the first appellate court.

From an emotional perspective this stands to reason. Cases that ended in arbitration were cases whose emotions had been settled or stilled. Cases that endured for any length of time and ended in a sentence were almost invariably cases involving intense emotions that would have been exacerbated by

[150] ADBR 3B 803, fols. 126r–128v, case opened 1 Nones of July. The procedural error arose from the fact that the defendant, Raymondet Berengier, was a citizen of the upper city and not within the jurisdiction of the criminal court of the lower city, the court that had sentenced him to death.

[151] ADBR 3B 802, fol. 44r–v, May 1290.

**Table 1.8 Average Number of Civil Appeals per Year, 1264–1409**

| Time Period | Months Covered by Registers in Sample | Number of Civil Appeals | Average Civil Appeals Per Year |
|---|---|---|---|
| 1264–1342 | 55 | 59 | 13 |
| 1351–58 | 60 | 72 | 14 |
| 1365–86 | 32 | 40 | 15 |
| 1400–1409 | 62 | 103 | 20 |
| Total | 209 | 274 | 16 |

*Sources:* as for Table 1.7.

an unfavorable sentence. For this reason, as we will see in the next chapter, talk of anger and hatred is most prevalent in appellate court registers.

In this chapter I have argued that users of the civil courts around the middle of the fourteenth century were spending at least 2,860 pounds to 4,400 pounds annually in litigation. In all probability the actual investment in legal pursuits was considerably higher. Compared with state finances this was a considerable sum, easily more than the direct tax of 1,661 pounds collected by the municipal government in 1360–61 and, at the upper end, approaching the seven to eight thousand pounds collected by the Angevin crown from indirect taxes.[152] The criminal court was far less significant: apart from the brief period in the early fifteenth century when the Angevin crown temporarily tightened the fiscal screws, proceeds from the operations of the criminal court tended to hover around five hundred pounds per year. Whereas criminal fines ended up in the treasury, the costs associated with litigation enriched the personnel of the court.

As this comparison suggests, the personnel of the civil courts had fiscal interests in the operations of the court that exceeded those of the crown. It is easy to appreciate why they might have encouraged civil litigation. But to return to a question raised in the introduction, why did ordinary men and women invest in the civil courts? Pursuing a dispute through the various forms of self-help—gossip and innuendo, insults and threats, assaults and even killings—was generally cheaper. As argued above, the civil courts offered one major service to its users, namely leverage. We can safely assume that 15 to 33 percent of all cases of litigation in Marseille ended in arbitration, a reasonably successful outcome. But in other respects the civil courts

[152] For these figures see Alain Droguet, *Administration financière et système fiscal à Marseille dans la seconde moitié du XIVe siècle* (Aix-en-Provence, 1983), and my "The General Taille of Marseille, 1360–1361: A Social and Demographic Study," *Provence historique* 49 (1999): 473–85.

were markedly ineffective in achieving their stated aims, and consumer investment remains difficult to explain. Only 10 to 15 percent of all cases ended in a sentence, and not all of these would have been in the plaintiff's favor. Sentences, moreover, weren't necessarily the end of the affair, since many were appealed. Measured according to their ability to generate arbitrations and favorable rulings, the civil courts were something of a failure, at least from the perspective of plaintiffs.

A purely economic perspective on courts of law in late medieval Europe would hold that the growing investment in civil litigation was a function of an expanding economy. A growing range of contracts required mechanisms for enforcement, and the extension of rights in land to non-nobles such as Bertran Vital fostered property litigation at many levels of society. Citizens invested in lawsuits to protect their rights. However persuasive, this model cannot easily accommodate the fact that civil litigation failed more often than it succeeded. Roman-canon procedural law offered defendants like Jacme Niel and his mother Reseneta Cambale too many ways to dodge the impeccably argued cases of their adversaries, and arbitrations, at least in Marseille, were not as significant a practice as we might have assumed. So little trust had Guilhem de Podio in the civil courts that he and his allies sought, and gained, an arbitrary ruling from the seneschal of Provence in their case against Antoni d'Ays. It was this ruling, not the money spent at court, that won him his victory.

Yet plaintiffs continued to use the courts, and by all accounts this investment continued to grow over the centuries. Perhaps the success rate grew as well. But as far as late medieval Marseille is concerned, we cannot explain court use solely in terms of the desire to recover debts or property holdings—that was too much to ask of the system. The frequency of abandoned initiations—35 percent of all cases were three pages or fewer in length, and most of these could not have terminated in arbitration—suggests that the initiation of a lawsuit was, in part, intended primarily as an inimical gesture, a public warning, a sign to all and sundry of a budding animosity. It was an investment, to look at it one way, in a summons or a series of summons, an opportunity to harass or humiliate an adversary on a very public stage, a rough equivalent to the everyday insult or assault and perhaps more fashionable than malicious gossip. Through initiating a suit, one could better assess the support of friends, neighbors, and kinfolk: the ritual had its integrative effects. It was also a gesture designed to repair lost dignity or shore up tottering morale. The gesture had these effects regardless of whether the plaintiff decided to pursue a suit to its conclusion, or even as far as the evidence phase. I suspect that most plaintiffs had little idea in advance where the gesture would lead: as seen above, only a few had the stamina and the social capital to persist in litigation. Seen this way, the secular courts of civil law were seamlessly integrated into a much wider cultural system for transacting enmity. Procedure formed the language for expressing this kind of transaction, and both evidence and outcome played, at best, minor roles in the larger drama.

# CHAPTER TWO
# STRUCTURES OF HATRED

I f love and friendship formed the warp of Marseille's basic social fabric, hatred and animosity supplied the woof. Such competitive tension is built into all societies.[1] "Groups are in competition with one another for power and resources," Sally Falk Moore remarks, "and individuals likewise compete with one another for valued social positions and goods. These competitions can be long-term or short-term, cool, smoldering, or flaming, but they are always in the background."[2] Bloodfeuds, raids, bloody brawls, insults: these are instances when the underlying animosity, the urge to seek redress, temporarily surfaces, like the fruiting bodies that reveal the existence of a vast underground fungus in the act of replicating itself. Vengeance is a state, not a set of discrete actions.

By the middle of the fourteenth century, acts of animosity were becoming increasingly costly, thanks to the meddlesome intervention of an Angevin legal system that prosecuted acts of violence and had enough coercive force to impose fines on those it deemed to be lawbreakers. The fines issued for

---

[1] David Cohen provides a very accessible summary of the literature, highlighting its relevance to the study of litigation, in his introduction to *Law, Violence, and Community in Classical Athens* (Cambridge, 1995), 3–24. Simon Roberts, "Introduction," in *Disputes and Settlements: Law and Human Relations in the West*, ed. John Bossy (Cambridge, 1983), 4, sums up the transactionalist viewpoint in this way: "Disputes, far from being pathological, were normal and inevitable as people struggled to secure their objectives." Elsewhere (18): "Quarrels were seen as normal and inevitable, rather than signs that something had gone wrong which needed to be put right." As his choice of verb tense implies, Roberts was somewhat agnostic about the value of the transactionalist perspective.

[2] Sally Falk Moore, *Law as Process: An Anthropological Approach* (London, 1978), 108.

brawling and insults, of course, may have been imposed counterproductively, for they were announced at public parlements and thus unwittingly served the crucial goal of all violent behavior, that of publicizing an animosity. But I do not doubt that one of the effects of Angevin penal sanctions was to encourage men and women to search for different, less costly ways to transact animosity. Not coincidentally, the law provided just such an arena. I turn again to Moore: "The legal wrong, because of its specificity in time, place, and circumstances, can provide the occasion for action. The legal wrong, moreover, makes it possible to have a showdown without necessarily acknowledging the deeper long-term motives or objectives which may accompany such action."[3] Here, speaking of African societies, Moore is using "legal wrong" in its most universal sense, but the observation applies very well to the specific legal circumstances under which someone could sue or denounce an adversary in Marseille's courts of law. Seen from the perspective of the user, in short, there is a basic equivalency between brawls, insults, and lawsuits. All are ways to instantiate and publicize an existing animosity.

The structures of hatred that motivated active confrontations are not vague suppositions imposed willfully on the sources. Both love and hatred appear from time to time in testimony given before civil and criminal courts in late medieval Marseille. These crucial bits of testimony reveal that networks of friendship and animosity engaged men and women at all levels of society, ranging from urban notables, who advertised their animosities through feuds and factional violence, to artisans and shopkeepers, laborers and herders, judges, notaries, Jews, Christians, priests, nuns, servants, and former slaves who typically found other ways to pursue their hatreds. Testifying at court, men and women routinely used the language of love and hatred as the filter through which they made sense of the fundamental patterns of their own social universe. Their depositions, translated from the vernacular into Latin by the notaries of the court, are consistently marked by an emotional vocabulary, one in which love, friendship, and goodwill (*dilectio, amicitia,* and *benevolentia*) were contrasted to the dark emotional world of hatred, unfriendship, and ill-will (*odium, inimicitia,* and *malivolentia*). These nouns had counterparts in other parts of speech that surface frequently in proceedings: nouns used for identifying men and women (e.g., *inimicus, -a; amicus, -a; benivolus, -a, malivolus, -a*), adjectives for qualifying those nouns (e.g., *odiosus, -a*), and the corresponding verbs (e.g., *inimico, -are, diligo, -are*). Use of this vocabulary shows the existence of a kind of emotional sociology or social epistemology, a way of thinking about and categorizing social relationships that used the language of emotions to characterize social bonds

[3] Ibid., 108–9.

and social divisions.[4] In this sociology, we find that ego-centered groups—binding others to an individual by love and affection, ever dissolving, always reconstituting—were counterpoised against other individuals and their equally transient groups.

To speak of a society described by contemporaries through a language of emotions is not to deny the significance of the bonds of kinship, fictive kinship, and neighborhood.[5] These ties were real and much talked about by contemporaries. But kinship and neighborliness were considered particularly concrete instances of a higher-order abstraction: love or affection. Beyond that, people could and did hate their neighbors and kinfolk, and they loved others wholly unrelated to them by formal bonds of kinship, spiritual kinship, or neighborliness. What mattered most in legal settings was whether one's actions at court were motivated either by hatred or love: hatred for the defendant, love for the plaintiff, love for the victim of murder, and so on. Formal ties such as kinship or spiritual kinship were not wholly irrelevant, for they were sometimes used to prove the existence of affectionate emotions. But it was emotional structures, notably the structures of hatred, that mattered most at law.

Since the practice of law and justice is inextricably associated with social formations and relationships, the use of the law courts in medieval Marseille

[4] As much recent work has shown, a social epistemology based on emotions was a European-wide phenomenon; see Otto Brunner, *Land and Lordship: Structures of Governance in Medieval Austria*, trans. Howard Kaminsky and James Van Horn Melton (Philadelphia, 1992 [4th rev. ed., 1959]), 17; Richard M. Fraher, "Conviction according to Conscience: The Medieval Jurists' Debate concerning Judicial Discretion and the Law of Proof," *Law and History Review* 7 (1989): 23–88, here 37, 39, 41 and notes; William Ian Miller, *Bloodtaking and Peacemaking: Feud, Law, and Society in Saga Iceland* (Chicago, 1990); Claude Gauvard, *"De grace especial": crime, état, et société à la fin du Moyen Âge*, 2 vols. (Paris, 1991), 2:686; John Hudson, *The Formation of the English Common Law: Law and Society in England from the Norman Conquest to Magna Carta* (London, 1996), 171–72; John Bossy, *Peace in the Post-Reformation* (Cambridge, 1998); Robert Bartlett, "'Mortal Enmities': The Legal Aspect of Hostility in the Middle Ages," T. Jones Pierce Lecture, University of Wales (Aberystwyth, 1998), 8–9.
[5] Such social bonds and networks have been stressed by several decades of medieval social history. Important works include D. V. Kent and F. W. Kent, *Neighbours and Neighbourhood in Renaissance Florence: The District of the Red Lion in the Fifteenth Century* (Locust Valley, N.Y., 1982); Jacques Heers, *Family Clans in the Middle Ages: A Study of Political and Social Structures in Urban Areas*, trans. Barry Herbert (Amsterdam, 1977); F. W. Kent, *Household and Lineage in Renaissance Florence: The Family Life of the Capponi, Ginori, and Rucellai* (Princeton, 1977); Harry A. Miskimin, David Herlihy, and A. L. Udovitch, eds., *The Medieval City* (New Haven, 1977); Ronald F. E. Weissman, *Ritual Brotherhood in Renaissance Florence* (New York, 1982); David Nicholas, *The Domestic Life of a Medieval City: Women, Children, and the Family in Fourteenth-Century Ghent* (Lincoln, Neb., 1985); Nicholas A. Eckstein, *The District of the Green Dragon: Neighbourhood Life and Social Change in Renaissance Florence* (Florence, 1995).

cannot be understood independently of the structures or scripts of hatred and love that motivated all of the assaults, threats, and insults prosecuted by the court of inquest, most of the denunciations that drew them to the attention of the court, and many of the lawsuits heard before the civil courts. Recovering these emotions, of course, is a perilous enterprise, since most do not appear in the record and must be inferred. This doesn't mean that we should not infer them. Marseille's notaries, like many such record-keeping bureaucracies, tried to record the world in a wholly impersonal way. Procedural law is an emotionless architectonic form or grid that imposes itself on all stages of a given trial. Plaintiffs cannot sue simply because they are feeling angry or vengeful. They first must identify a debt or an injury; having done so, they must pursue satisfaction according to procedural rules. As a result, emotions are usually hidden in the formal structure of court transcripts. In vain does one look for them in the opening moves of Johanet Salvayre's lawsuit described in chapter 1. Why many record-keeping bureaucracies see the world in this way is an interesting historical question in its own right. The effort to put emotions back into history will always be hampered by the fact that the emotions themselves were and are routinely elided in administrative records.

But as I noted earlier, references to emotions do push through the emotional neutrality of the record from time to time. There are good reasons why this is so. The moral climate of the fourteenth century was decidedly hostile to excessive emotions. It did not take fourteenth-century litigants and defendants long to figure out and exploit this moral condemnation of excessive emotions, and they used it to undercut the legal standing of their adversaries and their arguments. Use of this tactic means that a fair amount of emotion bubbles to the surface of the extant court records in spite of the institutional obstacles.

Talk of love and hatred, therefore, can be found in a number of places in the civil and criminal court records from late medieval Marseille. Such talk surfaces most often in articles of proof, witness interrogations, and especially in witness exception procedures, discussed at greater length in the first section below. These references make it clear that people in Marseille were fully conscious of their emotional relationships and kept track of them in much the same way that they kept track of their credits and debts. "I am more a friend of theirs than an enemy, because they've never done anything against me," acknowledged a witness named Micael Magni, when asked at court in 1403 to say whether he favored a certain party.[6] Friendship, evidently, was the default setting. It was also useful to know one's en-

_____

[6] ADBR 3B 138, fol. 104v, case opened 28 Apr. 1402 on fol. 55r: "est potius amicus quam inimicus quia nunquam contrarium sibi fecerunt."

emies, if and when one acquired them. One's enemies were not chosen indiscriminately. They did not, for example, constitute all the members of some disfavored minority group, as the literature on medieval persecution would lead one to believe. Enemies were real people. They had dangerous friends, carried sharp swords, and paid for court summons. This hard-edged reality led litigants and witnesses to speak about "my enemy" or "his or her enemy" or "their enemies," using possessives in a distinctive way. Enemies were publicly announced. In 1413, Matieu Vital was fined fifty-five shillings for saying to an official of the court, "You show ill-will; know that I hold you as a mortal enemy" (Vos manez mala voluntat et sapias que yeu voz ay por ennemie mortal).[7] This statement presumably put the official on his guard—a meridional version of what was a necessary and formal procedure of the customary law of Beauvaisis in northern France—but also served to advertise news of the hatred among all those who happened to be before the lower gates of the church of the Blessed Mary of Accoules at the time of the statement.[8] It is true that some people may have had no active hatreds at any given moment. Friendships were always more in evidence. Hatreds could and did end. But enemies were only too easily remade. Few people, certainly few people with any claim to honor and standing, would have gone through life without acquiring several enemies along the way.

No great insight was necessary to remember one's own emotional relationships. But keeping track of others' was just as important and mattered just as much at law. In 1401, the nobleman Peire Raynaut complained to a judge about some witnesses who were refusing to testify on his behalf. He had found out that they were in a state of hatred with Raymon Aymes, the notary of the court who would be responsible for interrogating them.[9] How could he know this? Moral philosophy tends to assume that emotions are internal states of mind. So does the modern psychophysiological study of emotions. This, obviously, is not how Peire Raynaut understood love and hatred.

Depositions in witness exception procedures discussed in the second section show that loves and hatreds, according to vernacular classification, were like clothes: rich in significance, worn on the outside of the body for all to see, and easily changed. These depositions show that one advertised one's emotional relationships by means of certain scripted performances that were continually perceived and interpreted by those present as meaningful

[7] ADBR B 1947, fol. 51v.
[8] *The* Coutumes de Beauvaisis *of Philippe de Beaumanoir*, trans. F. R. P. Akehurst (Philadelphia, 1992), 613.
[9] ADBR 3B 1016, fol. 169v, case opened 7 Feb. 1401 on fol. 149r.

statements about social relations. Given the existence of this system of signs, it was far easier for Peire Raynaut to keep track of the emotional relationships of his potential witnesses than we might imagine.

One of the most noteworthy features of the social epistemology of emotions is that hate and anger, the sort of emotions said to generate the blood-feud, were not reserved for men. Depositions discussed below in section three give numerous examples of women who had both loves and hatreds toward unrelated men and women. They acted on them in the public sphere. The gestures or performances deemed to be proof of love or hatred, moreover, were only lightly stereotyped according to biological sex. The commonplace ascription of public emotions to women has considerable significance because the ability to have hostile emotions in public in any society is usually the mark of a free and honorable individual. Servants, slaves, and Jews surely had hostile emotions in medieval Europe but they were not supposed to express them in public. Peasant revolts were frightening precisely because peasants broke this fundamental rule.[10] As seen in chapter 1, the law courts constituted a major public venue at which women could speak and be heard. The ability to have a public hatred was another such venue. Women engaged in this as freely as men.

The emotional sociology found in witness exception procedures offers us insights into the vernacular sociology of medieval Europe. Much of this chapter is devoted to reconstructing this emotional sociology. But the emotion talk had a legal purpose as well. As I will make clear in this chapter, evidence from late medieval Marseille's civil and criminal proceedings shows that various forms of legal initiations and behaviors were gradually entering into the standard emotional lexicon. Put differently, many vernacular performances served to advertise emotions, and various actions at law were rapidly becoming performances that served similar publicizing ends. It is easy to appreciate why denunciation to the criminal court was considered a convenient way to announce or pursue an enmity and why the script was widely interpreted as such. But even civil litigation was interpreted by many as a scripted performance designed to display hatred. Various clues suggest that this sentiment had grown especially strong by the early fifteenth century. Litigation was not only costly for the defendant, it was also potentially humiliating, a useful vehicle for putting an enemy in his place regardless of its outcome. There are several reasons why this was so. Returning to one of the themes of the first chapter, during bouts of litigation the defendant was always at the beck and call of the plaintiff, who could

---

[10] Paul Freedman, "Peasant Anger in the Late Middle Ages," in *Anger's Past: The Social Uses of an Emotion in the Middle Ages*, ed. Barbara H. Rosenwein (Ithaca, 1998), 171–88.

THE CONSUMPTION OF JUSTICE

issue a summons at any moment, tying the defendant to the house or requiring costly arrangements for a procurator or other representative. This
placed defendants in a powerless or humiliating posture. Defendants, of
course, found ways to seize the initiative and harass plaintiffs in similar
ways, and as a result the litigating process was marked by the tit-for-tat
characteristics of the vengeance game. In discussing the basic your-
turn–my-turn structure of the Icelandic feud, William Ian Miller notes
how the person who set the tempo could profit from this position, causing
the adversary to slink about in constant fear of life and limb, never knowing
when the blow might fall.[11] Much the same pattern holds for fourteenth-
and fifteenth-century litigation in Marseille.

Beyond this, public humiliations were built in to the basic patterns of litigation. Exception procedures often included acid commentary on the
morals and manners of the adversary's witnesses and hence, by association,
on those of the adversary. These moralizing observations, so tropic as to be
essentially interchangeable, presumably circulated in somewhat less scripted
forms as gossip. The outdoor court offered a stage for publicizing and vali-
dating this gossip. This was a legally sanctioned procedure for delivering an
attack on someone's character. The fact that criminal courts throughout Europe routinely prosecuted insults and other acts of defamation seems to suggest that courts wanted to promote good social relationships and penalized
those who broke this happy rule of life. Nothing could be further from the
truth. Public attacks were quite acceptable to courts and sovereigns as long
as they were constrained by the grammar of Roman-canon procedural law
and conducted in legally sanctioned public spaces.

## KINSHIP AND THE WITNESS EXCEPTION PROCEDURE

The exception procedure, as discussed briefly in the first chapter, was a
feature of Roman-canon procedural law that allowed defendants to protest
certain procedural errors of adversaries. Exceptions or related procedural
ploys like these were common enough in judicial procedures in Europe before the twelfth-century revival of interest in Roman-canon procedural law.
We find evidence of challenges to the status of witnesses in early medieval
pleas and in medieval Icelandic procedural law, and similar challenges, based

[11] Miller, *Bloodtaking and Peacemaking*, 193.

on misspoken testimony, are found in various customary procedural laws.[12] Exceptions play an important role in Roman-canon legal proceedings from the thirteenth century onward; certainly most civil and appellate court cases of any substance from fourteenth-century Marseille have an exception of one kind or another.[13] The exception was one of the key features of late medieval Roman-canon legal procedure that allowed judges *not* to make a ruling based on a strict reading of facts. In this regard, the exception and related rulings on procedural flaws, such as failure to lodge an appeal within the time span allowed by statute, joined with practices of arbitration, fines for contumacy, and banishment to limit the number of judgments based on the facts of the case in late medieval Roman-canon law courts. Successful exceptions effectively eliminated the legal standing of the adversary's case. Like other features of Roman-canon procedural law, exceptions were not forced on anyone by jurists or judges. Instead, they were an aspect of procedural law that canny lawyers and their clients learned how to exploit and manipulate from the twelfth century onward.

Exceptions could be made for any type of procedural error, including the fact that a plaintiff or a witness was in a state of excommunication. As we saw in chapter 1, Gilet Alfans successfully pleaded an exception to the suit lodged against him by Ugo Gaydon by proving that Ugo had been excommunicated for sorcery. Other exceptions included objections to the trustworthiness of documents. The most common types of exception, though, were based on an objection to the words or status of witnesses (*dicta et persona testium*). The procedure based on such exceptions, sometimes known as the *reprobatio testium* (recusal of witnesses), allowed defendants in both civil and criminal cases to challenge the adverse testimony of hostile witnesses.[14] As Bernard Schnapper's survey of juristic sources has shown, such exceptions could be based on a number of factors.[15] Tancred's 1215 treatise on Roman-canon procedural law, the *Ordo iudiciarius*, nominally prohibited the

[12] See, for example, the discussion of formalism and witness testimony in Miller, *Bloodtaking and Peacemaking*, 248–55; see also Chris Wickham, "Land Disputes and Their Social Framework in Lombard-Carolingian Italy, 700–900," in *The Settlement of Disputes in Early Medieval Europe*, ed. Wendy Davies and Paul Fouracre (Cambridge, 1986), 105–24, here 111.

[13] In addition to works based on normative evidence cited elsewhere, see the brief discussion of practical applications of witness exceptions in Patricia MacCaughan, "La procédure judiciare à Manosque au milieu du XIIIe siècle," *Revue historique de droit français et étranger* 76 (1998): 583–95, here 588–90.

[14] For an example of this expression see the list of "recusation articles" (*titulos reprobationes*) that inaugurated a recusation procedure in ADBR 3B 859, fol. 132r, case opened 26 Apr. 1408 on fol. 105r.

[15] Bernard Schnapper, "*Testes inhabiles*, les témoins reprochables dans l'ancien droit pénal," *Tijdschrift voor Rechtsgeschiedenis/Revue d'histoire du droit* 33 (1965): 575–616.

testimony of the unfree, women (in criminal cases), minors, the insane, the infamous, the poor, and infidels (against Christians), domestic servants, and others.[16] Guillame Durand covers the entire spectrum of exceptionable witnesses in his more detailed treatment of the subject in the *Speculum iudicale*, written and revised in the late thirteenth century.[17] Most of these restrictions were incorporated directly into Marseille's statutes, compiled in 1253.[18] Both love and hatred stand out among the potentially exceptionable witness qualities in Marseillais practice. Durand phrases the situation in no uncertain terms: "enmity, or conversation or kinship with enemies, render testimony null" (inimicitia, seu cum inimicis conversatio, aut consanguinitas, reddunt testimonium nullum), and he also noted that a friend may not testify (*amicus etiam non potest esse testis*).[19]

To expose potentially unqualified witnesses and perhaps to forestall the exception procedure itself, judges and notaries of the court in Marseille responsible for witness interrogations routinely asked witnesses to identify themselves and to describe their relationship to the two adversaries in the case. The questions were posed according to the following formula and its variations, which in turn were based closely on procedural manuals:

Has anyone coached, instructed, or suborned you? Has anyone offered you a reward or a future compensation? Are you currently excommunicated? Are you a kinsman or a domestic of the person who cited you?

[16] Tancred, *Ordo*, 2.6 (pp. 222–28).

[17] Durand's treatment of witnesses runs to fifty-nine pages in his *Speculum iudicale* I de teste (1:283–341). Durand's discussion aims to set out the categories of acceptable and unacceptable witnesses; any of his strictures could then form the basis for a successful exception. Exception procedures are discussed later in the *Speculum iudicale* II de exceptionibus et replicationibus (1:509–31).

[18] Pernoud, *Statuts*, 87–88; see the statutes entitled *De forma in qua debeant produci testes in Massilia vel extra Massiliam, Qui non admittuntur ad testimonium*, and the following statutes *De eodem* and *De testibus cogendis et non cogendis*.

[19] The statement regarding hatred comes from the repertory at the beginning of the first volume: Durand, *Speculum iudicale*, 1:lvi. This phrase in turns refers to III de inquisitione § Inquisitio qualiter impugnetur. The section begins with the phrase "An inquisition may be impugned or annulled in many ways"; § 1.19 explicitly proscribes the testimony of enemies and those who reside with enemies or are their accomplices or kinfolk. The same proscriptions applied in civil suits as well; see I de teste § Quae possunt contra testes opponi, which opens "Opponitur autem contra testem, quod est inimicus" and then proceeds to discuss other exceptionable categories. The prohibition on the testimony of a friend is noted a few lines further on. See also Tancred, *Ordo* 2.5.1. (p. 141). Modern discussions of this exception can be found in Charles Donahue, "Proof by Witnesses in the Church Courts of Medieval England: An Imperfect Reception of the Learned Law," in *On the Laws and Customs of England: Essays in Honor of Samuel E. Thorne*, ed. Morris S. Arnold et al. (Chapel Hill, 1981), 127–58; Bartlett, " 'Mortal Enmities'," 9–12.

How old are you? How much are you worth? Which of the two parties do you favor? Have you testified out of love, fear, hatred, or anger?

Much the same kinds of restrictions applied also in customary law courts in the north of France.[20] For the most part these formulaic interrogations elicited nothing useful in Marseille's courts. No witness ever admitted that his or her testimony had been coached or rewarded or motivated by love or hatred. Similarly, no witness ever admitted to being in a state of excommunication, though a few admitted to favoring one of the parties, and there are several cases of servants admitting a domestic relationship to the plaintiff. Queries about kinship and domesticity were somewhat more fruitful, for these did elicit a fair number of responses and exposed some potentially disqualifying relationships. A witness heard in a case from 1355, the nobleman Laurent Ricau, when asked whether he was related in any way to the plaintiff, Johaneta Bonipara, responded that he wasn't, but admitted that Johaneta was a god-kin (*commater*) of his. Moreover, he was a widower, and his late wife was a cousin of Johaneta.[21] In another case, Bonafos Chaulet responded to a similar question from the judge by explaining that the plaintiff, Bertrana Berengiera, was the wife of his father-in-law (a second wife, it seems). In a third, Johan Vivaut explained that Amiel Bonafos was a relation "inasmuch as" Amiel's wife was the daughter of a certain cousin of his. In the same trial, and speaking of the same girl, Ugo Vivaut, a relation of Johan, "said he was not related to Amiel except that Amiel had married his cousin."[22] Use of expressions like "except" (*nisi*) and "inasmuch as" (*in tantum quod*) reveal the sense that these relationships were on the fuzzy border where kinship gave way to something else.

But given the evident reluctance of witnesses to disqualify their own testimony, it was normally up to defendants to expose disqualifying relationships by means of the witness exception procedure. To challenge one or more witnesses, the interested party compiled a list of witness exceptions (*exceptiones contra testes*) and proved these by means of his or her own witnesses. As seen in the next section, many of these exceptions were based on affection and hatred. But exceptions based on kinship and other formal ties were also relatively common and worth exploring in greater detail.

In several trials from the 1350s, the *clavaire* of Marseille, the official responsible for defending sentences of the criminal court against appeals,

<hr />

[20] Gauvard, "*De grace especial*," 1:129–31; also Claude Gauvard, "La declinazione d'identità negli archivi giudiziari del regno di Carlo VI," in *La parola all'accusato*, ed. Jean-Claude Maire Vigueur and Agostino Paravicini Bagliani (Palermo, 1991), 170–89.

[21] ADBR 3B 58, fol. 98v, case opened 19 Feb. 1355 on fol. 92r.

[22] ADBR 3B 820, fol. 76r, case opened 7 July 1356 on fol. 8r.

pleaded exceptions to several witnesses summoned by the appellants. The legal basis of these exceptions was kinship and factional association. In the appeal lodged in 1356 by one of the captains of the Vivaut party, Amiel Bonafos, the clavaire challenged two of the witnesses, Johan Macel and Carle de Montoliu, by showing that they were consanguines and house-mates of Amiel.[23] Johan was indeed a cousin on his mother's side, we learn. One witness to this exception, not knowing the precise degree of kinship, declared simply that Johan was a member of the *parentela* (kin-group) of Amiel.[24] Later in this same case, the witness Carle Athos, when asked whether he was related to Amiel Bonafos, said no, "although it is true that Amiel took as his wife the sister of the witness, who is now dead, and from her no children survived."[25] The implication here is interesting: had children survived, then Carle might have felt himself more closely related to his former affine. In another case, a defendant named Johan Girman tried to refute the hostile testimony of one Ugueta Segueria by claiming that Ugueta was the niece of the opposing litigant, Jacma Thomasia, a tavern keeper. Jacma eventually admitted to a relationship, although we find out that Ugueta was in fact Jacma's husband's niece and not her own. Marin de Morlans, the goatherd in chapter 1 who suffered a heart attack in the Marseilleveyre and was accused of allowing his flock to trespass on the land of others, pleaded an exception to the hostile testimony of Ugo Raymon and his son Andrieu by claiming that they were related in the second degree to his accuser. The two witnesses he summoned to speak on this point showed that the men in question were affines, related through the wife of one of the men.[26]

As these examples indicate, kinship was a powerful ideology. In the case of the murder of the merchant Guilhem Tomas by Guilhem de Belavila, which I discussed at length in the first chapter and will return to below, one witness sought to undermine the testimony of another by arguing that she behaved toward the murder victim, Guilhem Tomas, "as if she were of his blood" (*ac si esset de sanguine dicti condam Guillelmi*).[27] Curiously, though, kinship was not always easy to know or prove in exception procedures. Kinship, after all, is not an identity naturally inscribed on the body. In a world without written archives of birth, marriage, and death, kinship was sometimes proven in exception procedures by reference to certain patterns of behavior, such as speech behavior, gifts, co-residence, and the devolution of

---

[23] Ibid., fol. 90r: *consanguiney, domestici, et familiares dicti Amelii.*
[24] Ibid., fols. 90r, 93v, 95r.
[25] Ibid., fol. 74v.
[26] ADBR 3B 43, fol. 12r, case opened 12 July 1341 on fol. 10r.
[27] ADBR 3B 825, fol. 112r, case opened 13 May 1365 on fol. 35r.

property, which was common knowledge (*publica fama*) in the city. When Amiel Bonafos needed to protect his father from prosecution after Amiel had hidden in his father's house following the murder of Peire de Jerusalem in 1356, a crime that rocked the city and shut down all factional warfare for several years, he argued that his father was behaving like any loving father. To prove this argument, Amiel needed to show that his father *was* his father. He did so by arguing that his father was openly and publicly held and judged to be just that.[28] Similar ideas crop up in a suit heard in 1407, during the course of which a Jewish auctioneer named Cathon pleaded an exception to the hostile testimony of a fishmonger named Antoni Robaut by showing how the witness "was bound in an affinity and a great affection" with Cathon's adversary, Margarita de Altu.[29] To prove the affinal relationship, Cathon claimed that Margarita spread the news (*dicit et reputat*) that Antoni was her nephew (*nepos;* actually, he was her late husband's nephew) and that Antoni did likewise, calling Margarita his aunt (*avuncula*). According to Cathon's argument, it was their speech behavior—in this case, their public exchange of formal titles of kinship—that made their relationship significant and knowable. All social relationships, in short, were ultimately sets of actions, gestures, or behaviors in the eyes of witnesses, a principle that was universal in the Continental common law, as Thomas Kuehn has shown with the problems of identity arising from accusations of illegitimacy.[30] Even kinship, in other words, was a relationship that was known and displayed through performance.

## EMOTIONAL STRUCTURES

This is even more the case with exceptions based on hatred or affection. As seen in witness exception procedures, emotional states in late medieval Marseille were never seen as internal states of minds. The only possible exception to this is certain emotions, such as anger, that were occasionally said to have been motivated by the devil. Instead, the key jural emotions of love and hatred were seen as patterned behaviors and performances. Love and

---

[28] ADBR 3B 820, fol. 47r, case opened 7 July 1356 on fol. 8r: "Petrus Bonifacii est pater et legitimus et naturalis dicti Amelii et pro tali habetur et reputatur habitus est et reputatatus palam et publice inter notos et vicinos."

[29] ADBR 3B 859, fol. 133r, case opened 26 Apr. 1408 on fol. 105r.

[30] Thomas Kuehn, "*Fama* as a Legal Status in Renaissance Florence," in *Fama: The Politics of Talk and Reputation in Medieval Europe*, ed. Thelma Fenster and Daniel Lord Smail (Ithaca, 2003), 27–46.

affection were typified by patterns of behavior based on speech, gestures, and commensality: thus, two people said to be affectionate were described as conversing frequently, sharing food and wine, sleeping in the same house or the same bed, and generally acting as housemates.[31] Affection, curiously, was never proven by the exchange of gifts, apart from hospitality. Latin or Provençal equivalents of the word "gift" rarely appear in witness exception procedures. Given the emphasis on gifting in modern sociological literature—given, too, the predominance of gifting as a way to define social relationships in contemporary literary texts—the absence of the gift in such contexts is rather curious.[32] I would expect to find that the jural language of social relationships in other Mediterranean jurisdictions included the gift as a public manifestation of affection or departed from Marseille's norms in other ways. Hatred was also proven by means of performances or gestures such as assaults and certain forms of speech behavior like insults and threats. Isolated gestures like emptying large jars of excrement before the doorways of one's enemies crop up from time to time. One of the most interesting behaviors cited as evidence for hatred was no speech at all: the refusal to greet, the refusal to converse, an exact counterpart to the conversations deemed to be evidence for affection.

Examples of exceptions based on both love and hatred can be found in a criminal appeal lodged in 1365 arising from the murder of Guilhem Tomas.[33] Guilhem Tomas was a merchant; later in the trial, we find out that he was also a member of the de Jerusalem faction. He lived with his wife Johaneta, née de Fonte, in a part of the city known as the Spur, a neighborhood of well-to-do artisans located on the border between the upper and lower cities just a few blocks east of Negrel street. His greatest rival in the Spur was a neighbor who lived just across the way, a public notary named Guilhem de Belavila, at the time the officially appointed notary of the palace court. By 1365, relations between the two men were tense. Testimony located the origin of the enmity in a fraudulent contract drawn up by Guilhem de Belavila a year or two earlier that Tomas had denounced to the court. But the two men were predisposed toward enmity in any event, since they were the two leading figures in the Spur. In a pattern that repeated itself in many neighborhoods throughout the city in the mid-fourteenth century, the two men pursued their enmity by associating themselves with rival

[31] The Latin word used to impugn a witness as the "housemate" of the plaintiff was *domesticus, -a*. Context shows that although *domesticus, -a* could mean servant it more usually meant someone who routinely shared a living space with another with no implications of servitude.

[32] See Natalie Zemon Davis, *The Gift in Sixteenth-Century France* (Madison, 2000).

[33] ADBR 3B 825, fols. 35r–188r, case opened 3 May 1365.

noble factions: de Belavila allied himself with the Vivaut, and Tomas turned to the de Jerusalem. This association may have been long standing: Tomas's wife's maiden name suggests kinship with the merchant Esteve de Fonte, a committed member of the de Jerusalem faction.

Matters came to a head on 8 February 1365, when the two men confronted each other on the street outside their houses. Thanks to the careful eyewitness testimony of a Dominican named Raymon de Sappo we have a reasonably accurate account of what happened next. Brother Raymon's testimony went something like this:

> I was coming from the episcopal court. When I was in front of Guilhem Tomas's house in the street of the Spur I noticed Guilhem de Belavila, and a lance throw away there was Guilhem Tomas, coming after him and saying certain words that I could hardly make out. De Belavila responded "You lie through your throat." Walking along, as master Guilhem de Belavila was in the space just before his house, and Guilhem Tomas in front of the doorway to his house, the same Tomas suddenly threw the parcel of meat he was carrying into his house and came as fast as he could toward master Guilhem de Belavila, his knife drawn. Seeing this, master Guilhem whipped back his cloak and with knife drawn said in a loud voice toward the witness and his friend, "O Lords, you be witnesses for me that this ribald wishes to kill me." (fol. 122r–v)

Seeing the fight, de Belavila's brother-in-law, Fulco Robaut, then rushed out of his house, and was joined by his wife Johana and her sister, Uga, who was de Belavila's wife. Most of the testimony given in the case was more or less consistent with this depiction of the early stages, though the deposition by de Belavila makes it clear that he also was returning from the market with meat.

Witness accounts diverge abruptly from this point onward, frustrating the judges, who made a number of querulous marginal notes noting how the depositions contradicted each other, and making it difficult to extract a reasonably coherent narrative. Some witnesses who favored the dead man claimed that Tomas was then held by the two women, allowing de Belavila to stab him to death. Witnesses for de Belavila claimed that other people had assisted the victim, including Tomas's wife Johana, and argued that Johana Robauda and Uga de Belavila had only tried to separate the two men. Furthermore, it was Fulco Robaut, not Guilhem de Belavila, who delivered the killing blow with a weapon described variously as a sword and a broad knife, two digits in width. The weapon had been left in the wound—Tomas, according to one witness, plucked it out himself. Surgeons reported that it was two-and-a-half palms in length and had entered the body to the width of a palm. Fulco acknowledged ownership of the knife, though there is some suggestion that he did so to protect his brother-in-law.

All accounts agree that Fulco and Guilhem immediately fled the scene and took sanctuary in the church of St. Antoine. The fama soon reached the court, located just a few blocks to the south, and the judge of the palace court, Leonardo da Siena, accompanied by a judge of one of the lesser courts, Johan de Quinciato, came to inspect the body of the dead man. Surgeons palpated the wounds and inspected the weapons. Leonardo then went to the church to interrogate Guilhem and Fulco; following their testimony, he then drew up five indicia pointing to Guilhem's guilt, as paraphrased below:

(1) Guilhem de Belavila was Guilhem Tomas's mortal enemy, daily pursuing his destruction, because the previous year Tomas had had him pursued in court on the charge of making a false instrument. (2) Tomas was struck by a sword belonging to Guilhem de Belavila; many recognize this as his. (3) The two men fled and took sanctuary in a church. (4) De Belavila has been accused of many crimes and was arrested last year. (5) All this is the public talk and fame (fol. 60r–v).

Testimony taken on these indicia also pointed to the guilt of Fulco Robaut and the two sisters, Johana Robauda and Uga de Belavila.

Fearing the wrath of the de Jerusalem faction and, as Guilhem explained, the "turpitude of the court," both Guilhem and Fulco prudently fled town, and as a result could not defend themselves during the criminal inquest. On 7 May 1365, they were sentenced to heavy fines of 500 pounds each. Uga de Belavila and Johana Robauda, however, had not fled, and were being held under house arrest. It was not customary in Marseille for women to take flight following an assault or a homicide, presumably because they were normally exempt from vengeance killings. In addition, Uga had been wounded during the battle and Johana was breast feeding a small boy. Since both women were present at the criminal inquest, they were allowed to make a defense against the charges brought against them. The depositions taken during the course of their defense, which began late in the month of March, were subsequently used as evidence in the appeal lodged by Guilhem de Belavila later in May of 1365.

To challenge the accusations made against Uga and Johana, Esteve Agulhenqui, a notary like Guilhem and the procurator for all four of the accused, found it necessary to plead an exception to three of the most damaging witnesses heard during the original inquest, namely Uga Bernarda, Alazays Antonia, and Alazays Rogeta. Following the norms of the witness exception procedure, Esteve argued that two of the women were in a state of hatred with Guilhem and Uga de Belavila and with Johana Robauda. Two of them, moreover, were in a state of friendship with the victim, Tomas. These exceptions, if proven, would have been sufficient to invalidate their testimony, exculpating not only Johana and Uga but also Guilhem and Fulco.

In the overall list of twenty-four arguments the seven relevant witness exceptions were expressed in this way.[34]

> (1) Uga Bernarda is an ill-wisher and capital enemy [*malivola et inimica capitalis*] of the couple, Guilhem de Belavila and Uga his wife . . . (3) Uga was a god-kin [*comater*] of Guilhem Tomas while he lived, his well-wisher and a friend [*benivola et amica*]. (4) While Guilhem Tomas was still alive, this same Uga acted like a family member of his [*ac si familiaris illius existeret*]; they conversed together daily, drinking, eating, and doing other homely and family-related things . . . (7) Alazays Antonia is a servant of Uga Bernarda. (8) She also conversed, resided, and spent time with Guilhem Tomas in his house as if she were a family member of his, eating, drinking, and doing other necessary things with him [*et alia necessaria faciendo cum illo*]. (9) Uga Bernarda and Alazays Antonia live facing the house of the said Guilhem Tomas as neighbors and well-wishers [*benivole*] of the said Guilhem Tomas. (10) Alazays Rogeta . . . is a capital, malevolent enemy of Guilhem and of his wife and sister-in-law. Owing to the hatred and malevolence she bore and still bears against them, she hasn't spoken to them and still does not speak to them and refuses to, owing to a fight or conflict that took place about ten years ago. (fols. 99v–100v)

This argument is interesting for many reasons, not the least of which is the suggestion that the enmity between Alazays Rogeta and the de Belavilas had independent origins and was much older than the enmity between Guilhem de Belavila and Guilhem Tomas. Here, as in the case of Antoni d'Ays, what appears in court as an enmity between two big men turns out, on closer inspection, to be inextricably associated with enmities between networks of women. Esteve, incidentally, seems to have been entirely successful. There is every indication that Johana or Uga were declared innocent. Among other things, the condemnation of 7 May includes only the names of Guilhem de Belavila and Fulco Robaut.

---

[34] These weren't the only exceptions lodged against these women; other points of the cedula accused the last two of being loose women.

From the point of view of the exception procedure, the most prominent feature of the list is an emotional polarization embedded in key expressions or terms. On one side is a group of friends, housemates, and well-wishers who converse, eat, and drink together and move freely in and out of one another's living spaces. Despite the assertion that Alazays Antonia did "useful things" for Guilhem Tomas there is no hint that the two women were his servants. Among other things, Uga appears to have been an independent proprietor or leaseholder and both women were treated as neighbors. Uga, moreover, was Tomas's god-kin, a spiritual relationship that would more or less exclude the possibility of a profound social gulf between them. Nor is there any hint of a sexual liaison either in the articles or in the ensuing witness testimony, despite the accusation, made in article five, that Alazays Antonia was a prostitute. Their friendship, in turn, was mirrored by their hatred and antagonism for Guilhem and Uga de Belavila and Fulco and Johana Robaut. The mirror effect was embedded in the language: in the articles against Uga, "well-wisher and friend' (*benivola et amica*) was echoed by "ill-wisher and enemy" (*malivola et inimica*), an echo that persists throughout the articles.

This conventional language of enmity and friendship is found, with slight variations, in many witness exception procedures and elsewhere in the records from fourteenth-century Marseille. An enemy was routinely identified as an *inimicus, -a* or *malivolus, -a*, nouns sometimes qualified as "capital" or "deadly" (*capitalis*) or "willful" (*voluntarius*). Such enemies were often described as *inimicatus*, "hateful toward," or *malivolus*, "ill-willed" or "evilly intentioned." They held either *inimicitia* or *odium capitale et malivolentia*, "mortal hatred and ill-will." This language was vernacular as well as Latin. The language and orthography of love and hatred in legal records, tellingly, was often more standardized than the orthography of personal names and place names. In this record, Guilhem de Belavila's surname was spelled in several different ways, including *de Bellavilla*, *de Belavilla*, and, most often, in the Latinized form *de Pulchravilla*. The orthographic routinization of hatred is persuasive evidence for the degree to which an emotional vocabulary figured in legal procedures.

All the witnesses who were summoned to confirm the points made on behalf of Guilhem de Belavila were women. None of them offered any evidence of actual baptismal sponsorship to sustain the claim of god-kinship. One, Dousa Euzeria, called Uga a "god-kin of Guilhem Tomas and his special friend," as if god-kinship was more or less identical to strong friendship.[35] With a few exceptions they also ignored the procurator's claim of

[35] For the ensuing examples see ibid., fols. 112r–114v.

neighborly friendliness, probably because all the people involved in this case, killers and victim alike, were close neighbors. Most of the testimony centered on other gestures deemed to be more powerful evidence of affection or hatred. Dousa Euzeria, asked to elaborate on her claim of a special friendship between Uga and Tomas, explained that Uga had once loaned the victim ten pounds, and therefore "she believed her to be more a friend than an enemy." To prove the enmity between Uga and Guilhem de Belavila and his wife, another witness, Garcendis Dalmacia, explained that she had often heard Uga blaspheming them and their daughters. The friendship, in turn, was amply confirmed by the fact that Uga treated Tomas's house "as if it were her own." Biatris Rollanda elaborated on this point by arguing that Uga ate and drank regularly with Guilhem Tomas and his wife. Adding detail to this otherwise colorless expression, she went on to say that "they continually ate together in birthday celebrations in his house" (continue comedebant in festivitatibus natalitie in suo hospicio). Testimony regarding the absence of polite conversation between Alazays Rogeta and the defendants is especially interesting. Several witnesses confirmed this claim. Biatris Rollanda reported that she had once heard Alazays Rogeta having malicious words with Guilhem's wife and her sister; she went on to say that she did not know whether, at the time of the murder, they were still enemies, or whether they were once again speaking to each other (tamen nescio si tempore rixe erant inimice aut si loquebantur adinvicem). This testimony is particularly interesting because it shows how women like Biatris kept track of conversations in their neighborhood and inferred from them whether people were in a state of hatred or friendship. Uga Moressa, like Biatris Rollanda, also kept track of conversations; she considered Uga Bernarda to be an enemy of Guilhem de Belavila's wife and sister because she didn't speak with them.

In this case an entire neighborhood appears to have been riven by complementary and mutually reinforcing friendships and animosities. We cannot be sure of this: to make the exceptions work, Esteve had to describe the neighborhood in a way that fitted the demands of procedural law. All the same, the manifestly public nature of all trials in Marseille ensures that arguments could not wholly abandon verisimilitude. By the same token, one cannot help feeling that even if the adversaries of the de Belavilas were not hateful toward them *before* the trial, they surely became so *after* Esteve was through with them. The demands of the procedural law, according to this argument, may have served to harden sentiments that could have been less extreme before the trial.

Let us, for the purpose of the argument, accept Esteve's characterization as a reasonably accurate portrayal of the emotional structures of the neighborhood. The existence of common enmities in the Spur served, among other things, to refresh and firm up the friendships, and the friendships complemented and extended kinship groups to the point where a group of friends would avenge one of their own by means of hostile testimony. The emotional relationships may have crystallized around the rivalry between two big men, namely the notary Guilhem de Belavila and the merchant Guilhem Tomas, but they were nourished by vicious disagreements among the women. The men expressed their well-known hatred by means of assaults, insults, and threats. The women normally participated in the hatreds and friendships in a different way, largely through malicious barbs and hostile testimony, though they were not averse to joining in the street battles. All parties used public coldness to put their hatred on display.

The performative sociology used by the witnesses in this case, which evokes the sociological observations of Erving Goffman, is typical of a number of other trials.[36] A woman named Vivauda de Nercio attempted to prove to the judge that many suits lodged against her in 1354 had their origin in her distant cousin and enemy, Bertran Montanee. As her procurator explained, "Bertran, like any enemy, had ceased to speak to Vivauda during the entire period in question, apart from several injurious words."[37] In an appeal lodged on behalf of several residents of the burg of St. Augustine, condemned by the court of inquest for participating in a homicide on 20 May 1342, their procurator, Ugo Micael, sought to damage the testimony of several witnesses at the inquest by showing that the hostile witnesses were in a state of hatred with the accused men. One witness summoned by Ugo echoed Vivauda de Nercio's claim that insults were evidence for formal hatred: he explained that he knew of the capital enmity because of insults he had heard exchanged between the hostile parties in the plaza of the Palace.[38] Several other witnesses confirmed that the two hostile witnesses—Peire Ferier and Jacme Raynaut—were capital enemies (*inimici capitales*) of the accused.[39] One witness, Peire Clerici, was asked how he knew this. The notary recorded Peire's response in this way:

[36] Erving Goffman, *Presentation of Self in Everyday Life* (New York, 1959).
[37] ADBR 3B 54, fol. 47r, case opened 12 July 1354 on fol. 6r.
[38] The case is ADBR 3B 808, fols. 123r–159r, case opened 23 July 1342; this reference is to fol. 131v.
[39] The original claim that the testimony was tainted by hatred was made by the procurator on fol. 125v and confirmed by Esteve de Viens on fols. 126v–127r and by others elsewhere. Esteve was a neighbor of the accused and hence claimed full knowledge of the situation; he was able to trace the origin of the hatred to the fact that the accused had wounded the butcher Antoni Raynaut, the brother of Jacme Raynaut, some time earlier; Antoni had evidently died of his wound. Thus, according to the witness, Jacme was out for revenge.

He knows this because the said Peire and Jacme do not speak to the condemned, nor do they address words to them when they can avoid it [nec verbum dant eis quando obviantur] . . . . Whenever he went about with the condemned men or with either one of them, Jacme Raynaut and Peire Ferier did not wish to give them any word of greeting [nolebant eis aliquod verbum salutationis dare]. (fol. 128v)

Judges were interested in this argument for public coldness. A witness to an exception procedure lodged in the course of Johanet Salvayre's 1408 suit, discussed at length in chapter 1, observed that Antoni Dalmas and his wife were in a state of hatred with Reseneta Cambale. The witness, Peire Barbesaure, had heard Antoni and Reseneta quarreling publicly and trading great insults. "From that time onward," the witness said, "Antoni and his wife have been enemies of Cambale without the one speaking to the other apart from when they have a fight" (absque eo quod unus alteri loquetur nisi sit dum habunt simul rixam). He was interrogated further on this point: "How does he know that Antoni and his wife and lady Cambale do not speak?" Peire, according to the transcript, responded, "By my own sight and hearing, because I am a neighbor and would have often heard if the one had spoken to the other in good friendship" (respondit visu proprio auditu quia vicinus est et audivisset pluries si bona amicitia unus alteri locutus fuisseret).[40]

The insults and assaults traded by Antoni and Reseneta were negative gifts, and their refusal to converse normally was a refusal to exchange the gift of words. As seen already in the appeal of Guilhem de Belavila, the negative gifts used to describe enmities were mirrored by the positive exchanges, notably commensality and conversation, that gave shape and public expression to friendships. The ritual sharing of food and wine was perhaps the most meaningful of these. The sharing of food and wine was commonly used to mark certain liminal moments or punctuate the recategorization of relationships.[41] A case from 1360 shows three men sitting down to a meal of bread, cheese, and red wine before attempting to resolve a long-standing debt arising from the sale of sheep. Two witnesses, Jacme Bernat and Andrieu Scoffier, described the meal in some detail.[42] Such rituals could later be used to prove the existence of a strong affectionate bond. When a plaintiff named Peire Veyrier sued Johan de Portale for a debt, Johan challenged the testimony of one of Peire's witnesses by showing that

[40] ADBR 3B 147, fols. 93v–94r, case opened 24 Feb. 1407 on fol. 21r.
[41] Maurizio Lupoi, *The Origins of the European Legal Order*, trans. Adrian Belton (Cambridge, 2000), 222–23.
[42] ADBR 3B 62, fols. 109v–110r, case opened 18 Jan. 1360 on fol. 100r.

he was a close associate (*socius*) of the plaintiff. Johan's witness to this claim explained that he had frequently seen the plaintiff and *his* witness eating and drinking together from one bread and one wine (*uno pano uno vino*).[43] The judge asked how he knew they drank and ate together from one bread and one wine. The witness, Nicolau Gracie, responded that it was the custom in Marseille that when any partner or mariner returned from a voyage, the other partner or patron of the boat would share bread and wine with him.[44]

Friends, relatives, and members of a household shared food and drink on a much more regular basis and the ritual significance of such exchanges was even more powerful: most exceptions based on commensality refer to these exchanges, not the episodic meals described by Nicolau Gracie. In the case from 1360 mentioned previously, in which a promise to repay a debt was attested by the ritual exchange of bread, cheese, and red wine, the defendant objected to the plaintiff's witnesses, Jacme Bernat and Andrieu Scoffier, on numerous grounds, including the fact that they regularly shared food and drink with the plaintiff, Ugo Perdigon.[45] In two separate suits, two agricultural laborers named Jacme Raynaut and Raymon Dedieu challenged fines leveled against them for trespass by arguing that their denouncers, Augustin Peire and Guilhem de Matis, were close associates (*socios*) of the men of the tribunal, "going about, chatting, and drinking with them" (*eundo, conversando, bibendo cum eisdem*).[46] All the witnesses attested convincingly to the relationship. In a similar case discussed earlier, the defendant, Peire Clerici, impugned two witnesses as close associates of the plaintiff, "very frequently eating, sleeping, and drinking with them" (*comedentes sepe sepius et sepissime iacentes et bibentes cum predictis*).[47]

Exceptions provided in the case of Antoni d'Ays give some of our best evidence for the ritual meaning of commensality, though in this case the exception was being used not to impugn witnesses but rather to undermine the legitimacy of a suit. During his counterarguments, Antoni sought to prove that he and Dousa had formerly been accepted as friends by those same neighbors. The current suit, he claimed, was a piece of vengeful

---

[43] An expression used in Tuscany to define kin; see Christiane Klapisch-Zuber and Michel Demonet, "*A uno pane et uno vino*: The Rural Tuscan Family at the Beginning of the Fifteenth Century," in Christiane Klapisch-Zuber, *Women, Family, and Ritual in Renaissance Italy*, trans. Lydia G. Cochrane (Chicago, 1985).

[44] ADBR 3B 34, fol. 121v, case opened 18 Oct. 1338 on fol. 111r.

[45] ADBR 3B 62, fol. 115r, case opened 18 Jan. 1360 on fol. 100r.

[46] ADBR 3B 52, case of Jacme Raynaut, fols. 100r–128v, case opened 19 Nov. 1353; ADBR 3B 57, case of Raymon Dedieu, fols. 142r–162v, case opened 16 Feb. 1355; ADBR 3B 818, appellate hearing of Raymon Dedieu, fols. 87r–122r, case opened 12 Sept. 1355.

[47] ADBR 3B 808, fol. 128v, case opened 23 July 1342 on fol. 123r.

hypocrisy designed to punish him after friendly relationships had deteriorated into hatred.[48]

Numerous witnesses testified on Antoni's behalf, and many sought to illustrate the formally friendly relationships by referring to commensality. Consider the words of Jacme Gavot, a shoemaker who did not live in Antoni's neighborhood. According to the transcript of his deposition concerning the friendship between Antoni, Dousa, and the men and women of Negrel street, Jacme had said the following words:

> I have seen and heard . . . Guilhem de Podio, Gilet Alfans, Ugo de Podio, and many other shoemakers of Negrel street, neighbors of Antoni and Dousa, having good, peaceful, and honest relations with Antoni and Dousa, eating and drinking with Antoni, and their wives with Dousa. (fol. 181v)

The commensality extended to Antoni's suppliers. The leather-worker Antoni Beromes was reported to have said the following:

> Very often, over a great stretch of time, when the witness used to go to the house of Antoni to receive payment for cured leather, he saw Antoni and Dousa conversing with the neighboring shoemakers, those neighbors eating and drinking with Antoni and Dousa and chatting peacefully and quietly with them, and often they would call him over so that he might eat and drink with them. (fol. 180r)

Commensal relations implied very strong affective bonds. Ugo Saornin summarized his testimony in this way: "So much were Antoni and Dousa loved [*diligebantur*] by the said neighbors that if these same neighbors were related by blood to Antoni and Dousa they could not love them more" (fol. 178v).

Some witnesses, like Jacme Gavot, kept Antoni's feasting relationship with the men separate from Dousa's relationship with the women. Johan de Trets, according to his deposition, "saw the said Antoni d'Ays and Dousa in Negrel street conversing peacefully and quietly with the neighbors of the street . . . , the men eating and drinking with the said Antoni and the women . . . of the neighborhood eating with the said Dousa and otherwise conversing and chatting together" (fol. 175r). Several witnesses stressed how Dousa ate and shared fruit with the other neighborhood women. This testimony, first given by the witness Paulet Faber, was later supported by Ugo

[48] ADBR 3B 41, fols. 164r–187v, case opened 16 Aug. 1340.

Saornin, who twice talked about *incenia fructuum* (formal feasts of fruit). The next witness, Jacme Gavot, used the expression *maxime fructus*, and the notary Johan Augier explained that Dousa and the other women ate and drank together, "especially sharing fruits" (*specialiter fructus*). The sharing of fruit, in the testimony of Ugo Saornin, also corresponded with giving Dousa the title "lady" or "mistress" (vocando eam dominam Dousam et inceniam fructuum eidem Dulcie transmitendo et fructus simul comedendo) (fol. 178v). By referring to this title, usually reserved for married or widowed women, the witness recalled to everyone's attention that Dousa, though a maid, was also a respectable widow. He was also suggesting by the context of his remarks that marriage was not the sole principle behind respectability. Respectability, instead, was the common acceptance afforded by one's gender and neighborhood peers, as symbolized, among women, by the sharing of fruit.

The case of Antoni d'Ays, with its frequent allusions to the gentle conversations among close neighbors, shows how the sharing of words was just as important as the sharing of food. Conversation does not show up in exception procedures as often as ritual commensality, but it surfaces often enough to show a basic awareness of the mirror opposition between hostile exchanges or coldness on the one hand and friendly conversation on the other. Both conversation and commensality, in turn, were often bolstered by allusions to domestic or familial relations. Returning to the case of Guilhem and Uga de Belavila, witnesses against the couple were said to have treated the victim's house as if it were their own, as if they were housemates or household members. The suggestion crops up in many other exception procedures. In some cases, it was made concrete by the suggestion that two men slept in the same house. It was used frequently in cases in which a servant was giving testimony on behalf of a master or mistress. In such cases, as with the poor or the very young, the state of dependency implied by domestic servitude should have been sufficient to throw doubt on a witness's testimony. However, defendants who posed exceptions evidently did not think it sufficient to establish the fact of servitude alone, for they routinely added conversation, commensality, and co-residence to the list of reasons for doubting the testimony. Thus, in a case from 1355, the draper Guilhem de Montels, a de Jerusalem faction member, challenged the testimony of a women named Viventa not only because she was a prostitute but also because, despite her oath to the contrary, she was a servant of Guilhem's adversary for whom she testified, living in his house, eating, drinking, and chatting with him.[49] In another case, Bernat Raymbaut challenged the hos-

[49] ADBR 3B 58, fol. 105v, case opened 19 Feb. 1355 on fol. 92r.

tile testimony of one Jacma Colrata by arguing that Jacma was a maid of the plaintiff, Jacma Bernicia, living in her house and eating and drinking and talking with her.[50] In 1351, Raynaut de Conchis challenged the hostile testimony of Berengiera Lamberta by arguing that she was a maid of the defendant Garcenda Imberta, eating, drinking, sharing a bed, and performing her service.[51] Poverty was a related accusation, since it implied dependency. In one case, the judge Peire Dalmas thought it necessary to ask the witness Aycarda Sallona, a poor woman, whether she was a servant of the litigant Jacma Thomasia: was she "eating and drinking the bread and wine of the said Jacma"? She answered no.[52] But as seen in the case of Guilhem de Belavila and others, the suggestion that two people shared a household was not limited to master-servant relationships.

How successful were exceptions based on love and hatred? Given the absence of extant books of sentences it is difficult to tell, but all the clues suggest that witness exception procedures based on a disqualifying relationship were normally very successful. Esteve Agulhenqui seems to have been successful in his defense of the de Belavilas and the Robauts. Raymon Dedieu won his appeal on the basis of the exceptions he argued against his adversary's witnesses. The victory of Reseneta Cambale over Johanet Salvayre, discussed in chapter 1, is particularly striking, for any reading of the evidence of the case against Jacme Niel and Reseneta would suggest that Johanet's arguments were sound. By showing that the depositions of Antoni Dalmas and his wife were motivated by hatred, though, Reseneta at a stroke brought Johanet's case crashing down and garnered a favorable ruling from the judge of the case.

Presumably no one was surprised to learn that some witness testimony was motivated by hatred. But the use of the courts to pursue a hatred was hardly limited to occasional acts of hostile testimony. Records from the fourteenth century are filled with exceptions of various kinds showing that civil suits themselves, not to mention denunciations to the court of inquest and imprisonments for debt, were thought to be motivated by hatred.[53] In 1341, for example, Marin de Morlans, the goatherd encountered in chapter 1, was denounced yet again to the court of the ban. This time he had allowed an ox to stray into a field where it caused damage. In his defense, Marin noted that the denouncer, Guilhem Sycart, was an enemy of Marin and Marin's children. A witness sustained this exception by observing that Guilhem was enraged because Marin (or perhaps one of his sons) had wounded

50  ADBR 3B 816, fol. 44v, case opened 17 June 1353 on fol. 12r.
51  ADBR 3B 43, fol. 31r, case opened 30 Aug. 1341 on fol. 21r.
52  ADBR 3B 37, fol. 267v, case opened June 1339 on fol. 264r.
53  Compare to Gauvard "De grace especial," 2:671.

Guilhem's brother.[54] In 1409, the goldsmith Nicolau Antoni complained how his enemy, Duranta Johanna, "moved by wrath," first insulted him openly on the street, then flung a rock at his head, and finally denounced him to the court of inquest on the basis of an injury that she faked, thus catching him up in the toils of the law.[55]

A royal letter from Queen Isabella in 1435 notes explicitly how numerous denunciations against people of good fame were being secretly procured by those full of envy or ill-will.[56] Names of denouncers were normally published in an attempt to expose the practice of hateful denunciation but people had evidently figured out ways to denounce their enemies "secretly"—through the offices of someone not known to be an enemy of the victim of the denunciation. It would be charitable to assume that at least some lawsuits and denunciations were initiated for disinterested or emotionally neutral reasons. But in some respects this is beside the point, for regardless of the motives or intentions of initiators, victims automatically interpreted such practices as hostile gestures that gave *them* the right to claim the existence of a hatred and act accordingly. Such claims formed the basis for exceptions that attempted to negate the legal standing for a libel or a denunciation, for as noted earlier, according to Roman-canon procedural law—and the procedure of the English common law as well—neither suits nor denunciations could be motivated by capital hatred.[57]

In Antoni d'Ays's 1342 suit defending his right to keep Dousa as his maid, Antoni accused his adversaries of being his "capital enemies" and argued that their suit against him was motivated by "vindictiveness, malice, and gross injustice."[58] Witnesses agreed. The mere act of initiating such a suit could be used later to prove the existence of hatred. In 1407, a witness was challenged on the grounds that he was an enemy and ill-wisher of the defendant: among other things, he had earlier litigated against the defendant.[59]

In the appeal of Guilhem de Belavila, one of his original defenses was based on the fact that Guilhem Tomas hated him and "daily pursued his destruction." A witness confirmed this, and when the interrogating judge

---

[54] ADBR 3B 43, fols. 10r–16v, case opened 12 July 1341.

[55] ADBR 3B 862, fols. 333r–46r, case opened 28 June 1409.

[56] AM FF 3, also AA 5, fol. 80, act dated 12 September 1435: "quod cum plerumque contingat processus criminales formari per curiam regiam dicte civitatis seu eius officiales contra bonas personas fame laudabilis honeste et conversationis ad instigationem seu procurationem secretam et latentem invidorum aut malivorum suorum."

[57] See Naomi D. Hurnard, *The King's Pardon for Homicide before A.D. 1307* (Oxford, 1969), 350–52, and in general appendix 1, "The Writ *De Odio et Atia*," 339–74.

[58] ADBR 3B 41, fol. 174r–v, case opened 16 Aug. 1340 on 164r.

[59] ADBR 3B 858, fol. 148r–v, case opened 7 May 1407 on fol. 23r: *dictus testis alias litigavit cum dicto Thome.*

asked him how he could be so sure, the witness responded "because the said Guilhem Tomas expressed hatred toward him and once lodged a suit against him in the court."[60] In a related effort to establish the victim's bellicosity, another witness reported that Guilhem Tomas "fought daily with Guilhem de Belavila, and the witness had heard it said in the village of Caderia that he had killed a man, that he litigated with two or three others in the same place, and had brought others to poverty. Many people of the village say as much."[61] Here, we get a strong sense of the contemporary idea that hatred and litigation were cut from the same cloth. That a prior suit was considered grounds for assuming the existence of a hatred is also made clear in another appeal for murder from 1342 that involved a number of accused men from the burg of St. Augustine. A witness for the appellants explained that he knew that hostile testimony given at the inquest was motivated by hatred because earlier he had seen the two witnesses, Jacme Raynaut and Peire Ferier, prosecute the accused in court.[62] In 1356, the Vivaut captain, Amiel Bonafos, was being persecuted by leaders of the de Jerusalem faction and sought to prove that his enemies were pursuing him unjustly, motivated by capital hatred.[63] A witness named Primar Mirapeis confirmed that the de Jerusalem faction was pursuing Amiel out of capital hatred. Primar, who was himself a judge in one of the city's lesser courts, justified his claim by saying that "he had seen and was present when the party of the de Jerusalem lodged a suit against Amiel in court; they even demanded a copy of the judge's ultimate sentence in the case."[64]

The principle also applies in criminal inquests. Here, the accusation was that individuals either denounced their enemies to the court or "made part" with the court during the inquest. Antoni Dalmas evidently assumed that Reseneta Cambale had denounced him to the criminal court out of hatred, and responded accordingly. In the St. Augustine case described just above, another witness confirmed the existence of hatred by reporting that Jacme Raynaut had once had the accused arrested and thrown in prison.[65] Jacme Raynaut had good cause, for the men accused in this case had killed his brother, Antoni Raynaut. This, however, was seen as irrelevant, since the norms of procedural law could not legitimate any hatred, whether expressed through revenge killing or through denunciation. The appeal of Guilhem de Belavila contains several powerful statements indicative of a widespread

---

[60] ADBR 3B 825, fol. 115v, case opened on 13 May 1365 on fol. 35r.
[61] Ibid., fol. 119r.
[62] ADBR 3B 808, fol. 130v, case opened 23 July 1342 on fol. 123r.
[63] ADBR 3B 820, fol. 47r, case opened 7 July 1356 on fol. 8r.
[64] Ibid., fols. 68v–69r.
[65] ADBR 3B 808, fol. 133r, case opened 23 July 1342 on 123r.

perception that people assisting the criminal court during an inquest did so out of hatred for the defendants, Guilhem and Fulco.[66]

> Guilhem de Montels, Jacme his brother, Restezin Johan, and those fishermen named de Fonte have pursued them capitally. Asked how he knows, the witness answered that he saw Guilhem de Montels and the others above coming to the court to denounce and prosecute Guilhem and Fulco. Guilhem de Belavila wrote to the witness that he refused to appear out of fear of the power of the de Montels. (testimony of Guilhem Bavilis, fols. 160v–161r)

> Augier Viadier, a cousin of Guilhem de Montels, and Guilhem de Montels were friends of Guilhem Tomas while he lived. When he died, as capital enemies of Guilhem de Belavila, they have persecuted him and still do persecute him in the royal court . . . so as to avenge the death of Guilhem Tomas, making part with the court, plotting, and providing information against Guilhem de Belavila when he was condemned for contumacy. Afterward, they urged the court to seize Guilhem's goods and auction them off. They have also been prosecuting the appellate case against Guilhem notoriously, publicly, and openly, making part with the court against him. (testimony of Lois de Bonils, notary, fol. 165r)

> Peire de Fonte and others of that name and Restezin Johan, cousins and affines of the late Guilhem Tomas, along with Guilhem de Montels, have persecuted and still persecute Guilhem de Belavila and Fulco . . . as their enemies in the royal courts of this city of Marseille, both in the court of the lord viguier and in the court of first appeals, so as to avenge the death of the said Guilhem. (testimony of Antoni Bort, fol. 169r)

The threat of the corporal punishment wielded by the criminal court could also serve as a useful device for forcing recalcitrant enemies to humiliate themselves and make peace. To judge by the brief summary of a case, found in the clavaire's register from 1407, a resident of Marseille named Monet Blete was involved in a dispute with Jacme Bosquet. This dispute was serious enough to require that a formal peace be made between the two antagonists. In Marseille, not to mention Florence and Siena, evidence that peace had been made was sufficient to terminate formal assault charges by

---

[66] ADBR 3B 825, case opened 13 May 1365 on fol. 35r.

the criminal court.[67] Jean-Marie Carbasse shows how medieval French kings struggled, in vain, against the practice.[68] But this custom, as Monet knew only too well, gave the victim of assault a potent bargaining chip. At Monet's behest, Jacme had been seized and locked up by officers of the court, and Monet, speaking through the bars, had threatened Jacme with these words: "Unless you make peace with me I will ensure that you lose a foot or a fist" (nisi concordaret se cum eodem quod ipse faceret quod perderet pedem vel pugnam).[69] This, evidently, was going a bit far: Monet's threat was overheard, and he was fined a considerable sum of money, although the fine was reduced by the viguier to 7 pounds 10 shillings since Monet successfully pleaded benefit of the clergy.

An even more compelling civil court case from 1403 shows that enemies were suspected of bribing the courts to torture their enemies.[70] The facts of the case, naturally, were contested, but let us assume that the plaintiff, Jacme Babot, was telling a reasonably believable story. At some point during the course of his long-running feud with a hatter named Jacme Robert, Jacme Babot was captured by the court and tortured on three or four different occasions. The torture seems to have been unusual in one regard, for at several places in the transcript Babot suggests that it was carried out in such a way that he was rendered permanently enfeebled (perpetuo remaneret inpotens). Babot was also told that he would be tortured again and again until he agreed to a peace with his enemy (quod nisi pacem faceret ipse iterum et iterum torqueretur). He finally caved in. What he didn't know at the time, though, is that Jacme Robert had bribed the court with twenty-five florins so as to force him to make peace through torture (ignorabat quod adinstanciam dicti Jacobi Roberti captus fuisset et demum tortus pecunia mediante).

What all these cases show is that litigation, denunciation, and the practice of making part with the court, just like insults, threats, assaults, public coldness, and hostile testimony, were routinely interpreted as inimical gestures. By the early fifteenth century, there was a widespread and growing perception that the courts were thoroughly contaminated by the exercise of vengeance. This perception manifested itself linguistically in the increasing use of the insult baratier, cognate of the English "barrator," meaning one who either defrauds another, accepts bribes, or falsely accuses another in court. The first two uses of the expression were somewhat more common in

---

[67] Laura Ikins Stern, *The Criminal Law System of Medieval and Renaissance Florence* (Baltimore, 1994), 27; Peter Raymond Pazzaglini, *The Criminal Ban of the Sienese Commune, 1225–1310* (Milan, 1979), 94.

[68] Jean-Marie Carbasse, *Introduction historique au droit pénal* (Paris, 1990), 213.

[69] ADBR B 1943, fol. 25r.

[70] ADBR 3B 141, fols. 128r–145r, case opened 16 Oct. 1403.

Marseille's records.[71] Barratry, however, could also mean nasty litigiousness, a meaning captured in the insult that Johan Bohier hurled at Peire Venel in the midst of a lawsuit: "You've committed a great barratry against me."[72] Contemporaries elided all distinctions between these meanings—any misuse of legal apparatus was liable to be called barratry. Tellingly, the word was entirely absent as an insult earlier in the fourteenth century, and only begins to show up regularly as an insult in Massiliote records from the early fifteenth century, when complaints about legal and judicial abuse were rife.[73]

## GENDERING HATRED

One of the most remarkable features of the emotional scripts of fourteenth-century Marseille is how freely they were applied to both men and women. Beyond that, and even more significantly, the actions that formed the basis of the language of love and hatred were scarcely gendered at all. Men routinely used speech behavior to advertise loves or hatreds. Women often engaged in acts of violence. Recent work in feminist studies and sexuality has suggested that medieval European thinking about sex and gender acknowledged two sexes but only a single sliding gender system based on what one might call the individual's degree of forcefulness.[74] Most people, including boys, old men, Jews, peasants, servants, and clergy, were publicly gendered as weak, dependent, and "feminine." Free, middle-aged, Christian men were more likely to be considered forceful, aggressive, "masculine." Since gender ideologies did not inhere in differences of biological sex, certain women could be gendered as masculine. In the language of Marseille's court records, such women were considered fully capable of hating. One can, of course, hate in the privacy of one's home, muttering curses and threats as witches were said to do, and no one should be surprised to learn that women could hate. What is most important is that it was considered normal for women to act publicly in pursuit of that hatred. So normal was it

[71] E.g., ADBR B 1945, fol. 14r.

[72] ADBR B 1943, fol. 45v: "dixerat in iudicio contra Petrum Venelli quod ipse fecerat eidem unam magnam barateriam."

[73] In 1407 a notary chided a judge for his incompetence, saying "I've been doing business in this court for sixteen years, but never have I seen it so badly run as it is now" (lo a xvi ans que jeu acostumi aquesta cort, mays jamays jeu non la vi si mal gouvernada coma es al jorn duey). See ADBR B 1947, fol. 44r.

[74] Carol Clover, "Regardless of Sex: Men, Women, and Power in Early Northern Europe," in *Studying Medieval Women*, ed. Nancy F. Partner (Cambridge, 1993), 61–85.

for women to have hatreds that no witness from fourteenth-century Marseille ever evinced the least hesitation in ascribing public hatred to a woman, and the nouns used to name an enemy were routinely and normally feminized to identify female haters: *inimica, malivola*, and so on.

Hatreds did not just pit women against women, though this was common enough. All the women on both sides of the Guilhem de Belavila case hated one another with gusto, exchanging barbs and insulting one another's daughters. In a case discussed shortly, Vivauda de Nercio identified Micaela Berarde as an enemy and an ill-wisher (*inimiosua et malivola*). Records of fines paid show that woman-on-woman confrontations, and not just those between prostitutes, were quite common. But rather more significant than woman-woman hatreds are those situations where women hated men and vice versa. Some of these hatreds involved couples or complex groups. In the case of Guilhem de Belavila, hatreds were said to exist between the four defendants on the one hand—Guilhem and Uga de Belavila, and Fulco and Johana Robaut—and, on the other, Guilhem Tomas and his female friends Uga Bernarda, Alazays Antonia, and Alazays Rogeta. One result of the nature of the witness exception procedure is that the record does not describe a group hatred so much as strands of individual hatreds, but one suspects very strongly that there were group alliances involved. The record treats all subsidiary antagonisms as a function of the major hatred between Guilhem de Belavila and Guilhem Tomas, itself predicated on the Vivaut/de Jerusalem divide, though, as noted above, the women's hatred might well have existed independently or prior to that of their male friends and relatives.

Several cases show that single women were perfectly capable of having and maintaining hatreds with other individuals or couples. Such women were usually prominent members of the community, like Vivauda de Nercio, a member by blood and marriage of several notable families, or the prominent merchant Reseneta Cambale. Reseneta was so widely known and influential that her shop bore her name (*apotheca domine Cambale*), not that of her son, according to a long-standing practice among merchants whereby shops were named after "the oldest and most worthy member of the society" (*denominantur ab antiquiore et digniore de societate*).[75] In finishing off her adversary Johanet Salvayre, Reseneta proved that two of his witnesses, the apothecary Antoni Dalmas and his wife Batrona, were capital enemies and ill-wishers of Reseneta and her son Jacme Niel. All four people involved, like the antagonists in the Guilhem de Belavila case, were near neighbors. The enmity arose five years earlier when Reseneta denounced Antoni to the court of inquest, and since that time Antoni and Batrona hated Reseneta bit-

---

[75] ADBR 3B 147, fol. 48r, case opened 24 Feb. 1407 on fol. 21r.

terly and, according to witnesses, sought every evil against her and refused to make peace.[76] The major axis in this hatred was clearly that between Antoni and Reseneta. An equally interesting case described a hatred between Antoni Vinsens and Agneta Beroarde, a nun in the monastery of Syon. As noted in chapter 1, the hatred arose when Agneta had Antoni excommunicated for late payment of rent and subsequently took his land away from him.[77]

Although single women involved in hatred were typically of higher status there are exceptions and none more remarkable than the case of the caulker, Peire Uguet, and Magdalena, wife of a cobbler.[78] During the course of this 1407 trial, nominally over small debts but motivated by tremendous bitterness, Magdalena, for understandable reasons, found it necessary to undermine Peire's argument that she was his slave, purchased some years ago in Naples, and to do this she had to plead an exception to one of Peire's witnesses, a barber-surgeon named Nicolau de Sala. Nicolau was something of a personage in early fifteenth-century Marseille, prominent enough to have lent his name to a whole block of houses located near the port. He claimed to have witnessed the purchase of Magdalena. Magdalena challenged this testimony by offering the depositions of two women who claimed that Nicolau hated Magdalena.[79] According to the two women, the origin of this hatred lay in an event that took place several years earlier. On that day, Magdalena had gone to the barber to retrieve some razors that she had left there to be sharpened. Nicolau asked her "to go upstairs with him." Understandably concerned that Nicolau might cause shame to Magdalena, the two women, who were present, pressed her to refuse, which she did. It was this humiliating rejection, the two women claimed, that caused Nicolau to nourish a hatred for Magdalena.[80]

Women, clearly, were not excluded from public hatred by virtue of their biological sex. But also significant is a gender issue, for the actions considered proof of the existence of a hatred were not routinely or overtly gendered. Public coldness was associated with women such as Alazays Rogeta in the trial of Guilhem de Belavila but was equally ascribed to men such as Peire Ferier and Jacme Raynaut, who wouldn't greet the men of the burg of St. Augustine, and Bertran Montanee, who refused to speak to his cousin Vivauda de Nercio. Insults and public abuse, similarly, were used indiscriminately by both men and women. Witnesses reported that Antoni Dalmas and

[76] Ibid., fols. 90r–95r.
[77] ADBR 3B 147, fol. 175v, case opened 15 Mar. 1407 on fol. 136v.
[78] ADBR 3B 858, fols. 178r–263r, case opened 16 Aug. 1407.
[79] Ibid., fol. 246v.
[80] Ibid., fols. 248r–249r.

Reseneta Cambale fought publicly on the street, hurling insults and abuse, and records of fines collected give numerous examples of such actions.

Most significantly, spontaneous violence, though commonly practiced by men, was also available to women. Like public coldness, insulting words, litigation, and denunciation, spontaneous violence was routinely interpreted as good evidence for the existence of a hatred, and hence crops up relatively often in witness exception procedures. Several civil and appellate trials reveal situations where women assisted their menfolk in killing an enemy, or, like Johana Robauda and Uga de Belavila, were accused of having done so, and other cases can be found in the records of fines assessed by the criminal court and collected and recorded by financial officers of the crown. Men engaged in spontaneous violence more commonly than women, it is true, and women rarely or never used male weapons such as knives or swords. But they were free in their use of wooden bars, stones, and of course hands and fists.

## MORAL CONDEMNATION

The law courts of medieval Marseille, criminal and civil, offered fruitful opportunities for the public humiliation of adversaries. Those found guilty of crimes by the court of inquest were routinely and publicly shamed by having their sentences read out in public spaces. The pursuit of debt offered creditors the chance to have debtors taken from their houses and thrown in jail. But humiliations or veiled insults could be engineered more directly by actors at court, notably in exception procedures.

The several lawsuits of Vivauda de Nercio are interesting for what they reveal not only about the hatred-generating quality of litigation but also about the strategic use of legally sanctioned attacks on the character of witnesses and adversaries alike. Between 26 July 1352 and 19 July 1354, Vivauda, the daughter of Raymon Montanee and the wife of Raymon de Nercio, was involved in four lawsuits, both as the plaintiff and as the defendant. The first suit set Vivauda against her brother Johan over their maternal inheritance, and although the suit seems to have ended amicably enough—Vivauda had to pay Johan thirty florins to cover roughly half of his court costs but she got her inheritance—her litigious demeanor apparently antagonized some of her kinfolk, laying the groundwork for the next three suits.[81] Anger against

---

[81] ADBR 3B 48, fols. 323r–344v, case opened 26 Apr. 1352.

Vivauda may also have been kindled by the death of Johan shortly after the conclusion to the suit, for we learn in later suits that Vivauda had become Johan's heir. In the next suit, which opened on 11 December 1353, Vivauda was sued by a distant cousin, Bertran Montanee, over a plot of land that Bertran claimed was his by right of inheritance.[82] Vivauda countered that Bertran had sold it to her brother Monet, from whom she had inherited it, and provided evidence to the effect that she and her brother possessed the land peacefully, harvested its fruits, and paid the annual rent to the lord, the cellarer of the monastery of St. Victor. The record of the case ends with no apparent resolution, as many such records do.

But that was not the end of the story, and the fizzling of the legal case in no way implies a waning of the vengeful emotions that motivated it. The following July, in an apparently unrelated move, a man named Felip Francisci and his brother sued Vivauda for a debt of 168 florins.[83] The situation was complex. The two brothers, Italian merchants who did business in Marseille, had temporarily stored four large jars of sugar worth 168 florins in a house they subleased from a resident Italian merchant named Tanno Sorbi, who in turn had leased it from Vivauda's brother, Johan. At some point in 1349, they claimed, Johan took the jars out of the house and sold them. It is not clear whether he stole them or simply sold them on the merchants' behalf, but in any event money was owed. Vivauda, as Johan's heir, inherited this debt. That they took five years to lodge the suit is a little suspicious in itself. Even more suspicious is a witness list that included Bertran Montanee.

Felip's witnesses also included two friends, Tanno Sorbi and another man named Mayfren Rolant, and the entire set of witnesses adequately proved the seizure and sale of the jars of sugar. Vivauda's first attempt at a rebuttal did not produce any convincing witnesses. The articles for this rebuttal have been lost, although subsequent testimony reveals Vivauda's basic argument: Johan's seizure of the jars was justified because Tanno was behind in his lease payments, and it was up to Tanno to reimburse his sublessors. But the testimony was fragmented and unconvincing. Confronted with this initial failure, Vivauda's procurator, Albert Champoni, opened a new line of defense. First, he argued, Bertran Montanee is Vivauda's known enemy and ill-wisher; he has sued her in court and has tried to prevent her from inheriting from her late brother Johan. Bertran also ordered the nominal plaintiff, Felip, to come from Avignon to Marseille to initiate the suit. Albert then turned against other key witnesses, Tanno Sorbi and Mayfren Rolant, and the principal himself, Felip Francisci.

[82] ADBR 3B 52, fols. 150r–171v, case opened 11 Dec. 1353.
[83] ADBR 3B 54, fols. 6r–50v, case opened 12 July 1354.

(6) Tanno Sorbi is and has been a man accustomed to hang about in the taverns of the poor; he is almost continually in these low-status taverns. He has also been a debtor of Vivauda's for a long time, for rent of the house in question. (7) Mayfren is a man who frequents poor and hopeless taverns of low status and dishonest way-of-life [*conversationis inhoneste*]. (8) Mayfren is Felip's cousin, housemate [*domesticus*], and associate, eating and drinking almost continually in the city of Marseille. (9) Felip lives and sleeps with and resides in Mayfren's house. (10) Mayfren and Tanno are defamed men. (fol. 32v)

Witnesses easily sustained these points. One of them, Johan Bausan, reported in some detail how on numerous occasions last year, in the plaza of the Palace, he had heard Bertran Montanee announce publicly, in the presence of many people, that he would inflict every harm or injury he could on Vivauda, and that when the current suit was stilled many others would be initiated (fol. 35r). Felip's response was to defend Bertran's probity; he argued that Bertran was a good and honest man who, as Vivauda's cousin, would naturally preserve her honor (fol. 40r). Vivauda's procurator responded in turn by repeating the argument that Bertran had secretly conspired to initiate the suit against Vivauda and had offered Felip money for doing so (fol. 46v). From the time of the original lawsuit onward, according to further articles, Bertran had been threatening to disinherit Vivauda of everything she owned, and Felip knew this. Finally, as mentioned earlier, the procurator noted that during the entire time period Bertran had ceased to speak to Vivauda just as any enemy would.

This case, too, ended abruptly, though with suggestions that Vivauda was coming out on top. Her troubles were not over yet, though, for Bertran also offered hostile testimony in yet another suit that opened a week later and was running concurrently with Felip Francisci's case.[84] Vivauda was suing Johana de Caturcio to recover a small debt of eleven florins originally owed to Johan Montanee, and Johana defended herself by calling witnesses to say that the debt had been repaid. In addition to Bertran, against whom Vivauda lodged a by now familiar set of exceptions, the witnesses included the unimpeachable Peire Deodat and the rather more dubious Micaela Berarda, a maid. Vivauda's exception to the deposition of Micaela ran this way. Four months ago, Micaela had stolen numerous things from Vivauda's house, including a certain notarial instrument, and on account of this theft Micaela and Vivauda had had words with one another. For this reason, Micaela has been and is Vivauda's enemy and ill-wisher. Beyond that "Micaela is the

[84] ADBR 3B 54, fols. 62r–73v, case opened 19 July 1354.

poorest of women, of evil fame and defamed, and is called 'vielh destral' by many people" (Michaella est mulier pauperima male fame et diffamativa et per pluries vielh destral nominatur). This particular case ends with a judge's ruling that security be taken from Johana to pay the debt, so there is every reason to believe that Vivauda won her case.

Vivauda's two years in court are interesting for what they say about hatred and litigation, but the cases also provide examples of what are, to all intents and purposes, legally sanctioned assaults on another's character. This exception, which shows up in a number of trials from the fourteenth century, has equivalents in classical Roman and early Arabic law as well as early medieval procedural law.[85] The defamation exception challenged witnesses on the grounds that their behavior or way of life had brought them to a condition of ill fame (*mala fama, mala vita*) and so eliminated their standing as witnesses. As the examples from Vivauda's trials show, the exception was used selectively, either against those who really were low-lifes or those whose behavior was capable of such an interpretation. In the sugar-jar trial, there may have been no point in attacking Felip himself—he was the principal party in the suit, not a witness whose testimony needed to be excepted—but Vivauda's procurator did not include two other witnesses, Johan de Vaquiers and Alrassa Montanea, Johan Montanee's widow, presumably because their characters were unimpeachable. Micaela Berarda also offered testimony in the sugar-jar trial but, for whatever reason, her testimony was not excepted on that occasion. In the debt case, it would have been foolhardy for Vivauda to attack the character of one of the hostile witnesses, the respectable nobleman Peire Deodat, hence the exception fell on Micaela Berarda. Such selective usage did not weaken the procedure: numerous cases show that judges tended to think that one witness's moral turpitude infected the entire set of depositions, even those given by unimpeachable witnesses. The defamation procedure, even if used selectively, cast an aura of moral turpitude over an entire case, tarring the plaintiff as well as the witnesses in question.

Moral turpitude, unlike hatred, was partly gendered according to biological sex, for the tropes assigned to men were different from those deemed

[85] In general see Edward Peters, "Wounded Names: The Medieval Doctrine of Infamy," in *Law in Medieval Life and Thought*, ed. Edward B. King and Susan J. Ridyard (Sewanee, Tenn., 1990), 43–89; Francesco Migliorino, *Fama e infamia: problemi della società medievale nel pensiero giuridico nei secoli xii e xiii* (Catania, 1985); Jeffrey A. Bowman, "Infamy and Proof in Medieval Spain," in *Fama*, ed. Fenster and Smail, 95–117. As Jeannette A. Wakin notes, the importance of witness testimony as a method for enforcing good moral character in Islam was so great as to limit the turn to written instruments; see Wakin, ed., *The Function of Documents in Islamic Law* (Albany, 1972), 7–8.

characteristic of women. The first accusation made against both Tanno Sorbi and Mayfren Rolant, that of drinking in ill-famed and "hopeless" (*inops*) taverns, was a common attribute of defamed men. Nearly as common were two other accusations, that of fornicating (or pimping) and gambling; other accusations include quarrelsomeness, blasphemy, mendacity, and begging. In a defamation procedure heard during a 1352 appeal, three hostile witnesses were challenged on the grounds that they were "men of low status, dice-players, great deniers of God, and frequent tavern-goers." Beyond that, they were also capital enemies of the defendant.[86] Another appeal later in 1352 invoked the defamation procedure against a set of witnesses, arguing that they were gamblers and tavern-goers and biased toward the plaintiff.[87] The witnesses on these points were surprisingly ambivalent. Johan Julian said that he didn't know if the hostile witnesses really were gamblers or tavern-goers, although he admitted that he often saw them eating and drinking with the plaintiff, because he himself often ate and drank with them.[88] Several other witnesses disclaimed all knowledge, and only two witnesses fully confirmed the defendant's argument. Defamed men were also said to quarrel and fight a lot and associate routinely with low-lifes. Defamed men were often characterized as having *mala conversatio*, literally "bad conversation" or "evil speech," often translated as an "evil way of life." In 1334, a priest named Guilhem de Cina testified in court about a notarial instrument he had read out loud to its owner. His testimony was then excepted on the grounds that he was an abject man and a beggar, accustomed to making his living by begging from door to door, also a frequenter of taverns and brothels, "who on account of his vile life and conversation was once ejected from the castrum of Ginhaco and from other places."[89] Perhaps more central to the case being made against him, he was also called "rude and idiotic, almost wholly ignorant of Latin."

Another set of accusations lodged against defamed men referred to their economic failures. Accusations of being a spendthrift were somewhat less common in witness exception procedures than lifestyle accusations and the logic was different, although defendants sometimes linked the two behavioral complexes because men who drank, gambled, and fornicated could be assumed to be spendthrifts. The conventional accusation was that such men "badly managed their wealth," literally "their assets" (*substancia sua*) or "their goods" (*bona sua*). Occasionally, defendants argued that defamed witnesses had no economic assets whatsoever and had to live off their labor

---

[86] ADBR 3B 811, fol. 130r, case opened 4 Feb. 1352 on fol. 116r.
[87] ADBR 3B 812, fol. 31r, case opened 1 June 1352 on fol. 26r.
[88] Ibid., fol. 33r.
[89] ADBR 3B 29, fol. 45r, case opened 28 June 1334 on fol. 35r.

alone. A good example can be found in the proceedings of a 1360 suit over a disputed sale of sheep. The suit was initiated by Ugo Perdigon, who accused the butcher Jacme Raynaut of failure to pay for the sheep and, beyond that, failure to repay a small loan of 29s.[90] Two witnesses for Ugo named Jacme Bernart and Andrieu Scoffier adequately confirmed the existence of the sale and the loan. Jacme Raynaut accordingly attacked their credibility with a witness exception that is a classic of the genre. Though only the first accusation is related to work habits the exception is worth considering in full:

> For the purpose of annulling, breaking, and eliminating the depositions of the corder, Jacme Bernart, and Andrieu Scoffier, alias de Valansola, given by Jacme and Andrieu in the active suit between Ugo Perdigon and Jacme Raynaut: (1) Jacme Bernart and Andrieu Scoffier, who gave testimony in the suit, are poor men of low status, bearing the burden of such duties that they could not make a living without great labor. They are also foreigners from other parts. (2) They are cousins and affines of Ugo Perdigon of that same place, namely the castrum of Valansola. (3) These witnesses for some time hence have made part with Ugo against Jacme Raynaut . . . (4) Ugo eats and drinks with the said witnesses, especially with Jacme Bernart, the corder, even sleeping in his house as a cousin, affine, and housemate. (5) They have made threats against him. (6) As a poor man, Andrieu Scoffier is the sort of man who is accustomed to hang about with men of low status and dishonest life in taverns and other dishonorable places. (7) Andrieu the witness is a player of dice who is accustomed to betting his shirt in taverns and other most vile places. (8) All this is the public talk and fame. (fols. 114v–115r)

The accusation that the two men could scarcely make a living even with their great labor (qui non possint vivere sine maximo eorum labore) suggests how dependent they were on others.

The nominal purpose of what I shall call the "witness defamation procedure" was to except the testimony of hostile witnesses. The procedure was quite effective. But quite apart from this the procedure also managed to tar the plaintiff for associating with such individuals. Ugo Perdigon does not come off well for having shared a house, even a bed, with a drinker and gambler such as Jacme Bernart. Other kinds of procedures attacked the character and probity of one of the principal parties more explicitly. As noted in previous sections, a plaintiff's hatred was frequently used against him or her. In other cases it was the defendant whose moral standing took a beating.

---

[90] ADBR 3B 62, fols. 100r–116r, case opened 18 Jan. 1360 on fol. 100r.

This is notably true of suits for the recovery of dowries, where the defamation of men was a stock formula. As discussed in the next chapter, some dotal suits were clearly intended to publicly penalize erring husbands.

The most fascinating case of this kind evokes many of the same characteristics attributed to defamed witnesses. The case was initiated in 1334 in one of the lesser courts by Laurens Giraut. On behalf of his daughter Sileta, Laurens was attempting to recover a dowry of one hundred pounds from his in-law, Bertran Vital, who as Sileta's father-in-law had taken control of her dowry. Invoking his right to hold the lesser court judge in suspicion, Bertran had the case removed from that court's jurisdiction. His countersuit, formally initiated in the palace court in July 1334, lasted for over eight months.[91] In his list of articles, Laurens argued that Bertran Vital and his son (probably by a previous wife) were going bankrupt, hence the need to recover Sileta's dowry of one hundred pounds before it disappeared. Various clues suggest deeper marital problems: among other things, Sileta and her own two children had left Bertran and were living with her father. A parade of witnesses on Laurens's behalf showed up to attest to the rumors of Bertran's bankruptcy that were circulating in the city. As these witnesses pointed out, Bertran had been selling off his properties and had large debts. "A great *fama* works against Bertran [*magna fama viget contra predictum Bertrandum*] because he sold and alienated the properties mentioned above," remarked one unimpeachable witness, the notary Peire Mayin (fol. 41r–v). "He is badly using his assets," observed another notary, Paul Giraut (fol. 43v). One of the most interesting features of the case made by Laurens is that he brought five notaries to attest to property transfers they had drawn up for Bertran. At issue was not the existence of the transfers: the notarial instruments could have served that purpose just as well. More significant was the fact that each notary interpreted these transactions as the desperate measures of a man on the verge of bankruptcy. Perhaps such impersonal observations helped counter the suggestion that the hostile witnesses were motivated by hatred for Bertran. Several witnesses were closely interrogated by the judge on this point: Does the public talk and fame proceed from Bertran's enemies or ill-wishers? "I didn't know that Bertran had any enemies," responded one witness, the cobbler Peire Asami (fol. 39v).

The accusation that husbands badly managed the dowries of their wives or daughters-in-law was conventional in dotal suits. In his defense, Bertran made a series of arguments to the effect that he was a decent person, reputed by his neighbors to be a man of wealth and good standing, and if it could be proven that he did alienate the properties in question this was for the pur-

[91] ADBR 3B 28, fols. 29r–70v, case opened 12 July 1334.

pose of making money and also for putting together his daughter's dowry. Witnesses amply sustained these points. So Laurens tried a new and even more hostile tactic:

(1) Bertran is a tavern-goer, drinking and eating in taverns. (2) Bertran has recourse to prostitutes and spends his *bona* dishonorably. (3) Bertran manages his assets badly. (4) All this is the public talk and fame. (fol. 57r)

Linking these character traits is an idea that is characteristic of a number of such accusations, namely that a man is badly managing his assets precisely because he has been wasting it all on alcohol and prostitutes. What followed after this revelation was a series of witnesses all of whom attested in great detail to the taverns and houses where Bertran was seen drinking, the tripe and the types of fruit he ate (quinces, peaches, and figs), even the color of the wine he drank. As Guilhem Rogier observed, "A year ago he, with two other people and Bertran, drank and ate in the house of the ladies of the beguinage next to the house of Raolin Vivaut where red wine is sold. A year ago they drank in the house of Bertran Gayrier where white wine is sold" (fol. 59r). This line of reasoning got Laurens nowhere. Following procedural rules, Bertran was able to have each witness interrogated on the suitability of this behavior. Was Bertran drinking dishonorably in these taverns? Do other respectable men, namely those who manage their assets well, use the taverns of neighbors and friends in a similar way? "He drank and ate well and honestly in these taverns," the witnesses for Laurens all agreed, "just as a good man is able to drink and eat." "It is the custom among the men of the burg to drink in a similar way in the taverns of their neighbors and friends" (fol. 58r–v).

By this point in the trial Laurens's dander was up, and his next series of arguments all attacked the person of the witnesses brought by Bertran earlier in the suit: one was a public usurer; another was Bertran's relation, a housemate and family member; another was a spiritual kinsman and a man of vile speech, drinking in and frequenting taverns dishonestly and publicly; yet another had been publicly defamed for homicide. The witnesses for Laurens, again, were unconvincing, and the trial drew to a close shortly after Bertran complained to the judge about the vexations he had suffered. The judge ruled in his favor, though Laurens appealed the decision and the eventual outcome is unknown.

With the notable exception of hatred or anger, character failings configured as deadly sins are surprisingly rare in exception procedures. Jacme Bernart and Andrieu Scoffier were considered less than worthy because they worked too hard rather than too little. Accusations of drinking and eating in vile taverns never include the suggestion that one is consuming too much, nor is the word "gluttony" ever used. The moral fault here was either wasting one's wealth or associating with low-lifes. Envy is never referred to, and on the only occasion where I've run across the word avaricious (*cupidus, avarus*) the adjective was being used to describe a Jewish auctioneer.[92] Witnesses were accused of consorting with prostitutes but this was not configured as lust so much as an evil association, though one exception procedure from 1413 does accuse a hostile witness of adultery.[93] Guilhem Tomas was accused of being proud (*superbus*) but otherwise this word, too, is absent in court records. What exception procedures suggest is that, with the major exception of hatred and anger, vernacular character attributes had little to do with Christian moral virtues and sins.

Like men, defamed women were often accused of fornication or prostitution. In sharp contrast to men, though, women were never accused of hanging around in taverns, gambling, physical assaults, or associating with low-lifes. Nor were they ever defamed as incapable of managing their economic assets. Most commonly, women were defamed for their inability to govern their mouths: they were accused of being verbally quarrelsome or gossipy, as with Alazays Antonia, accused in the case of Guilhem de Belavila of being a gossipy woman (*mulier locax*) of evil fame, low status, dishonest life, poor, one who suffers from lust just like a prostitute.[94] The accusation was not tropic. The next witness excepted in this trial, Alazays Rogeta, was not considered gossipy, though she was considered lustful and poor. One witness, Marita Venella, confirmed the exception against Alazays Rogeta, though she did call Alazays a gossip (*lauzengeria*), an accusation not found in the exception (fol. 117r). Other witnesses were surprisingly unwilling to condemn the two women: Guilelma Pelhana remarked that she considered Alazays Rogeta a good lady, and Dousa de Gorda noted that although Alazays Antonia was a gossip she was not "vile of her body" (*vile de suo corpore*) and basically a good woman (*bona mulier*) although poor.[95] Here there is also some overlap with men, since men were similarly accused of being quarrelsome. The dif-

---

[92] ADBR 3B 859, fols. 131v–132r, case opened 26 Apr. 1408 on fol. 105r.

[93] ADBR 3B 151, fol. 93v, case opened 15 Sept. 1413 on fol. 86r. The witness, whose name is not readable, was accused of having been caught in adultery (*fuit aprehensus in adulterio*).

[94] ADBR 3B 825, fol. 100v, case open 13 May 1365 on fol. 35r.

[95] Ibid., fols. 116v, 119v. See also the favorable testimony of Sanxia Rigauda on fol. 118r. Jaumeta Pellissier similarly considered Alazays Antonia a good lady though gossipy; see fol. 121r.

ference lies more with the weapon used: tongues in the case of women, swords and knives in the case of men. The use of the same set of adjectives (*rixosus, -a*, etc.) shows that observers did not draw a great distinction between tongues and knives.

The defamation procedure was mirrored by a procedure that painted the good fama of the defendant. This, the character-witnessing procedure, can be found in many lists of articles. In 1341 Raymon de Gordono called himself "a youth of good fame and condition, good conversation and life, and not quarrelsome."[96] Girart de Buco called himself "a peaceful man of good life and fame and honest conversation and the sort of man who is never accustomed to committing or sponsoring homicides" in an appeal in 1356.[97] Adhemar de Furno, a farrier accused of having killed a gray pony through his own negligence, called himself "a good farrier, and a lawful man of good name and good fama in Marseille and elsewhere."[98] A series of appeals from 1355 show that all the accused men were good and peaceful men of good conversation, not accustomed to fighting or doing evil, prone to flee from street battles (*fugiens rixas*), obedient to the court (*obediens curie*), and so on.[99] Uga de Belavila and Johana Robauda, accused of assisting in the murder of Guilhem Tomas, were called women of good fame who avoided street battles.[100] Uga's husband Guilhem de Belavila was an especially good man, adding simplicity (*homo simplex*) to the array of favorable character traits. Witnesses spoke favorably of his goodness: "He freely gives alms to the poor," said one. "I know him and have noticed his lifestyle. He is never accustomed to fighting *rixas* or *pelegias;* he doesn't run around in taverns or other inhonest places; he goes to church often to hear the divine offices, especially to the Church of St. Louis," remarked another. "I've known him since he was a boy and talk to him a lot," said a third.[101]

Dominating the list of good traits is peacefulness, good conversation, honesty, and of course good fame. "Lawful," reflected by the adjective *legalis, -e*, shows up in a number of instances.[102] Though more often used to describe men such as Adhemar de Furno it was also used by women, notably women who engaged publicly in some form of retailing or other commercial activity. The wine-seller Jacma Thomasia described herself in 1339

---

[96] ADBR 3B 808, fol. 70v, case opened 6 March 1341 on fol. 68r.
[97] ADBR 3B 820, fol. 161v, case opened 12 July 1356 on fol. 133r.
[98] ADBR 3B 45, fol. 24v, case opened 23 May 1343 on fol. 24r.
[99] See ADBR 3B 819, passim.
[100] ADBR 3B 825, fol. 102r, case opened 3 May 1365 on fol. 35r.
[101] Ibid., fols. 162v, 165r, 169r.
[102] See Charles E. Odegaard, "Legalis Homo," *Speculum* 15 (1940): 186–93.

as "a lawful and honest woman of good life and laudable condition and good fame and held as such in the city of Marseille by acquaintances and neighbors."[103] Rarely, again, are there allusions to the seven virtues, though simplicity borders on humility and the modesty or chastity of women is embedded in the adjective used most often to describe women, namely "honest" (as in *honesta mulier*). The appeal of Guilhem de Belavila is one of the few that seem to have been influenced by Christian virtues and vices, for Guilhem attributed to himself the virtue of charity in much the same way that he assigned to his victim the vice of pride. Vernacular moral philosophy, like its intellectualized Christian counterpart, did make a pairing of virtues and vices though not with such consistency. The pairings run roughly as follows.

| *Vice* | *Virtue* |
|---|---|
| Quarrelsome (*rixosus, -a*) | Peaceful, Lawful (*legalis, -e*) |
| Lustful | Honest |
| Lying (*mendax*), Gossipy (*locax*) | Good speech (*bona conversatio*) |
| Wasteful with money, drinks, gambles | Manages money well |
| Must do manual labor to live | Has *bona*, does not need to work |
| Has bad fama | Has good fama |
| Associates with low-lifes | Leads a good life (*bona vita*) |

Defamation proceedings in medieval and early modern European courts are a commonplace. A plausible argument for the frequency of such proceedings is that authorities wished to clamp down on uncivil behavior, an argument that is fully consonant with the conclusions of Norbert Elias and others who have assumed the existence of a civilizing process. One of the problems with this argument is that it tends to assume an omniscient court, able to witness and hence prosecute every insult that took place in the streets. But most insults would have to be denounced to come to the attention of the court at all. Defamation procedures, in short, must also be read as instances in which the objects of insulting words have chosen to use the courts to get back at their enemies, as Martin Ingram and others have argued.[104] But beyond that, the witness exception procedure and related procedural moves made in the courts of law of late medieval Marseille show clearly how the court, as a moral entity, had no principled objection to attacks on the character of others. Such attacks were fully legal

---

[103] ADBR 3B 37, fol. 266v, case opened in June 1339 on fol. 264r.
[104] Martin Ingram surveys much of the literature in his "Law, Litigants, and the Construction of 'Honour': Slander Suits in Early Modern England," in *The Moral World of the Law*, ed. Peter Coss (Cambridge, 2000), 134–60.

and allowable as long as they were done according to the rules set by the court itself.

⋖⋗

One can write the history of western European penal law as a history of state-sponsored courts supplanting, delegitimating, and marginalizing age-old practices of self-help and bloodfeud, which nonetheless persist in the margins for centuries to come. There may be a certain institutional truth to this argument. Certainly it corresponds to what rulers *thought* they were doing. But the argument is too sanguine in its casual and unstated assumption that emotions thrive only in the feud and disappear when they are written out of the disputing procedure, to be replaced with the emotionally neutral architecture of legal procedure. The emotions that drove and continue to drive disputes never went away. They persisted across the late medieval period of institutional transformation, and adapted themselves easily to the new intellectual and emotional architecture of the procedural law used in state-sponsored law courts. The courts were readily adopted by consumers as the new language or expression of vengeance. Denunciations, summons, cedulas, articles, exceptions, depositions: these procedural gestures became the means for expressing hostility. The procedural norms of Roman-canon law and the local customs of Marseille's courts determined how these gestures would be strung together in sequence. They acted like a grammar or syntax that structured this new lexicon of hostility.

One objection to the idea that people used courts to pursue hatred is that this procedure could easily backfire. Among other things, litigation was expensive for both parties, not just the defendant. Even more to the point, success was never guaranteed, since a judge might well rule against the plaintiff, or, more commonly, make no ruling at all. This objection does not bear the weight of scrutiny. One could just as well point out that feuds were expensive and could easily backfire and thereby prove that feuds were not motivated by hatred. Beyond that, as I argue throughout this book, plaintiffs could achieve their objectives even when lawsuits failed to result in a favorable verdict against adversaries. Most lawsuits never resulted in a sentence, but knowing this, litigants still chose to invest in the process, because the chance to perform an enmity publicly—through initiations and summons, through witness depositions, through exceptions—was a sufficient end in itself.

Given the options at their disposal, including arbitration and many forms of self-help, why did litigants choose the theater of the court? Emptying jars of excrement on an adversary's doorstep served as an adequate expression of hatred. Routine insults, street violence, and acts of customary vengeance did so as well. Giving an enemy the cold shoulder was entirely cost free. These gestures, not acts of litigation, were the solutions preferred by most. But part of the reason why certain people chose to invest in litigation lies in its publicity. Hatreds and social sanctions of all types are useless unless they are advertised to a general public, and the courts of law were geared toward publicity. The court convened six days a week in a very visible, open-air setting, near the commercial and symbolic heart of the city. The system of criers ensured the rapid diffusion of news beyond the court itself. As a performance, litigation was arguably a more efficient form of communication than insults, assaults, vengeance-takings, and other inimical gestures restricted to smaller neighborhood spaces.

The model I am developing here proposes a form of competition in the marketing and distribution of hatred, pitting courts of law against conventional or vernacular institutions. This economic metaphor can be pushed even further. Centralizing states in many societies commonly seek to control the marketing of goods. Markets serve as useful sources of indirect revenue, but beyond that the ability to regulate markets is a powerful symbol of state power. Though Carolingian capitularies show evidence of market regulations, the practice became far more normal from the twelfth century onward, in tandem with the growing economy and the growing power of kings and states. Negative gifts such as insults and assaults were also transacted in an open, public market—the street, the plaza, the tavern—and the forms of exchange were just as scripted or culturally bound as the marketing of goods. The prosecution of insults and assaults in fourteenth-century Marseille was, in a sense, a state-sponsored effort to shut down an alternative marketplace for the transaction of hatred. Courts were being offered as the new market. On the whole, men and women were not unwilling to shift their resources into this new market. The effect was profound. Centralized markets generally serve to increase the circulation of goods. The metaphor holds for emotional transactions as well. Contrary to the assumptions of a civilizing process in European history, courts of law did not repress emotions. Instead, law courts in late medieval Marseille allowed individuals to pursue emotional satisfaction, though in the form of an acceptable and professionalized script, and provided ample new opportunities for transacting humiliations and insults.

# CHAPTER THREE
# THE PURSUIT OF DEBT

Economics and enmities often generate overlapping metaphorical fields. In many human societies, the bloodfeud and the vendetta, as sets of exchanges between two parties, are metaphorically configured according to the language and practice of the gift and the counter-gift. "Gifts have been given to you, father and sons alike," remarks Bergthora of *Njal's Saga* to her sons, speaking of a grievous insult, "and you would scarcely be men if you did not repay them."[1] The gift exchange involves more than just the thing being exchanged, for the giving of the gift creates an obligation that colors the ensuing relationship until the gift is requited. Although the obligation itself may be a material thing, the sense of obligation, the burden of being the receiver of a gift, is an emotion or a moral sentiment. Positive gifts often elicit emotions of gratitude and respect, though they can also promote feelings of envy or ill-will. Negative gifts, in the form of injuries, are even more efficient in creating ill-will and hatred, though Judeo-Christian moral philosophy envisages the heroic possibility that negative gifts might generate love.[2] Both types of gift, positive and negative, lend rich emotional hues to the texture of social relationships. The men and women of medieval Marseille, as seen in the previous chapter, routinely kept track of these emotional hues, in much the same way that they kept track of who owed what to whom, and for much the same reason. In so doing, they acted like accountants of the emotions, toting up the balance sheet of loves and hatreds so as to appraise the value and social worth of the person in question.

[1] *Njal's Saga*, trans. Magnus Magnusson and Hermann Pálsson (London, 1960), 115.
[2] Proverbs 25:21–22; Romans 12:17–21.

To judge by the records of fourteenth-century Marseille, the gift had long since lost ground as the fundamental metaphor of exchange, replaced instead by a slightly different though fully congruent economic metaphor: the relationship of creditor and debtor. Much the same was true for fourteenth- and fifteenth-century Florence, where merchants in their *libri di ricordanze* toted up their credits and debts in much the same way that they wrote out lists of their friends and enemies. This metaphorical shift from gift to credit reflects the fact that the economic world of late medieval Mediterranean Europe had been monetarized for several hundred years. It would be surprising if economic metaphors did not evolve accordingly. In Marseille, the language and metaphor of credit and debt was never used in the explicit Florentine fashion, but economistic ideas nonetheless suffuse emotion talk and never seem to have been far from the minds of litigants and witnesses. Asked in 1403 if he was an enemy (*inimicus vel odiosus*) of the party against whom he had just testified, the notary Laurens Aycart remarked, "I am hated by no one, nor do I believe that I have any enemies."[3] He could just as well have been congratulating himself for being neither creditor nor debtor. The apparent redundancy in what he said seems to suggest that, for Laurens, hatred was like envy or debt in having a single vector, from injured party to injurer. He therefore had to deny a position on both sides of the vector. Although it was convenient in the previous chapter to think of hatred as something shared between two people, and although some records, notably those pertaining to enracinated feuds, do talk this way, many instances of emotion talk reveal a similar vectoring of hatred that is fully congruent with a metaphor of debt.

But the overlap between economics and emotions was more than metaphorical. To begin with, relationships of credit in Marseille were suffused with friendly emotions. The pattern is typical of many human societies. Describing a meeting of a Javanese institution called the "rotating credit institution," Clifford Geertz calls it "a feast, a small gathering of friends, neighbors, and kin," particularly in villages, where it is "commonly viewed by its members less as an economic institution than a broadly social one whose main purpose [is] the strengthening of community solidarity."[4] Emotional

---

[3] ADBR 3B 138, fol. 107r, case opened 28 Apr. 1402 on fol. 55r.

[4] Clifford Geertz, "The Rotating Credit Association: A 'Middle Rung' in Development," in *Economic Development and Cultural Change* 10 (1962): 241–63, here 243. Much of the literature is conveniently surveyed in William Chester Jordan, *Women and Credit in Pre-Industrial and Developing Societies* (Philadelphia, 1993), 1–2, 85–86; see also Paul Millett, *Lending and Borrowing in Ancient Athens* (Cambridge, 1991). A section of *Annales: histoire, sciences sociales* 49 (1994) devoted to credit in early modern rural European society contains much evidence on the social dimension of credit.

relationships like marriage are structured as debt relationships in dotal societies. In Marseille, as elsewhere, the successful conclusion of a business deal was capped with a drink, a public sign of mutual friendship. In a different vein, the extension of credit was one of the behavioral patterns or signs that suggested to onlookers the existence of affection. As I noted in the previous chapter, a woman named Dousa Euzeria, testifying on behalf of her good friend Guilhem de Belavila in 1365, confirmed one of Guilhem's most important claims, namely that one of the hostile witnesses, Uga Bernarda, had been a god-kin and a very special friend of the victim. "She once loaned the victim ten pounds," Dousa explained, "and for this reason, I believe her to be more his friend than his enemy" (*credit ipsam esse magis amicam quam inimicam*).[5] As this remark suggests, material transactions such as loans were not interpreted as wholly impersonal transactions. They helped define and publicize social relationships to bystanders.

But credit relationships were also debt relationships, and friendly emotions could easily sour. In a 1359 trial, a witness named Pellegrin Calfat reported how one day, when he was in the shop of the Italian merchant Marcho Marchi, "Alexi Bernat came by and said to me 'You should know that Vivaut has repaid me the remainder of the ten pounds he owed me.'" Speaking of an otherwise unknown third party named Biatris, Alexi went on to say, "The lady has had a peace made (*fecit fieri pacem*) between me and him, and together we drank."[6] Repayment of the debt was tantamount to the payment of a composition that reestablished a peace. Not all soured debts were so happily resolved. According to arguments made in the case of Guilhem de Belavila, one of the hostile witness, Johaneta Chaulete, was a capital enemy of Guilhem and his wife Uga. The enmity arose from a debt they owed her that had not been repaid. To get her money back, Johaneta insinuated herself into their house and carried away some goods. Guilhem, in response to this and other injuries, struck her, and a hatred was born that would result in her perjured testimony against Guilhem.[7]

To those watching, credit relationships implied affection. The withdrawal of credit marked an emotional transformation that turned affection into hatred. The withdrawal of credit was interpreted as a hostile gesture, much like the insults and assaults that shamed the victim and promoted retaliation in kind. Guilhem and Uga's refusal to repay a debt; Johaneta's act of private distraint and her insults; Guilhem's blow; Johaneta's perjured testimony: all were routine exchanges in hatreds that had coagulated around

[5] ADBR 3B 825, fol. 112r, case opened 13 May 1365 on fol. 35r.
[6] ADBR 3B 62, fol. 45r, case opened 22 Oct. 1359 on fol. 36r.
[7] ADBR 3B 825, fol. 126r, case opened 13 May 1365 on fol. 35r.

embittered credit relationships. What Johaneta did not do was litigate, though she did make use of the law in other ways. But for many people, litigation for debt was a thoroughly appropriate and satisfactory way to get back at, sanction, or humiliate an enemy. This usage has been noted by other historians of debt litigation.[8]

These are points worth stressing at the very outset of a chapter on late medieval debt litigation because much of the literature on the subject has not been overly concerned with the social or cultural implications, let alone the emotional overtones, of credit and debt. There are important exceptions, such as Elaine Clark's pathbreaking study of the social dimensions of lending in England.[9] As William Chester Jordan has argued in his study of consumption loans and networks of sociability, "There is no doubt whatever that strong networks, supported by kinship, friendship and respect, often existed within the world of male lending and borrowing, among women borrowers and lenders, and sometimes among women and men involved together in credit transactions."[10] But for the most part, the history of medieval credit has centered on commercial capitalization and Jewish lending, fields of study that focus on the institutions, mechanisms, and belief systems that lay behind the extension of impersonal forms of credit outside social networks rather than within them. Commercial historians from the 1920s onward found it important to stress how medieval advances in banking and law made possible the accumulation of productive capital. Their findings, consciously or not, tended to support a sociology that made the decay of kin groups and other ritual associations a key feature of late medieval urban society.[11] Michael Postan, writing in 1928 on then-current

----

[8] On interlocking metaphors of vengeance and debt pursuit in ancient Athens, see Millett, *Lending and Borrowing*, 7; for concrete examples showing how debt litigation could be used to pursue vengeance, see Keith P. Luria, *Territories of Grace: Cultural Change in the Seventeenth-Century Diocese of Grenoble* (Berkeley, 1991), 181–83; Laurence Fontaine, "Espaces, usages et dynamiques de la dette dans les hautes vallées dauphinoises (XVIIe–XVIIIe), *Annales: histoire, sciences sociales* 49 (1994): 1375–91, here 1389.

[9] Elaine Clark, "Debt Litigation in a Late Medieval English Vill," in *Pathways to Medieval Peasants*, ed. J. A. Raftis (Toronto, 1981), 247–79.

[10] Jordan, *Women and Credit*, 13–49, esp. 26. In contrast to Clark, who tends to stress the horizontality of creditor-debtor associations (e.g., "Debt Litigation," 265), Jordan argues for the unbalanced or biased nature of credit networks (*Women and Credit*, 27).

[11] For useful introductions to the field, see Michael Postan, "Credit in Medieval Trade," *Economic History Review* 1 (1928): 234–61; Raymond de Roover, *Money, Banking, and Credit in Mediaeval Bruges: Italian Merchant-Bankers, Lombards, and Money-Changers* (Cambridge, Mass., 1948); Kathryn L. Reyerson, *Business, Banking, and Finance in Medieval Montpellier* (Toronto, 1985). On the rationalistic perspective generally adopted in this literature, see Craig Muldrew, "Interpreting the Market: The Ethics of Credit and Community Relations in Early Modern England," *Social History* 18 (1993): 163–83.

theories regarding the historical emergence of credit, sought to illustrate the modern, sophisticated, and impersonal dimensions of medieval credit.[12] The large literature on Jewish lending has been motivated by a different set of concerns, but for the most part this literature proceeds from the assumption that Jewish-Christian debt relations are interesting precisely because they were impersonal.[13]

The economic perspective has an easy explanation for the prominence of debt litigation in high and late medieval courts of law: a growing economy naturally requires the extension of credit, and debt litigation is therefore a reflection of the size and sophistication of the medieval European economy. The argument is persuasive and logical but not complete. In an innovative argument Robert Palmer has suggested that rising debt litigation in post-plague England does not reflect economic concerns so much as the perfection of a legal-coercive system designed to recover debts.[14] R. H. Britnell, in turn, has explained the rise in debt litigation in post-plague Colchester as a function of several factors, including increased numbers of disputes over noncommercial debts arising from social relations, labor contracts, and land rentals.[15] Building on these observations, I will argue in this chapter that economic arguments for debt litigation tend to overlook the social function of debt and, by the same token, the social implications of debt recovery.

Several studies have emphasized how credit relationships were influenced by a social system of trust, reputation, and honor.[16] Craig Muldrew, for example, explains the high levels of debt litigation in England between 1530 and the eighteenth century as the result of the vast extension of trust across a wide field of social relations, larger than a face-to-face community,

[12] Postan, "Credit in Medieval Trade."

[13] Works I consulted include Richard W. Emery, *The Jews of Perpignan in the Thirteenth Century: An Economic Study Based on Notarial Records* (New York, 1959) and Joseph Shatzmiller, *Shylock Reconsidered: Jews, Moneylending, and Medieval Society* (Berkeley, 1990), both of whom emphasize the positive aspects of Jewish lending. William Chester Jordan, by contrast, is more concerned with the economic ideologies that foster pariah-group lending and lie behind the persecution of Jews; see *The French Monarchy and the Jews* (Philadelphia, 1989). Jewish money lending and ideas of usury often go hand in hand, and indebtedness in preindustrial and peasant societies is often seen as a pathology; for a discussion of some of the literature on "malignant indebtedness," see B. A. Holderness, "Credit in English Rural Society before the Nineteenth Century, with Special Reference to the Period 1650–1720," *Agricultural History Review* 24 (1976): 97–109, here 97–98.

[14] Robert C. Palmer, *English Law in the Age of the Black Death, 1348–1381: A Transformation of Governance and Law* (Chapel Hill, 1993), 62–103, e.g., 89.

[15] R. H. Britnell, *Growth and Decline in Colchester, 1300–1525* (Cambridge, 1986), 98–114, esp. 98–102.

[16] On the meaning of credit and its relationship to trust see Britnell, *Growth and Decline*, 104; Jordan, *Women and Credit*, 28; Millett, *Lending and Borrowing*, 7.

and the consequent need for court intervention to enforce trust.[17] Following Muldrew's formulation, it is easy to appreciate that any public act of
debt recovery, however much it may be motivated by the unemotional logic
of financial rationality, will have implications for the debtor's honor and is
therefore bound to be resented. "Public knowledge of an arrest or attach-
ment could seriously damage the credit of a household . . . Arrests were
treated seriously, and such encroachment upon a person's body was considered socially very shameful."[18] Only a creditor extraordinarily deaf to the
ordinary social conventions of late medieval and early modern European society could be unaware of the social implications of public litigation for
debt. A creditor who pursued debt recovery, therefore, had to assume either
that the debtor's dishonor needed to be exposed to the general public, or
that the debtor was so beneath contempt that her or his resentment was not
worth bothering about. Which was more important to the creditor, the
money or the moral and social sanction? A purely economic perspective
would suggest the former. The fact that creditors were typically selective
about whom they chose to sanction, and did not necessarily follow the dictates of financial rationality, suggests the latter.

Finally, the economic argument assumes that most cases of debt litigation
involved impersonal credits. To the extent that one can judge the social relationships behind extensions of credit it is fair to say that a number were to
some degree impersonal, but a great many extensions of credit were wholly
personalized. This is the fundamental point made by Clark, namely that
many human societies, including late medieval ones, consist of dense webs
of interlocking credits and debts between friends, neighbors, and kin. This
model applies very well to late medieval Marseille. Although creditors and
debtors were hardly averse to using the courts to pursue or resist debt
claims, and although the mere threat of debt litigation was a useful way to
promote an amicable settlement out of court,[19] litigants were nonetheless
aware of the social implications of debt recovery, and used the courts to
punish individuals with whom they had fallen out. Debt litigation, in short,

[17] Craig Muldrew, *The Economy of Obligation: The Culture of Credit and Social Relations
in Early Modern England* (New York, 1998), 3.
[18] Ibid., 275, 276. This argument is crucially developed in the chapter on credit and
reputation, 148–72.
[19] On this process, see Clark, "Debt Litigation," 253; Maryanne Kowaleski, *Local
Markets and Regional Trade in Medieval Exeter* (Cambridge, 1995), 218–19; Carole Rawcliffe, "'That Kindliness Should Be Cherished More, and Discord Driven Out': The Settlement of Commercial Disputes by Arbitration in Later Medieval England," in *Enterprise and Individuals in Fifteenth-Century England*," ed. Jennifer Kermode (Stroud, U. K.,
1991): 99–117.

mirrors the tendency to use the courts to pursue hatred as discussed in chapter 2.

## TISSUES OF CREDIT AND DEBT

The impersonal loans deemed typical of commercial investment and Jewish banking or lending account for only a certain proportion of the webs of credit and debt in late medieval Marseille. Between the years 1337 and 1362 there are seventy extant notarial casebooks from Marseille containing around sixty-six hundred contracts. Of these, 1,514 or 23 percent are contracts involving some form of credit—namely loans, debts, or commercial investments—and another 991 or 15 percent are quittances of various types.[20] Since the survival rate of notarial casebooks may have been as low as one in fifteen, these figures suggest that Marseille's notaries recorded as many as 22,710 credit contracts over a period of twenty-six years, or a maximum figure of 873 notarized credit contracts per year.[21] Similar calculations yield a maximum figure of 572 notarized quittances per year. Around 14 percent of all credit contracts were related to commenda contracts and therefore centered on a commercial investment or a transaction among merchants, though the figure is probably higher than this because commercial loans were not always formally distinguished from noncommercial loans. Around 250 creditors in all credit contracts between 1337 and 1362 were Jewish, 17 percent of the total. On the face of it, therefore, 31 percent or roughly a third of the 1,514 credit contracts fit the profile of the impersonal contract. The remaining two-thirds linked Christian creditors and debtors in exchanges that were not primarily commercial in nature. Similarly low percentages of impersonal credit can be found elsewhere in Europe. Analyzing debts listed in wills from the English village of Terling, Keith Wrightson

[20] See my "Notaries, Courts, and the Legal Culture of Late Medieval Marseille," in *Urban and Rural Communities in Medieval France: Provence and Languedoc, 1000–1500*, ed. Kathryn L. Reyerson and John Drendel (Leiden, 1998), 23–50, here 36–37. Credit contracts are most easily defined by the notarial formulas used, bearing in mind that form does not determine function—a commenda contract, for example, could be defined as a kind of loan, and a deposit could be used for a commercial investment.

[21] For the reasoning behind my maximum ratio of one in fifteen, see my "Common Violence: Vengeance and Inquisition in Fourteenth-Century Marseille," *Past and Present* 151 (May 1996): 28–59, here 44. In general, see Louis Stouff, "Les registres de notaires d'Arles (début XIVe siècle–1460): quelques problèmes posés par l'utilisation des archives notariales," *Provence historique* 25 (1975): 305–24, here 307–10.

and David Levine concluded that 67 percent were between neighbors, 17 percent between kin, and only 16 percent, involving a creditor or debtor outside of Terling, have the appearance of impersonality.[22]

The formal qualities of loans and other credits do not tell us whether the creditors and debtors liked and esteemed one another. In a small village such as Terling it is reasonable to assume that most people knew one another and, therefore, that loans between neighbors and kin reflect some degree of affection between the parties involved. Things were different in a large city such as Marseille, where the presence of a number of professional Christian lenders—the banker Antoni Vinsens, Bertomieu Bonvin, the priest Bertomieu Folco, the de Sant Jaume family, and Peire Martin, among many others—ensures that many Christian-to-Christian loans were motivated by profit or, in the case of priests, impersonal charity rather than immediate friendship or kinship. But by the same token, one should not assume that commercial capitalization and Jewish banking were necessarily impersonal. Jews and Christians did not routinely share food and wine, the most potent symbol of friendship, but, as Joseph Shatzmiller has pointed out, Jewish bankers like Bondavin de Draguignan needed to establish reputations for probity and therefore cultivated a network of Christian well-wishers apparently without much difficulty. The ease with which Bondavin assembled a large group of witnesses to attest to his good qualities reflects Bondavin's high standing among Christians.

Even more personalized were commercial loans and capitalization strategies among Christians. There is a simple reason for this: factional allegiance in medieval Marseille played a significant role in commercial capitalization. Members of the great mercantile families of fourteenth-century Marseille were prominent in the ranks of the two great noble factions, the Vivaut and the de Jerusalem. Consider Esteve de Brandis, described by Édouard Baratier in his justly renowned volume in the *Histoire du commerce de Marseille* as "certainly the most astonishing figure among Marseille's merchants in the latter half of the fourteenth century."[23] This observation is correct in more ways than one, because in his youth, before he made his vast wealth and become an intimate of King Louis I of Anjou, Esteve pursued a rather sporting interest in factional warfare as a member of the Vivaut party. On one occasion, as we read in a court case from 1351, he was chased up and down the streets of Marseille by a sword-wielding minion of the de Jerusalem party. Esteve's close associate in mercantile activity, a distant

---

[22] Keith Wrightson and David Levine, *Poverty and Piety in an English Village: Terling, 1525–1700* (New York, 1979), 100–101.

[23] Édouard Baratier and Félix Reynaud, *De 1291 à 1480*, vol. 2 of *Histoire du commerce de Marseille*, ed. Gaston Rambert (Paris, 1951), 69.

affine of his named Johan Casse, was also a member of the Vivaut party and was arrested for the murder of Marques de Jerusalem early in the 1350s and barely avoided being slaughtered by the vengeful de Jerusalem. Johan, in turn, was the son-in-law of Boneta Sarda, a member of a great merchant family and also, as it turns out, a kind of oral historian attached to the Vivaut party. Called to testify on behalf of a Vivaut partisan about past de Jerusalem iniquities, she dug up events committed over forty years earlier against what she calls "our party." The person for whom she obligingly narrated this history, Amiel Bonafos, was the son of a great merchant capitalist and was linked by marriage to the Martin family, also famous in the pages of Marseille's economic history. Baratier identifies nine great merchant families in thirteenth- and fourteenth-century Marseille. Seven of the nine had at least one member who fought in Marseille's factional quarrels between 1349 and 1356. Baratier lists, in addition, thirteen particularly prominent fourteenth-century merchants. Seven had factional allegiances; two others were linked by blood. More generally, out of 225 men (and a few women) who were involved in various ways in factional warfare—laborers, nobles, apothecaries, fishermen, even judges and notaries—thirty were merchants, more than one in eight. It is almost impossible to overestimate the close relationship, on the level of personnel, between the world of commerce and the world of faction in mid-fourteenth-century Marseille.

These factional relationships, in turn, spilled over into capitalization and financing, for commercial contracts often show us one member of a faction arranging commenda contracts or commercial loans with another member.[24] Even more telling, when merchants fell out with one another, they built ties to the opposing factions in order to gain supporters, ties that are reflected in witness lists in subsequent cases of litigation. Merchants, like other men and women of Marseille, found ways to exploit the structures of hatred described in the previous chapter.

For all these reasons, the formal characteristics of loans—who was lending what to whom—can only give us a dim idea of the emotional textures of credit relationships. It suffices to say that a great many loans and other credits were *capable* of reflecting the kind of friendship described by Dousa Euzeria. The reason is that credit is vital to many preindustrial societies, and the relative absence of professional lenders means that those with cash at hand readily lent to their kin, friends, and neighbors on the assumption that the favor would be returned in the future. Many of the acknowledgments of debt that show up in Marseille's notarial archives were the sale credits so

---

[24] I have analyzed these credit relationships at greater length in my unpublished paper "Merchant Disputes and Factional Allegiance in Medieval Marseille."

common in cash-poor societies.[25] Some of the simple loans were presumably distress loans. Others can be identified as loans needed to finance an extraordinary expense arising from marriage, pilgrimage, death, or the like. As B. A. Holderness observes, one function of credit "is to provide the means to pay for excessive commitments to conspicuous expenditure in the form of feasts and social gatherings."[26] Still others, and possibly a plurality, arose from the natural rhythms of a largely agrarian economy. On 22 May 1338, a widow named Cecilia Guiberta took out a loan of seven pounds 5s. from the merchant Guilhem Arnaut to pay "to cultivate and work her vineyard," an example that shows how agrarian cycles lay behind Marseille's lending patterns.[27] As in fourteenth-century Montpellier and Perpignan, fourteenth- and fifteenth-century Salon-de-Provence, and fifteenth-century Carpentras, loans in Marseille followed a cyclical pattern: less common in June and July, they peaked in April and May and again in October and November.[28]

The judicial system was an important factor in the creation of debts. As discussed at greater length in the next chapter, late medieval Continental law courts used monetary sanctions more often than blood sanctions. In Marseille, in the fiscal year 1331, more than five hundred men and women paid criminal fines averaging 25s., and about half the fines were greater than 20s., an important threshold, as I will describe shortly.[29] Such fines were hard to pay, and recourse to loans was often inevitable. In 1353, a laborer named Guilhem Johan, found guilty of wounding another man, was unable to pay either the 250s. fine assessed by the court or the 160s. composition owed to his victim, and therefore acknowledged a debt of 410s. to his pledge (*fideiussor*).[30] This anecdote, incidentally, brings up a further issue, for extrajudicial processes of arbitration and settlement also created significant numbers of debt relationships that were not always immediately paid off. Several cases of debt litigation from mid-fourteenth-century Marseille turn on just this issue. In September of 1353, Lois Orlet was being sued in the palace court by the chief financial officer of the Angevin crown in Marseille, the

---

[25] See the discussion of cash and trust in Muldrew, *Economy of Obligation*, 6.

[26] See Holderness, "Credit," 98.

[27] ADBR 391E 12, fol. 9r–v, 22 May 1338. A closer analysis is not possible because loans in Marseille rarely explain why the loan is necessary, Cecilia Guiberta's loan contract being atypical in this regard.

[28] The patterns in all locales are slightly different; in particular, loans in Marseille and Carpentras peaked in April and May, whereas they did not in Perpignan and Montpellier. See Emery, *Jews*, 64; Reyerson, *Business*, 78–79; Monique Wernham, *La communauté juive de Salon-de-Provence d'après les actes notariés, 1391–1435* (Toronto, 1987), 116; G. Castellani, "Le rôle économique de la communauté juive de Carpentras au début du XVe siècle," *Annales E.S.C.* 27 (1972): 583–611, here 601.

[29] See ADBR B 1940, fols. 74r–139v

[30] ADBR 381E 79, fol. 126r, 8 Dec. 1353.

**Table 3.1 Number of Loans per Month in Notarial Casebooks, 1337–1362**

| Month | Number of Loans | Month | Number of Loans |
|---|---|---|---|
| January | 65 | July | 33 |
| February | 58 | August | 78 |
| March | 43 | September | 55 |
| April | 78 | October | 89 |
| May | 82 | November | 92 |
| June | 36 | December | 64 |

*Sources:* ADBR 351E 3–5, 642–645; ADBR 355E 1–12, 34–36, 285, 290–293; ADBR 381E 38–44, 59–61, 64bis, 72–75, 79–87, 384, 393–394; ADBR 391E 11–18; AM 1 II 42, 44, 57–61.

*clavaire*, on behalf of Johan Robert.[31] During a fight Lois had cut off Johan's left hand and arbitrators had fixed composition at forty pounds, a sum of money that Lois had not yet paid.

The need to raise money to pay composition was probably the motivating factor in a notarized loan from 1356.[32] In this contract, the draper Guilhem Elie loaned seventy-eight florins to the nobleman Carle de Montoliu. No reason was given. However, close study of the people involved reveals the following situation. First, Guilhem and Carle are identified in other records as belonging to the same noble faction, the Vivaut party. The loan was transacted in the house of Franses de Casals, a man readily identifiable as a member of the adversary faction, the de Jerusalem party. The witnesses included one leading member of the de Jerusalem party, Johan de Jerusalem, one leading member of the Vivaut party, the merchant Johan Aycart, and a third man, Johan Macel, who was linked by marriage to the Vivaut party. The fourth witness, Matieu Symondelli, was an influential merchant with no known ties to either party; he may well have been an arbitrator. Clearly, the loan was embedded in the context of peacemaking between the two parties.[33]

However numerous they were, notarized loans and debts represent only a portion of the lending that went on in late medieval Marseille. For one thing, plenty of anecdotal evidence exists for small, unnotarized hand loans and pawns. If we look closely at the 750 notarized loans extant from the period 1337 to 1362, we find that the median loan was around 260s.,[34] and only three were less than 20s., a threshold imposed by the costs associated with notarization. Twenty shillings, in mid-fourteenth-century Marseille, was a good deal of money. According to wage limits set by the city council in 1351—probably honored more often in the breach than otherwise, but

[31] ADBR 3B 52, fols. 12r–20r, case opened 2 Sept. 1353.

[32] ADBR 355E 8, fols. 65v–66r, 14 Jan. 1356.

[33] Factional conflict was intense at this time; see ADBR 3B 819 and 820.

[34] The mean is about 580s., right-skewed because of the large size of many commercial loans.

*The Pursuit of Debt* [ 143 ]

nonetheless a useful benchmark—it took a male agricultural laborer about a week and a female laborer almost two weeks to earn 20s.[35] Small loans of less than a week's wages were surely very common and virtually all such loans were handled by means of hand loans and pawns. Here, it is also important to acknowledge the social breadth of lending. Several individuals, both Jews and Christians, stand out as professional lenders, but there was scarcely any monopoly: both notarized contracts and the meager anecdotal evidence show that virtually anyone was capable of lending money or goods.[36]

Notarized credit contracts, small hand loans, and pawns constitute voluntary or willful extensions of credit on the part of the creditor. It is important to realize, however, that numerous debts and obligations arose circumstantially. The best example of what I will call "circumstantial credit" is the dowry: most men were permanently indebted to their mothers, wives, and daughters-in-law by virtue of the dowries and paraphernalia assigned to or managed by men but owned by women.[37] Indeed, the most significant single category of creditors in medieval Marseille was almost certainly women. Debts such as dowries were meaningful only if enforced, hence it is important to recall, from chapter 1, that litigation arising from contested dowries was a significant element of the caseload of the palace court, amounting to 11 percent of all cases filed (86 in 796 cases). As far as we can tell, the women in these cases almost always won. The dowry was but one of many forms of circumstantial indebtedness. Among others were unpaid legacies as well as a range of long-term contracts that required periodic payments, such as wages, land rents, and leases, all of which could turn into debts whenever they went unpaid. Circumstantial credit has been noted by other historians. As Britnell observes, "often indebtedness arose without any intention on the creditor's part to give credit." Examples he gives include unpaid rents and wages.[38]

By analyzing notarized quittances it is possible to offer a crude but useful

---

[35] As noted in chapter 1, shortly after the Black Death, in January 1349, the city council fixed the maximum wages of male agricultural laborers at 4s. per day; female laborers could earn 2s. 6d. (Mabilly, *Inventaire*, 50). The order was reiterated on 16 Feb. 1362, shortly after the second plague (ibid., 91–92); see also the discussion of wages in Georges Lesage, *Marseille Angevine* (Paris, 1950), 164, and my "Accommodating Plague in Medieval Marseille," *Continuity and Change* 11 (1996): 11–41, here 30–31.

[36] On this see, among others, Wernham, *Communauté juive*, 131–32.

[37] See Andrée Courtemanche, *La richesse des femmes: patrimoines et gestion à Manosque au XIVe siècle* (Montreal, 1993); Eleanor S. Riemer, "Women, Dowries, and Capital Investment in Thirteenth-Century Siena," in *The Marriage Bargain: Women and Dowries in European History*, ed. Marion A. Kaplan (New York, 1985), 59–79, here 63.

[38] Britnell, *Growth and Decline*, 98–114, esp. 98–102.

### Table 3.2 The Origin of Debts in Notarized Quittances, 1337–1362

| Source of Debt | Number |
|---|---|
| Voluntary credit | |
| Loans | 61 |
| Sales of movables | 55 |
| Sales of immovables | 52 |
| Commenda contracts | 19 |
| Deposits | 9 |
| Partnerships | 5 |
| Subtotal | 201 |
| Circumstantial credit | |
| Legacies | 66 |
| Dowries | 57 |
| Inheritances | 23 |
| Land rents | 16 |
| Settlements and arbitrations | 12 |
| Leases | 10 |
| Wages | 9 |
| Estate administrations | 7 |
| Pensions | 4 |
| Subtotal | 204 |
| Total | 405 |

*Sources:* as for Table 3.1.

measure of the relative importance of both voluntary and circumstantial in-debtedness. There are 991 extant notarized quittances from the mid-fourteenth century, and 405 of these identify the origin of the debt. Of this total, 201 arose from voluntary extensions of credit and the remaining 204 originated in circumstantial forms of credit such as unpaid legacies, dowries, and land rents (table 3.2).

The ambiguity of notarized quittances makes it difficult to compare the sums involved—debts are often identified by means of such non-pecuniary expressions as "all debts" or "the house named in my father's legacy to me"—but if frequency is any guide then we can assume that around half of all debts significant enough to require notarization arose circumstantially. Court caseloads suggest that voluntary credits were somewhat more common but not greatly so. Simple debt litigation and commercial disputes typical of voluntary credit constituted 41 percent of the caseload of the palace court over the same time period, between 1337 and 1362, compared to 31 percent for disputed legacies, dowries, rents, leases, and other forms of circumstantial credit.

The nature and function of circumstantial credit is crucial to our understanding of tissues of credit and debt in late medieval Marseille. Unlike voluntary extensions of credit, circumstantial credit did not have fixed terms of repayment and could be carried for extended periods of time. To hold this kind of long-term credit over others is to have a permanent lien on their behavior.

Voluntary loans and debts can also function in much the same way if they are carried for extended periods of time. Thus, it is important to ask how quickly voluntary credit was repaid. Let us look at simple loans. These loans, in Marseille, were typically due at the end of one year,[39] but many were never formally acquitted: only 32 percent of all loans made between 1337 and 1362 were canceled in the casebook, and there are not enough quittances to make up the difference. The loans that were canceled show that half were paid off within eight months and 63 percent within a year, but 37 percent lasted longer than a year, and of these, 20 percent required two years and more. Noël Coulet shows that repayment was even more delayed in Aix-en-Provence over the years 1430–1435: 12 percent of the loans were paid off within the allotted time period (usually between one and nine months were allowed); 38 percent were paid off within a year of the nominal due date; and 50 percent were more than a year overdue, sometimes (7 percent) requiring more than ten years.[40] Whenever voluntary credit extended beyond the nominal due date it could behave more and more like circumstantial credit, for the decision to extend credit depended not only on the financial interests at stake but also on the creditor's goodwill.

Estate inventories and testaments confirm the fact that a number of people could carry large numbers of long-standing credits arising from both notarized loans and hand loans. The grain merchant Guilhem Gili is a case in point, for the inventory made after his death in June 1347 yielded no less than seventy-four debts owed to him. Most were over a year old, and one extended back sixteen years.[41] Many were proven by means of a judicial mandament, or a court order, and not by a notarial instrument or even a

[39] Loans were also commonly made due at the discretion of the lender. On this topic see Reyerson, *Business*, 80–81. In fifteenth-century Carpentras, Castellani has shown that 97 percent of all debts to Jewish creditors were nominally due within one year; see "Rôle économique," 598–99; a similar situation holds in Salon-de-Provence (see Wernham, *Communauté juive*, 158–163). For Aix-en-Provence, see Noël Coulet, *Aix-en-Provence: espace et relations d'une capitale (milieu XIVe s.–milieu XVe s.)*, 2 vols. (Aix-en-Provence, 1988), 1:517.

[40] See his *Aix-en-Provence*, 1:516–18. For all debts in Salon-de-Provence, the figures show somewhat more rapid repayment: within the allotted time period, 12 percent; within a year after the due date, 62 percent; more than a year overdue, 26 percent. See Wernham, *Communauté juive*, 164. Compare Castellani, who finds for Carpentras that three-quarters of the loans due to Jewish lenders were paid within six months: see "Rôle économique," 599.

[41] AM 1 II 58, fols. 110r–120r, 4 June 1347. On the use of inventories for studying patterns of debt, see Peter Spufford, "Les liens du crédit au village dans l'Angleterre du XVIIe siècle," *Annales: histoire, sciences sociales* 49 (1994): 1359–73.

handwritten note. There is a tangential point here: Guilhem acquired mandaments from the court system but then did not choose to pursue them aggressively. He acquired mandaments because his extensions of credit evidently included a number of non-notarized hand loans or other insecure loans, and he used the courts as a kind of post facto notarization device. But why did people such as Guilhem not insist on an aggressive pursuit of their rights? Perhaps he anticipated interest, but another answer lies in the prestige associated with *not* being avaricious. Testaments reveal that the forswearing of small debts was a not uncommon type of legacy; to give one example, in June 1361 the shepherd Johan Talon forgave Raymon Durant a debt of 40s., noting "the good things he has done for me."[42] The prayers of relieved debtors such as Raymon constituted a useful spiritual investment. Hence forswearing a loan, like making the loan in the first place, could have a powerful charitable dimension.[43] This leads us to an important conclusion: unrepaid debts do not always reflect the weakness of the legal system.[44] Johan Talon never did get his 40s. from Raymon Durant, but he did get "many good things" in exchange.

Credit, in short, was a form of power, whether it arose voluntarily or circumstantially. Yet we should not imagine a distinct class of creditor-patrons like Guilhem Gili benevolently lording it over their debtor-clients. For one thing, as Shatzmiller has made clear, debtors able to sue for usury possessed a certain amount of power over the good fame of creditors.[45] Hence, even if credit relationships were sometimes skewed, the power and influence in these relationships worked in both directions. Nor were all credit relationships necessarily skewed: plenty of evidence anecdotally confirms one of Elaine Clark's most important observations, namely that people could be both creditors and debtors simultaneously, muddying the seemingly clear distinction between creditor-patrons and debtor-clients.[46] In some notarial casebooks we see people using a credit to pay off a debt. There even existed a notarial formula called a *vanamentum* designed explicitly for this process of debt transfer: twenty-four such contracts are extant between 1337 and 1362. Such exchanges could be handled by means of different contracts, however, such as a loan in which the debtor provides a debt owed him by an-

[42] ADBR 355E 293, fols. 35v–36v, 14 June 1361.

[43] On this see Aaron Kirschenbaum, "Jewish and Christian Theories of Usury in the Middle Ages," *Jewish Quarterly Review* 75 (1985): 270–89; Jordan, *Women and Credit*, 24–32.

[44] See, for example, Reyerson's analysis of the procedures for and difficulties of recovery of debt in *Business*, 95–105; also Kowaleski's important study of transaction costs in her *Local Markets*, 179–221.

[45] Shatzmiller, *Shylock Reconsidered*.

[46] Clark, "Debt Litigation," 265–71.

other as security. In one example, Lois de Avinione borrowed six florins from Aycardeta Senequiera and gave as security a twelve-florin debt owed him by Peire Bonet.[47] These debt exchanges are also implicit in certain cases of back-to-back quittances where the creditor in the first act is the debtor in the second. Sometimes debtors and creditors simply switched roles, as in a loan from 1359 for two florins, in which the creditor, Antoni Feraut, stipulated that an existing debt of eight florins owed by him to the debtor, Guilhem Blancart, be canceled. Antoni had paid Guilhem ten florins, thereby extinguishing the existing debt and creating the new one in the amount of two florins.[48] Testaments show us individuals passing on credits to their heirs and simultaneously leaving sums of money to pay off their debts. As Shatzmiller has pointed out, when reading notarial registers and other records from southern France one often gets the impression that "virtually everyone was permanently in debt."[49] Most estate inventories included both credits and debts: even Guilhem Gili owed two important debts, both over twenty-two pounds.[50] To live in such complex and interlocking networks of credit and debt was to accept all the obligations and responsibilities assigned to the roles of creditor and debtor alike. Put differently, it was neighborly to borrow and to lend, and a charitable act not to insist on rapid repayment of voluntary and circumstantial credit. As Wrightson and Levine conclude, "relationships of debt and credit thus helped to bind together the village community."[51] To spurn the culture of credit and debt would be to claim to live above the likes and dislikes of your friends, neighbors, and colleagues.

## DEBT LITIGATION AND SOCIAL SANCTION

The foregoing has shown how the decision to pursue a debt did not have to arise from the impersonal desire to recover a sum of money. Both credits and debts were valuable commodities; they gave one power over the behavior of others. Many cases of debt litigation, therefore, can be construed as occasions on which this power was exercised. Debt litigation, in other words, could be intended or interpreted as a hostile gesture, a form of humiliation and social sanction. But the power did not operate in a single di-

47 ADBR 381E 81, fol. 40v, 1 Aug. 1358.
48 See ADBR 381E 82, fol. 2v, 27 Mar. 1359.
49 Shatzmiller, *Shylock Reconsidered*, 71.
50 AM 1 II 58, fols. 110r–120r, 4 June 1347.
51 Wrightson and Levine, *Poverty and Piety*, 101.

rection alone, for debtors' countersuits, both for usury as well as accusations of double-dipping, were powerful tools for retaliation.

Most creditors did not have to litigate to recover debts owed to them. The large number of canceled loans and other debts in notarial contracts shows that many were paid off amicably enough within a reasonable time frame. The vanamentum contract and related practices also show how debts could, in effect, be bought, sold, and traded, and how they therefore acted as a kind of paper currency, useful precisely because the debts in question went uncollected. Pawnbrokers sold items left them as security for a loan. Some creditors, like Johaneta Chauleta, chose simply to enter the house of a debtor and distrain goods to the value of the debt, though it is difficult to judge the frequency of this extracurricular activity. Some cases of private distraint ended up in court as accusations of theft made by the debtor, suggesting that the practice was not uncommon. Ricarda Borgella, the wine merchant discussed in chapter 1, was sued in 1323 by her step-children for having taken several large jars of wine from the house of her late husband without permission; she countered with the argument that the wine was hers.[52] In 1352, Jacma Augelerie was charged with the theft of some movables that she claimed formed part of her dowry.[53]

In situations where creditors had no security and were unwilling, for whatever reason, to exercise private distraint, there were public mechanisms for the recovery of debts that fell short of litigation. The public system of debt recovery was extremely efficient and sophisticated, though since it was used indiscriminately to pursue debts arising from criminal fines as well as civil debts I will delay discussion of it until the next chapter. Of prime significance here is that the system, exceptionally visible, naturally occasioned a certain amount of resentment on the part of the humiliated debtor. The emotional neutrality of the record-keeping bureaucracy ensured that most such emotions were written out of case transcripts, but from time to time the emotions push through. A case in point involves a laborer and cleric named Guilhem Bonafos who was the subject of a criminal inquest by the ecclesiastical court in 1401.[54] Guilhem owed a certain sum of money to a cleric and gardener named Guilhem Gautier, who had chosen to call in the debt. Encountering Gautier one day at the market, Bonafos said to him, "You have done evil since you have had items taken in security from me" (male fecistis quia me fecistis pignorari). Gautier responded in kind: "You

---

[52] ADBR 3B 16, fols. 60r–82v, case opened 16 Mar. 1323.
[53] ADBR 3B 812, fols. 26r–37r, case opened 1 June 1352
[54] ADBR 5G 772, fol. 73r, case opened Dec. 1401.

vile shit, I have accorded you grace many times, as you will not deny" (O vilan merdos yeu tay fach mays de gratia que non denias), whereat Bonafos leaped on Gautier and would have done him an injury had not bystanders intervened.

Given the efficient system of debt recovery, creditors did not need to embark on lawsuits to recover simple debts. Cases of debt litigation, therefore, typically reflect situations in which debtors had made some resistance to the claims of creditors, whether the plaintiff was the creditor or the debtor. Other instances of debt litigation involve creditors' attempts to recover circumstantial credits, because these, unlike loans, did not have built-in deadlines and therefore could not be presented as loans past due. Many such suits represent a falling out between spouses, friends, relatives, business partners, and colleagues. These suits were not about money so much as they were about moral issues and the pursuit of budding hatreds.[55] The evidence is necessarily anecdotal and suggestive rather than conclusive. Nonetheless, it all suggests that money was less at issue than was emotional satisfaction or moral sanction. For the sake of the argument, I will assume that the public system of debt recovery involved contempt, humiliation, and resentment, emotions that operated across emotional planes or social strata or served to set the creditor in a superior position to the debtor. Debt litigation, by means of which the debtor laid claim to a dignity or status roughly equivalent to that of the creditor, tended to involve the more egalitarian emotions of hatred and anger.

There is little need to stress the importance of reputation or, to use contemporary language, "good fame" (bona fama) in lending, given Joseph Shatzmiller's study of Bondavin de Draguignan. Bondavin was a Jewish banker highly visible in Marseille's records between the 1320s and 1350s who made it a point to defend his good fame in court. Shatzmiller's study, in turn, was motivated by some of the conclusions of R. W. Emery.[56] What is particularly significant about Shatzmiller's reconstruction of Bondavin's lending business is that Bondavin appears to have accorded considerable favor (gratia) to honorable and upstanding clients who were too poor to repay their debts to him. Shatzmiller describes how a witness on Bondavin's behalf reports that Bondavin, on hearing of the great poverty of one of his debtors, "gave back to the woman a great quantity of money, as the witness

---

[55] As Clark points out, careful management of credit extensions and debt litigation could also be used in a hostile way to acquire land and create a relationship of debt servitude; see Clark, "Debt Litigation," 264. I have not yet seen obvious examples of this use of debt litigation in Marseille.

[56] Richard W. Emery, "Le prêt d'argent juif en Languedoc et Roussillon," in Juifs et judaïsme de Languedoc, Cahiers de Fanjeaux, vol. 12 (Toulouse, 1977): 85–96.

himself saw."[57] It is clear in turn that the laborer, Laurent Girart, who lost his usury case against Bondavin, was something of a low-life. The evidence is indirect, and stems from the fact that the sole witness he called on his behalf, Peire Guizot, was, during an exception procedure, widely judged by Christian witnesses to be a man of ill-repute and illicit life: in short, an *infamis*.[58] Peire was an in-law of Laurent's and lived in Laurent's house, thus implicating Laurent in his *infamia*. What we have, then, is the distinct likelihood that Jewish lenders listened carefully to Christian talk of reputation and selectively sanctioned those with bad fame while according favor to those with good fame. This is critically important information: it shows how even Jewish debt litigation could function as a form of sanction against defamed Christian individuals.

A less remarkable though nonetheless interesting case from 1339 shows how other instances of debt litigation could similarly turn into a reputation contest. The case, a disputed quittance, was initiated by Johan Girman and his nephew Esteve Girman, who claimed a debt of 7 pounds 12s. 2d. from a wine-seller or tavern-keeper (*thabernia*) named Jacma Thomasia for a purchase of wine.[59] Relations were already tense before the opening of the suit, for Jacma, physically or verbally harassed by Esteve, had denounced him to the court of inquest and Esteve had been thrown in jail. In making his arguments, Johan sought to prove "that Esteve and Johan are men of good repute who customarily abstain from lying and from asking others to pay off debts that are not owed," and this was the public talk and fame in Marseille (fols. 264v–265r). Johan and Esteve brought forward three witnesses to attest to their virtues. All gave glowing reports.

In response, Jacma assembled her guns. In a tidy two points she argued simply: 1) That she had paid off the debt fifteen days ago at the doorway of her house; 2) That she was a lawful and honest woman, of good life and praiseworthy standing, and judged to be so by acquaintances and neighbors. On her behalf she brought in three witnesses, all women, all of whom vigorously confirmed that the debt had been paid off in their presence and all of whom attested in equally glowing terms to her character and probity. "Jacma is a lawful and honest woman [*mulierem legalem et honestam*] and is held and named as such in the city of Marseille, especially among Jacma's neighbors and acquaintances," remarked Bertomieua Anone (fol. 267r). Other cases of debt litigation involve a similar situation in which a debtor used a countersuit to defend her or his reputation. In Jacma's case, a vigor-

---

[57] Shatzmiller, *Shylock Reconsidered*, 112–18, especially 114.
[58] Ibid., 35–40.
[59] ADBR 3B 37, fols. 264r–269r, case opened in June 1339.

ous defense of her reputation as one who paid her debts promptly would have been vital to the success of her wine-selling business.

As I will argue at greater length in chapter 5, Johan and Esteve had difficulty assembling witnesses to the facts of the case because the space in front of Jacma's tavern was a female space: the clientele from whom she recruited her witnesses was a largely female clientele who seem to have had little sympathy for the aggressive behavior of the two Girman brothers. Another case from the same year also suggests how aggressive behavior by a lender could be sanctioned by unsympathetic witnesses.[60] The case centered on a bed loaned by a man to his kinsman; the borrower died, and the lender had to sue the widow for the return of the bed. He claimed that the dying man had acknowledged the loan. Things went badly for his case, however, because the only witnesses available were neighbors and professional colleagues of the dying man who had gathered in anticipation of the vigil. Put off by the high-handed and thoughtless behavior of the lender, they refused to testify on his behalf. The judge had his own suspicions, asking one witness whether she was an enemy of the lender—naturally, she said no.

As the judge's query in this case suggests, debt litigation could be used to pursue a nascent hatred. As discussed at length in the previous chapter, two suits for recovery of debt were lodged against Vivauda de Nercio in the 1350s, and in both cases she was able to trace the origins of the suits to the hatred of a distant cousin who had dug up potential litigants and pushed them into suing.[61] A case from 1355 nominally centered on a debt arising from an unpaid land rent, but witnesses called by the defendant reveal that it too was motivated by a deeper hatred, in this case the feud pitting the Vivaut and the de Jerusalem which, in 1355, was at its worst. The case was initiated by Augier de Soliers, a procurator acting on behalf of his mother-in-law Johana Bausana, who was suing the draper Guilhem de Montels for failure to pay nine pounds rent on a garden that formed part of her dowry.[62] As witnesses, Augier called the noblemen Laurens Ricau, Bertran de Buco, and Augier Bonipar, along with a woman named Bertranda Viventa. That the case was motivated by hatred is suggested by Bertranda's attempt to deflect the accusation. Asked whether she was an enemy of Guilhem de Montels or hateful toward him (inimica dicti Guillelmi de Montiliis aut inimicatus eidem), she said no, adding that when she wished to buy any cloth she preferred going to the workshop of Guilhem rather

60  ADBR 3B 43, fols. 37r–65v, case opened 10 Sept. 1341.
61  ADBR 3B 54, fols. 6r–50v, case opened 12 July 1354; also ADBR 3B 54, fols. 62r–73v, case opened 19 July 1354; ADBR 3B 816, fols. 6r–11v, case opened 21 June 1353; ADBR 3B 820, fols. 201r–202v, case opened 4 July 1356.
62  ADBR 3B 58, fols. 92r–112r, case opened 19 Feb. 1355.

than anyone else's (fol. 101v). Guilhem did not push the accusation of hatred but it was evident from other aspects of the trial. Guilhem was one of the leading members of the de Jerusalem faction. *All* his male opponents were associated in some way with the rival Vivaut/Martin faction.[63] Guilhem did accuse Laurens Ricau of pushing Johana Bausana to sue and therefore of being the instigator of the suit by stealth. The implications behind Guilhem's exception are obvious.

The existence of this suit raises an important question, for how had the debt arisen in the first place? The debt—unpaid land rent—was a form of circumstantial credit because all proprietors were indebted to direct lords on an annual basis. The factions were exceedingly well defined in this period and most people would have avoided falling into a long-term credit relationship like this with a member of the opposing faction. As it turns out, Guilhem de Montels was not the original proprietor of the garden. It had been owned for the past twenty years and more by a gardener named Guilhem Peire and, after his death, by his son Bertran, neither of whom was in any way associated with factional violence. Bertran, in turn, left the garden to Guilhem de Montels in his will. Why he did so is unclear, especially since it is unlikely that they were related—Bertran was a laborer and Guilhem de Montels a notable draper. It is likely that the garden was left in legacy as repayment for an unspecified debt owed to Guilhem arising from the sale of cloth or some such purpose. At any rate, Guilhem had only recently succeeded to the property in question, thus precipitating the events that followed.

An earlier case, from 1354, nominally involved a debt of forty-two pounds 6s. 8d. but also turns out to have implicated factional enmity.[64] The plaintiff in this case was none other than Guilhem de Montels, who was suing the merchant Guilhem Mercier for a debt that arose from the sale of cloth. The de Montels family, associated with the de Jerusalem faction, and the Mercier family, associated with the Vivaut faction, were bitter rivals, and again one wonders how the debt could have arisen in the first place. As it turns out, the debt was originally owed by the former sub-viguier, Peire Guibert, and Guilhem Mercier became burdened by the debt as Peire Guibert's pledge. The sub-viguier, like many other Angevin officials, was a stranger to the city doing an annual tour of duty, and one explanation for the existence of the debt is that it was transacted before Peire Guibert declared himself for the Vivaut party and acquired Guilhem Mercier as his

[63] Augier de Soliers, Laurens Ricau, and Augier Bonpar were committed Vivaut party members and Bertran de Buco was implicated by kinship.
[64] ADBR 3B 57, fols. 2r–19v, case opened 8 Oct. 1354.

pledge. One wonders whether tensions arising from this debt helped turn the sub-viguier against the de Montels family and the entire de Jerusalem faction. That Peire Guibert was associated with the Vivaut party is evident from a number of court records, for he had assassinated a member of the de Jerusalem party a short time before and was nearly killed in retaliation, and Guilhem Mercier made his defense in part by arguing that several witnesses for the plaintiff were capital enemies of Peire Guibert. In both of the suits involving Guilhem de Montels, therefore, debts reasonably innocent of strong emotions at their origins were subsequently transferred and became overlain with enmities. These enmities both impeded repayment and motivated the ensuing litigation.

In other cases, litigation for debt took place when a credit relationship between two formerly friendly individuals decayed over time, as in a telling case from 1341 involving two merchants. Merchants did not enter into commenda contracts with known enemies, and the case of the young merchant Bertran Gontart and his older colleague Johan Esteve, heard in the summer of 1342, shows how a souring relationship gradually became factionalized, as first Bertran and then Johan turned to the opposing factions for assistance in their thorny and ongoing squabble.[65]

The facts behind the case are not terribly clear, in part because the register in which the case appears was damaged by water and the ink has run. A plausible reconstruction follows. Johan Esteve was a fairly minor merchant capitalist. At some point in 1341, he and his rather more important colleague Antoni Catalan sent Bertran off to Genoa with a shipment of wine. Just twenty-two years old, Bertran may not have known of the troubles that would result if word got back to one's financiers that one had put water in the wine, for that is what he did, and the shipment, as the record puts it, "lost value." Bertran claimed that he made amends to his financiers in the amount of forty-six florins and other goods. Johan Esteve denied receiving any repayment of the commenda, and had Bertran criminally prosecuted and publicly sentenced for fraud. Then, seeking to press his advantage, Johan, the older man, forced young Bertran to bring the case before arbitrators so as to square accounts.

Here, Johan may have abused his power a little, for he somehow engineered the election of two arbitrators, a draper and a merchant, who had extremely tight links to the de Jerusalem party. The matter might have ended here with a simple decision in his favor if Antoni Catalan had not in the meantime fallen out with his colleague Johan, whom he suspected of trying to steal his money. So embittered had their former partnership become that

[65] ADBR 3B 42, fols. 14r–31v, case opened 24 July 1341.

at some point in the preceding year, Antoni had had Johan subjected to the humiliation of arrest, and as the two of them stood before a judge one even suggested to the other that they simply step outside and settle things like real men (*vadamus extra et videamus quis erit valens homo*).[66] Given this state of affairs, it was only natural that Antoni sided with young Bertran in his dispute with Johan, and it was only natural, in turn, for Antoni Catalan to turn to his friends, all of whom were members of the Vivaut faction.

Antoni was never formally listed as fighting on behalf of the Vivaut, and he never gave testimony in any extant court cases involving the Vivaut, but whenever we find him in the records from the period he is almost always associated with the Vivaut in some way: he lived on a street dominated by the Vivaut, he was the direct lord of a vineyard owned by a Vivaut party member, he acted as a procurator for another, he was a god-kin of another man with similar ties to the Vivaut, and so on. As it happens, young Bertran's father-in-law also had similar ties to the Vivaut, so it may not have been Antoni alone who pushed the young man in that direction. In any event, named to arbitrate the dispute was a third man who, like Antoni Catalan, had some ties to the Vivaut faction (Laurens Garcin, Antoni's father-in-law). The plan, apparently, was for this man to refuse to be part of a joint decision made by the arbitrators, thereby allowing young Bertran the possibility later to claim that what had become a null decision proved his innocence. This is what transpired: the arbitrator played his part to perfection, refusing to agree to the inevitable decision against Bertran, and when, in 1342, Johan brought the case into the courts, the arbitrator testified on behalf of his young friend, as did Antoni and another man.

Johan subsequently pleaded an exception on the grounds that the three witnesses brought against him were his public enemies (*inimici capitales*), known to favor Bertran's cause and, by implication, willing to lie for him. He brought a series of de Jerusalem faction members to testify on his behalf, and in the end won the case. We hear no more about Johan Esteve after this suit, but the story has an interesting epilogue in Bertran's case, for the factional associations that developed during his yearlong dispute with Johan ripened over time. In particular, Bertran became a very close friend and affine of the notary Raymon Audebert, a confirmed Vivaut party member, and when he died in the plague at the age of twenty-nine he had named the notary Raymon as the guardian of his young daughter Catharina. In 1353, the girl, assisted by her tutor, sold her stake in a ship to a Vivaut party member, Johan Casse.

The circumstances found in this case replicate themselves in four or five

[66] Ibid., fol. 24r.

other merchant disputes from the period.[67] All suggest how instances of debt litigation were motivated by a growing hatred between two former associates. Other types of long-term and formerly harmonious relationships were equally prone to dissolving into vengeful litigation for debt. Suits for the recovery of a dowry, though not strictly speaking cases of debt litigation, are the most notable examples. Such cases require some delicacy of analysis because women or their heirs sometimes sued with the connivance of their husbands or fathers in order to defraud the other creditors of an insolvent estate.[68] But hostility is evident in other cases. In 1353, a widow sued her son for the return of her dowry, and the testimony in the case reveals a pattern of mutual hostility and harassment.[69] In another case from the same year, a son sued his father for his dead mother's dowry; the libel complained of unjust behavior "contrary to the duty and piety of a father."[70] Hatred, frustration, or anger was also implicit in a third case from 1353 involving a woman who had gained a formal separation from her husband.[71] Although the husband was not required to repay the dowry, the episcopal court had assigned the woman the yearly profits from a dotal vineyard and house and a yearly payment of 10 percent of her dowry of 120 pounds. She was suing to force him to make good on these obligations. Other cases show women sanctioning their husbands' bad behavior by suing for their dowries, as in a case from 1355 in which a woman sued to recover her enormous dowry of 1,000 pounds, accusing her husband of adultery and physical abuse.[72] In perhaps the most interesting case involving a woman sanctioning a man, Guillelma Bandina sued her father-in-law in 1354 for the restoration of her dowry of eighty pounds.[73] Her case consisted of two simple claims: first, her father-in-law some three years ago had become a demented and unreasonable vagabond (*demens et incensatus et vagabundus*); second, owing to this demen-

---

[67] E.g., ADBR 3B 62, fols. 110r–116r, case opened 18 Jan. 1360; this case centered on a disputed sale of some sheep, and the case reveals how a former friendship between seller and buyer descended into threats and perjured testimony.

[68] See my "Démanteler le patrimoine: les femmes et les biens dans la Marseille médiévale," *Annales: histoire, sciences sociales* 52 (1997): 343–68.

[69] ADBR 3B 52, fols. 24r–39v, case opened 12 Oct. 1353. A few months earlier the son had also sued the mother; see ADBR 3B 50, fols. 204r–205r, case opened 8 Apr. 1353.

[70] ADBR 3B 52, fols. 77r–88r, case opened 7 Nov. 1353; the dispute is continued in ADBR 3B 822, fols. 102r–103r, case opened in late December 1357.

[71] ADBR 3B 50, fols. 207r–209r, case opened 17 May 1353. See also a similar case, this time heard in the court of first appeals: ADBR 3B 816, fols. 1r–5r, case opened 15 Sept. 1352; a related case in this same dispute can be found later in the same register, fols. 69r–81v, case opened 2 July 1353. This case speaks explicitly of the hatred (*rancor et odium*) between husband and wife (fol. 71v).

[72] ADBR 3B 57, fols. 96r–104r, case opened 26 Jan. 1355; see also a similar dotal retrocession arising from wife-beating in ADBR 3B 62, fols. 28r–29r, case opened 9 Oct. 1359.

[73] ADBR 3B 52, fols. 190r–193v, case opened 21 June 1354.

tia, he had ceased earning money and food as a goldsmith and instead had become a jongleur, singing songs on street corners and frequenting taverns. She won easily.

The animus implicit and sometimes explicit in many cases of debt litigation among Christians is set in relief by the cases of debt litigation involving Jews and Christians. A total of fifty cases, about 6 percent of the caseload of the palace court, set Christians against Jews and vice versa. These cases never involve talk of anger or hatred. The suits are usually quite short, evidence that they had not engaged the emotions: between 1323 and 1416, the average length of suits between Jews and Christians was 7.52 pages and the median was 4 pages, considerably shorter than the overall average length of 12.92 pages and median of 6 pages. Only one suit exceeded twenty-two pages. This one, a relatively long usury suit the proceedings for which took up ninety pages, was brought before the palace court in 1339. It was filed by the Jewish physician Salamon de Palermo against the Christian Jacma de Fontiayris, widow of the late Ugo de Fontiayris.[74] The case arose because several years prior to this, Ugo had supposedly deposited a sum of 160 florins with Salamon and several other Jews, and after Ugo's death Jacma, representing a number of heirs, had sued to recover the unrepaid amount of 144 florins. Salamon claimed that the amount deposited really only amounted to eighty florins; besides, he had repaid a large part of his own share of thirty-two florins. He brought a number of Christian witnesses to attest to this. All the circumstances suggest that the suit and countersuit were based on a misunderstanding: evidently, Ugo had kept his wife in the dark about his financial transactions.

⟨≷⟩

Historians working with late medieval and early modern secular court records typically divide the business of the courts into separate spheres: criminal and penal on the one hand, civil on the other. This is a natural thing to do, since the courts divided their own competencies along these lines. The resulting profile of cases looks very different. In criminal courts throughout medieval and early modern Europe, one finds violence, bloodfeud, assault, insult, and other subjects of cultural and microhistorical works. In secular civil courts one finds cases of debt and not much besides, used most often by economic historians. But the formal and disciplinary distinction between criminal and civil courts collapses when the law courts are viewed through the eyes of their users.

[74] ADBR 3B 38, fols. 90r–134v, case opened 20 July 1339.

As I have suggested in this chapter, men and women in late medieval Europe thought about their emotional relationships using convenient economic metaphors. Their economic relationships, similarly, were suffused with public and meaningful emotions. It was natural for Dousa Euzeria, in 1365, to assume that the extension of credit implied friendship. By the same token, the withdrawal of credit was a hostile gesture. In this epistemology, all public transactions—words and deeds, civil suits and criminal denunciations, money and blood—were of a piece. All served to generate, regenerate, and redefine emotional relationships. Debt litigation in the public, open-air courts of late medieval Marseille was no less a performance than any private hostile gesture and was arguably more effective in achieving its goal, that of advertising current social relationships and social standing for the benefit of observers.

The sense of obligation that underpins both gifts and debts is not unique to settled societies. Among the Mbuti, a hunter-gatherer people of the central African rainforest, when hunters kill an elephant, the entire clan assembles in short order, and a loud discussion ensues.[75] People haggle over the kinship connections that determine the distribution of choice tidbits and quarrel over the honors of the hunt. Newcomers busily remind the hunters of their debts and obligations. This makes sense. A carcass is often larger than hunters alone can process and consume before it spoils, and the institution of obligation is a vitally important way for successful hunters to store up favors against future bad luck. Some of the most significant work done by evolutionary psychologists has stressed the evolution of cooperation—how and why basic trust and the culture of reciprocity first emerged in ancestral societies.[76] The flip side of trust is sanction, for trust is operative only if those who break it can be readily identified and sanctioned.

Though the men and women of fourteenth-century Marseille were more accustomed to transactions involving money rather than elephant meat the principle is the same. They routinely kept track of their mutual obligations and transactions and assumed, as a matter of course, that both friendship and enmity would follow lines of credit and debt. They could punish those who defaulted in several ways: through the spreading of rumors, a deliberate assault on their fama; through the private distraint of goods; and through the pursuit of debt in court.

Arguments for the rise of debt litigation in medieval or early modern Eu-

[75] John Reader, *Africa: A Biography of the Continent* (New York, 1998), 107–8.
[76] The perspective is rooted in the work of the evolutionary biologist William Hamilton; useful introductions include Robert M. Axelrod, *The Evolution of Cooperation* (New York, 1984); Robin Dunbar, *Grooming, Gossip, and the Evolution of Language* (Cambridge, Mass., 1996); Steven Pinker, *How the Mind Works* (New York, 1997).

rope typically start with the idea that an expanding market economy generates a demand for credit, thus creating a culture of credit and debt.[77] There is undoubtedly some correlation between markets and debt litigation. Yet the proposition, insofar as it is based on the principle that debt can be usefully expressed *only* in the language of money, is not quite right. What these historians are really describing, I think, is not the creation of a culture of credit and debt ex nihilo, but instead a fundamental transformation in the nature of the metaphors of obligation. Human societies are always marked by cooperative and competitive relationships that are instantiated and publicized through a variety of somatic gestures as well as in more ritualistic, culture-bound ways: gift and counter-gift, bloodtaking and peacemaking, the potlatch, and so on. This is the balanced-exchange model of human relations.[78] The rise of market culture brought with it, for a time, a new transactional metaphor, that of credit and debt, which became the intellectual filter through which men and women understood and interpreted the nature of their social relations. The rise of debt litigation is simply a function of the growing tendency of people to express transactional imbalances in monetary terms and to pursue their social envies and personal enmities through the courts.

At the same time, the growing range of material goods available on the European market—fine clothing, furniture, household silver—coupled with the manners and social refinements necessary for their proper use became, in the ensemble, crucially important ways to pursue both status identity and social competition. In looking for explanations for the European-wide decline in rates of litigation in the eighteenth century, I am inclined to suggest that the eighteenth century marks the age when Europeans finally became accustomed to expressing social competition through manners and material goods, largely obviating the need to use either self-help or the courts for this purpose. A very schematic argument, surely, but one that at least has the merit of underscoring the competitive nature of many human rituals and social processes, lawsuits among them.

[77] See Richard L. Kagan, *Lawsuits and Litigants in Castile, 1500–1700* (Chapel Hill, 1981), xix: "The rise of a market economy in the twelfth and thirteenth centuries created new reasons for lawsuits." See also Muldrew, *Economy of Obligation*, 3: "The origin of this culture of credit began in about the mid-sixteenth century and was a result of rapid economic change."

[78] William Ian Miller articulates the balanced-exchange model (though limiting it to the feud) in *Bloodtaking and Peacemaking: Feud, Law, and Society in Saga Iceland* (Chicago, 1990), 184–85.

# CHAPTER FOUR
## BODY AND *BONA*

The system of coercion and sanction as it was practiced in fourteenth-century Marseille was built around the simple principle that whereas people were mobile their property was not. It was easy for a person to escape the law. Outside the walls of the city, the jurisdiction of the courts ended at the fuzzy boundary between the city's territory and the world beyond. Inside the walls, jurisdiction ended abruptly at the threshold separating the secular space of street and plaza from the ecclesiastical space of church and monastery. Criminals and bankrupts made free use of these boundaries, and the system of coercion and force was built around their existence. Sanctuary, exile, and banishment were the norms in this legal world: murderers were expected to run away, and other men as well if circumstances warranted so drastic a decision. Women too, though rarely, and more to escape abusive husbands than the law. From afar, those in exile used their wives, relatives, and procurators to make peace with their enemies or recover as much of the estate as possible. Assessed unreasonably large contumacy fines by the criminal court, they negotiated reductions and scraped together the cash to pay off the fine. Once things had quieted down they slipped back into the city and reassembled what they could. Incarceration was available for women and also for men who were too inept to flee in a timely fashion, had no network of support in the countryside, or preferred their chances of resisting the accusations and the torture that might accompany them. Corporal punishments—limbing, ear-cutting, whipping through the streets, and even hanging on occasion—did exist. They were typically used on the unlucky, the unconnected, and the exceptionally wicked: foreigners, vagabonds, and out-and-out ruffians of whom an example was to be made. As many people suggested with some bitterness, torture was also applied to those unfortunate enough to have made enemies of officials of the court. But such punishments were not common. The punishment inflicted on Damiens the regicide, used to such effect by Michel Foucault in the introduction to *Discipline and Punish*, cannot but leave one with the impression that premodern legal systems routinely punished the body and delighted in so doing.[1] Compared to this, the judicial system in fourteenth-century Marseille was decidedly squeamish about the body. Men and women missing fingers, hands, ears, or eyes or marked by scars on the breast, the left side of the head, and on the left arm, shoulder, or leg would not have been an unusual sight in fourteenth-century Marseille, but on the whole these scars were inflicted in face-to-face combat by their right-handed enemies, not by the courts. The body was eminently sanctionable in late medieval Marseille. On the whole, though, it wasn't the state that did the sanctioning.

The state-sponsored apparatus of coercion and punishment that formed an element of the penal system of fourteenth-century Marseille, thus, was not principally organized around the body of criminals or debtors. Instead, it was organized around their *bona*. The Latin word *bona*, always in the plural, occurs thousands of times in the extant judicial records. It does not translate well into English. Its semantic range starts with goods, property, rights, assets, and inheritance, but extends beyond this to encompass the very source of one's social position and fama. As seen in chapter 2, to say that a man was incapable of managing his bona was to strike at the very roots of his public being. Some of the symbolic weight of one's bona came from the fact that one did not really possess it. Instead, it was attached symbolically to one's family or descent group and served an important economic role. Most people, especially women and nobles, relied on inherited bona to supplement what they could make from trade, artisanal production, retailing, or labor, and their community standing depended on this source of wealth. The symbolism was powerful and, in the form of allusions, surfaces often in the records. To seize bona, in this world, was not only to collect a criminal fine or recover a debt. It was to strike at the very roots of an adversary's community standing and that of his or her descendants and potential heirs.

Bona were the ready objects of penal fines and civil pursuits because they were not very portable. One's bona consisted of one's houses, vines, lands,

---

[1] Michel Foucault, *Discipline and Punish: The Birth of the Prison*, trans. Alan Sheridan (New York, 1977). For an extended critique, see Richard Mowery Andrews, *Law, Magistracy, and Crime in Old Regime Paris, 1735–1789*, vol. 1, *The System of Criminal Justice* (Cambridge, 1994).

rents, instruments of credit, beds, bedclothes, tables, chairs, chests, clothing, jewelry, weapons, dishes, jars of wine and oil, and in the case of artisans, tools, looms, and other devices. Long, itemized lists of bona sometimes fill the pages of the judicial registers, an intrusive accounting that laid bare the fractured lives of dissolute husbands, bankrupt merchants, or criminal fugitives. It was through bona that the courts regulated and sanctioned criminals, and typically it is only when bona failed, when a person's infamy was such that he or she had neither bona, nor credit, nor friends and kinfolk willing to intercede with gifts and loans, that blood sanctions applied. When ordinary men and women used the law courts to pursue their hatreds they expected their adversary to suffer some degree of aggravation or humiliation. If things went very well it was even possible to punish an adversary through his or her bona.

This property-oriented system of coercion and sanction collapses the formal distinctions between civil and criminal procedures that I took pains to establish in chapter 1. Civil and criminal procedures were initiated in different ways and involved different premises but arrived at a similar result, namely the attempt to sanction the miscreant through the seizure of bona. All those who lost a civil trial became beholden both to their former adversaries and to the courts and either paid up or suffered a distraint of property. Criminals were similarly transformed into debtors, and sanctions were then applied to them as if they were debtors. It is here, in the practice of forcible distraint, that the state in Marseille first developed a true monopoly on coercive force. Put another way, the state's monopoly on coercive force in Marseille did not begin with control over the body. Instead, impelled by exigent creditors, one of which was the criminal court itself, the state's apprenticeship in systems of coercion began with the practice of forcible distraint, a form of violent coercion exercised on passive and unresisting bona. By contrast, the effort to police violence, and control or sanction the body of the criminal, or to enforce a hypothetical peace, was clumsy and inept, less sophisticated than existing practices of family-based coercion and vengeance, and indeed heavily dependent on both family and faction in the effort to police the city.

In this chapter I will begin by exploring the body-based systems of coercion that did exist. It is important not to dismiss the very real threat posed by the existence of a police force. People did not like incarceration and feared torture, and the occasional excision of a hand or foot, or even a hanging, showed that the state could and did sanction the body. Nonetheless, as many historians have noted, family, faction, and neighborhood remained very prominently in view as institutions of coercion, and public retaliation and vengeance remained the conceptual norm throughout the fourteenth century, despite Angevin efforts to delegitimize such practices. It was family force, I will argue, that gave criminal justice its teeth in Marseille. From there, I turn to the well-developed bona-based system of forcible distraint used by the criminal court, which was closely related to and certainly grew out of the system of debt recovery discussed briefly in chapter 3. From the perspective of the criminal court, at the heart of the bona-based system of sanction was the practice of condemning absent malefactors for contumacy, notably murderers and other perpetrators of especially violent crimes who, fearing the vengeance of their victims or the victims' families, had fled the city. But all behaviors now deemed to be criminal were penalized by means of fines, fines that were growing over the course of the fourteenth century as the criminal court became more and more confident of the ability of the coercive apparatus to seize the bona of the miscreant and distrain this fine.

But the practice of justice was a two-way street, and one should never imagine any development without its corresponding reaction. As the weight of Angevin penal law pressed down ever more heavily on the city and its population there emerged a culture of evasion built on a sophisticated system of financial shelters, a culture explored in the third section. Here, we depart from one of the major themes of this book: we are not dealing with the *use* of justice so much as the response to the system as it was used by others, namely the adversaries who denounced one to the court and the officials of the court itself who sometimes proceeded ex officio. In this system of financial shelters two practices stand out. One of these, clerical status, is well known to historians of medieval Europe. The use of dotal or other legal shelters, a second practice, is less well known. These parallel systems of financial shelters were already in place by the early fourteenth century and grew more elaborate over the course of the century as the threat to bona became ever more serious.

## COERCIVE FORCE

The apparatus for applying or evading coercive force was complex. One's tendency is to assume that there must have been a distinction between the public force that operated on behalf of the state and the private force that operated on behalf of individuals or groups. In Marseille, only with hindsight is it possible to say that there were two kinds of force invested in different institutions. The distinction was less obvious to contemporaries. In 1342, a shoemaker named Bernat Martin was sentenced by the criminal court to pay a reasonably heavy fine of 60s. for having beaten his apprentice,

Johan de Lione, a fine he subsequently appealed.[2] According to the inquest, the apprentice had tried to make off with a pair of shoes and 5s. Bernat, in pursuit, knocked Johan to the ground and thrashed him, causing a wound to the face from which blood flowed. The theft was not in question: the problem, evidently, was the use of excessive force. As it turns out, though, Bernat had requested and received formal permission from the court to pursue his apprentice and was even accompanied in the chase by a messenger of the court. He, at least, felt that his private exercise of coercive force had been justified by public authorities.

The power to use coercive force was officially delegated to the sub-viguier and members of his household, his *familia*, from at least the early fourteenth century. In 1308, the defendant in a successful criminal appeal, Raymondet Berengier, was able to prove that the sub-viguier and his servitors had forcibly extracted him from the cathedral church of La Major, thus violating the immunity of the church.[3] This is the earliest reference to the policing activity of the sub-viguier that I have found. References become relatively frequent after this date. Many are similarly paradoxical: the sub-viguier stands out for his many acts of murder and mayhem. Other officials of the court were not supposed to intrude on the sub-viguier's monopoly on coercive force. An interesting argument made during a case from the year 1405, for example, shows that the power to make an arrest was vested exclusively in the sub-viguier: "It is ancient custom in Marseille that men are captured and taken to jail by the sub-viguier and his servitors and not by other messengers deputized in service to the royal court."[4] The one official exception was the viguier himself, who, as the direct representative of the crown, was free to take up arms.

As the case of Bernat Martin suggests, the sub-viguier and his servitors did not normally interest themselves with theft or property damage. Instead, they were drawn to street battles known, in the records, under a variety of roughly interchangeable words such as *rixae*, *pelegiae*, *querelae*, *murmures*, and especially *rumores*. Little distinction was made between squabbles, murmurs, and rumors on the one hand and battles involving knives and swords on the other. In 1341, a dispute broke out between the abbess of St. Sauveur, Maria de Tornafort, and Bertomieu and Raolin Martin over the ownership of a portion of a house located in the Fishmongery.[5] The abbess, accompanied by her prioress, many nuns, and a number of priests, marched to the house in question to confront the brothers. Though

---

2 ADBR 3B 808, fols. 167r–173r, case opened 17 Sept. 1342.
3 ADBR 3B 803, fol. 127r–v, case opened 1 July 1308 on fol. 126r.
4 ADBR 3B 856, fol. 9v, case opened 27 June 1405 on fol. 5r.
5 ADBR 3B 808, fols. 228r–272r, case opened 25 Oct. 1342.

there is no mention of weapons the ensuing quarrel was called a *rixa*. Nine years later, on the evening of 22 July 1351, a violent battle broke out between dozens of armed members of the Vivaut and de Jerusalem parties and resulted in many bloodings.[6] This, too, was called a *rixa*, though it was also called something even more serious, a *briga*. *Rumor* was the most common word. Any *rumor* could range from a simple fuss to a killing. In the latter case the notary might relent and allow that it was a *magna rumor*.

Semantic distinctions between word-battles and weapon-battles were difficult in part because all battles generated a hue-and-cry, the clamor, murmur, or rumor spoken of in the records. To observers, the fight itself was conceptually indistinct from the public outcry it invariably occasioned. There is a good deal of evidence to show that women had the major responsibility for making the public clamor and did so for the purpose of inciting intervention. Some ducked this responsibility. In 1365, Comptessa Comptesse admitted that she had heard a rumor and a fuss outside her house one day but "she believed it to be women who were fighting and thus didn't bother to go out."[7] Guilhem Tomas lost his life in this fuss. Never is it recorded, though, that women went directly to the sub-viguier or viguier, though the rumor itself may have been designed to draw the attention of the court. Instead, they went to neighbors, and most of the fights for which we have records were stopped by neighbors rather than by the sub-viguier. So systematic is testimony on this issue that there was clearly a well-developed culture of intervention. A witness to a fight in 1402 reported that he was standing with others in the boutique of a spice-merchant located not far from the *rumor* when a woman came running up, crying, "O lords, run to the street where Jacme Albin lives to break up the fight [*ad dividendum rumorem*] that's taking place there!"[8] In this same fight another witness who had been heading away from the battle ran back upon hearing the hubbub and arrived just in time to prevent a blow to a man lying prostrate on the ground.[9]

Methods for stopping a fight varied. A common tactic was to insert a heavy staff (*baculus*) or bar (*barra*) between the fighters. In 1342 two fishermen used one or more bars to intervene during a fight, earning the gratitude of Julian Marquet, one of the men involved. Julian claimed that his enemies would have killed him without this intervention.[10] The bar in this case was

---

[6] ADBR 3B 811, fols. 15r–101v, case opened 12 Dec. 1351.

[7] ADBR 3B 825, fol. 69v, case opened 13 May 1365 on fol. 35r.

[8] ADBR 5G 772, fol. 93r, case opened 20 Aug. 1402 on fol. 81r.

[9] Ibid., fol. 92v

[10] ADBR 3B 808, fol. 50v, case opened 5 Mar. 1342 on fol. 32r. For other references to bars or staffs in this trial see fols. 35r, 43r, 44v, and 53v.

wielded with sufficient violence as to break the middle finger of Julian's principal adversary.[11] In another case, Margarita de Alesto watched as a fight developed and then ran into the nearest house, not her own, with the intention of grabbing a bar so as to divide the fighters.[12] Evidently she expected the average house to be furnished with bars, though in the event she found none. In still another case, from 1401, a woman named Johaneta Rostagne did find a bar, but since her son was in the battle she wielded it rather energetically on his behalf, striking her son's adversary, Bernat Berengier, on the head and shin and causing him to fall to the ground.[13] Bars were not the only device useful for intervention. One bystander threw a cloak over a fighter.[14] Another defended a prostrate man on the ground by threatening his adversary with a knife, and for his pains was wounded on the left hand.[15]

As these examples indicate, women used bars just as often as men and, furthermore, did not hesitate to intervene with their bodies. As soon as Bernat Berengier had been knocked down by Johaneta Rostagne, his wife Guilhelmona cast herself on her prostrate husband, crying out to the man now threatening him, "O false friend, you're killing my husband" (*O fals compayre, ausiras mon marit*). In the event her intervention did her husband little good because the assailant, Nicolau Jausap, managed to slip in a knife blow, giving Bernat a mortal wound.[16] Uga, the wife of Guilhem de Belavila, similarly intervened in the battle between her husband and his adversary Guilhem Tomas, crying out, "Kill me instead of my husband." She lost a finger.[17] Johaneta Tomasia, wife of the victim, also tried to intervene, crying out, "Aie, Mary, that's my husband!" (*Ay Marida aysso es mon marit*), or, according to another witness, "For God's sake don't kill my husband!" and received several knocks.[18] Such injuries were not uncommon. Women were considered perfectly capable of assuming an aggressive posture—Johaneta Rostagne is a case in point—and in the heat of the battle it may have been difficult to distinguish friendly intervention from assault. Several witnesses in the appeal of Guilhem de Belavila reported that both his wife and his sister-in-law held the victim as he received his death-wound. Subsequent testimony shows that the witnesses were probably wrong or lying but clearly such behavior by women was within the realm of possibility. Intervention, in

[11] Ibid., fol. 59v.
[12] ADBR 3B 825, fol. 167r, case opened 13 May 1365 on fol. 35r.
[13] ADBR 5G 772, fols. 24v and 26r, case opened 16 Dec. 1400 on fol. 24r.
[14] Ibid., fol. 73r, case opened Dec. 1401.
[15] Ibid., fol. 93r, case opened 20 Aug. 1402 on fol. 81r.
[16] Ibid., fol. 27r, case opened 16 Dec. 1400 on fol. 24r.
[17] ADBR 3B 825, fols. 74v–75r, case opened 13 May 1365 on fol. 35r.
[18] Ibid., fols. 61v, 66r.

short, was dangerous, and demanded considerable courage. Not all were up to the task. Numerous instances of witness testimony show that women, on hearing a hubbub in the street and opening their doors, shut them again just as quickly when it was clear that weapons were involved. Ugueta Jeorgia was standing on her doorstep when Guilhem Tomas met Guilhem de Belavila. As soon as knives were drawn, she hastily reentered her house (*confestim intravit hospicium suum*).[19]

The common practice of intervention shows that the duty to keep the peace was not, in the minds of ordinary citizens, a prerogative of the sub-viguier. This is critical: the state was not considered to have held a complete monopoly on the exercise of coercive force. Instead, the legitimate exercise of coercive force continued to reside within families and neighborhoods, and the criminal law system was, in practice, built on the existence of this force.

Another important point buried in these examples confirms an observation made by Claude Gauvard, namely that most fights, even homicidal assaults, took place during daylight hours and in very public spaces, often near markets, in the presence of enough witnesses to account for the great clamor or loud rumor that witnesses often spoke of.[20] Examples are legion. Guilhem Tomas honorably accosted his adversary, Guilhem de Belavila, in the small plaza of the Spur, as one or both of them was on his way back from market. Johan Areat was on his way back from market one day in 1403 when he was lethally assaulted by his enemy, Jacme Albin, and two associates.[21] The three men staged their ambush on the street of Caysarie, one of Marseille's major thoroughfares, and killed their adversary in the presence of numerous witnesses. Slayers did not secretly murder their enemies in their beds. A similar scrupulosity can be found in many premodern societies, for there is little point to having an enmity that is not well publicized.[22] The evident lack of shame or hesitation about fighting in public is yet another tacit denial of the sub-viguier's putative monopoly on coercive force, and a sign that the exercise of violence was still beholden to the rules and rhythms of customary vengeance.

Though the sub-viguier usually arrived too late to stop a fight he would take into custody any assailant still on the scene. This was sometimes resented by friends of the captive, and efforts might be made to secure the

[19] Ibid., fol. 69v, case opened 13 May 1365 on fol. 35r.
[20] See Claude Gauvard, "*De grace especial*": *crime, état, et société à la fin du Moyen Âge*, 2 vols. (Paris, 1991), 1:281.
[21] ADBR 3B 140, fols. 229r–273v, case opened 11 July 1403.
[22] One of the key points made by William Ian Miller, *Bloodtaking and Peacemaking: Feud, Law, and Society in Saga Iceland* (Chicago, 1990).

captive's release.[23] The knifesmith Colin de Bosco was accused of doing just so in 1405.[24] A public proclamation from 1341 forbade anyone, under pain of a one hundred pound fine, from daring to follow the servitors of the court when they were in the process of taking someone to jail, suggesting that the practice of intervention was common enough.[25] Records of the court of inquest show that the assailants captured by the sub-viguier who were successfully prosecuted by the criminal court were usually guilty of relatively minor assaults and assessed correspondingly small fines—small, at any rate, by comparison with the hundreds or even thousands of pounds that surfaced in homicide cases. In a few cases involving homicide, the sub-viguier did manage to reach the scene in time to arrest the killer. In 1356, during a criminal inquest into the murder of Peire de Jerusalem, partisans of the Vivaut faction sought to justify the killing by stories of past de Jerusalem atrocities, and a favored story was that of the young merchant Johan Casse. Several years earlier, Marques de Jerusalem had been murdered by adherents of the Vivaut faction. Johan had actually been seized by the viguier, the sub-viguier, and their little band of men, and was being taken off to the court for questioning. On the way to the court the group was violently attacked by a number of de Jerusalem faction members bearing drawn swords. Johan prudently ducked into a nearby shop and the sub-viguier, Peire Guibert, defended the door, saying, "You shall not have him unless I am dead first!"[26] But this exception proves the rule. First, Johan may have allowed himself to be captured because he stood little chance of escaping the de Jerusalem on his own. Second, the sub-viguier was actively associated with the Vivaut party and was later accused of killing a de Jerusalem faction member. Johan, incidentally, went on to become one of Marseille's leading merchant-capitalists of the latter half of the fourteenth century, a success story that shows how an honest or open homicide was never held against one.

It was far more normal, in Marseille as elsewhere in Europe, for assailants to flee the scene immediately after any serious assault in search of sanctuary or self-imposed exile.[27] Legal and social historians have repeatedly noted the existence of this practice.

---

[23] Nicole Gonthier discusses other forms of resistance to police in *Délinquance, justice et société dans le Lyonnais médiéval de la fin du XIIIe siècle au début du XVIe siècle* (Paris, 1993), 262–63.

[24] ADBR 3B 856, fol. 7v, case opened 27 June 1405 on fol. 5r.

[25] AM FF 165, fol. 3r.

[26] ADBR 3B 820, fol. 74r, case opened 7 July 1356 on fol. 8r.

[27] On this practice see Peter Raymond Pazzaglini, *The Criminal Ban of the Sienese Commune, 1225–1310* (Milan, 1979); Randolph Starn, *Contrary Commonwealth: The Theme of Exile in Medieval and Renaissance Italy* (Berkeley, 1982); Thomas Kuehn, *Law, Family, and Women: Toward a Legal Anthropology of Renaissance Italy* (Chicago, 1991), 150–51; Kathryn

Most people charged with major crimes [in Bologna] fled rather than respond to the summons to appear in court.[28]

But obviously flight was the best way to elude justice, because it was very difficult for judges to pursue legal action beyond their jurisdictional limits.[29]

Although the late fourteenth- and early fifteenth-century Florentine criminal justice system was very aggressive in capturing criminals, compared to medieval standards, many criminals remained at large.[30]

Often, however, the killer fled, perhaps directly from the scene of the crime . . . Other times the guilty party waited for days or weeks while the victim nursed his wounds, probably compensating him and his angry family with a payment, and then when death occurred, "fearing the rigors of justice," fled out of the jurisdiction, the region, and sometimes even out of the kingdom of France.[31]

These are just the casual observations. Bernard Guenée considered contumacy a key element in what he called *la justice impuissante* (impotent justice) of late medieval Senlis. "What can justice do against a guilty party who cannot be bodily seized," he asks rhetorically. Little, it seems: "The contumacious individual was normally banned. But this banishment had no personal consequences, because the judicial system of one seigneurie could

---

L. Reyerson, "Flight from Prosecution: The Search for Religious Asylum in Medieval Montpellier," *French Historical Studies* 17 (1992): 603–626; Robert Bartlett, "'Mortal Enmities': The Legal Aspect of Hostility in the Middle Ages," T. Jones Pierce Lecture, University of Wales (Aberystwyth, 1998), 14. On the relationship between flight, banishment, and contumacy, see Kenneth Frederick Meredith, "The Penalty of Banishment in Medieval France and England," Ph.D. diss., University of Virginia, 1979, 318–87. For England, see Naomi Hurnard, *The King's Pardon for Homicide before A.D. 1307* (Oxford, 1969), 131–51. For older perspectives on contumacy in medieval French criminal law, see Adhémar Esmein, *A History of Continental Criminal Procedure with Special Reference to France*, The Continental Legal History Series, vol. 5, trans. John Simpson (Boston, 1913), 73–77.

[28] Sarah Rubin Blanshei, "Crime and Law Enforcement in Medieval Bologna," *Journal of Social History* 16 (1982): 121–38, here 123.

[29] Jacques Chiffoleau, *Les justices du pape: délinquance et criminalité dans la region d'Avignon au quatorzième siècle* (Paris, 1984), 44.

[30] Laura Ikins Stern, *The Criminal Law System of Medieval and Renaissance Florence* (Baltimore, 1994), 59.

[31] Natalie Zemon Davis, *Fiction in the Archives: Pardon Tales and Their Tellers in Sixteenth-Century France* (Stanford, 1987), 7–8.

only banish someone from that seigneurie."[32] Claude Gauvard, who has studied the question in a more deliberate fashion, has calculated that more than 45 percent of those who obtained letters of remission in late medieval northern France did so as fugitives.[33] In Florence, the contumacy rate fluctuated between 58 percent in the period 1380–83 and 42 percent in the early fifteenth century.[34] In Mantua between the years 1460 and 1462, two-thirds to three-fourths of all sentences were based on contumacy. Certain crimes had even higher contumacy rates. In a sample of 261 individuals declared guilty of homicide between 1444 and 1463, 228 (87 percent) were contumacious.[35]

In the absence of the accused, courts in Marseille and elsewhere had little choice but to declare the individual guilty and impose a fine for contumacy that sometimes involved seizure of bona, a practice discussed at greater length in the next section. In some jurisdictions, the condemned might also be executed in effigy. The frequency of effigy executions in Auvergne in 1665—out of a total of 347 death sentences, 324 were carried out in effigy—provides yet another indication of the normalcy of contumacy.[36]

Though contumacy rates are impossible to establish for Marseille, evidence for the systematic practice of sanctuary and exile coupled with court-imposed contumacy fines and peacemaking procedures is overwhelming. The sole homicide inquest in eighty-four cases heard by the criminal court between May of 1380 and January of 1381 was characteristic of the genre.[37] Four people—two shoemakers and two prostitutes or concubines—were charged with the murder of a Catalan woman named Mathea Sadaroni. The notary of the inquest noted that a messenger had been sent to summon the four suspects. Only one showed up at court and she was found innocent. Mathea's slayers, quite evidently, had taken flight, and a marginal note in the record, though damaged by humidity, suggests that two hundred pounds had been collected from the abandoned estates by virtue of this contumacy.[38]

Many other documents from Marseille, notably court proceedings, fiscal

[32] Bernard Guenée, *Tribunaux et gens de justice dans le bailliage de Senlis à la fin du Moyen Âge* (Paris, 1963), 293–95.

[33] Claude Gauvard, "*De grace especial,*" 1:163.

[34] See Stern, *Criminal Law System*, 210, citing (for the first of the two periods) Umberto Dorini, *Il diritto penale e la delinquenza in Firenze nel sec. XIV* (Lucca, 1923), 154–55. The contumacy rate for political crimes in Florence was especially high, 78 percent; see Stern, *Criminal Law System*, 222.

[35] David S. Chambers and Trevor Dean, *Clean Hands and Rough Justice: An Investigating Magistrate in Renaissance Italy* (Ann Arbor, 1997), 65–66.

[36] Jean-Marie Carbasse, *Introduction historique au droit pénal* (Paris, 1990), 215. See also Chiffoleau, *Justices du pape*, 45.

[37] ADBR 3B 96, fols. 10r–13r, case opened 11 June 1380.

[38] Ibid., fol. 13v.

records, and notarial instruments, record the practice of taking flight. Like hatred, flight (*fuga*) was a formal legal condition; like hatred, it generated a precise set of terms and expressions in these records. Those in self-imposed exile were conventionally said to have "taken flight" or "put themselves into flight," the language used in an act from 1364 describing how three clerics named Giraut Alaman, Andrieu Bonvin, and Marques Borgondionis killed Lois de Jerusalem and then "took flight" (*in fugam se constituerunt*).[39] Exile was often preceded by ecclesiastical sanctuary; here, the expressions become "he saved himself in the church" (*se salvavit in ecclesiam*), or "he rescued himself in the church" (*se reduxit in ecclesiam*). Use of reflexive verbs is particularly distinctive.

Why take flight? The threat of bodily punishments may have been a factor. In Marseille, however, flight was motivated most often by fear of the family and friends of the victim, not out of fear of capture and incarceration by the sub-viguier.[40] In his 1365 appeal arising from the murder of Guilhem Tomas, Guilhem de Belavila argued strenuously that it was far too dangerous for him to return to the city in answer to the summons:

> It was and is notoriously well known in Marseille that, at the time of the sentence and during the trial, there were and are many capital enemies of Guilhem who were persecuting him out of a notorious ancient and capital hatred. Powerful friends of the late Guilhem Tomas pursue many plots against Guilhem de Belavila and might kill him, and thus it was perilous, and death would have been imminent, if perchance he had returned to Marseille.[41]

Fearing immediate vengeance from the close friends of the victim, both Guilhem and his brother-in-law, Fulco Robaut, sought sanctuary first in St. Antoine, then in the cathedral of La Major, and later made their way out of the city through paths known only to themselves, eventually reaching Aix-en-Provence. Fear of the might of the de Jerusalem faction was an essential element in the appeal of Amiel Bonafos in 1356, though there was an added twist: the viguier was Amiel's mortal enemy and, furthermore, in league with the de Jerusalem faction.

> It is common and public opinion in the city of Marseille that if the said Amiel should come into the hands of the said viguier, the viguier him-

[39] AM FF 14.
[40] Gauvard makes a similar argument; see "*De grace especial*," 1:165.
[41] ADBR 3B 825, fol. 42v, case opened 13 May 1365 on fol. 35r.

self would put Amiel in jail and the party of the de Jerusalem would execute him, through their own action and on their own authority, with the approval of the viguier.[42]

Fear of enemies was not restricted to those in factions. Consider Fulco Alelin, a recent immigrant to Marseille from Nice who was implicated in the murder of Bertomieu de Nantes in 1380. Bereft of kinfolk and friends and fearful of the power of his enemies—not only his victim's friends but also personal enemies who might choose to profit from his distress—Fulco fled to sanctuary in the Carmelite monastery. From the safety of its walls he then engineered a reduction in his contumacy fine, negotiated a royal pardon, and successfully sued for the return of his house and other goods that had been seized by officials of the crown.[43]

The role assigned to victims' families and friends in this process was not formalized in any way but clearly served an important customary role that met with the tacit approval of the courts. In a very real way, therefore, policing was done not by the sub-viguier but rather by the families and friends of victims.[44] Testimony in the appeal of Amiel Bonafos records how tight the association between private and public force could be. Following the assassination of Peire de Jerusalem, leaders of the de Jerusalem faction ringed the city with a huge militia force in an effort to track down the killers, and did so, according to witnesses, with the open approval of the viguier.[45]

Court proceedings began after the assailant was safely in exile. At the same time, slayers and assailants opened peace negotiations with the family of the victim. Such peace negotiations figure commonly in Mediterranean municipal statutes: proof of peace was a necessary precondition for the lifting of the banishment.[46] Sarah Rubin Blanshei has even argued that, in homicide cases, the primary role of government in thirteenth-century Italian city-states "was to reconcile criminal and victim rather than to punish the offender," the situation that held in Marseille throughout the fourteenth century.[47] Marseille's thirteenth-century statutes, still in force in the four-

[42] ADBR 3B 820, fol. 47r, case opened 7 July 1356 on fol. 8r.
[43] ADBR 3B 94, fols. 307r–314v, case opened 31 Jan. 1380.
[44] Blanshei describes this aptly as the "modified vendetta system," "Crime and Law Enforcement," 121.
[45] ADBR 3B 820, fols. 49r–82v, case opened 7 July 1356 on fol. 8r.
[46] On this see Massimo Vallerani, *Il sistema giudiziario del comune di Perugia: conflitti, reati e processi nella seconda metà del XIII secolo* (Perugia, 1991), 99–105; see also Daniel Lord Smail, "Common Violence: Vengeance and Inquisition in Fourteenth-Century Marseille," *Past and Present* 151 (1996): 28–59, here 41–42.
[47] Blanshei, "Crime and Law Enforcement," 121.

teenth century, explicitly required a formal peace made with four to five members of the victim's family and the payment of the contumacy fine.[48]

Even those historians who are aware of the frequency of the practice of self-imposed exile consider incarceration and trial as the "normal" path of late medieval criminal justice, and treat self-imposed exile as a failure of the state's security apparatus.[49] In Marseille, it was quite the reverse: the system of self-imposed exile followed by contumacy was the normal practice, and the incarceration, trial, and execution of the accused was clearly the exception. The situation in Marseille throws into doubt a basic presupposition of some strands of criminal justice history, namely that officials of the court always wanted to capture, incarcerate, put on trial, and execute murderers. Speaking of decisions reached by the Parlement of Paris, Claude Gauvard notes that "the penalty of death is rare and, when the decision is reached, it can still be the object of changes that transform the ritual."[50] Her magisterial synthesis *De grace especial* shows that late medieval French kings built their political legitimacy on their ability not to execute, but to pardon, a practice that served to promote peace.[51] Killers, certainly, found their lives made miserable by royal officials. The process that led up to the granting of a royal pardon was a long and humiliating one and cost a good deal of money. All the same, the practice of pardoning, coupled with a fine and some form of humiliation, was the "normal" path of criminal justice.

The frequency of contumacy and banishment is the key to the proper working of the system. Judges and other local officials in Mediterranean Europe had many reasons for tacitly allowing the accused to get away. First, the absence of the accused meant that the criminal court did not have to make a judgment based on the facts of a case: a sensible solution, insofar as judgments may have inflamed passions. Peter Raymond Pazzaglini, furthermore, notes that systematic contumacy also reduced the court's caseload and

[48] Pernoud, *Statuts*, 178.
[49] A characteristic example of this tendency can be found in Guido Ruggiero's brief discussion of contumacy in *Violence in Early Renaissance Venice* (New Brunswick, N.J., 1980), 23.
[50] Claude Gauvard, "L'honneur du roi: peines et rituels judiciaires au Parlement de Paris à la fin du Moyen Âge," in *Les rites de la justice: gestes et rituels judiciaires au Moyen Âge occidental*, ed. Claude Gauvard and Robert Jacob, Cahiers du Léopard d'Or, no. 9 (Paris, 2000), 99–123, here 99–100. Elsewhere, speaking of the Parlement, Gauvard observes that "the court preferred banishment;" see "Les juges jugent-ils? Les peines prononcées par le Parlement criminel, vers 1380–vers 1425," in *Penser le pouvoir au Moyen Âge: VIIIe–XVe siècle*, ed. Dominique Boutet and Jacques Verger (Paris, 2000), 69–87, here 74.
[51] Gauvard, *"De grace especial."*

helped preserve judges from the threat of retaliation; he argues throughout his work for the adaptive nature of the Sienese ban.[52] Second, judgments were easily contested. As noted in chapter 2, judgments based on the testimony of two or more eye-witnesses were particularly difficult to uphold in Marseille's appellate court, for testimony could easily be excepted: homicides were often witnessed by groups of individuals who were partial to one party or the other, and hence most witnesses were exceptionable on some ground or another. Self-defense was another ready-made grounds for evading a criminal inquest or overturning a decision. Third, application of a contumacy fine allowed the court to evade the two-witness rule of Roman-canon legal procedure. Use of a fine made homicide cases equivalent to *delicta levia*, the petty crimes for which judges in the Roman-canon legal system did not need to have the testimony of two unimpeachable witnesses and could instead use their own discretion.[53] As a result, killers could be readily condemned on the circumstantial evidence of their flight, a known state of hatred with the victim, the existence of a prior threat, and so on. Fourth and finally, the practice of self-imposed exile and contumacy fines allowed for the easy mitigation of the harsh penalties nominally assigned by statute. Few judges or even citizens wished to see an upstanding member of the community executed for an honorable homicide.

The repatriation of slayers was the final stage of the system of exile and contumacy. Natalie Zemon Davis mentions how, after the successful negotiation of a letter of pardon, killers might be required to stay away for a year or two but were eventually restored to their communities as well as their prior good fama.[54] In Italy, the situation was more complex: as many have noted, the more stringent conditions imposed by many city-states led to the formation of a class of bandits, more or less permanent by the seventeenth century.[55] In fourteenth-century Marseille, the repatriation of the killer could be astonishingly rapid and thoroughgoing. I have already mentioned how Johan Casse never looked back after the murder of Marques de

[52] Pazzaglini, *Criminal Ban*, 71 and 101.

[53] Here I follow Langbein, who argues that "free judicial evaluation of the evidence" had been in place throughout the middle ages in any case involving *delicta levia* that would result in a fine or minor corporal punishment rather than blood sanctions; see *Torture and the Law of Proof* (Chicago, 1977), 48–49. Richard M. Fraher discusses the similar conclusions of the fifteenth-century legal scholar Gandinus in "Conviction according to Conscience: The Medieval Jurists' Debate concerning Judicial Discretion and the Law of Proof," *Law and History Review* 7 (1989): 23–88, here 42.

[54] Davis, *Fiction in the Archives*, 11.

[55] See esp. Osvaldo Raggio, *Faide e parentele: lo stato genovese visto dalla Fontanabuona* (Turin, 1990).

THE CONSUMPTION OF JUSTICE

Jerusalem. Amiel Bonafos, complicit in the murder of Peire de Jerusalem in 1356 and fined two thousand pounds in contumacy, was elected as one of the city's three syndics just five years later.[56] Banned for the killing of Bertomieu de Nantes in 1373, Fulco Alelin spent less than a month in sanctuary (23 November to 20 December).[57]

A similarly rapid rehabilitation is revealed during the appeal lodged by Jacme Albin, a smith, for the killing of Johan Areat. The case is very interesting from a number of angles and well worth considering in detail. Johan was a caulker by trade, and probably lived in or near the Caulkery, located near the port and to the west of the city's major centers. Early on the morning of 27 February 1403 Johan went to market with his small son to buy some mutton. Along the way, his son noticed a woman buying some fish, and, with a prescience fatally ignored by his father, pointed her out, saying, "There is the wife of the smith," Jacme Albin. Though witnesses did not explicitly say so there is more than a hint in the subsequent testimony that Jacme's wife, Fransesa, was acting as a lookout for her vengeance-minded husband. Presumably informed of his enemy's movements by his wife, Jacme set an ambush along the street of Caysarie, the route Johan would have to follow while returning to the Caulkery from the market. As Johan passed by, near the garden of Peire Audebert, Jacme and his two associates leaped out of an alley and attacked with swords, inflicting fourteen wounds on Johan's head and body before fleeing to the cathedral. We can only imagine what Johan's small son was thinking as he watched the butchery. Johan survived long enough to testify against his enemy. Jacme, safe in exile, was assessed a contumacy fine of four hundred pounds by the court of inquest. It was this fine that he subsequently appealed.

The long and lawyerly arguments made on Jacme's behalf, though unusual, were fully consonant with the state of penal practice in Marseille. The procurator began by pointing out that Johan had killed Jacme's brother, Guilhem Albin, the previous year, and had been condemned in contumacy and banished. Jacme, accordingly, had killed Johan so as to avenge the death of his brother (*vindicans mortem fratris sui*). Citing multiple precedents, the procurator went on to argue that such a killing was licit because Johan was still under the ban of homicide and, moreover, remained under the ban be-

[56] See the record of elections in AM BB 23, fols. 1–10. This was not simply because the Vivaut faction had taken control of the city council. Peire Carbonel, Vivaut de Jerusalem, and Guilhem de Montels, all related to the de Jerusalem party, were nominated to important offices on the council.

[57] ADBR 3B 94, see the instruments of banishment and appeal copied out on fols. 310r–313r, case opened 31 Jan. 1380 on fol. 307r.

cause he had *not* negotiated a peace with Jacme.[58] A copy of the instrument of Johan's banishment, dated 15 February 1402, was included in the record.[59]

The circumstances of the case show that the revenge killing, in an Italian fashion otherwise unusual in Marseille, took place near the anniversary of the original murder, and the space chosen—the street of Caysarie near the garden of Peire Audebert—was very near the spot where Jacme's brother Guilhem had died. We know this thanks to the existence of the record of an ecclesiastical inquest into that killing.[60] The transcript of this inquest reveals that the fight between Johan Areat and Guilhem Albin had broken out nearer the port. Both inflicted serious wounds on the other. Seeking sanctuary in the cathedral, Guilhem had been running along the street of Caysarie when he fell down dead from his wounds.

As far as banishment goes, though, the remarkable thing about these two records is that they show how Johan, himself a murderer, was absent from the city for less than a year, perhaps only a few months. It is doubtful that he had paid his own contumacy fine of three hundred pounds. Evidently, he had simply decided to return at some point during the year, and the court had shown little interest in pursuing him. So confident was he in his own security—a misplaced confidence, as events were to prove—that he freely went to market accompanied only by a small boy.

The thoroughly ingrained custom of seeking sanctuary and self-imposed exile meant that the court did not normally control, or even seek to control, the body of violent assailants. Marseille had a jail, of course, but it was described in several places as flimsy and seems to have been used more often to hold impecunious debtors at the behest of their creditors rather than assailants.[61] Arguments in the trial of Amiel Bonafos were made to the effect that the jail was so weak that his enemies could have easily broken in and killed him had Amiel chosen to return to the city to face criminal charges. Some observers, moreover, felt that it just wasn't necessary to imprison respectable people. In 1405, Colin de Bosco saw fit to protest when a friend of his was being taken off to jail by officials of the court. "You can find him any day. He is a servant of the knight Lazarus Deodati, and it would please Lazarus not to have him taken away."[62] For his pains, Colin was charged in court with hindering a lawful arrest.

The fact that late medieval justice, on the whole, preferred monetary

[58] ADBR 3B 140, fols. 267r–269r, case opened 11 July 1403 on fol. 229r.

[59] Ibid., fols. 269v–270r.

[60] ADBR 5G 772, fol. 91v, case opened 20 Aug. 1402 on fol. 81r.

[61] See ADBR 3B 820, fols. 47r, case opened 7 July 1356 on fol. 8r, and ibid., fol. 161v, case opened 12 July 1356 on fol. 133r.

[62] ADBR 3B 856, fol. 7v, case opened 27 June 1405 on fol. 5r.

penalties to blood sanctions does not mean officials handled all criminals with kid gloves. Blood sanctions were too useful an exemplum to forego entirely, and literary and visual sources ranging from the poems of Ronsard to the paintings of Brueghel show that, at least by the sixteenth century, the state's use of blood sanctions did not fail to make an impression on the intended audience. Statutory and customary laws from the Continent are filled with descriptions of gruesome punishments, some of them illustrated in lavish detail, and some states, such as Venice, seem to have punished or executed homicides at an exceedingly high rate.[63] From time to time Marseille's courts, too, opted for blood sanctions. The registers of the clavaires record payments made to executioners for certain corporal punishments. In 1316 Johan de Nicia lost his foot and the executioner received 18d. for his efforts. Later in the year, a barber named Johan de Paris was whipped and a thief named Ugo de Monpelier whipped and mutilated in an unspecified way.[64] Over the course of several days in 1290 Ugo Gaudin committed a series of aggressions against some unnamed Jews in the Jewry and was condemned to pay a fine of twenty-five pounds or lose his left hand. His wife Maria appealed the sentence, citing their poverty as an extenuating factor, and the fine was reduced on appeal to ten pounds.[65] It is not known whether he was able to pay the fine and keep his hand. On 6 May 1331, a carpenter named Guilhem Ugo was paid 8s. to build a platform for the purpose of excising the feet, ears, and hands of malefactors.[66] An appeal from 1319 reveals that a weaver named Raymon de Narbona was to be whipped through the streets, perforated through his tongue, and placed in the stocks from midday till evening if he failed to pay a fine of twenty-five pounds within three days, although in the event Raymon successfully appealed this sentence.[67] The success of his appeal suggests that such savage sanctions were usually doled out for form's sake rather than with any serious intention of applying them. Even so, Monet Blete could not have used the threat, "Unless you make peace with me I will ensure that you lose a foot or a fist," to force his incarcerated enemy Jacme Bosquet to make peace with him unless this were at least within the realm of possibility.[68]

There are even a few instances of capital punishment. Some of these,

---

[63] Ruggiero, *Violence in Early Renaissance Venice*, 47–49. It is not clear whether the figures cited represent penalties actually carried out or penalties imposed by the court, though the discussion suggests the former.

[64] ADBR B 1939, fols. 12v–13v.

[65] ADBR 3B 802, fols. 41v–42v, case opened May 1290.

[66] ADBR 3B 1940, fol. 202r.

[67] ADBR 3B 804, fols. 3v–4r, case opened 19 Jan. 1319.

[68] ADBR B 1943, fol. 25r.

again, are recorded in the financial registers of the clavaires. On 1 February 1316, Johan de Charchasona was hung, and the record notes a payment of 4d. for the rope. Later in the year, both Isnart Raynut and Giraut Ugo were hung, the latter because of his many crimes.[69] A register from the fiscal year 1330–31 reveals a payment made on 12 December 1330 to a Genoese canvas-maker named Mathieu for the purchase of enough canvas to make two sacks for drowning malefactors (*saccos duos pro malefactoribus submergendis*), an element of classical Roman penal law, though there is no record of them actually being used. Early registers of the court of first appeals include several appeals arising from condemnations for homicide. In one of them, from 1308, Raimundet Berengier was condemned to be hung for both murder and theft, though the condemnation was annulled on appeal.[70] Another appellate case from 1357 shows that a foreigner named Boryaca or Buryata was hung.[71]

How does one measure the frequency of blood sanctions versus monetary sanctions? As Jacques Chiffoleau has remarked, blood sanctions usually do not show up in fiscal records and thus have a tendency to be underreported.[72] The logic is impeccable. In the case of Marseille, such reasoning would suggest that the near-total absence of remits for homicide in the records of the clavaires—a subject I will address at greater length in the next section—is evidence that homicides were punished capitally. I would be inclined to agree with Chiffoleau were it not for the fact that the system of sanctuary, exile, and contumacy fines is so very well defined in the records and so clearly and wholly superseded blood sanctions. The lesson to be learned from the records of payments made to executioners, moreover, is that limbing, whipping, and hanging *did* cost money and do show up from time to time in financial records, perhaps especially so in Angevin realms where the fiscal obsessions of Charles I of Anjou led to the creation of one of the most sophisticated accounting systems of the later middle ages.[73] Given the existence of this system the paucity of references is good evidence for the paucity of blood sanctions. The record for the year 1316 includes a total of three hangings and three mutilations or whippings.[74] Another of the clavaires' registers, this one from 1330–31, has a neatly demarcated section of

<hr>

69 ADBR B 1939, fols. 12v–13v.

70 ADBR 3B 803, fols. 126r–128v, case opened 1 July 1308.

71 ADBR 3B 822, fols. 25r–35v, case opened 18 Sept. 1357.

72 Chiffoleau, *Justices du pape*, 148.

73 In general, see Édouard Baratier, *Enquêtes sur les droits et revenus de Charles Ier d'Anjou en Provence, 1252 et 1278* (Paris, 1969).

74 ADBR 3B 1939.

expenses called "On Executions."[75] This records the hanging of two men and one woman and five mutilations inflicted on three men and two women. The total expenses came to one pound 10s. 10d. There is every evidence that this was a complete accounting. Eight cases over the course of a year in a city of twenty to twenty-five thousand people, though doubtless spectacles of considerable interest to Marseille's citizenry, represent a singularly unimpressive application of blood sanctions. A record from 1409 includes a single payment for a ladder and other expenses for hanging Augustin Nodot.[76] The sole surviving record of the secular court of inquest confirms the paucity of blood sanctions. This records only one potential blood sanction in fifty-four verdicts of guilty over the space of seven months, and this against a habitual thief named Nicolau del Foliayret.[77] Blood sanctions, in short, were relatively uncommon in late medieval Marseille.

Blood sanctions—like torture, as it turns out—were almost invariably used on unconnected foreigners like Boryaca and out-and-out ruffians like Nicolau del Foliayret. The presence of relatively unusual "foreign" names among the examples recorded above—Johan de Nicia, Johan de Paris, Ugo de Monpelier, Johan de Charchasona—is itself indicative of this tendency. Records of remits paid to the clavaires show that the vast majority of "crimes" in Marseille were committed by ordinary citizens in the pursuit of ordinary hatreds. Such men and women rarely, if ever, suffered bodily sanctions. But how was one to know who was who? What distinguished the respectable from the disreputable was fama, the things that people said, a subject that already came up in chapter 2, and one to which I will return in chapter 5. Structures of affection and hatred, of course, more or less ensure that everyone had bad fama with at least someone, so it is well to stress that a person was truly infamous only if she or he was infamous in the eyes of all. The rotation of judges means that judges were usually incapable of distinguishing the fama of those who appeared before them. Some of the work of identification may have been done by notaries and other permanent residents who staffed the courts. But the system also had a built-in famadetection system. First, the outdoor venue meant that judges could assess the community response and make decisions about torture and blood sanctions, perhaps unconsciously, on the grounds of what they heard and saw.

[75] ADBR 3B 1940, fol. 243r.

[76] ADBR 3B 1944, fol. 49r–v.

[77] ADBR 3B 96, fols. 158r–160v, case opened 7 Nov. 1380. It is true that corporal punishments could be applied if an individual failed to pay the fine assessed, though there don't seem to have been many if any such cases in this record. A multitude of marginal notes all confirm that the fines were collected (*collecta sunt* is the expression).

Second, individuals unable to pay a fine and hence subjected to blood sanctions would prove their infamy not just because they were poor and without bona but also, and far more importantly, because they were without friends or pledges willing and able to lend them money. As argued in chapter 3, most men and women in Marseille were enmeshed in networks of both credit and debt. These networks revealed to judges and other observers that the people in question were embedded in networks of trust and hence were well-spoken of and had good fama. Such was the case with a butcher named Durant Imbert, condemned in 1413 to suffer a whipping and the loss of his left ear, followed by banishment, for theft. The whipping, the ear-cutting, and the banishment were successfully bought off by his friends who paid twenty pounds composition on his behalf to the courts.[78] Failure to find lenders and pledges was proof of infamy. The need to maintain one's fama so as to avoid blood sanctions adds yet another anxious dimension to the practice of debt litigation: through pursuit of debt, creditors attacked the fama of debtors. Debtors, in turn, proved their own good fame by publicly resisting creditors' claims in various ways.

There is one major exception to the rule that blood sanctions were only applied against marginal figures, an exception that brings us to torture. Corporal punishment was always inflicted outdoors. Torture, by contrast, was always performed indoors, out of the public eye. For this reason it was easier for officials to get away with ignoring the fama of the person at hand.

Standard works on the role of torture in Roman-canon procedural law suggest that torture was both a necessary and a common form of proof in the regions of late medieval Europe that adhered to Roman-canon law.[79] Several references in the records from Marseille indeed show that people were afraid of torture and bitterly resented the denunciations of their enemies that led them to be tortured. Recorded instances of torture, however, are relatively rare. The sole surviving record of the court of inquest shows one instance of torture in eighty-three inquests, involving the thief Nicolau, and there are no extant depositions made by tortured defendants in any of the several dozen surviving criminal appeals. Appellate records do record some interesting appeals arising from torture cases. In one case from 1357, a young man and pauper named Guilhem Robaut appealed a condemnation for homicide on the grounds that torture had caused him to admit to a crime he hadn't committed and that torture should not in any event have been inflicted on one less than twenty-five years of age.[80] In another case, torture was inflicted on a res-

---

[78] ADBR B 1947, fol. 25r.
[79] Notably Langbein, *Torture and the Law of Proof.*
[80] ADBR 3B 822, fols. 84r–85r, case opened 15 Dec. 1357.

ident of La Ciotat thought to be guilty of the murder of a citizen of Marseille in Naples, and he was released from torture when he called out to the notary, asking that an instrument be made to the effect that he was not under the jurisdiction of Marseille's court and was therefore being tortured illegally.[81] In a third, a Jewish obstetrician (*obstetrix, abstetrix*) named Floreta appealed a ruling of the court of inquest that she be tortured in a case involving the death of one of her clients.[82] The case is stunning and, most unfortunately, all too short. Her client, a woman named Gasseneta Aymbarda, had failed to deliver the afterbirth. A female Christian obstetrician tied the umbilical cord to Gasseneta's thigh but then called in Floreta to give advice and assistance in the case. Numerous witnesses reported that in an effort to dislodge the placenta from Gasseneta's uterus, Floreta had inserted her hand up to the elbow, but the cord broke when she gave it a tug from inside and Gasseneta subsequently bled to death. Floreta categorically denied this accusation but the judge ruled that there was sufficient evidence to torture her. His reasoning is unclear to me, since there were more than enough eyewitnesses to sustain a conviction. This was the ruling that Floreta, following normal procedures, appealed. Her appeal is not extant.

As Edward Peters has observed, and as these cases illustrate, judicial torture was law-bound.[83] But more than that, it was culture-bound. Torture was characteristically inflicted on the marginal and unconnected: a poor man, a foreigner, a Jewish woman. A similar situation holds in the nearby Provençal town of Manosque, where Steven Bednarski notes only four instances of torture in more than fifteen hundred criminal inquests between 1340 and 1403, all of them used on foreigners.[84] Servants in Marseille were also fair game. Complaining bitterly in 1356 about the tendency of the court to favor members of the de Jerusalem faction while allowing the Vivaut to linger in jail, Ugo Vivaut went on to say that the viguier had even had a servant of Jacme de Galbert "raised on the horse," the common euphemism for torture.[85] An interesting reference in a witness defamation procedure in 1355 shows that the fact of having been tortured became subsequent proof of infamy. Asked to say something about the fama of a hostile witness Antoni de Pontu, Esteve Vassal remarked that Antoni had often been arrested for various crimes and "lifted on the horse" (*in eculeo elevatus*).[86] Judicial torture, in

[81] ADBR 3B 811, fols. 3r–13r, case opened 26 Nov. 1351.
[82] ADBR 3B 140, fols. 2r–16r, case opened before 23 March 1402.
[83] Edward Peters, *Torture* (New York, 1985).
[84] Steven Bednarski, "Crime, justice et régulation sociale à Manosque, 1340–1403" (Thèse [Ph.D.], Université de Montréal, 2002).
[85] ADBR 3B 820, fol. 75v, case opened 7 July 1356 on fol. 8r.
[86] ADBR 3B 819, fol. 15r, case opened 23 May 1355 on fol. 9r.

short, was almost exclusively applied to those with little *fama*, just as the jurist Gandinus later prescribed in his fifteenth-century "Treatise on Crimes."[87] In this regard the exercise of judicial torture paralleled that of the ordeal in earlier centuries, which, in the rare situations where it was used at all, was characteristically employed as a mode of proof only in cases where the suspect was not oath-worthy or did not have sufficient standing to merit trial by battle.

Questioning arguments that torture was a vital element of the Roman-canon law of proof in late medieval Europe, Richard Fraher notes that "torture was not employed as often as one would have expected if it were the only means of escaping the inefficiencies created by the scholastic law of proof."[88] In Provence, likewise, torture was rare: the vast majority of defendants hauled before the criminal court were simply not considered torture-worthy. Torture may also have been rare in northern France: a late fifteenth-century record of the Châtelet indicates twenty instances of torture in six hundred cases, and torture was applied in just 17 percent of the cases heard before the Parlement of Paris in the mid-sixteenth century.[89] Despite the low rate of torture in Marseille, however, proof was not a problem. As discussed below, most men or women accused of simple crimes simply confessed. Some were found guilty on the basis of eyewitness testimony and some were let go for insufficient proof. But in virtually all serious cases—severe wounds, the amputation of limbs, and murders—the accused simply fled the city and paid fines for contumacy.

There is one caveat to this rule: extrajudicial torture. A few records reveal the existence of a belief that officials of the court had no scruples about using torture against their own personal enemies and on behalf of their friends and factional associates. Ugo Vivaut, attesting to the torture of the servant of Jacme de Galbert, also noted that Guilhem Chabert, a member of the Martin party, which was closely allied to the Vivaut, had been tortured by the viguier in the absence of any judge (*sine iudice*). This was proof of the vengeful and illegal nature of this torture.[90] Guilhem, probably a cobbler, was certainly no servant and normally not torture-worthy. There is a good deal of evidence suggesting how normal it was for officials of the court to have enemies and hate them, and the power to torture personal enemies

---

[87] Fraher, "Conviction," 47.

[88] Ibid.

[89] Cited in Gauvard, "*De grace especial*", 1:162 and 1:157. Ruggiero also argues for a low torture rate in the case of Venice; see *Violence in Early Renaissance Venice*, 24. Cases of theft were an exception (29).

[90] ADBR 3B 820, fol. 75v, case opened 7 July 1356 on fol. 8r.

who had fallen under their power was, in some cases, evidently too tempting to pass up.

Assuming that such accusations were at all justified—and there is no particular reason for doubting them—what they show is that officials of the court were just as embedded in structures of hatred as anyone else. Given that members of Marseille's factions each had representatives among court officials, one could also say that the factions themselves invested in the state-sponsored system of coercive force as part of an investment in their own vengeance games. They certainly showed every willingness to denounce and testify against their enemies at court. The Vivaut and the de Jerusalem did not constitute a mafia with a concept of *omertà* and a perception that the state is the common enemy. Factions happily worked hand-in-hand with the courts to avenge themselves on their adversaries.

None of this comes as any surprise to historians familiar with the situation in Italy, where Guelfs and Ghibellines made free use of the courts against their enemies. What is also interesting about Marseille is that those who filled the office of the sub-viguier were themselves widely perceived—and not only by their victims—as violent and criminous individuals who trampled on the liberties and privileges of Marseille's citizens. Several complaints about illicit behavior were heard by the city council, as in 1351, when Amiel Bonafos asked the viguier to imprison the sub-viguier and punish him for his enormous crimes.[91] Evidently the normal alliance between the sub-viguier and the Vivaut was not working this year. Elsewhere the sub-viguier and his servitors were accused of destroying rented property, theft, unpaid debts, excessive force, and, in 1355, the murder of Jacme Bertran.[92] In keeping with this hostility, the policing activities of the sub-viguier seem to have been perceived as moves in the vengeance game. It felt like a feud. It just so happened that the adversary consisted of a crown official and his *familia*, but it was a feud nonetheless.

With historical hindsight, it is just possible to imagine a distinction between private, family-based violence on the one hand and public, law-based coercion on the other. In practice, the distinction barely existed in the eyes of contemporaries. Among other things, the criminal court in certain respects relied as much on private force as it did on the sub-viguier. In a nutshell, public force was shot through with private interests and private force served public interests. No formal distinction between the two kinds of force can be made.

[91] Mabilly, *Inventaire*, 67. The original is AM BB 21, fol. 146.
[92] Examples include AM FF 170, fol. 11r–v; ADBR 3B 49, fol. 11r–v; 3B 57, fols. 2r–19v, case opened 8 Oct. 1354; AM FF 16, liasse dated 28 Apr. 1429; and ADBR 3B 819, passim.

# BONA

At the end of an interrogation, as discussed in chapter 2, a witness in civil cases was routinely asked a series of questions designed to help the judge decide how trustworthy the witness was. The questions varied from one case to another and could include interrogations requested by the adversary. Several questions, however, were more or less universal, and one of these was how much bona a witness possessed. The answers to this question, "How much does s/he have in bona" (*Quantum habet in bonis*) were thoughtful and, presumably, reasonably accurate, since the urge to inflate one's worth would have been tempered by concern lest the tax collector find out. Answers range from a high figure of three thousand pounds, the assessment given by Alexander Giraut in 1352, to twelve pounds.[93] A thirty-six-year-old married woman named Johaneta Marine, in her response to an interrogation in 1380, distinguished between the two hundred pounds she owned outright and the one thousand pounds she owned by virtue of her dowry.[94] A number of witnesses, perhaps concerned about the tax collector, were said to have guardedly replied, "He [or she] is secure with what he has" (*est contentus de sua*), and several young witnesses reported that they were worth nothing because they were still in *patria potestas*.[95]

The posing of the question serves as a useful reminder of the tight association between personal worth and community standing that is characteristic of many premodern societies. Worth was measured not in annual salary but rather in bona, the goods that one possessed. Friends, kinfolk, neighbors, and enemies were keenly aware of the current value of someone's bona and gossiped about it endlessly. For wives and creditors this gossip served a basic economic function, for it was on the basis of such talk that the decision to extend or withhold credit was determined. A concerned wife typically initiated a claim for a dotal retrocession with the observation that it was public knowledge that her husband had been "badly using his substance" (*male utitur substancia sua*), thus justifying her attempt to recover her dowry from the insolvent estate. Evidence for the social evaluation of bona is abundant and could easily fill an entire chapter in its own right. The practice itself is common in human societies and, like hatred and love, was something people

---

93  For Alexander Giraut, see 3B 812, fol. 32v, case opened 1 June 1352 on fol. 26r.
94  ADBR 3B 94, fol. 272v, case opened 9 Dec. 1379 on fol. 193v.
95  For example, ADBR 3B 152, fol. 72v, case opened 18 Nov. 1416 on fol. 47r.

talked about quite a lot. In the present context, I make the observation only to point out why a system of penal sanction based on the payment of fines, and if necessary the forcible distraint and auctioning off of bona, was both punitive and, in the context, morally appropriate.

Given the infrequency of corporal punishment, the penal sanctions applied in late medieval Marseille consisted almost entirely of fines. This is true elsewhere in Provence and generally in late medieval Europe.[96] Discussing northern Italian cities, Fraher notes that "it is clear that the city-states imposed fines and exile rather than corporal punishment, even for homicide. Possibly, this was to escape the stringency of the law of proof in criminal cases involving corporal sanctions, but it might have been that fines and exile were socially preferable to sanguinary punishment."[97] Especially significant is the fact that, in Marseille, the fine was understood by contemporaries to be the normal penalty in homicide cases. We know this thanks to a remarkable argument made in a suit heard in 1334. The defendant in this suit lodged an exception against one of his adversary's witnesses on the grounds that he was publicly defamed as a homicide, and called his own witnesses to prove the defamation. The plaintiff was well within his legal rights to insist that bad fama alone was not enough. Witnesses to the exception had to prove that the homicide really had taken place, and were asked to give corroborating details: the name of the victim, how the homicide was committed, which viguier announced the condemnation, and the sentence applied. Here's the crucial bit: Witnesses were not asked whether he was sentenced to any bodily mutilation. Instead, they were asked to identify the amount of the fine in which he was condemned (quantam fuit illa quantitas in qua fuit condempnatus).[98] As this chance bit of testimony so clearly records, the normal sanction for homicide was understood to be a fine, not mutilation, still less an execution.

Five itemized records of fines received by the crown have survived be-

---

[96] For Provence, see Rodrigue Lavoie, "Endettement et pauvreté en Provence d'après les listes de la justice comtale, XIVe et XVe siècles," *Provence historique* 23 (1973): 201–16, here 204. See also the fuller discussion in his "Les statistiques criminelles et le visage du justicier: justice royale et justice seigneuriale en Provence au Moyen Âge," *Provence historique* 115 (1979): 3–20. For northern France, see Gauvard, *"De grace especial"*; for the Lyonnais, see Gonthier, *Délinquance, justice et société*, 228; for southwestern France, see Leah Otis-Cour, "'Terreur et exemple, compassion et miséricorde': la repression pénale à Pamiers à la fin du Moyen Âge," in *Justice et justiciables: mélanges Henri Vidal*, Recueil de mémoires et travaux, vol. 16 (Montpellier, 1994), 139–64.

[97] Fraher, "Conviction," 43. See also the discussion in Chambers and Dean, *Clean Hands*, 72–74.

[98] ADBR 3B 28, loose page between fols. 68–69, case opened 12 July 1334 on fol. 29r.

**Table 4.1 High, Low, and Median Fines for Criminal Acts, 1330–1413**

| Selected Categories | High | Low | Median |
|---|---|---|---|
| Insult, threat | 3 li. | 10 s. | 1 li. |
| Throwing rocks (no bloodshed) | 3 li. | 1 li. | 2 li. |
| Other assaults (no bloodshed) | 10 li. | 10 s. | 3 li. |
| Women's adultery | 10 li. | 5 li. | 5 li. |
| Assault with bloodshed or assaults to the head | 50 li. | 1 li. 12 s. | 10 li. |
| Theft | 25 li. | 5 li. | 14 li. |

*Sources:* ADBR B 1940, 1943, 1944, 1945, 1947.

tween 1330 and 1413 and these give us a good sense of the tariff of penalties applied in cases of assault.[99] Insults and threats were the least heavily penalized, with a median payment of one pound, representing five to ten days of work for an average citizen. Rock throwing was a crime that shows up relatively often in the sources and was usually penalized around two pounds unless blood was shed. The shedding of blood dramatically increased the size of all fines. By way of comparison, women's adultery was penalized less heavily than assaults leading to the drawing of blood, whereas property theft was much more severely penalized.

Strikingly absent from these records, however, are any remits explicitly for the crime of homicide. The closest we get is a remit of six pounds paid in 1331 on behalf of little Guilhem Guis, an eleven year old who chased after and tried to stab a man fatally wounded by Guilhem's brother, Johanet Guis. Johanet himself does not show up in the record. The total absence of remits for homicide is in no way the product of a penal system based on blood sanctions. Instead, it reflects both the system of sanctuary and exile as well as the tendency for homicides to end up in the ecclesiastical court, a subject discussed at greater length in the next section. Killers may well show up in these financial records but if so they are being fined for crimes such as bearing illegal arms, making illicit congregations, and going about at night without a lantern.

The one exception to this consists of several remits for contumacy. Anyone who failed to answer a summons was liable to a sentence for contumacy. This goes for violent assailants in sanctuary and exile, bankrupts who had fled their debts, and, for that matter, anyone who just happened to be absent from the city at the time of the summons and had made no arrangements for a procurator. One remit for contumacy is recorded in 1331, when Garsens Audite paid a fine of eight pounds on behalf of Johan Andree for wounds he had inflicted on the body of Pelegrina Blanquerie some six years earlier, in

---

[99] Such tariffs, which tended to limit judicial discretion, were a commonplace in southern French legal practice from the thirteenth century onward; see Carbasse, *Introduction*, 90. For the tariff of nearby Manosque, see Bednarski, "Crime, justice."

1325.[100] Johan, it seems, had been formally banished for this entire time, though given the example of Johan Areat this does not necessarily mean that he was gone the entire time. The small size of the fine suggests that the victim had not died of her wounds. Later, in 1407, a register noting that a mariner named Bernat Viguier had paid off a contumacy fine of forty pounds explicitly states that the victim, Peire Garet, had died of his wounds, which prompted Bernat to take flight.[101] Bernat evidently was allowed to pay in installments because this register records the receipt of only twenty-five pounds. The register from 1412–13 is exceptional in that it records seven remits for contumacy. The reasons for these charges of contumacy are not always given, but several of the original fines—one for three hundred pounds and one for five hundred pounds—are high enough to suggest that they arose from homicides.[102]

Records from the first appellate court provide clearer details on contumacy fines. They show that the fines assessed for contumacy in murder cases ranged from fifty pounds to as high as seven thousand pounds. In 1308 a group of cousins, all from the Engles family, took flight after the murder of Peire Raymon and were assessed between fifty pounds and two hundred pounds each for their contumacy.[103] Another appellate case from this register reveals that a miller named Peire Bibaygas was condemned by the court to a fine of one hundred pounds for contumacy.[104] This case clearly indicates that Peire had been arrested and subsequently banished before his trial. The factional violence that set in from the 1340s through the 1360s raised contumacy fines to new heights. For the murder of Peire de Jerusalem in 1356, Amiel Bonafos and Giraut de Buco were each assessed a contumacy fine of two thousand pounds and heavier fines of four thousand pounds and seven thousand pounds were issued to the Martin brothers.[105] Guilhem de Belavila was assessed five hundred pounds for his contumacy following the murder of Guilhem Tomas in 1365.[106] Such variation suggests that the social standing of the victim had a bearing on the fine. Peire de Jerusalem was one of the most noteworthy men in the city at the time, as were his killers. Guilhem Tomas and Guilhem de Belavila were, comparatively speaking, small fry. It remains possible that contumacy fines, follow-

[100] ADBR B 1940, fol. 95r.

[101] ADBR B 1943, fol. 22v.

[102] ADBR B 1947, fol. 53r.

[103] ADBR 3B 803. There are three consecutive appeals in this register beginning on fol. 109r, case opened 17 June 1308.

[104] Ibid., fol. 122v, case opened 11 Kalendas of July 1308 on fol. 122v.

[105] ADBR 3B 820, fols. 1r and 8r. Giraut de Buco's fine is at fol. 133r, case opened 12 July 1356.

[106] ADBR 3B 825, fol. 35r, case opened 13 May 1365.

ing older rules, were assessed at the rate of one-third of the delinquent's estate.[107] Whatever the practice, subsequent fines for contumacy in Marseille never quite reached the dizzying heights of the 1350s.

Contumacy fines were very hard to resist. In Marseille and elsewhere in Mediterranean Europe a contumacious individual could not be represented by a procurator.[108] Judges of the court of inquest in Marseille applied this rule systematically and refused to hear procurators representing clients in sanctuary or exile. This created a legal impasse, because appellants like Amiel Bonafos and Guilhem de Belavila, citing the danger posed by the victim's friends and kin, uniformly insisted on the impossibility of returning to face charges. Guilhem de Belavila added a twist to this argument by pointing out that he *had* testified before a judge on the charges made against him. The palace judge, Leonardo da Siena, had personally come to the cathedral where Guilhem and Fulco Robaut had taken sanctuary in order to take down their testimony.[109] The judge, clearly, didn't think this qualified as a formal appearance. Underlying this apparently superficial difference of opinion are rich sets of ideas about courts as spatial entities. Guilhem seems to be arguing that the court was a portable space forming around the body of the judge and moving with him. The judge, in turn, seems to have thought that a court was a gravitational center to which a humbled defendant must be drawn.

Given that Alexander Giraut, with goods valued at three thousand pounds, was one of the richest men in Marseille, the fines assessed against Amiel Bonafos and the Martin brothers were ludicrously high and probably beyond their capacity to pay, even assuming heavy borrowing from friends and relatives. Did the court seriously think that these fines for contumacy would ever be paid? As it turns out, many fines for contumacy, if paid at all, were reduced on appeal and sometimes voided altogether. All the contumacy fines appealed in 1308 were reduced by some degree. Jordan Engles, for example, had his contumacy fine of fifty pounds reduced on appeal to fifteen pounds, ten pounds of which was for the contumacy and five pounds for the deed itself (*factum principale*). His cousins' fines were similarly reduced. In this same register, a goldsmith named Sifren Ugo had fled the city

---

[107] For this rule see *The Liber Augustalis; or Constitutions of Melfi, Promulgated by the Emperor Frederick II for the Kingdom of Sicily in 1231*, trans. James M. Powell (Syracuse, 1971), 58: "We order that in the future the contumacious person, regardless of rank, who has been accused in a civil or criminal case, should be fined the third part of his movable goods." Later, rules and procedures regarding contumacy were strengthened (see 65–73).

[108] See Catherine Guimbard, "Exil et institution du *comune* à Florence dans la seconde moitié du XIIIe siècle," in *Exil et civilisation en Italie (XIIe–XVIe siècles)*, ed. Jacques Heers and Christian Bec (Nancy, France, 1990), 21–31, here 25.

[109] ADBR 3B 825, fol. 71v, case opened 13 May 1365 on fol. 35r.

following a street battle; his victim did not die, and on appeal his contumacy fine of eight pounds was reduced to six pounds.[110] Later appellate records do not provide sentences so it is a little difficult telling what happened, say, to the fines assessed against the Martin brothers. The seven remits for contumacy from 1412 and 1413, however, all reveal important reductions in the fines. The laborer Guilhem Bonafos paid only twelve pounds 10 shillings out of an original contumacy fine of one hundred pounds. Another laborer, Peire Raynaut, had a contumacy fine of three hundred pounds reduced to twenty-nine pounds.[111] Other reductions were less spectacular, ranging from a half to a third of the original fine. The record of the bishop's court from 1400 shows that a cleric was fined thirty-five pounds for homicide, suggesting that the courts in the early fourteenth century could normally expect to get at least a few dozen pounds out of a homicide. In the case of the killers of Mathea Sadaroni, the record notes that two hundred pounds had been seized from the estates of the three who had fled the city.

A significant point here is that contumacious individuals were not normally stripped of all their bona. Kenneth Meredith has noted that the *coutumiers* of northern France "usually called for the confiscation of the property of both executed criminals and persons who had been forbanned." The possessions of the contumacious individual, in theory, were seized, ravaged by the crown, and returned to the lord.[112] In Florence, banishment was considered equivalent to infamy and civil death.[113] By comparison, the contumacious individual in Marseille was treated with considerably more leniency. As discussed in the next section, it often proved very difficult for the court to carry out a seizure of goods.

This system based on sanctuary, exile, and contumacy fines was already well established by the early decades of the fourteenth century and remained more or less intact throughout the fourteenth and fifteenth centuries. As a method for dealing with serious violence it has a lot to recommend it. Among other things, homicides were probably very difficult to prosecute. As noted above, most killings were shot through with hatreds that would have rendered suspect much witness testimony. Fines for contumacy were a different matter, for they were assessed for nonappearance.[114] The facts of the case, in short, were neatly deflected onto a wholly uncontestable terrain. It has been suggested that the ordeal could function as a

---

110 ADBR 3B 803, fols. 147v–148v, case opened 23 Dec. 1308.
111 ADBR B 1947, fols. 30v and 53r.
112 Meredith, "Penalty for Banishment," 329.
113 Guimbard, "Exil et institution," 25.
114 For comparison with the northern French customaries, see Meredith, "Penalty of Banishment," 327–29.

form of proof insofar as it transformed arguments about wrongs into arguments about scars. The practice of transforming killers into contumacious individuals fits this model even better than do ordeals. The coercive force wielded by victims' friends and families played a tacit role in this transformation from murderer to contumacious individual, since it was fear of vengeance that prevented the assailant from facing the charges against him. As this shows, family-based violence was built into the basic system for handling homicides in fourteenth-century Marseille.

The use of contumacy fines means that virtually every crime successfully condemned by the court of inquest, ranging from the mildest insult to the gravest homicide, was transformed into a debt. Words, deeds, debts: these were all one in a cultural system of reckoning that assessed transactions not by their content but by the resulting transactional imbalance. The practical consequence of this system is that virtually all men and women condemned by the court of inquest were transformed into debtors and then handed over to the system of public debt recovery. Like the rest of Provence and other parts of Europe, Marseille had an efficient public mechanism for debt recovery from the late thirteenth or early fourteenth century onward.[115] Creditors who showed up in court with reasonable evidence for the existence of a debt—a notarial contract, a handwritten note, a shop cartulary—could acquire a mandament demanding repayment of the debt either from the debtor or the debtor's pledge. The criminal court, as a creditor, could move more directly. In all cases, the court's role in the act of recovery began with a simple summons. If this failed to encourage repayment, judges ordered the forcible distraint of the debtor's bona, a responsibility that fell on the shoulders of messengers of the court (*nuncii*), sometimes accompanied by servitors of the sub-viguier. For small debts, messengers were instructed to go to the house of the debtor and seize small, portable items. If a trial was ongoing and the debt promised to be large, a house might be sealed with tape and the goods removed and temporarily stored with trustworthy individuals, such as officials of the court or their wives or even their widows.[116] If the movables were insufficient, then the debtor's real property could be seized, assessed, and a percentage equal to the amount of the debt transmitted to the creditor. Once a verdict was reached, goods were either handed over to the creditor or auctioned off by Jewish pawnbrokers and auctioneers (*corraterii et inquantatores*), with the proceeds going to the creditor. Records of oaths taken by the auctioneers in the 1350s and 1360s show that they

[115] Joseph Shatzmiller, *Shylock Reconsidered: Jews, Moneylending, and Medieval Society* (Berkeley, 1990), 12–14.

[116] For an instance of the latter practice see ADBR 3B 839, fols. 68r–77v, case opened 22 Sept. 1386.

swore to auction goods openly, so as to ensure that debtors' bona were not fraudulently undervalued.[117] A case heard in 1386 turns on precisely this issue: a golden vessel studded with pearls and other precious gems was allegedly seized for debt and auctioned off for less than its value of two thousand florins.[118]

Further safeguards against the possibility of fraudulent auctions were provided by public mechanisms for assessing the value of goods taken. Though messengers seem to have had considerable latitude when taking security, the assessment of both movables and immovables, especially in cases of large debts, was formally the responsibility of a body of officials known as the general assessors of goods (*extimatores generales bonorum*). Thirty-one rulings of these officials are preserved in a cartulary extant from the year 1421, an example of which follows:[119]

The honorable men Ugo dal Templo, Peire Dalmas, and Montolevet de Montoliu, general assessors of goods in the city of Marseille, reported to the noble and honorable lord Guilhem de Mellomonte, judge of one of the lesser chambers of the palace court of the city of Marseille . . . , that by the order of the said lord judge and at the insistence of Leo Vidas, Jew of this city, they assessed for Leo Vidas [*extimasse eidem Leoni Vidas*] in and on the goods of Greardus de Avinione, a laborer, and Maritona his wife, citizens of Marseille, up to the amount identified in the mandament written below, the tenor of which follows.[120]

Where property was involved, a notarized contract known as an *extimatio* (assessment) was subsequently drawn up on behalf of the new proprietor. Sixty-six such contracts are extant in the notarial archives from the years 1337 to 1362, suggesting that this period saw an original total of between six hundred and fifty and one thousand such contracts, around twenty-five to forty per year. Usually an entire house or plot of land was assessed and transferred to the creditor, but in some cases the creditors received only a portion, as in a contract from 1344 in which the creditor, Resens Gauteria, received one-third of a house belonging to the estate of the late Andrieu Tollays.[121] The assessments could be quite precise. In 1347, Raymon Bonvin received exactly ten palms and ten and three-quarters digits of a house for-

---

[117] AM FF 166.
[118] ADBR 3B 839, fols. 3r–40v, case opened 11 Sept. 1386.
[119] AM FF 1009.
[120] Ibid., fol. 29r.
[121] ADBR 381E 394, fol. 51r, 17 Feb. 1344.

merly belonging to Peire de Roussillon.[122] Fragments of houses or plots of land show up from time to time in the cartularies of direct lords. A record of properties held under the direct lordship of the Angevin crown, from the year 1331, reveals a workshop half of which was owned by Symiona Romete, and half by Bondavin de Draguignan.[123] This was clearly a situation where half the workshop had been transferred to Bondavin to extinguish a debt.

The process of distraint was itself expensive and costs were assigned to the debtors, adding to their woes. In 1358, to take just one example, a debtor named Biatris de Tollono was ordered by the court to repay not only the debt she owed to her creditor but also a total of 3s. 5d. to two notaries and three messengers for writing out and delivering the summons and mandaments.[124] The record of the general assessors of goods mentioned above carefully itemized not only the principal debt but also the additional costs of recovery.

The act of distraining goods and property could be quite violent and created a *rumor* indistinguishable, in the minds of observers, from the *rumor* that accompanied any street battle. In 1453, a messenger named Johan Conte with the revealing alias "lo grant Johan" or "Big John" was sent to the house of Guilhem Revel to collect security for a small debt of four florins.[125] Guilhem's pregnant wife Loiseta pleaded with him to take a lien on the house and then, when that failed, asked him not to take a large jug that she and her husband needed for drawing wine. Lo grant Johan swore at her and then struck her in the belly, causing her water to break and bringing a criminal inquest down on his head. Ordinary citizens like Loiseta and her neighbors viewed the messengers as little better than a body of predatory officials, and several witness called this particular sequence of events a *rumor*.[126] Growing resistance offered to the messengers, discussed below, shows how deeply resented was this predation.

This bona-based system of debt recovery worked in part because all citizens in Marseille were required to invest at least one-third of their bona in urban property. This investment served as security for future business dealings and other debts, and the court's ability to seize this bona was a fundamental aspect of the system of debt recovery. But not everyone had made such an investment, including merchants from other cities currently residing in Marseille and children in patria potestas. One's bona, moreover, did not always match one's debts, a situation that would become manifest dur-

---

122 ADBR 381E 75, fol. 16r–v, 24 Apr. 1347.
123 ADBR B 1940, fol. 185v.
124 AM FF 536, fols. 6r–7v, 15 Sept. 1358.
125 AM FF 21, fols. 1r–18v.
126 Ibid., fols. 8r, 16r.

ing bankruptcy proceedings. Bankrupts were thought eminently capable of fleeing the city, abandoning their bona to the courts and their creditors.

Flight for bankruptcy was exceedingly common. Bankrupts, in short, were like killers. So normal was it for bankrupts to seek sanctuary and exile that the willingness to remain and undergo incarceration was probably taken as a sign that the debtor intended to resist the charges made against him or her in court. Whenever a bankruptcy was discovered, criers would be sent to public squares and street corners to announce the news, requiring that all men and women with an interest in the estate appear before the court within ten days. Judges in such cases were faced with the unenviable task of deciding the order in which creditors would be repaid, a process known in the records as "priority and posteriority of creditors" (*prioritas et posteritas creditorum*).

One result of this predilection is that debtors with itchy feet could be imprisoned at the behest of the creditor. In a typical case from 1402, the creditor, a moneychanger named Johan Mayne, asked the court to imprison Bertomieu and Simon Simondel for an enormous debt of one thousand florins. The judge did so, noting that they would have to stay there until they had arrived at a concord (*donec se convenerint et concordaverint*) with Johan.[127] In 1353, a debtor named Jacme Andree, a merchant and citizen of Arles, was imprisoned by the court at the behest of his creditor, Johan de Laureis, because he had bona in Marseille only to the value of ten florins whereas the sum under dispute amounted to over one hundred florins.[128] The two parties compromised shortly afterward. Abuses were possible. In 1399, Louis II of Anjou issued a letter patent requiring that debtors not be imprisoned unless the value of their movables and immovables was insufficient, clearly implying that punitive jailing was not uncommon. He also required that the name of the denouncer be appended to the mandament, a measure taken to prevent individuals from using the system against their enemies.[129]

The foregoing shows that the practice of debt recovery was shot through with coercive force. Goods could be violently and humiliatingly distrained; houses seized; debtors imprisoned at a word from their creditors. The comparison between this system and the system of coercive force exercised on the body is striking. Bona were very roughly handled by the court. Paradoxically, bodies were most liable to coercive force when a debt was at stake. Though statistics are difficult to assemble, it is entirely safe to say that

[127] ADBR 3B 138, fol. 18r–v, case opened 11 Mar. 1402.
[128] ADBR 3B 53, fols. 19r–21r, case opened 16 Sept. 1353.
[129] AM 26/6, liasse dated 27 Aug. 1399.

debtors awaiting trial or slow to negotiate a compromise were jailed at a far higher rate than were killers.

It is worth noting that the soul was not entirely exempt from coercion, for another important element in the public system of debt recovery was the practice of excommunication for debt. Scattered records reveal that excommunication for debt was common, the idea being that refusal to repay debt constituted a violation of one's sacred oath. A long and bitterly contested inheritance dispute from 1401 and 1402 reveals at one point that both Guilhem de Troys and Antoni de Raude, who owed some money to Catarina, wife of Guilhem Mathey, had been excommunicated some five years earlier at Catarina's behest.[130] The articles of proof note that the excommunications had been duly announced every Sunday and feast day in the churches of Marseille. Antoni's excommunication was particularly pertinent to the case because he was the sitting palace judge when the case opened in 1401.

As the system of debt recovery grew ever more efficient over the fourteenth and early fifteenth centuries resentment and resistance grew with it. One of the most striking features of the remits collected by the crown, in fact, is not the absence of remits for homicide but the remarkable growth in resistance to the taking of security for debts. Such acts of resistance are completely absent from 1330 and 1331 and show up in numbers only in 1407. By way of example, in 1407 Antoneta Faveria was fined 40s. because she refused to open her door to the messenger charged with the task of taking items in security, and a few years later Ugona Guiste was fined ten pounds for assaulting a messenger who was attempting to seize goods from her son's house.[131]

The changing weight of Angevin fiscal oppression is almost certainly related to the arrival of the second house of Anjou following the War of the Union of Aix in 1386. The details of the change of regime need not concern us here; suffice it to say that the second house of Anjou was desperately strapped for cash and eager to restore comital revenues lost during the failing years of the reign of Queen Jeanne. Officials working on behalf of Louis II of Anjou uncovered rents owned by the crown that had gone uncollected for decades, owing to the turmoil of the 1380s. They sued proprietors for rents owed and, in some cases, sought to seize houses that had been sold without the official approval (*laudatio*) of the crown. The increasingly heavy weight of criminal fines is part and parcel of this changing fiscal environment, and the marked increase in remits paid to the crown around this time (table 1.6) indicates the success of the new policy. Contemporary complaints

---

[130] ADBR 3B 136, fol. 189r, case opened 27 June 1401 on fol. 151r.
[131] ADBR B 1943, fol. 18r, and B 1944, fol. 35r.

by debtors also show that Angevin judicial machinery was being wielded not only on behalf of the crown but also on behalf of creditors.

Overzealous judges were not above a little legal chicanery in an effort to increase payments to the crown. By the early 1400s, judges of the criminal court had gotten into the habit of fining individuals an amount that was less than 60s. Records sometimes indicate a payment of 60s. less one *obole*. In other cases, they split a criminal condemnation into several headings and hence several fines, each of which was less than 60s. The reason for this, as noted in chapter 1, is that according to statute no sentence involving a sum of less than 60s. could be appealed. For civil cases this was not a problem since no case worth 60s. would ever show up in the court anyway. Criminal fines were a different matter because the majority of fines were less than 60s. Royal letters patent reveal the extent of the bitterness that arose from this practice, and efforts were made to prevent judges from exploiting the rules in this way.[132] An injunction to this effect was reiterated as late as 24 November 1485 by Charles VIII of France.[133]

Both private citizens and city council members complained about this practice, and one result of these complaints was the increasing frequency of general amnesties. Amnesties can be found in the early fourteenth century but become more common in the fifteenth century.[134] In 1413, for example, Louis II issued a general pardon for "all crimes and excesses committed by Marseillais," including public and private theft, homicides, insults, arson, evil deeds, usury, the uprooting of trees, seizures and violations of highways and prisons, rape, adultery, incest, the defloration of virgins, and so on.[135] Excepted were a condemnation of two hundred pounds against a nobleman named Vivaut Bonafos and a sentence of contumacy and parricide issued against the son of the late Raynaut Vassal. On 18 March 1446, King René issued a general amnesty for all crimes except lèse-majesté, incest, premeditated homicide, notarial fraud, and highway robbery.[136] A probable result of this growing custom was the gradual decrease in remits for condemnations that is evident by the middle of the fifteenth century.

An alliance between the city council and its condemned citizens can be found in other contexts. In 1336, two syndics presented a formal complaint to the court about its treatment of a fisherman named Johan de Fonte. Having killed Bernart Raynart, Johan fled the city, refused to respond to the

[132] See, for example, AM FF 3, liasse dated 12 Sept. 1435, and FF 4.
[133] AM FF 4.
[134] The earliest I have found is from 1351; see AM AA 137. Siena issued general amnesties from 1302 onward; see Pazzaglini, *Criminal Ban*, 87.
[135] AM FF 16, liasse dated 4 Feb. 1413.
[136] ADBR B 1950, letter of amnesty issued at Saumur, dated 18 Mar. 1446.

summons, and was subsequently fined one hundred pounds for contumacy. The syndics complained about certain procedural irregularities—among other things, the judges had not required all the necessary summons and had not submitted the charge in writing. The penalty was remitted.[137] In 1351, shortly after the Black Death of 1348, ambassadors representing the city council before Queen Jeanne and her husband Louis complained both about the dearth of citizens and the unbearable weight of prosecutions for fights and scandals and gained a temporary cessation of criminal inquests.[138] Early in the fifteenth century the municipality simply paid off a fixed sum to the crown as composition for the outstanding fines owed by all criminals. The figure negotiated by the crown and the syndics in 1411 was three hundred florins.[139] There is no evidence suggesting that noblemen and patricians benefited to the exclusion of artisans and workers: in these amnesties, it was often noblemen like Vivaut Bonafos whose deeds were explicitly excluded from the amnesty. Such practices, once again, throw doubt on the common assumption that, at the origin of the historical development that led to the state's monopoly on legitimate violence, ordinary men and women favored a criminal court that aggressively pursued and punished crime.

## EVASION

People did not like to have their ears or feet cut off and did what they could to encourage the court to transform body-based sanctions into fines. The early records of the court of first appeals show how bodily sanctions were frequently evaded by transforming them, on appeal, into fines. But by the same token, people did not like to see their bona spiral away into the hands of the crown and other creditors. As the system of public debt recovery developed over the course of the thirteenth and fourteenth centuries, so too did practices of evasion.

Before the union of the upper and lower cities in 1348 the jurisdictional boundary between the two cities was freely exploited by debtors eager to escape their creditors. The court of one city could not act directly against the

---

[137] AM FF 13, liasse dated 17 Nov. 1336.
[138] AM 137, 1 May 1351.
[139] AM FF 16, referred to in two liasses dated 16 Mar. 1411 and 4 Feb. 1413. See also AM FF 16, liasse dated 20 June 1409, which reveals the existence of a similar general amnesty in 1409.

citizens of the other city, and to pursue debtors a judge in one city had to write to his counterpart in the other asking for his cooperation.[140] The sub-viguier and the jailer of the lower city were chastised and fined in 1338 for having imprisoned a citizen of the upper city at the behest of a lower city resident.[141] The problem, of course, was knowing who was who. Late in the year 1325, Augier Bernart was imprisoned at the behest of his creditor, Arnaut Maurel. The judge of the Praepositura, yet another special jurisdiction in Marseille, wrote to the palace court judge to complain: the imprisoned man, he claimed, was a resident of the Praepositura. But Arnaut responded to this claim vigorously, protesting that Augier was a citizen of the lower city, as proven by the fact that his wife, children, and servants made this their residence. If it appears that Augier changed his residence, Arnaut asserted, he did it fraudulently so as to avoid his creditors.[142]

Even though Augier got caught it seems likely that the loophole was both known and exploited by debtors, in much the same way that residents of one state in the United States might keep a residence in another state so as to evade state income taxes or high auto insurance rates. In Marseille, this loophole was closed in 1348 with the political union of the cities. Spatial boundaries of this sort are not practical in societies that use law courts to pursue debts. Put another way, the interest of creditors promotes ever-larger jurisdictions where boundaries are further away and harder to cross, and in this regard dovetails with the expansionist interest of states.

The most obvious technique for evading or at least frustrating both civil and criminal pursuit, in Marseille as elsewhere, was the claim of clerical status. This could be done legitimately but it also could be done fraudulently, as in the case of Peire de Bemia, a layman who was fined twelve pounds in 1400 for having tonsured himself so that he could sue his adversary in the episcopal court.[143] Clerics could not be sued in secular courts and several records show that defendants used this privilege to avoid prosecution—at least temporarily, because the suit could be initiated all over again in the ecclesiastical court. This had its downside, of course, because a cleric could not use the civil courts to pursue his own debtors, and defendants sometimes nullified a suit by raising this objection. In 1402 Jaumet de Signa was successfully prosecuted in the ecclesiastical court because, despite being a cleric, he litigated in the royal court with Antonet de Noto and Antonet's

---

140 See AM FF 15, two liasses dated 13–14 October 1285.
141 AM FF 13, 1338.
142 ADBR 3B 19, fol. 13r, case opened 23 Dec. 1325 on fol. 11r.
143 ADBR B 1944, fol. 24v.

mother Douseta over a pony.[144] The best thing, of course, was to be a cleric selectively. A case from 1323 suggests that two men chose to be clerics to defend themselves against criminal inquests but divested themselves of their clerical status when they wished to move against debtors in the secular court.[145] In his own defense, one of these men, Esteve Flori, argued that he was entitled to act in the secular court because a full year ago he had ceased wearing the garb of a cleric and had ceased claiming clerical privilege.[146]

Claims of clerical status show up far more commonly in criminal contexts. The claim of clerical status did not allow the cleric in question to evade prosecution entirely but did allow him to negotiate a reduction in the fine paid. In 1413, for example, a total of twenty-three men claimed clerical status in order to reduce the amount of the fine paid to the crown. Condemned to pay forty pounds for a nasty assault on Peire Penot, the cleric Peire de Castres successfully negotiated a reduction to five pounds, and another cleric named Peire Boysson reduced the fine levied against him for slapping a girl named Clareta from ten pounds to three pounds.[147] These fines were not technically coerced. A record concerning a man named Peire Bonaut notes that his fine of 60s. was reduced to 16s., an amount "which he freely paid notwithstanding his clerical status."[148] Some records hint at a certain amount of negotiation behind the scenes. In 1407, Lazaret Bannier was fined 50s. for an assault on one of the agents of the sub-viguier. The record notes that "because he is a cleric not bound by secular law [*clericus solutus*], the clavaire, with the permission of the lord viguier, composed with him [*composuit cum eodem*] in the amount of 25s."[149]

One of the major reasons for the absence of remits for homicide is the startling number of homicides that were prosecuted in the ecclesiastical court. A number of extant registers and charters recording a variety of negotiations or outcomes attest to the frequency of claims of clerical privilege.[150] The best evidence comes from several registers from the early 1400s

[144] ADBR 5G 772, fol. 74r, case opened 10 Jan. 1402.

[145] For an example see AM FF 15, fols. 3v–4r, case opened 3 Aug. 1323 on fol. 1r. The situation is complicated. Jacme de Fagiis, a tax collector, moved in court against two bakers. According to arguments made on behalf of the bakers, he did so illegally because he was a cleric and had often defended himself against criminal inquests on these grounds (fol. 4r).

[146] Ibid., fol. 15v.

[147] ADBR B 1947, fols. 19r and 22r.

[148] Ibid., fol. 23v: "quos gratuiter soluit non obstante clericatu de condempnatione 60s."

[149] ADBR B 1943, fol. 3v.

[150] Cases discussed above and in earlier chapters, involving Johan Areat, Nicolau Jausap, and others, are cases in point. Other examples include a charter arising from a homicide investigation in 1336; see ADBR 3HD H2, liasse 1; the date is torn but appears to

that record ecclesiastical inquests. These include several homicides and a wide array of other crimes, including arson, adultery, and theft, all of which were committed by clerics.[151]

Were clerics a particularly criminous lot? Did these claims of clerical status constitute polite legal fictions? Answers are not easy to come by. The frequency of the claim suggests an understanding that the ecclesiastical court was gentler than the secular court, though, as we've seen, the secular court itself was no great punisher of either the body or the bona of killers. More likely is the fear that the secular court was more readily influenced by one's enemies than was the ecclesiastical court. Officials of the secular court, as noted earlier, used extrajudicial torture from time to time against their enemies, outside the presence of judges. The ecclesiastical court may have been free of this sort of vengefulness.

The use of clerical status as a legal shelter elsewhere in medieval Europe is well known and needs no further comment here.[152] More interesting is a second system that exploited certain features of contract law to which people had access through the system of public notaries. It worked in several congruent ways. One practice was to make a temporary donation of one's bona to another person, such as a friend or a mother. Several cases show that this could be used to stymie one's creditors in the ordinary course of affairs.[153] It was an especially useful device when the creditor was the royal court. A good example of the practice comes from a letter of the viguier issued in 1314, scolding the clavaire for seizing the bona of a killer named Johan Rebol. Johan had previously donated all his goods to his mother, Resens, and thus legally owned no bona that could be seized by the court.[154] In 1330, members of the Grifen family sought to avoid a fine on the grounds that Albert Grifen, the contumacious individual, had donated all his goods to his brothers, Guilhem and Nicolau.[155]

That there was trickery in such cases is made clear by a suit and counter-

---

be the 20th of a certain month in 1336. A similar charter is AM FF 14, liasse 2, dated 9 May 1364. Defenses in appellate records based on clerical status include several arising from the great Vivaut/de Jerusalem street battle of 1351; see ADBR 3B 811, fols. 41r–42v, 56r–59v, 71r, and passim in the witness testimony. Seven men tried to be excused in this way: Antoni Vassal, Nicolau Vassal, Ugo Ode, Johan Catrelengas, Lois Athos, Bertran Castilhon, and Johan Raynaut.

[151] See ADBR 5G 771, 772, and 775.

[152] See esp. Hurnard, *King's Pardon*, appendix 2, "Clerical Excusable Homicides," 375–80.

[153] E.g. ADBR 3B 34, fols. 192r–195r, case opened 5 Nov. 1338, in which the creditor protested a factitious donation made by the debtor to his mother.

[154] AM FF 1, liasse dated 22 Mar. 1314.

[155] ADBR 3B 25, fols. 117r–122v, case opened 6 Sept. 1330.

suit that turns on just this issue. The first suit was initiated in May 1334 by Jacme de Amilhano against his brother Vivaldon, who in turn countersued Jacme in August.[156] At issue was the estate of their late brother Bernat, worth roughly one hundred and fifty pounds. The dispute arose from a fraudulent donation that Bernat had made to an Italian named Gambino Lambertini, a servant of King Robert of Naples. If we accept the arguments made by Jacme in both trials the facts are as follows.

Bernat had been wounded by Peire de Lambesc and several accomplices some three years earlier, in 1331. Planning his vengeance, Bernat announced in the presence of his friends and kinfolk that he was going to give all his *bona* to Gambino. His intention was as follows: should he succeed in his vengeance, then the royal court would have no rights over his *bona* ("ad illum finem quod se accideret quod aliquam vendictam faceret de dictis vulneribus quod curia regia super bonis suis que tunc habebat nullum ius ex inde consequi posset"). The donation, therefore, was factitious (*factitiam et simulatam*), and Bernat continued to possess the estate peacefully after the donation. Numerous witnesses in the first trial attested to the nature of the donation. One witness, the draper Simon de Apt, reported that Bernat had said the following words: "Friend, I wish to make a donation of all my goods to Gambino so that I might preserve my goods, since I intend to avenge myself on Peire de Lambesc."[157] Simon, as Gambino's procurator, was also specifically instructed to defend Bernat's estate against the royal court should Bernat be accused of any crime. Problems arose, though, when Bernat died—perhaps in a failed attempt to avenge himself. For reasons that are not clear, Gambino chose to donate all Bernat's goods to Vivaldon, rather than splitting the estate between Vivaldon and Jacme, the situation that motivated Jacme to go to court. In pursuit of his dead brother's estate Jacme even traveled to Naples, met with Gambino, and said to him:

You know well that that donation of goods which the late Bernat de Amilhano made to you had been done factitiously [*simulata*]. It was made only because, if Bernat should be able to avenge himself on his enemies and commit a crime, then you would be able to defend Bernat and his goods. They were not supposed to remain with you.[158]

---

156 For the two suits see ADBR 3B 28, fols. 75r–83r, case opened 19 May 1334 (Jacme as plaintiff) and ADBR 3B 29, fols. 94r–113r, case opened 11 Aug. 1334 (Vivaldon as plaintiff).
157 ADBR 3B 28, fol. 79r.
158 ADBR 3B 29, fols. 112r–113v, case opened 11 Aug. 1334 on fol. 94r.

A possible explanation for this turn of events is that Jacme and Gambino had had a falling out after the death of Bernat, prompting Gambino to exclude Jacme when it came time to return the factitious donation.

Donations are very common in notarial casebooks from the period. Some of these, notably donations made by insolvent debtors to their creditors, were relatively benign and not intended to defraud either creditors or the royal court. But the cases discussed above show that at least some of these donations were factitious donations. It is difficult to know how many cases there were because the parties involved normally had a vested interest in hiding factitious donations. A crucial feature of donations is that they had to be planned well in advance, as in the case of Bernat de Amilhano, who carefully divested himself of his bona well before his failed attempt to take vengeance. They were less useful if the act of violence was sudden or unplanned.

It is for this reason that the most significant and the most abundantly documented form of property shelter was provided by dotal law. Most men were indebted to their wives or daughters-in-law by virtue of their dowries, a major form of the permanent or circumstantial form of indebtedness discussed in the previous chapter. As I have argued elsewhere, this shelter worked against creditors of all kinds, and there is some evidence that women and their husbands were complicitous in this attempt to shelter an estate.[159] To take one example, in 1335 a woman sued her husband, Jacme, who was on the verge of bankruptcy, for recovery of her dowry of thirty-five pounds and that of her mother, worth ten pounds. The judge clearly ruled in her favor and there is no evidence that the husband ever contested the charges made against him.[160] But the practice was especially effective when used against the royal court. Most creditors understood how women's dowries could be used as shelters, and therefore lent money not just to husbands but to husbands and wives, giving the creditor a lien on the woman's dowry. In the case of debts created by criminal inquests, especially the larger debts for cases of homicide and serious assaults that were largely committed by men, the royal court had no such lien.

Several cases of civil litigation reveal situations in which women used their dotal rights to prevent the seizure of their husbands' estates. In March 1330, for example, a group of men joined in the killing of Jacme Gayraut. Following their flight they were charged with contumacy, and royal officials

---

[159] See my "Démanteler le patrimoine: les femmes et les biens dans la Marseille médiévale," *Annales: histoire, sciences sociales* 52 (1997): 343–68, here 366–68.

[160] ADBR 3B 30, fols. 31r–32v, case opened 6 July 1335.

subsequently initiated procedures for seizing the abandoned estates. On 12 June, two women showed up at the palace court to defend their dotal rights. Bertomieua, the wife of Antoni Guillissoni, resisted the attempt to extract a one hundred pound contumacy fine on the grounds that her husband was indebted to her for the value of a vineyard given him in dowry. In the next suit, Raymona, the wife of Ugo de Podio, noted that her husband's entire bona was obligated to her by virtue of her dowry of sixty pounds.[161] A few weeks later, Bermona, the widowed mother of Antoni Guillissoni, appeared at the palace court and demanded the return of her own dowry of one hundred and eighty pounds, which had passed into her son's hands at the death of her husband.[162] Shortly afterward, Raymona de Podio appeared once again, this time demanding the return of forty pounds given her by her husband in augmentation of her dowry.[163] This is a particularly interesting example for it shows how a man, in augmenting his wife's dowry, could shelter even more of his estate from possible crown prosecution. Though no sentences are given in these cases, various clues suggest that the clavaire did not vigorously contest the women's claims.

In the proceedings of a case from 1379 arising from the killing of the laborer Guilhem Cotaron by Ugo Jauselm, the notary pointedly mentioned how the killer's wife, Marita, was able to show the judge her dowry contract and thereby recover a fifty pound dowry from the estate of her contumacious husband. The next case shows that Ugo's daughter-in-law similarly recovered her eighty pound dowry.[164] Two other cases heard in 1330 which were apparently unrelated to the murder of Jacme Gayraut also reveal situations in which women were defending their dowries against charges of contumacy assessed to their husbands.[165] Similar cases show up in other records.[166] One record from December of 1354 notes that the killer, Pons

[161] ADBR 3B 25, fols. 60r–63v, first case opened 12 June 1330.

[162] Ibid., fols. 72r–77v, case opened 30 June 1330.

[163] Ibid., fols. 78r–83r, case opened 7 July 1330.

[164] ADBR 3B 95, fols. 170r–182r, cases opened 21 Nov. 1379 and 7 Nov. 1379 (not in chronological order).

[165] Ibid., fols. 104r–106r, case opened 13 Aug. 1330; in this suit, Adalays Isnarde was retrieving her dowry from the bona of her husband, Peire Pons, who had been arrested for wounding Ricarda Borgarelle. See also ibid., fol. 139r, case opened 7 Nov. 1330.

[166] E.g., ADBR 3B 28, fols. 11r–14r, case opened 22 Apr. 1334; ADBR 3B 29, fols. 128r–129r, case opened 18 Aug. 1334. In the former case, the woman was defending her three hundred and fifty pound dowry from the officials of the crown; in the latter, two women were sheltering dotal goods valued at one hundred and seventy pounds and a house. See also ADBR 3B 52, fols. 97r–99r, case opened 18 Nov. 1353. The circumstances of this case are not clear, though the woman's husband had fled the city for his "diverse crimes." In ADBR 3B 54, fols. 76r–78r, case opened late July 1354, Adalays Manganelle sought to recover her dowry of two hundred pounds from the estate of her husband Johan, who had fled the city following the murder of Guilhem Johan. See also two related suits defending

THE CONSUMPTION OF JUSTICE

Gassin, who almost certainly took flight after the murder of Alazays Borgona, was condemned to forfeit all his bona. His wife, Biatris, came to court to defend her dotal rights.[167] In this case we happen to have a peace instrument from the following April showing that Pons had successfully made peace with his victim's kin, a peace sealed by the marriage between the victim's son and a young cousin of Pons named Bertomieua Bohiera.[168] In none of these cases is there any indication that the women were separating themselves from their husbands. Killers normally disappeared for a few months and then returned to the city, resuming their normal lifestyle.

The use of the dowry in medieval Europe, and related subjects such as dotal inflation, have generated a large literature, in part because the practice is relatively uncommon in human societies. That the dowry was a form of pre-mortem inheritance is incontestable. But whatever the origins of the practice there is little question that some couples in late medieval Marseille were systematically using dotal law to shelter conjugal assets against creditors of all stripes, including, perhaps especially, the royal court. Note how this system was not just a loophole for patricians or aristocrats eager to escape the natural course of justice: all reasonably respectable citizens could hope to benefit from it. The weight of state prosecutions for violence, insofar as they resulted in contumacy fines, may well have spurred not only dowry augmentations but also dotal inflation. The more men were indebted to wives, daughters, and daughters-in-law, the more secure they were from criminal prosecution.

Whatever the shelter, the court was very open to the idea that the distraint of goods must be bound by law, and as a result worked to prevent or hinder illegal or overzealous distraint. Rogue officials of the crown sometimes seized property before they were authorized to do so and were penalized by the court. In 1314, for example, complaints were raised to the effect that the clavaire had made off with the bona of men condemned for homicide before the accused had had a chance to appeal.[169] Defendants who appealed their sentences to the court of first appeals could routinely ask for and receive a letter of inhibition from the judge of the first appellate court that prevented the clavaire from moving against his goods during the appeal.[170] If nothing else, the practice gave the appellant some breathing space

---

her dowry from Johan's creditors, ibid., fols. 84r–88v, case opened 9 Aug. 1354, and ADBR 3B 57, fols. 20r–22v, case opened 10 Oct. 1354.

[167] ADBR 3B 57, fol. 83r–v, case opened 18 Dec. 1354.

[168] ADBR 355E 290, fols. 20r–21r, 4 Apr. 1355. For the dotal act, see ibid., fols. 61r–62r, 4 Apr. 1355.

[169] AM FF 1, liasse dated 12 Apr. 1314.

[170] E.g., ADBR 3B 856, fols. 5r–6v, case opened 27 June 1405 on fol. 5r.

during which he or she had time to protect assets through shelters of various types.

⊰⊱

The development of these techniques for evading the bona-based sanctions of the civil and criminal courts is a pointed reminder that courts of law had a powerful impact on social customs and habits. In chapters 2 and 3 I argued that consumers gradually shifted resources into the courts as they became aware of how they could use the courts to pursue animosities and discipline their adversaries. Courts were not imposed on a passive citizenry by sovereign powers eager to build states and centralize power. Instead, caseloads were built by citizens. But these very same citizens were often at the receiving end of judicial pursuit, and found it necessary to develop modes of resistance to the courts whose actions they sponsored in other contexts. In a sense, practices of evasion were to bona what sanctuary and voluntary exile were to the body: customary devices that evolved for the purpose of avoiding sanctions. Both served to mitigate the potential excesses of the criminal court.

The evolution of a culture of evasion illustrates, from yet another angle, one of the central arguments of this chapter, namely that the criminal justice system in late medieval Marseille was heavily oriented around the imposition and collection of fines. That fines were preferred to corporal punishments in many jurisdictions in late medieval Europe is often interpreted by historians as a failure of the state—*la justice impuissante*, in Guenée's memorable phrase—and a sign of the corruption of the criminal justice system. Historians of the Angevin realms in Italy and southern France in the fourteenth century, to take an example close to home, have argued that the crown's growing reliance on fines represents one facet of the decay of strong government under the successors to Charles of Anjou. There are many problems with this argument, not the least of which is the difficulty of proving that thirteenth-century Angevin courts actually did impose bodily mutilations rather than fines. In a different vein, it is not immediately obvious to me that the degree of inflicted pain and suffering is a good measure of strong government, or that the supposed mildness of fines encouraged criminality.

Fines are often interpreted as though they were imposed in an effort to dissuade criminals. Certainly this is true to some degree. Curiously, in Provence and elsewhere, proceeds from the criminal justice system are found in fiscal records alongside listings of other forms of royal or comital revenue. Though fines may have had a moral component, in other words, they were actually categorized as a form of indirect taxation.

We can dismiss this association as a purely accidental result of the nature of record keeping. Out of curiosity, however, let us for a moment take this categorization seriously. What was being taxed? Two rough categories of criminal misconduct stand out, namely statutory infractions of one sort or another, notably evasions of market and craft regulations, and conflict of one sort or another, notably assaults, threats, and insults. It seems intuitive that we should distinguish these kinds of behaviors. Yet in both cases we see a crown jealous to defend its control of two marketplaces, namely the market in goods and the market in violence. In the same way that individuals were prosecuted for selling fish on the sly, to evade market taxes, so too were they prosecuted for transacting enmity in spaces uncontrolled by the crown. The crown sought to regulate the market in goods by requiring all marketing to take place in controlled market spaces. By the same token, the crown also sought to regulate the market in the transaction of enmity by requiring that enmity be transacted in courts. As I argued at length in chapters 2 and 3, lawsuits make the most sense if they are seen as instances in which enmity could be licitly transacted in controlled public spaces. That the court itself convened at candlers' booths, in market spaces, is a fitting symbol of this congruence of interests. Late medieval justice may have been *impuissante* as far as inflicting pain is concerned, but it looks far more efficient when seen as an institution designed to penalize illicit transactions made in unregulated markets.

For similar reasons, it is necessary to reevaluate the common suggestion that late medieval officials were corrupt. This assessment cannot be wholly wrong: contemporary observers themselves denounced the corruption of judges and other officials. But we should not take such accusations at face value. In the Gonzaga and Este states discussed by David Chambers and Trevor Dean, for example, the charge of corruption was issued in a highly politicized context in which noblemen, as enemies of the state, were manipulating the system so as to avoid criminal penalties.[171] In Marseille, there is little evidence suggesting that nobles and patricians were unusually favored. The practice of general amnesties requested by the city council served to protect the entire population (with the probable exception of infamous rogues) from the predation of overzealous judges. The council saw the fines as ruinously punitive, and after the great sack of 1423 even made the argument that the city could not be adequately repopulated unless fugitives

---

[171] See, for example, the index to Chambers and Dean, *Clean Hands*, s.v. "corruption."

could return under a general amnesty for all outstanding fines, an amnesty that was granted on 18 July 1424 by Charles of Maine.[172] The kings and queens of Naples sided with the Marseillais in their assessment of judges. It was not that judges were too corrupt. The problem seems to have been that they were not corrupt enough.

[172] AM FF 16.

# CHAPTER FIVE
# THE PUBLIC ARCHIVE

J udges of Marseille's court of inquest went to great lengths to uncover the facts in cases of homicide and serious assault. They conducted preliminary interviews in an effort to identify the likely suspect, fingered the blades used, and took the depositions of expert medical witnesses. The facts in place, judges then embedded them in a convincing storyline: "Mathea Sadaroni, a Catalan of Barcelona, was a friend of Maya de Anycellis, and she lived with her in the house of Druda de Lingris, one of the suspects, which is located in the Prostitutes quarter. There she shared a room with Maya, lying in the same bed, drinking and eating and sleeping with her by day and night." So begins one sad tale of treachery culminating in the murder of Mathea at the hands of two male friends of theirs in a dispute over clothing.[1] Other stories were just as artful. Sworn witnesses reaffirmed under oath what they had already suggested informally, and judges subsequently mulled over the resulting transcripts, annotating the margins copiously and confirming, or at times altering, the preliminary narrative of events.

But it was a curious thing to do, all this fact-finding. The public nature of virtually all homicides and assaults in fourteenth-century Marseille ensured the prior notoriety of all killers and assailants, a notoriety sealed by their very visible flight into sanctuary. Asked to say whether Peire Guibert was guilty of the 1355 killing of Jacme Bertran, one witness, a little surprised, replied, "It is common knowledge in Marseille that the sub-viguier is in the campanile of that church," perhaps pointing to the spire of St. Antoine's,

---

[1] ADBR 3B 96, fol. 11r–v, case opened 11 June 1380 on fol. 10r.

which may have been visible from the court space.[2] Peire's guilt, in short, was already manifest. The inquest procedure merely took the common fund of vernacular knowledge and burnished it with the scientific authority afforded by medicine, legal terminology, and a formal narrative. But the fact-finding was useless anyway because killers were almost always condemned for contumacy, not for homicide. Facts and stories were ancillary to this charge, which was wholly and easily proven simply by the absence of the killer. Reading through the inquest into the murder of Guilhem Tomas, it is hard to escape the impression that the fact-finding procedures that were so prominent a feature of this case were driven less by a desire of the judges to know the truth than by a desire of the victim's kin to blacken and besmear the name of their common enemy, Guilhem de Belavila.

From its inception in the twelfth century, Roman-canon law developed a sophisticated science of the fact, supposedly designed to root out hard-to-know facts. But in the vast majority of cases brought before Marseille's court of inquest, truth wasn't really a problem: the fanciful "hard cases" discussed in the law schools were simply irrelevant to the ordinary practice of justice in a city such as Marseille, where personal conflict remained a largely public affair.[3] Facts were similarly ancillary in the majority of civil trials. As noted earlier, most civil court cases ended in arbitration or simply fizzled out for one reason or another. In the case of arbitration, the threat of a sentence based on facts may well have pushed obstreperous litigants into more conciliatory postures. This surely happened in some cases. But if this were a commonplace one would expect to find a close correlation between the conclusion of the proof phase and the move to arbitration. There is no such correlation. Most cases never got to the proof phase at all, and either fizzled out or moved to arbitration well before facts were officially introduced into a case, suggesting that arbitration was not motivated by the need to minimize the damage posed by damning facts. Finally, many cases that did end in a ruling turned not on the facts of the dispute but rather on rulings over exceptions. An exception does not deny the relevance of facts to trial procedures. Like the ordeal, what the posing of an exception does is to change the facts under dispute. The issue becomes not one of "Did the defendant repay

[2] ADBR 3B 819, fol. 53r, case opened 28 May 1355 on fol. 50r.
[3] In his *Treatise on Fama*, the obscure thirteenth-century legal scholar Thomas de Piperata did address the probative value of publicity. In discussing a prototypical hard case involving an unwitnessed homicide, Thomas argued that the flight of the accused, coupled with *publica fama*, prior threats, and the existence of an enmity between accused and victim, constituted sufficient *indicia* for proving his guilt. See Richard M. Fraher, "Conviction according to Conscience: The Medieval Jurists' Debate concerning Judicial Discretion and the Law of Proof," *Law and History Review* 7 (1989): 23–88, here 39.

the loan to the creditor?" but "Does the defendant's witness love the defendant?" or "Is the witness morally fit to give testimony?" or "Was this suit motivated by hatred?" Growing usage of the exception procedure by lawyers and their clients meant that arguments about facts rapidly turned into arguments about public emotions, moral sentiments, and moral status. Such facts were not easily determined by legal norms and standards. The procedural manuals of the thirteenth-century jurists describe certain fact-finding procedures at great length. They provide far less guidance on how to identify love or hatred, and leave the determination of fama, or moral fitness, up to the community. One finds vague references to common knowledge and little else.

As this suggests, the practical epistemology of the law courts of late medieval Marseille, how judges actually determined what was a fact and which facts were important, departs considerably from the intellectualized epistemology of thirteenth-century jurists and their modern interpreters. But the epistemological issues go beyond this. The Roman-canon exception procedure, as used in civil courts, did not stop at difficult-to-know emotional and moral issues. Over the course of the fourteenth century, the growing expert class of procurators and lawyers, egged on by their paying clients, found that even simple facts, such as facts about birth, marriage, death, filiation, and property ownership, could be contested as a way to derail an adversary's case. "The adversary *claims* to have been married to the deceased but how do we know she wasn't just a maid or a prostitute?" "He says he is the nephew of the deceased but can he prove it?" "The plaintiff is younger than twenty-five and still in patria potestas and therefore has no standing at law." Exceptions like these, whether they were formally initiated or loomed, threateningly, on the horizon, cost the canny litigant little to pose but could delay or even derail an adversary's case. Perhaps in part to preempt such tactics, a number of fourteenth-century litigants, notably in cases involving inheritances and estate administrations, found they had to make arguments based on similar facts about age, marital status, death, filiation, and property ownership simply to recover their rightful property.

In modern Western-style nation-states, simple facts like these can be proven by means of certificates, titles, and other documents stored in official, authoritative state-sponsored archives. Should occasion arise these facts can be readily retrieved and brought to the attention of the court. But there was no such archive in medieval Europe. Marseille, like many other late medieval jurisdictions, routinely kept track of tax obligations, but for the most part basic life facts were almost wholly unarchived. Most people had little idea of their exact age and certainly had no document to prove it. Although dotal instruments in theory could be used to prove the existence of a marriage, in practice they rarely were. The absence of birth certificates and state censuses means that the facts of filiation were never recorded systematically on paper. Testaments might suggest when someone was approaching death but, by definition, provided no certain proof that the testator had died, and therefore could not serve as death certificates. Notarial casebooks, as a serial archive, provided some facts about property ownership but since casebooks were in the private possession of notaries this archive was dispersed and not easy to use. The most effective archive consisted of the instruments that notaries drew up for their clients, but instruments could be lost, stolen, or destroyed by fire or flood. In fourteenth-century Marseille, title in property was sometimes proven by means of a notarial instrument, but what is most striking about court proceedings is how many title disputes turned on witness testimony, not written instruments.

By the fifteenth century, some states, notably Florence and England, were beginning to develop the kind of massive state archive necessary to track basic facts like these systematically.[4] From the sixteenth century onward, such archives in the form of parish registers had become a reality in many parts of Europe. But for the first two hundred years or more of its existence, Roman-canon procedural law, whose fundamental epistemology assumed the existence of authoritatively known life facts, paradoxically had no official archives to draw on. Late medieval courts using Roman-canon procedural law were not embedded in the sort of state that could ever provide such archives. An archival vacuum was thereby formed. This vacuum may have contributed to the rise of state archives, but for the time being litigants and lawyers had to rely on a different sort of archive to fill the knowledge vacuum: the public archive of memory and gossip. All relevant facts, after all, were known by virtue of the things people saw and discussed among themselves. Given the archival vacuum, the memories and bits of gossip that formed the public archive of knowledge became an ever more important element in civil court procedures. It may be true, as Michael Clanchy has argued, that there was a shift from memory to written record across the twelfth and thirteenth centuries as far as certain state archives are concerned.[5] But one of the most striking features of the ex-

---

[4] In the summer of 1429, for example, Florence embarked on a program to record, on a quarterly basis, the names and birthdates of all minor citizens so as to resolve all age-related challenges in the future. See Andrea Zorzi, "The Florentines and Their Public Offices in the Early Fifteenth Century: Competition, Abuses of Power, and Unlawful Acts," trans. Corrada Biazzo Curry, in *History from Crime*, ed. Edward Muir and Guido Ruggiero (Baltimore, 1994), 110–34, here 121.

[5] Michael T. Clanchy, *From Memory to Written Record: England 1066–1307*, 2nd ed. (London, 1993).

tracts of witness testimony found in civil court proceedings from fourteenth- and early fifteenth-century Marseille is how the archival vacuum spurred an increasing reliance on memory and gossip, the public archive of knowledge.

What were the procedural norms governing this process of sounding out public opinion? Few procedural manuals discussed in any detail how Roman-canon judges should go about distinguishing authoritative from spurious talk, nor were there any guidelines telling lawyers and litigants how to set about providing such facts or how to defend themselves from exceptions. But we should not imagine that users of the law were conscious of any sort of archival crisis. There already existed an authoritative yardstick for testing the things said to be known, and that was public behavior: in a word, publicity.

The theme of publicity has run through all the preceding chapters. In this chapter, I would like to draw together these threads and describe the ensemble they constitute, namely the legal culture of publicity. The legal culture of publicity in late medieval Europe rested on the simple understanding that all facts worth knowing, especially legal facts, were public facts: known everywhere, at all times, and by all.[6] Couples married in public and, later, behaved together in the manner of married couples. Women gave birth before crowds of female witnesses and breast-fed their infants in public. Men and women performed their social emotions on the street, advertising their affections, filiations, and hatreds for all to see.[7] Lawsuits, sales, loans, quittances, insults, and assaults were transacted openly and publicly. When people died, whether peacefully in their beds or bloodily on the streets, they died in the public eye. All of this behavior was much discussed and analyzed in the gossip networks of the city, and the ensuing information was recorded in common knowledge or social memory. This knowledge was brought to light whenever witnesses attested to the fama circulating about a given set of facts. Judges inquired closely into fama. In fourteenth-century legal epistemology, things weren't really known or knowable until they had become the subject of public talk.

To appreciate how this legal culture worked, let us consider here just one

[6] The so-called Vincentian formula, named after the fifth-century bishop Vincent of Lérins. See Vincent of Lérins, *Commonitorium*, ed. R. Demeulenaere, vol. 64 of *Corpus Christianorum*, Series Latina (Turnholt, 1985), 149.

[7] On the publicity of emotions see Stephen D. White, "The Politics of Anger," in *Anger's Past: The Social Uses of an Emotion in the Middle Ages*, ed. Barbara H. Rosenwein (Ithaca, 1998), 127–52, here 139; Gerd Althoff, "*Ira Regis*: Prolegomena to a History of Royal Anger," in ibid., 59–74, here 74; Robert Bartlett, "'Mortal Enmities': The Legal Aspect of Hostility in the Middle Ages," T. Jones Pierce Lecture, University of Wales (Aberystwyth, 1998), 5.

example, a case that came before the palace court in 1338. The suit pitted a merchant named Peire Bonafos against his neighbor, Gandulfa Pisana. At issue was a drain that ran between Peire's house and a vacant lot belonging to Gandulfa, a drain that had fallen into a dilapidated state thanks to the inattention of Gandulfa's late husband and to Gandulfa's own vandalism. Peire was either appealing an earlier decision made by the mason-assessors or asking that their decision be enforced. To prove his case, he offered the palace court the proceedings of the original trial before the mason-assessors. One of the witnesses in this trial, Guilelma de Crusols, a young woman of twenty-four years, had said something like this on Peire's behalf:

At least twelve years ago, I saw a kind of small drain between the house (the house now belongs to Peire Bonafos, but it used to be mine) and the pasture belonging to Gandulfa. That drain took away the waste from the houses there. Everyone said the drain had always been there. The waste ran down to the street of St. Jacques. After I sold the house, the buyer asked me to help him out—the water was now draining into *his* house because Gandulfa had moved the drain. So I went there and asked Gandulfa why she had moved the drain. All she did was to say that if any drains were placed there again she would move them, showing me the tiled drainpipe in her hands. Lots of people who are now dead knew of this.[8]

Said another witness, Johan Senequier, a former mason-assessor, commenting on the plaintiff's claim that these facts were widely known, "All of this is public knowledge [*famam publicam*] in the city of Marseille among the people of the sixain of St. Jacques and among former mason-assessors." Asked what "fama" meant, he said "that which is publicly spoken among people."[9]

The facts of this case, we hear, are known by everyone, publicly shared. They are known everywhere, not only among the residents of the sixain of St. Jacques but even among the more geographically dispersed body of former mason-assessors. They are rooted in the past, in the memories of the living and the dead. There was, in fourteenth-century Marseille, no expert governmental survey or cadastral map; there were no records determining drain placement and maintenance. Knowledge, to *be* knowledge, had to be

[8] ADBR 3B 34, fol. 12r–v, case opened 22 Apr. 1338 on fol. 1r. I have paraphrased slightly and compressed the testimony to eliminate repetitions.

[9] Ibid., fol. 13v.

inscribed in the public archives of knowledge—known, that is, by many people both past and present throughout the city.

Many of the facts relevant to the law resided in this legal culture of publicity. As court proceedings from late medieval Marseille attest, the demands of this legal culture of publicity shaped behavior to a considerable degree. As shown in the first section below, ordinary men and women and even the law courts and the notaries needed to perform openly and in the public eye in order to inscribe facts in the memories and gossip networks that comprised the archive on which proof in subsequent legal quarrels might depend. Such public behavior created archives of knowledge based on memories that supplemented and extended the available written archives. The second section illustrates how these archives were put to use in litigation. A study of several cases suggests that litigants expected judges not only to listen to the facts presented by witnesses but also to pay attention to the social profile of the knowledge-bearing group assembled by litigants. Tellingly, litigants who were able to put together the most diverse group of witnesses consistently won their cases. As discussed in this section, diversity was measured in several ways: spatial separation, as measured by neighborhood of residence; degree of kinship, ranging from blood, affinal, and spiritual kinship to no kinship at all; and social separation, extending from nobles to workers. Successful witness groups also included both men and women, a feature that I will discuss in the third section. Litigants constructed diverse witness groups because this allowed them to illustrate in a relatively mechanical fashion how their claims fulfilled the impartial demands of a formula that equated truth with common speech and universal assent.

According to these arguments, the most characteristic quality of late medieval legal culture was neither orality nor literacy, but rather publicity. Put differently, the oral-written division that we customarily draw when describing medieval technologies for recording bits of knowledge is not helpful for understanding forms of knowledge and the use of knowledge in courts of law in fourteenth-century Marseille. More useful is a dichotomy that distinguishes public from secretive. These dichotomies are not identical: public is not necessarily oral, and secretive is not necessarily written. Written archives of knowledge acquired the authority of publicity when they were created in the public eye, as they were in fourteenth-century Marseille. Oral-memorial knowledge, by the same token, carried little authority in courts of law whenever it was seen as being limited to small, private groups of kin and dependents.

Men and women in medieval Europe broadcast information about their doings, identities, and possessions with an enthusiasm and energy that is difficult to exaggerate. Trousseaux were carted publicly through streets to allow neighbors to size up the bride's value and hence her father's status and generosity and to show that the dowry had been paid.[10] Clothes and hairstyle advertised social status, gifts were exchanged so that all could see, and finally, death, too, happened in the public eye.[11] A crucial feature of all these performances, all these acts of publicity, is that they could have important legal ramifications. In saga Iceland, homicides had to be committed openly and announced publicly if the killer was to avoid the stain of secrecy.[12] In Lombardy, the act of copulation, essential to the legal validity of a marriage, had to be viewed by witnesses.[13] All of these performances, coupled with the gossip they generated, created memories that subsequently served an archival function.[14]

Examples from the judicial records of fourteenth-century Marseille are rich enough to show that the need to be public in all that one did was a practice deeply embedded within local legal culture. We see this in the repeated usage of various forms of the word "public" and the use of the word "openly" (*palam*) in court records and notarial registers. In 1356, the city's viguier, we learn, openly and publicly (*palam et publice*) favors one noble faction.[15] A notary drawing up a loan displays coins on a table before him and then recites and publicizes (*recitavit et publicavit*) the debt just incurred, and another man openly and publicly acknowledges a debt of seven florins.[16] A

[10] Christiane Klapisch-Zuber, *La maison et le nom: stratégies et rituels dans l'Italie de la Renaissance* (Paris, 1990), 220–24.

[11] On clothing, see Diane Owen Hughes, "Regulating Women's Fashion," in *Silences of the Middle Ages*, ed. Christiane Klapisch-Zuber, vol. 2 of *A History of Women in the West*, ed. Georges Duby and Michelle Perrot (Cambridge, Mass., 1992), 136–58; on public death, see Georges Duby, *William Marshal: The Flower of Chivalry*, trans. Richard Howard (New York, 1984).

[12] William Ian Miller, *Bloodtaking and Peacemaking: Feud, Law, and Society in Saga Iceland* (Chicago, 1990), 249–50.

[13] Diane Owen Hughes, "Il matrimonio nell'Italia medievale," in *Storia del matrimonio*, ed. Michela de Giorgio and Christiane Klapisch-Zuber (Rome, 1996), 5–61, here 30.

[14] In general, see Piotr Górecki, "Communities of Legal Memory in Medieval Poland, c. 1200–1240," *Journal of Medieval History* 24 (1998): 127–54.

[15] ADBR 3B 820, fol. 46v, case opened 7 July 1356 on fol. 8r.

[16] ADBR 3B 38, fol. 110r, case opened 20 July 1339 on fol. 90r; ADBR 3B 147, fol. 259v, case opened 14 June 1407 on fol. 257r.

man is openly and publicly held to be the legitimate and natural father of his son among neighbors and those who know ("Petrus Bonifacii est pater et legitimus et naturalis dicti Amelii et pro tali habetur et reputatur . . . palam et publice inter notos et vicinos").[17] A brother and sister openly and publicly lease out stalls in the market ("locaverunt aliquas tabulas . . . palam et publice").[18] On the other side of the coin, a woman of loose morals is a prostitute as soon as she is considered a public prostitute (*meretrix publica*),[19] insults made openly and publicly are that much worse,[20] and to boast publicly of one's involvement in a murder is tantamount to a confession.[21] Similarly, to gather secretively and evasively (*clam et occulte*)[22] is no recipe for honest behavior, nor can one remove items from a house *clam et occulte* without drawing the suspicions of the neighbors.[23] One simply does not possess land in a secret way.[24] Matters of public record, such as council decisions and excommunications, were announced publicly in streets, marketplaces, and churches. All witches and spellmakers practicing their craft secretively and evasively (*clam et occulte*), we learn from a court case from 1343, were publicly excommunicated in the churches of Marseille on a regular basis.[25]

The frequent use of words such as *palam* and *publice* and their binary opposites, *clam* and *occulte*, offers simple evidence for the importance of publicity. Testimony in court cases reveals the importance of publicizing behaviors and deeds even when these words are not used. It was normal, for example, for a person's death to be proclaimed openly by their kinfolk, and this act of publicity was observed and much discussed by the neighbors. As a witness named Johan Barratan reported in one case:

Around two years ago he, the witness, was a neighbor of Guilelma Gamella, who was living in the house of her daughter Pellegrina. On a certain day that he does not recollect, around the time of the ringing of

<hr/>

[17] ADBR 3B 820, fol. 47r, case opened 7 July 1356 on fol. 8r.

[18] ADBR 3B 37, fols. 249v–250r, case opened 21 May 1339 on fol. 234r.

[19] E.g., ADBR 3B 58, fol. 105v, case opened 19 Feb. 1355 on fol. 92r.

[20] ADBR 3B 37, loose sheet between fols. 279–280, case opened 14 July 1339 on 280r: "Bernat . . . palam et publice in presencia multorum proborum et in pluribus et diversis locis dicte civitate . . . appellavit eundem Johannem bastardum."

[21] ADBR 3B 820, fol. 90r, case opened 7 July 1356 on fol. 8r: "Amelius publice diffamavit quod ipse est consocius mortis dicti Petri [de Jerusalem]."

[22] Ibid., fol. 12r.

[23] See, for example, ADBR 3B 16, fols. 60r–82v, case opened 16 Mar. 1323; ADBR 3B 816, fol. 24v, case opened 17 June 1353 on fol. 12r; ADBR 3B 64, fol. 9r, case opened 22 Oct. 1362 on fol. 6r.

[24] ADBR 3B 812, fol. 53v, case opened 28 July 1352 on fol. 42r. The plaintiff declared that he was holding a field in a non-secret (*non clam*) way.

[25] ADBR 3B 45, fols. 170r–180v, case opened 15 Oct. 1343.

the Ave Maria, while he himself was in his own home, he heard the daughter Pellegrina crying in a loud voice and lamenting her mother Guilelma, since she was on the verge of dying. Hearing Pellegrina crying and lamenting, he entered Pellegrina's house and found her as one half-dead, saying that Guilelma was dead.[26]

In another case, a witness heard it said "by all the people of the street" that death had come suddenly to one Girart Marro, and the dolorous expression "Mort es ses lenga, mort es ses lenga en Girart Marro" ("The voice of En Girart Marro is dead, his voice is dead") was on everyone's lips.[27] Time of death, an important legal datum, could be made known in other ways. In November 1362, shortly after a second outbreak of plague had devastated Marseille, an inheritance dispute hinging on time of death was settled in favor of the dead man's widow, for her female neighbors were able to testify that they had witnessed the bereaved woman "going to the church in the clothing of a widow, as is customary."[28] In a similar case, this time in the midst of the first plague in April 1348, neighborhood women were able to report that they had seen two successive funeral processions and, through their testimony, were able to prove the litigant's claim that his daughter died after his wife had died, thus making him the heir of both.[29]

Public performances like these created memorial archives that could then be drawn upon as needed in future litigation, as in these cases. There is no question that men and women were fully conscious of this archival function. "Bear in mind that you have seen me cultivating this piece of property," a laborer named Johan Trohin called out to a passing stranger one day in 1352.[30] He approached four other men with the same words and was later able to call upon his five witnesses to prove what he had been doing. Similar examples involving title, entry, debt repayment, and other events or transitions are numerous:[31]

[26] ADBR 3B 38, fol. 65v, case opened 14 Oct. 1339 on fol. 63r.

[27] ADBR 3B 45, fol. 147r, case opened 16 Aug. 1343 on fol. 142r. My thanks to Wayne Storey for the translation.

[28] ADBR 3B 64, fols. 50r–59r, case opened 8 Nov. 1362.

[29] ADBR 355E 292, fols. 48r–50v, 10 Apr. 1348.

[30] ADBR 3B 812, fol. 64v, case opened 28 July 1352 on fol. 42r: "recordete tibi ad memoriam quod tu me vides podantem istam possessionem."

[31] For the following examples see, respectively, ADBR 3B 825, fol. 122v, case opened 13 May 1365 on fol. 35r; ADBR 3B 41, fol. 46v, case opened 18 July 1340 on fol. 43r; ADBR 3B 41, fol. 269r, case opened 31 Oct. 1340 on fol. 268r; see also ADBR 3B 43, fol. 22r, case opened 30 Aug. 1341 on fol. 21r.

O lords, be witnesses for me that this man wishes to attack my person. (Guilhem de Belavila to two passing Dominicans as he was being attacked by Guilhem Tomas in 1365)

O Lord Raymon Natalis, be a witness that this Jew has acquitted me. (Andrieu Maurel in court with Crescas Pezati, before 1340)

O you others present here, be witnesses for my spiritual kinsman Julian, also here, if it is necessary to him, that I confirm the lease made to him by my father of a house located in the Fishmongery in which Julian currently resides. I wish that he himself hold the house just as he held it during my father's lifetime according to the form and manner of the lease made by my father to Julian. (Raolin Martin to Julian Marquet, following the death of Raolin's father Bertomieu in 1340)

We have no similar statements for events such as birth, marriage, and death, but the awareness of publicity was so great that there can be little doubt people understood the publicity attending these events as constituting a memorial archive.

The archive created, witnesses were available to testify in court on all life facts, including birth, age, death, legitimacy of parentage, and so on. In one case from 1339, discussed at greater length below, the plaintiff needed to establish that both his parents had died before he was twenty so as to prove that his elder sister, the defendant in the suit, had governed the estate on his behalf.[32] Another suit from 1362 over ownership of a house set a widow named Bertomieua Acharda against her daughter-in-law, Mandina Folquessa.[33] Following the death of her husband, Mandina had tried to evict Bertomieua from the house they had shared. Bertomieua countered that the house was really hers and had come to her from her own mother. To prove this, she related the following set of arguments, paraphrased and compressed below:

(1) Douselina owned the house and called Bertomieua "daughter" and vice versa. (2) Bertomieua was judged to be her daughter. (3) Douselina died last year. (4) She held the house alleged to have belonged to the adversary for thirty years and more. (5) She rented it out for a certain fee. (6) All this is public talk and fame. (fol. 66v)

[32] ADBR 3B 38, fols. 63r–66v, case opened 14 Oct. 1339.
[33] ADBR 3B 64, fols. 65r–71r, case opened 10 Nov. 1362.

This case is especially interesting for it involves three claims that, after the sixteenth century, came to form elements of state archives, namely title in property, filiation, and time of death. Witnesses amply corroborated her claims. Monet de Silans reported that Douselina often came to Bertomieua's house and "held her as a daughter" (fol. 67v). The shoemaker Razos Juven "saw them together as mother and daughter" (fol. 68v) and an old woman named Jacma de Rosono could even remember when Bertomieua was born (fol. 69v). A case from 1354 involving an estate administration included arguments about title, order of death, and age. The plaintiff's argument, compressed and paraphrased below, ran as follows:[34]

(1) A man named Guilhem Sabatier was a tutor for his young niece and nephew, Mathendeta and Guilhemet Sabatier. (2) Guilhem administered their estate. (3) He died. (4) His son Johan took over Guilhem's estate, including the children's estate. (5) Johan died, leaving his estate to his mother Guilelma. (6) Guilelma administered the estate. (7) Guilelma died, leaving the estate to her second husband, Peire Isnart. (8) Peire possesses the children's estate. (9) Mathendeta's little brother Guilhemet died. (10) Mathendeta is Guilhemet's heir and has been acting in this capacity. (11) She is old enough to do so because she is older than sixteen. (12) This is common knowledge. (loose sheet between fols. 304 and 305)

Most of these arguments were denied by Peire Isnart, so she had to prove each one. A series of witnesses came to court to attest to these facts. Yes, Guilhem died fourteen years ago. Yes, Johan died a year before the great mortality. Yes, Peire is holding some of Mathendeta's property. Yes, Mathendeta is older than sixteen. "How do you know this?" "Because I'm a neighbor of Mathendeta's and know her age sufficiently." "Because, as a relative, I raised her for some time in my own house."[35]

When Peire denied these arguments he did so not because he doubted the facts—as it turns out, he had a good defense to this charge—but because denying these facts forced Mathendeta to prove them, a procedure involving both time and expense. In a case heard in 1379, Johan Caprier denied similarly patent facts concerning his sister-in-law Ricardona and her husband, not because they were not true but because proving them might be difficult.[36] His adversary in this bitterly contested suit, Antoni Bertran, was forced to call witnesses for the following facts: Antoni and Ricardona were

34 ADBR 3B 53, fols. 300r–317v, case opened 9 May 1354.
35 Extracts from testimony in ibid., fols. 308r–312v.
36 ADBR 3B 94, fols. 193v–300r, case opened 9 Dec. 1379.

married; they had a daughter Bertomieua and acknowledged her as theirs; Ricardona died first, leaving the daughter as her heir; the daughter died, leaving Antoni as her heir. Antoni adopted a common strategy of proving his points by sheer weight of testimony: eight witnesses were summoned to attest to his arguments: "I was present at the wedding." "Ricardona and Antoni lived as a couple, eating, drinking, and sleeping together as husband and wife. They were named and reputed as husband and wife by neighbors and others in Marseille who knew them. On many occasions, I even came into their room and found them lying together in their bed as a couple." "I was present when Ricardona gave birth." "They openly and publicly said Bertomieua was their legitimate and natural daughter in the presence of me and all the neighbors." "I saw Ricardona breast-feeding her daughter." "I saw when Ricardona died one morning, and Bertomieua her daughter died the following night. I saw the cadavers and prepared them." "I sat vigil with the bodies with not a few neighbors." All were harassed by Johan's interrogatory questions in the hopes of catching them in an inconsistency: "Where was the marriage contracted? Where was it solemnized? Who was present?" "Did you actually see Bertomieua being born?" ("No," a male witness responded to this interrogation, "I'm no nurse, but the people in the house asserted that she had been born.") "Where was she baptized? Who baptized her?" And so on.

Questions of filiation flowed into questions of kinship, as in a case heard in 1343 in which a young man, Perrin Marro, needed to prove both that he was the nephew of the late Girart Marro and that Girart was the owner of a certain house.[37] The witness, Guilhem Castellana, noted that some sixteen years ago Girart was living in a certain house "which is commonly said by all to be Girart's." Guilhem himself lived just across the street, and "often, oftener, and most often (*sepe sepius et sepissime*) has he heard, from Girart's very mouth, in the presence of many people whose names he can't remember, that Perrin was Girart's nephew, son of his brother. Girart raised Perrin in his own house, giving him food and clothing." Raymon Bertran added that Girart had had Perrin instructed in good letters, customs, and doctrines by a teacher, further proof of the kinship said to exist between them. Other witnesses confirmed these points.

The ownership of movables was established by witnesses—friends, neighbors, servants—who had seen owners using them in an open fashion. The custom of asking neighbors to witness a dying person's last testament and then to stand vigil over the dead body was, as several cases show, a particularly important device for creating an archive of knowledge about indi-

[37] ADBR 3B 45, fols. 142r–152r, case opened 16 Aug. 1343.

vidual possessions.[38] Johan Barratan, whose testimony was cited earlier, went on to report as follows:

> The witness and all his neighbors who lived on Pellegrina's street stood vigil around the body or cadaver of Guilelma and stayed next to it for practically the entire night; and he believes that Pellegrina has held and controlled the bed on which Guilelma was lying and any other things or clothes that were in Pellegrina's house.[39]

Ownership of real estate was determined by similar rules. Both the early medieval common law and Roman-canon law allowed title to be proven by means of written documents. In most if not all medieval European legal systems, however, ownership was intimately associated with the useful enjoyment of the property in question, a use that created a presumption of possession that was sometimes in conflict with written documents. In cases of unwritten title, the Roman law of prescription specifically required that claimants enter into possession of property publicly and maintain it peacefully and openly.[40] Certain ritual forms dominated this process. An example of this ritual, worth exploring in some detail, can be found in a dispute over a *bastide*, a large Provençal agricultural holding that included a house and outbuildings. The case pitted a man against his uncle's widow. Sometime before 24 July 1343, when the case itself opened, the uncle, Jacme Macel, had died, leaving the bastide to his widow Biatris.[41] The dead man's nephew, Bertran, considered this loss a great injustice, and on the very day of his uncle's death he assembled a group of witnesses, including the notary Guilhem de Belavila, a friend named Peregrin Arnos, and his own brother-in-law, Jaufres Isnart, and marched into the countryside to enter into possession of the house. His actions conformed to the dictates of the Roman law that governed the entering of property, despite the fact that he apparently had no legitimate claim to the title of the bastide. Thus began a series of encounters all designed to impress upon witnesses the fact of his ownership.

[38] E.g., ADBR 3B 816, fols. 12r–67v, case opened 17 June 1353; ADBR 3B 43, fols. 21r–36r, case opened 30 Aug. 1341.

[39] ADBR 3B 38, fol. 65v, case opened 14 Oct. 1339 on fol. 63r: "Ipse testis et vicine sue omnes de carreria dicte Pelegrine corpus seu cadaver ipsius Guillelme vigilarunt et iuxta eam steterunt quasi per totam nocte; et credit quod lectum in quo ipsa Guillelma iacebat et alie res seu vestes si que erant in domo dicte Pelegrine, dicta Pelegrina habuerit et rexerit."

[40] Barry Nicholas, *An Introduction to Roman Law* (Oxford, 1962), 120–29; Thomas Kuehn, *Law, Family, and Women: Toward a Legal Anthropology of Renaissance Italy* (Chicago, 1991), 108–11.

[41] ADBR 3B 45, fols. 94r–141v, case opened 24 July 1343.

First, along the way he gathered up two female harvesters, Alazays Pelle-grina and Fransesa de Roceto, who were standing in the plaza of Lauret waiting for work. "Willingly," they said, when he asked them if they would like to harvest various fruits at his rural property. Somewhere along the way to the bastide, he called on the miller Johan Guilhem, working at his mill, to join him, and invited one of the miller's workers along too. Once there, he turned first to the miller and said to him, "Sir, know as a witness for me that I have entered and taken possession of this bastide of my uncle Jacme Macel, and of the entire land belonging to it." At this point, the notary Guilhem de Belavila, who had stopped to piss along the road, came hurrying up, in time for Jacme to say to him, "Make for me an instrument concerning how I enter and seize possession of this bastide and its land." Then he insulted Bi-atris's factor, who had reached the bastide before him, and demanded that the factor hand over the key. The factor complied, saying that he was unable to resist him. Meanwhile, the two women were busy harvesting fruit from the fruit trees, and Bertran eventually came to assist them. Together they loaded up an ass with a full burden of fruit to take with them back to the city. Later, he found some men passing along the road and asked if they would be willing to carry back three bushels of grain to the city to sell on his behalf. All this labor was evidence of use and possession; hence Bertran's desire to impress this upon the minds of witnesses.[42]

Bertran lost his case in the end, and his is one of the few extant cases from medieval Marseille in which a litigant seems deaf to the idea that a written act, in this case a testament, gave its beneficiary rights at law that would be recognized and defended by the courts. Here, what is significant is not the litigant's failed attempt at legal legerdemain, but rather the public nature of the entering process. Every new property owner, even those enjoying more legitimate claims to title than did Bertran, had to enact the rituals that cre-ated public awareness of the change in ownership. In the absence of a title claim based on a written instrument, as in cases of intestate succession, the highly publicized process of entering a property created a fund of memories that could later serve as proof of ownership.

To consider the issue more closely, let us take a brief look at further cases involving possession of a house or other urban property. On 8 November 1357, the laborer Peire Bermon brought a suit against Berengiera Girauda because Berengiera had not paid in full for a house that she had promised to

---

[42] For another example, see ADBR 3B 52, fols. 150r–171v, case opened 11 Dec. 1353. This case, a title dispute involving a plot of land and vineyard, includes statements and testimony to the effect that the land was peacefully harvested and otherwise usefully ex-ploited by the presumptive owner.

buy from him.[43] Peire did not produce a written document that would have established the nature of the transaction. As he argued before the judge, however:

> Berengiera, in the presence of many and diverse people, with Peire present, and carrying in her hand the God's pennies [the earnest money], said these words: "All you witnesses, know how I bought a certain house from Peire Bermon, present here, located in the street of the Tannery, for the price of one hundred and five florins, and the entry fee to be paid by Peire."

Then, according to Peire, Berengiera went to the merchant Johan Casse, the previous owner of the house. Johan had sold the house to Peire some time earlier, and as Berengiera told him, "O Lord, I bought from Peire Bermon the house you had sold to him, and since he said that he still owed you some money from the purchase, take from me the remainder." Johan answered her "Let us then conclude this together." Berengiera never showed up in court to defend herself, and the case closed when Peire asked the judge to cite her for contumacy. Peire had no particular need of the written act because the sale was established in the minds of many witnesses through the ceremonies that surrounded the transfer.

In a case from November 1352, Guilelma Scribauda, a citizen of Narbonne, came before the palace court to evict Bernat Bonafos from a house belonging to her late brother, Johan Scribaut.[44] The deceased brother had been a resident in Marseille for the past twenty years; he had lived and died, during the Black Death, in the house in question, which was located on the street of Malcohinat or the Lanternry, near the Coopery in the sixain of St. Jean. Guilelma had inherited the house when Johan died during the Black Death. She offered no written proof that Johan had actually owned the house. This mattered little, though, for she was able to argue that "he [Johan] lived in it as if he owned it" (*tanquam suum*); furthermore, the house was judged (*reputabatur*) by many men of Marseille to belong to her brother.[45] Yet here was Bernat, living, eating, and sleeping in the house and otherwise occupying it. Johan had been a hosteller. A plausible reconstruction of the case is that Bernat had been a guest or tenant of the house during the plague and had gone on living there quietly after the hosteller died. All

---

[43]  AM FF 534, fols. 17r–19v, case opened 8 Nov. 1357.

[44]  ADBR 3B 50, fols. 150r–153v, case opened 10 Nov. 1352.

[45]  Ibid, fol. 152r: "Ponit . . . quod domus predicta reputabatur per plures homines Massilie dicti Johannis Astribaudi et ita dictam domus nominabatur."

Bertran could say in response was that he had possessed the house peacefully and quietly for some time (*diu possedit pacifice et quiete quadam domum*),[46] which was the standard line used in such cases to establish ownership.

Once one possessed a piece of property one had to hold it openly and peacefully. There were a variety of ways for proving this. On 20 October 1338, the merchant Bertran Ricart brought an appeal to the palace court against a decision made by the mason-assessors.[47] The mason-assessors, in settling an argument over who owned a small stable located on Lanataps street near the Pilings, had ruled in favor of the painter Raynaut Adhemar. In the testimony on his behalf, Bertran sought to show how his ownership of the stable had been established through long usage. Thus, the merchant Raolin Martin, testifying for Bertran, claimed to have heard from the neighbors that the stable had belonged to Bertran for at least nine years.[48] The merchant Laurent Rostahn provided even better testimony. This witness regularly went to Bertran's house on merchant business. During his visits he had seen Bertran and his family possessing the stable in question (*possidentem stabulum de quo agitur*).[49] He also claimed to know that the stable and the attached house had been given in *accaptum* to Bertran by the lord Ugo de Jerusalem. The proof he offered was that he had seen Bertran pay the yearly rent ("prout dictum censsum vidit solvi . . . spacio v annorum et ultra"). Similar cases show that the paying of annual taxes was considered evidence for the useful and public ownership of property.[50]

In another case, a witness, Raymon Julian, was trying to help a litigant named Jacma Augeliera establish that a certain house had belonged to her late husband.[51] The witness reported that he had seen the deceased man, Johan de Tholosa, living in the house as if it were his own (*tanquam suo*) over the last seven years. When the judge inquired further into this point, asking him how he knew the house belonged to Johan, the witness answered that public knowledge held it to be so, and besides he had seen Johan pay the rent to an agent of St. Victor.[52] A second witness, Johan Julian, reported that he had seen Jacma entering and exiting the house and even possessing the key to the house, with Johan de Tholosa's full knowledge.[53] This is a partic-

---

[46] Ibid, fol. 151v.
[47] ADBR 3B 34, fols. 136r–148v, case opened 20 Oct. 1338.
[48] Ibid., fol. 141r.
[49] Ibid, fol. 141v.
[50] E.g., ADBR 3B 53, fols. 22r–25v, case opened 16 Sept. 1353.
[51] ADBR 3B 812, fols. 26r–37r, case opened 1 June 1352.
[52] Ibid, fol. 34v.
[53] Ibid, fol. 33r.

ularly interesting case because Jacma did not offer a dotal act to prove that she was married to Johan de Tholosa; her witnesses argued that they knew the couple to have been married since they (the witnesses) often shared food and drink with them in their house and saw them behaving as married couples do.

One of the most difficult facts to know was the financial health of a person's estate. Wives, widows, wards, and others whose wealth and property was under the administration of another had a vested interest in knowing how well the job was being done. This became a serious issue in the 1350s: many estates lost value following the Black Death through no fault of the husbands, tutors, and other estate administrators, but these were sued just the same in an effort to recover the estate. But how was one to know? The answer was fama: all a plaintiff needed to show was that there was common knowledge of the progressive dilapidation or impending bankruptcy. In November 1353, for example, Sparrona Carbonelle, the sister of the squire Peire Carbonel, moved against her husband Guilhem Benezeg on the grounds that his estate was losing value and that he was threatened by creditors. The positions presented on her behalf were simple: (1) Guilhem had been selling movable and immovable goods at a great rate; (2) common knowledge held that "he is verging on hopelessness" (*vergit ad inopiam*).[54] Guilhem had other debtors and naturally had absolutely no interest in defending himself from his wife's suit, so this trial, like most of its kind, concluded very rapidly and almost certainly in Sparrona's favor.

Marseille's legal culture, in many of its facets, was manifestly public in orientation, and thus an efficient mechanism for inscribing facts into the public record. As we have seen in all these cases, litigants were able to draw upon these facts when necessary. Publicity can be achieved unintentionally, of course, but the value placed on public behavior suggests that people were conscious of the need to be open.

One of the most remarkable features of the legal culture of publicity, as I have pointed out in earlier chapters, is that it encompassed the courts of law themselves, all of which convened out of doors. The publicity of legal function extends beyond the courts, for public notaries in Marseille and throughout Mediterranean Europe were just as public in their transactions. Subscription clauses from Marseille reveal that notaries frequently did business in the street before their houses or those of their clients. Rents owed to major lords were collected on a yearly basis by notaries hired to perambulate the city, knocking on doors of householders and drawing up acts on the spot, in the public eye. Acts were publicly read out loud in the presence of

[54] ADBR 3B 53, fols. 162r–167r, case opened 28 Nov. 1353.

witnesses.[55] Moreover, when selecting witnesses to notarial contracts, notaries and/or their clients commonly invited random strangers rather than close friends or kinsmen of the clients involved; this practice enhanced the open and public nature of the transaction. In the case of a notarized loan, a witness named Johan de Massilia gave the following testimony:

> Called by a certain woman whom he doesn't recollect, the witness went to a certain house belonging to Guilelma Cadella located in the street of the Upper Grain Market of Marseille where the said Ugonet and his wife used to live. There he found the notary Johan Guibert, junior, the said Ugonet, his wife, master Peire de Jovis, alias de Lhione, Jacme Juvenis, master Salamon de Palermo, and two other Jews and other Christians whose names he doesn't remember now. . . . This happened four or five years ago. On the table or desk of the house there was placed a certain number of florins that did not, it seemed, amount to eighty florins. . . . His name was written down as being a witness to the act and then the said notary read out loud and publicized how the said Jew acknowledged a debt of 160 florins to Ugonet. Hearing this, the witness whispered into Ugonet's ear that there wasn't eighty florins there, and Ugonet answered that for the eighty florins he was giving to the Jews they were going to owe him 160 florins.[56]

Johan was not involved in any way with the transaction, nor was he related to any of the parties involved, and his presence was an important element in Salamon's attempt to charge Ugonet with usury. The money was spread on the table in full view not only of the parties involved and of the two formal witnesses required for debts but also of several other people who came along to witness the transaction on behalf of their friends or co-religionists.

The great concern about fraud and forgery was one of the factors that encouraged notaries and their clients not to be secretive about the acts they drew up. The publicity that attended all forms of legal behavior in medieval Marseille reveals that even the law had to be open and public to avoid the cloud of suspicion that inevitably gathered around behavior that was seen to be secretive and evasive. Outdoor and open legal ceremonies contributed to the public and honest character of the law. Public behavior, in other words, joined with royal or governmental recognition to give notarial contracts and judicial pronouncements the authority they carried.

[55] E.g., ADBR 3B 19, fol. 132r, case opened 20 Feb. 1326 on fol. 119r: "Pluries et pluries vidit et audivit legi quoddam instrument aquitationis facte per dictum Amicum Vincentii generaliter Bartholomee Ruffe sorori Guillelmi Ruffi."

[56] ADBR 3B 38, fol. 110r, case opened 20 July 1339 on fol. 90r.

We have seen how the legal culture of publicity inscribed certain kinds of facts in the archives of memory. These memories sometimes duplicated written archives. More often, memories archived facts that were not readily available in writing. This is particularly true in cases involving age, parentage, ownership of movables, marital status, date of birth, and date of death, and is also true in many cases of title. In such cases, judges and litigants did not have access to a well-managed state archive. With the important exception of debt, judges in Marseille could rarely hope to base their judgments on a paper trail of written documents offering unambiguous evidence in support of a claim. Instead, the knowledge needed in such cases was diffused among innumerable archives composed, on a case-by-case basis, not only of any available written acts but also, and usually more importantly, of sets of witnesses and their memories—or, to be more precise, the ways these witnesses chose to interpret their memories in courtroom settings.[57]

Yet it was not easy, in the absence of modern forensic techniques, for judges to test whether the memories dredged up in court replicated the facts in some reasonably accurate fashion. It was not easy to decide which set of memories, which knowledge, was authoritative. Judges in southern Europe, of course, had a variety of tools for coping with this problem, one of which was torture. Another was to encourage arbitration, thereby avoiding a decision entirely. The stories of some litigants collapsed under the weight of their own inconsistencies. But not all cases provided easy solutions, and when all else failed it seems that judges sought to find out whether knowledge was known everywhere, always, and by all. If a state of affairs had been publicized in the appropriate fashion, if a litigant had been fully public in all he or she did, then knowledge of this should have seeped outside the confines of the litigant's immediate family, friends, and dependents and entered into the general archive of knowledge. Such knowledge was common knowledge, *fama publica*, "that which is publicly spoken among people," as Johan Senequier put it in 1337.[58] If this condition was met, then, logically speaking, the knowledge-bearing group, represented by the witnesses re-

---

[57] For many of these points see Sally Humphreys, "Social Relations on Stage: Witnesses in Classical Athens," *History and Anthropology* 1 (1985): 313–69.

[58] In jurisprudential treatises the role of fama, or rumor and reputation, was much discussed throughout the Middle Ages. The literature is discussed in Thelma Fenster and Daniel Lord Smail, eds., *Fama: The Politics of Talk and Reputation in Medieval Europe* (Ithaca, 2003).

cruited by litigants, should appear diffuse and pluralistic. By taking the measure of the knowledge-bearing groups, judges could ascertain which party had conformed most closely to the demands of publicity.

This is, of course, an argument from inference. We have very little direct evidence telling us that this is how judges sifted conflicting claims. Yet this is the most plausible way to explain why witness groups, in many cases of protracted litigation from medieval Marseille, bear the imprint of diversity. What seems clear is that litigants, in their attempts to sculpt the raw material of memory into a convincing case, took care to build a body of witnesses that made manifest the entirely public nature of the knowledge in question. The frequency of the practice suggests that it was a common and deliberate tactic used to influence the judge's decisions.

The judicial system of medieval Marseille was hostile toward memories that were bound up in small, intimate groups based on ties of kinship and dependency. The chief difficulty with a system that rigidly excludes the testimony of people closely associated with litigants, however, is that in many cases theirs is the best testimony. In the title dispute discussed briefly above, one witness named Alexander Girart gave testimony to prove that Jacma Augeliera was the widow of Johan de Tholosa. He revealed that he frequently drank and ate with the couple (*bibit et comedit cum eis*).[59] A subsequent witness, Johan Julian, when asked by the judge how he knew that Jacma had been married to Johan, also responded that he drank and ate often with them ("bibit et comedit pluries in hospicio cum eis").[60] If a judge were to rigidly exclude the testimony of such people, then it would be very difficult for any litigant to establish the facts of his or her case with any kind of authority.

A variety of cases from fourteenth-century Marseille reveal the following solution to this paradox: litigants routinely corroborated the possibly suspect but knowledgeable testimony of close associates, especially neighbors, with testimony from witnesses who were socially and geographically more distant. In the case of Bertran Macel described at length above, we have already seen how Bertran impressed the fact of his entering into possession of the bastide on a wide variety of people. These included an affine (his brother-in-law); his peers (a neighboring miller and a friend); his inferiors (the female harvesters, the passing carters, and the miller's worker); and the law (the notary Guilhem). All these people came to testify on his behalf in the subsequent court case. The resulting knowledge-bearing group was impressively diverse, ranging from a relative (his brother-in-law) to poor, female laborers.

[59] ADBR 3B 812, fol. 32v, case opened 1 June 1352 on fol. 26r.
[60] Ibid., fol. 33r.

Other witness groups, as we will see in the cases that follow, have remarkably similar social characteristics. The first case, from 1341, involved a dispute over ownership of a bed. At some point in August of that year, the shoemaker Guilhem Imbert was lying ill in his house.[61] The house was located in the shoemaker enclave known as the Shoemakery (Grolaria), in the sixain of St. Jacques above the New street. Guilhem's wife Garsens, sensing his impending death and wishing to gather the dying man's relatives, asked the shoemaker Guilhem Picart, who lived across the street, to go immediately to the houses of Alazays Ricaua and Raynaut de Conquis, the niece and nephew of the dying man, and tell them of their uncle's grave condition. Only the nephew Raynaut answered her summons. Arriving at his uncle's house and working his way through the press of neighbors that had gathered around the deathbed, Raynaut inquired of his uncle how he felt. Guilhem seemed to say that he was not too bad. The nephew tactlessly went on to ask the dying man, "Sir, do you recall the bed that I loaned to you some time ago?" At this point the testimony concerning the case diverges. According to Raynaut and his witnesses, his uncle's response was a vigorous "O Garsens, give the bed to Raynaut," to which Garsens answered that it would be done, whereat Raynaut turned to the people there and, following the principle that facts must be inscribed in the memories of witnesses, said, "Take heed on my behalf, you witnesses, of these words spoken by Guilhem and his wife, as you have heard." By contrast, the witness Guilhem Picart, who had accompanied Raynaut into the room, reported that Guilhem had said "It is upstairs, and if you find it, take it," but was half dead and bereft of his good sense (*de sua bona memoria derelictus*) at the time.

The dispute wound up in court. A variety of witnesses testified on behalf of the widow, Garsens. They included a maid who lived in the dying man's household, but the testimony of this close dependent was amply corroborated by a widening array of witnesses that featured neighbors, nonresident fellow shoemakers, and even a nobleman named Arnaut de Sant Jacme who lived several streets away. The only line of challenge open to the nephew Raynaut was to argue that the witness who had offered the most damaging testimony, Guilhem Picart, was, along with his wife, a member of the household or at least in the service of the dead man. But Raynaut's arguments could not be established by means of an equally persuasive array of witnesses and he lost his case.

The knowledge-bearing group assembled by Garsens, the widow, showed how events were known not only within the house but also in the neighborhood and even by a nobleman living several blocks away. The

---

[61] ADBR 3B 43, fols. 21r–36r, case opened 30 Aug. 1341.

telling case of Antoni d'Ays and his concubine, Dousa d'Esparon, also demonstrates how litigants were eager to establish that facts were known within the house and neighborhood, outside the neighborhood, and among different status groups.[62] The case, discussed at greater length in chapter 2, involved an attempt by certain shoemakers of Negrel street to evict Dousa, whom they accused of being a prostitute. The case began in earnest when Antoni's enemy, Guilhem de Podio, brought witnesses to prove that Dousa was a quarrelsome woman, overflowing with vice and wickedness, accustomed to insulting the good women of Negrel street, and she was therefore not worthy to live there. To prove this he called on six witnesses whose testimony was formulaic and interchangeable and remarkably lacking in chronological depth—one feature suggesting that who gave the testimony was more important than what that testimony revealed. Three of the witnesses were shoemakers and Negrel street householders: in effect, expert witnesses, people who knew the names of the "good women" who had suffered under Dousa's insults and could sketch out a simple topography of the householders on Negrel street.[63] Through the voices of the three men, Guilhem established the common purpose of all Negrel street shoemakers to have Dousa kept away. Yet this was clearly insufficient, for it had the effect of making the affair appear as a private quarrel among shoemakers. Accordingly, Guilhem sought out three further witnesses, one a glassmaker, one a former maid in Antoni's service, and one a merchant.[64] The maid, Aycelena d'Albanha, offered no new perspective despite her privileged post of observation, but was clearly used to show how even those in Antoni's service could turn against him. The testimony of the two men was even more important, for both enjoyed some standing and neither lived on Negrel street. Other sources reveal that the glassmaker, Peire Bermon, lived in the Old Glaziery, which stood at the head of Negrel street to the north. The merchant, named Jacme Bermon (unrelated to Peire), almost certainly lived on the street of the Upper Drapery, the street that cut across Negrel street to the south. By using their testimony, Guilhem de Podio was able to show, in a very spatial way, how word of Dousa's behavior had spilled beyond the confines of Negrel street both north and south and into the social world of glassmakers and rich merchants.

Ideally, knowledge of an event should circulate throughout the city, as we find in a fragment of a third case involving an affray in 1353.[65] The story ran as follows. A woman named Amelha became involved in a quarrel with Ay-

---

[62] ADBR 3B 41, fols. 164r–185v, case opened 16 Aug. 1340.
[63] Ibid., fols. 166r–168v.
[64] Ibid., fols. 169r–171r.
[65] ADBR 3B 50, unbound folios located at the end of the register.

carda Borgonha, the wife of the draper Andrieu Borgonho, on the doorstep of Aycarda's house. The quarrel ended with the lady Aycarda publicly insulting Amelha, calling her a whore. Bernat de Conchis, who was standing nearby, came to the defense of the insulted Amelha, and immediately Aycarda's husband Andrieu, her son Gilon, and a friend Lois Martin rushed out of the house. According to one inquisition witness, Amelha may have said to Bernat de Conchis, "Take hold of this boy since he is trying to kill me,"[66] presumably referring to the young Gilon, but it was Bernat who got the worst of it: Lois Martin struck him on the hand and arm, drawing blood.

The extracts of inquisition testimony from which this account can be reconstructed are followed by an appeal lodged by Andrieu, Aycarda, and Gilon Borgonho against the results of the inquisition. The family sought to build on testimony given by Andrieu himself in the original inquisition, namely that while he, Andrieu, was having a meal, Amelha came over and began insulting the "people of his house." Andrieu told her, "Madam, you shouldn't say those words to me in front of my own house" ("domina, non dicatis ante januam meam michi verba"). But what Andrieu was driving at in this inquisition testimony came out clearly when the time came for him and his family to make their own case: Amelha *was* in fact a vile whore. As a maid (*ancilla*) of the draper Johan Bernat, we learn, she regularly fornicated with a great many men. Aycarda, by contrast, was a good lady and Andrieu a peaceful man.

For our purposes the important features of this case lie, first, in Andrieu's ability to impugn the hostile testimony of three inquisition witnesses—all three were linked, by service and by blood, to Amelha's master, Johan Bernat—and, second, in the nature of the witnesses subsequently recruited on behalf of the Borgonho family. These included neighbors, nonresident drapers (Andrieu's colleagues), and two people who were not closely related in any way. The draper Folco Rainos and the furrier Guilhem Benezeg were evidently men of standing, for both had served at one point or another as rectors of the hospital of St. Esprit. The two distant witnesses included a notary and curial official, Johan de Montesalino, and the caulker Johan Isnart, who lived several blocks away. Andrieu's story, in short, was corroborated by a much wider community of knowledge that not only crossed status lines but also was distributed throughout the city. Although the final outcome is not given, the case ends in a way that suggests victory for the Borgonho family.

A final case, also discussed briefly in chapter 2, is fascinating for what it reveals not only about how paternity was known and proven in court but

[66] Ibid., testimony of Dulsona Rauqueta, fol. iv.

THE CONSUMPTION OF JUSTICE

also about the differing abilities of nobles and commoners to assemble socially and geographically distant witnesses. On 19 February 1355, the powerful nobleman Laugier de Soliers came before the palace judge, Pons Chays, to lodge a complaint of nonpayment of rent on behalf of his mother-in-law, Johana Bonpara. Johana was the wife of the nobleman Olivier Bonpar and daughter of Jacme Bausan.[67] The suit claimed that the owner of the estate of the late laborer, Bertran Peire, had failed to pay Johana nine pounds rent owed on a garden. A striking feature of the case is that no written proofs were offered for any of the arguments raised by either party. Laugier managed to assemble five witnesses to testify to the various points he raised.

The best testimony was provided by the first witness, the old nobleman Laurent Ricau, who was remarkably well informed about the original owners, the laborer Guilhem Peire and his son Bertran. The witness reported that the laborer Guilhem had received the land in question in dowry from his wife, Sileta Flora. To prove that he knew Guilhem well, the witness described the man's features: Guilhem was a man of ordinary stature, honest face, ancient, and partially blind. Asked by the court whether Bertran was in fact Guilhem's son, the witness answered yes, at least he was so judged by common opinion ("prout de eo erat publica vox et fama in civitate Massilie"), for Guilhem had raised him and nourished him inside his own home as a legitimate son. Regarding whether Bertran had in fact named Guilhem de Montels to succeed him, the witness explained that he himself had read the testament written by the notary Peire Verdelhon in which Bertran made Guilhem his universal heir.[68] He had also read the dotal act of Johana's mother Biatris, which is why he could confirm that the rent belonged to her and that she was indeed in a position to leave it to her daughter Johana. Furthermore, he had often seen Bertran paying the rent to Olivier Bonpar—the rent, he explained in a display of intimate knowledge, was not in fact nine pounds but had been reduced to seven pounds 4s. 1d.—and had even heard Bertran asking his workers to be sure and pick mature fruit for Olivier and Johana. The witness even named the fruits being harvested on their behalf: figs, pears, prunes, cherries, peaches, and other fruits.

At the end of Laurent's testimony, the judge, perhaps tipped off by the opposition, inquired into the relationship between Laurent and the litigants who had recruited his testimony. Was he related to Johana? Not exactly, explained Laurent, although she was a god-kin of his (*comater sua*), and Laurent's first wife had been a blood cousin of Johana's.

Testimony then followed from Jacme Bausan, who, as Johana's father,

---

[67] ADBR 3B 58, fols. 92r–112r, case opened 19 Feb. 1355.
[68] Guilhem de Montels's status—was he a legatee or an heir?—is never clarified.

was in a position to confirm the dowry. Then came Johana's maternal uncle, Bertran de Buco, who explained that it was he who had assigned the original rent in dowry to his sister Biatris, Johana's mother. The next witness was a woman named Bertrana Viventa. Her testimony was critically important to the case because all the other witnesses were related in one way or another to Johana and/or her son-in-law Laugier de Soliers. Bertrana explained that Guilhem Peire had been a neighbor of hers some three decades earlier, and she too gave a brief description of Guilhem. She also confirmed the general opinion that Bertran was widely considered to be Guilhem's son by their acquaintances. Asked how she was able to know that Bertran paid the rent regularly to Johana, she responded that she had seen installments of 52s., 52s., and 40s. 1d., and, as was usual, that he had named and called various people to witness the transactions (*nominabat et vocabat aliquos testes*). She had also seen Johana bringing to Bertran's house two empty baskets in which the fruit was to be collected in harvest season.

As in the case of Laurent above, the judge then asked her carefully about her status and her involvement in the case. Asked if she was hated by Guilhem de Montels or held him in hatred ("inimica Guillelmi de Montiliis aut inimicatus eidem"), she answered no, and explained that she even preferred to buy cloth from him rather than from any other draper. She was worth sixty to seventy pounds (in answer to other questions), was around forty years of age, and was not a servant of Johana or Laugier.

At this point the case seemed pretty clear cut: the payment of the rent had been established in long usage and the avenue by which ownership of the rent came down to Johana seemed to be unimpeachable. In contesting the case as set out by Laugier, the defendant Guilhem de Montels in fact chose not to contest any of this. Rather, his strategy was to impugn the testimony proffered against him.

First, he explained that Laurent Ricau was no innocent bystander but had instigated the suit and therefore should be barred from giving testimony. Second, Laurent had also led Johana to open the case, implying that he was using Johana as a means to persecute Guilhem. Third, Bertran de Buco had expressly joined sides with Johana (*partem expresse fecit*) and therefore his testimony should be discounted. And then possibly the most damaging set of points: "(4) Bertrana Viventa is a woman of vile standing and low life and a public prostitute; (5) she has even borne two children to one Johan Jaufres; (6) furthermore, Bertrana, despite her statement to the contrary, is a servant of Laugier de Soliers, eating, drinking, and living in his house."

The witnesses called by Guilhem all upheld various aspects of this argument. To prove Laurent's involvement in the suit, Guilhem de Sant Gili testified that one day, about a year ago, he had heard Laurent Ricau arguing with Guilhem de Montels in Guilhem's workshop on the street of the Upper Drapery. This argument was confirmed by the witness Pons Columbier. The third witness, Peire Martin, observed that two or three years ago he had seen Bertrana insulting her female neighbors on the street of the Steps, and then he had heard the neighboring women calling her a vile woman and a prostitute who had borne the illegitimate son of Bertran Jaufres (not Johan, as claimed in the articles of proof).[69] The witness had also seen Bertrana living in the house of Laugier. Last, a witness named Guilhem Borme reported that public rumor had it that Bertrana, while living in the house of Laugier's father Raymon, had borne twin sons for Bertran Jaufres, who was Raymon's bodyguard.

As this case suggests and others confirm, it is typical of the nobility that knowledge of their affairs was often restricted to a private space defined by their noble relatives or their servants. Why this is so is unclear. Guilhem de Montels managed to expose how the opposing witnesses and litigants constituted a coterie joined by blood, marriage, and service, and the rules of evidence made such testimony suspect, as discussed in chapter 2. Guilhem de Montels had much greater success in recruiting his own witnesses. Of the four men who testified on his behalf, one was a notary, Pons Columbier, theoretically public and impartial. Guilhem de Sant Gili was a nobleman with no obvious connection to the man who recruited his testimony. In all likelihood, he was a random passerby on the street of the Upper Drapery when he overheard the incriminating remarks that passed between Laurent Ricau and Guilhem de Montels a year earlier. This suggests how tradesmen profited from the public nature of their craft, from the constant coming and going in front of their workshops and houses. The remaining two witnesses were both residents of the street in question and therefore lived at some distance from Guilhem de Montels. Guilhem, in short, was remarkably adept at assembling witnesses from a broad social and geographical spectrum. Again, the outcome of the case is not given, but indications suggest that Guilhem was victorious.


## WOMEN'S KNOWLEDGE, MEN'S KNOWLEDGE


In the four cases discussed above I have explored how space, kinship, and status were important factors considered by litigants as they attempted to assemble diverse witness groups. The sex of witnesses was another factor.

[69] Ibid., fol. 109v.

When Maria Mayffrena testified on behalf of the Borgonho family in the case above, her testimony differed from that provided by the five male witnesses in a striking way. The men were able to testify to the general reputations of the men and women involved and to give some narrative of the events in the battle. Maria, however, was the only witness able to report on domestic affairs, namely that one of the hostile witnesses, Guilhem de Jerusalem, was in the service of a relative of the opposing litigant. In many court cases from medieval Marseille we find that women and men knew different things. In many cases, therefore, it was important to establish that the facts of one's case were known not only far and wide and across different status groups but also by men and women alike.

To begin with, almost every case that required testimony about time of birth or death was supported by the testimony of one or more women. A disputed inheritance that opened in December 1379 provides some of the most telling examples of testimony about time of birth.[70] Some of the arguments made toward the end of this long and fascinating case turn on the age of the deceased woman, Ricardona Bertrande. The articles of proof for this stage of the proceedings, unfortunately, have been lost, but it is clear from the testimony that her husband had refused to allow her to call a notary to acquit her sister and brother-in-law of an inheritance. He justified this refusal on the grounds that she was too young to call a notary without his permission. Three women and five men came to court to attest to her age at the time of her death in 1373. The testimony given by the five men confirmed Ricardona's age in general or vague terms. As the cobbler Jacme Johan said, "I believe her to have been less than twenty years old; she was said to be seventeen or eighteen." A buckler named Antoni Bocaran noted that he was aware of her age because he was a neighbor and knew both Ricardona and her father.[71] The three women, by contrast, gave much more detailed and confident testimony regarding Ricardona's age:

> Ricardona was eighteen when she died, according to what I know. She was born in the house where Johan Caprier now lives, and her father lived five years after she was born. Both her father and her mother died in the same plague. She was about seventeen or eighteen when she died. (testimony of Catherina de Auruolo, fol. 291r–v)

> She was seventeen or eighteen when she died. I know this because I breast-fed her with milk in her own house. She was seventeen or eight-

[70] ADBR 3B 94, fols. 193v–300r, case opened 9 Dec. 1379.
[71] For these two extracts see ibid., fols. 292v, 298r.

een when she died and if she had lived until now she would be twenty-four years of age. (testimony of Johaneta Sallone, fol. 292r)

It is true that she was seventeen or eighteen when she died . . . [She is asked which nanny raised her.] The nanny was someone who lived in the area of Cayssaria whose name is Aysselena Vuerna. (testimony of Benezega Stora, fol. 296r)

A case from October 1339 shows how neighborhood women kept track of both birth and death.[72] The case pitted Adhemar Gamel against his widowed sister, Pellegrina, in a dispute over the inheritance of their mother Guilelma.[73] The mother had died sixteen years earlier, around the year 1326. In her testament, she bestowed a few legacies on her married and dowered daughter, Pellegrina (chiefly clothes but also a bed and a few other things), and also gave a few things to Pellegrina's daughter, Jaumeta. Adhemar was Guilelma's heir. Pellegrina claimed she never received her legacies. Adhemar argued in turn that at the time of their mother's death, he was less than twenty-five years of age and had no curator. As a result, his elder sister, Pellegrina, had become curator of the estate by default. Given her power, she had been able to extract all her legacies at her leisure and in fact did so. Pellegrina denied seizing the estate. The case ended up hinging on Adhemar's age at the time of his mother's death.

The first witness, a neighbor named Sicilia Desderia, explained to the court that although she did not know when Adhemar was made heir, what she *did* know was that she had borne a son, Guilhem, around the same time that Adhemar and another neighborhood boy, Peire Rostahn, were born; all three boys were born within two months of one another. She knew this because she and the other two women all lived on the same street ("nam ipsa testis et Guillelma Gamella et Berengaria Rostagna mater dicti Petri Rostagni una carreria morabantur"). Her son was now age thirty-eight, which would have made Adhemar twenty-two at the time of the dictation of the testament.

The second and third witnesses, respectively Adhemar's wife Jacma and another neighbor, the caulker Johan Barratan, then testified that upon the mother's death, Pellegrina did indeed seize the bed and other items. Johan, hearing the news of Guilelma's death, came with other neighbors to perform the vigil, which gave him a privileged view of the goings-on in the

---

[72] This was particularly important in Roman law, where one's status at law was partly dependent on age. See Thomas Kuehn, *Emancipation in Late Medieval Florence* (New Brunswick, N.J., 1982).

[73] ADBR 3B 38, fols. 63r–66v, case opened 14 Oct. 1339.

house and made it possible for him to recognize the things, notably the bed, that Pellegrina now held. Despite being a neighbor of long standing, he did not testify on the question of Adhemar's age. The fourth witness, Berengiera Rostahna, returned to this question and provided essentially the same testimony as Sicilia Desderia. Last came Peire Rostahn himself, Adhemar's contemporary, although he was not asked to give his own age.

A final example, this one from 1348, also involves an effort to establish, at court, the fact of someone's decease. In this case, Jacme de Podio was trying to lay claim to the estate of his daughter-in-law Ugueta, the late wife of his son Peire, both of whom died during the plague without leaving testaments.[74] To lay his claim, he needed to show that Ugueta had died before the couple's daughter, Bilona. If this were the case, then Bilona would have been Ugueta's intestate heir. Peire, in turn, would have inherited his wife's estate from Bilona, and Jacme in his own turn from his son Peire. According to Jacme, Ugueta died around Lent. Bilona survived her mother by fifteen days, and her father Peire lived a mere two days further. The three witnesses to the order of deaths were all women; first, Ugueta Sperneria, the wife of Antoni Spernier, who claimed to know the correct order of deaths because she was a neighbor. Ugueta apparently reported the news to her neighbor Johaneta Bermunda, the next witness, who testified that she had seen Bilona going up and down the street after the death of the mother. Sanxieta de Galbert then testified that she saw Bilona being carried dead to the cemetery, following which she heard the news that Peire had died.

Women's authoritative knowledge over birth and death also made them arbiters of kinship and legitimacy of parentage. The case of Ricardona discussed earlier has numerous examples from earlier stages of the proceedings designed to show that a girl named Bertomieua was the legitimate offspring of Ricardona and her husband Antoni. Again, female testimony is both prominent and especially convincing. Agnes Johanna, for example, was able to report that she had been present when Ricardona gave birth to Bertomieua, and noted how both Ricardona and Antoni subsequently acknowledged Bertomieua openly and publicly. The subsequent witness, her husband, was only able to report that he knew of the girl's birth because his wife had been present and told him.[75] In a case that opened at court in 1335, witness testimony shows that the issue at stake was whether Raymon Malet and his wife Marquesia Martina were in fact married and treated all their children, including their daughter Gandulfa, as their legitimate offspring.[76]

---

[74] ADBR 355E 292, fols. 48r–50v, 10 Apr. 1348.
[75] ADBR 3B 94, fols. 213r–215r, case opened 9 Dec. 1379 on fol. 193v.
[76] ADBR 3B 30, fols. 112r–145v, case opened 7 Sept. 1335.

Witnesses included three women and one man. The man, Ferier Micael, was able to name the five children; he also reported that all the neighbors in the street of the Great Market held the children to be legitimate. The three women gave much stronger and more detailed testimony, Sicilia Maienqua even reporting how Marquesia nursed Gandulfa at her own breast.[77]

Women, like men, frequently entered the houses of their neighbors to chat and share food, and seem to have taken particular care to observe household possessions. An excellent case involving a great many relevant issues can be found in an inheritance dispute from June 1353, pitting Jacma, widow of the late laborer Peire Bernis, against Peire's heir, Bernat Raymbaut.[78] From the transcript we learn that Bernat's claim was the following: although the late Peire had left his widow Jacma a legacy of sixty pounds, she had forcibly seized a great many items (these were all enumerated) from Peire's house, items that were worth much more than sixty pounds. Jacma countered with the following:

(1) The house in which the couple lived was not Peire's but was in fact Jacma's dotal house, situated in the street of the Tannery. (2) Many things on Bernat's list came with the dowry [they were in the house at the time of marriage, the point implies]. (3) Peire had left her not only sixty pounds but also all that belonged in the house in question [arnesia ac totum froirum quae et quod erant infra dictam domum ... dotalem]. (4) With Peire dead, Bertran himself had violently seized several things belonging to Jacma. (5) All this is known by her neighbors. (fol. 29r–v)

Testimony suggests that Peire died in the plague, and that the dispute arose at least in part because of the uncertainties of possession caused by the plague. It also seems that Bertran, as heir, had in fact received very little by way of inheritance, and his anger appears to have stemmed from a mistaken belief that a woman's dowry belonged to the woman's husband and hence to his heirs. In Jacma's own defense of her dowry, she called upon four witnesses, two men and two women, although only the two women testified in the end. One witness reported how several elements of the dowry given on the list had originally belonged to Jacma Bernissa's mother, and that she had seen them in the house for at least twelve years. On the third point, this witness, Jacma Colrada, observed that she, along with many others, had been in the house when Peire dictated his testament and had heard the legacies

[77] Ibid., fol. 135v.
[78] ADBR 3B 816, fols. 12r–67v, case opened 17 June 1353.

made to Jacma. The other witness, Ermelina Barreria, gave similar testimony.

When his turn came, Bernat was strikingly incapable of summoning any convincing witnesses whatsoever. All three of his witnesses were men. A great deal of the testimony of the three men consisted of *nichil scire* (he knows nothing), and one witness, Raymon Pascal, even seems to have supported Jacma's claim. Bernat moved on to another tactic, that of impugning Jacma's witnesses, for he then claimed that Jacma Colrada was a servant of Jacma Bernissa, living in her house and eating, drinking, and chatting with her, as well as being worth less than the twenty shillings necessary for a witness. He called upon a woman to testify to this, who answered *nichil scire* to all three points.

These examples of types of female knowledge show that women controlled specific forms of socialization and were repositories of aural and visual information. To a certain extent, this afforded women a degree of power within neighborhoods, power unavailable to them in the larger city space, although the fact that men could and did testify on similar issues limits the extent of this power. All the same, it seems likely that not many men or women could afford to alienate the significant women of the neighborhood and still hope to marshal firm support in a lawsuit.

These issues are highlighted in a case from 1339 that set Johan Girman and his nephew Esteve Girman against Jacma Thomasia over a debt of seven pounds 12s. 2d. that had arisen from a purchase of wine.[79] At the time the record opened, Esteve was in prison at the behest of Jacma, and Johan was attempting both to get him out and to prosecute Jacma for failure to pay off the debt. According to Johan, Jacma had complained to the inquisition that Esteve had unjustly harassed her regarding the debt. Johan sought to prove:

(1) Jacma is a tavern-keeper. (2) Ugueta Segueria, the witness who had given testimony against Esteve, was less than twelve years of age . . . (3) Ugueta is also a niece of Jacma's. (4) Esteve and Johan are men of good repute who customarily abstain from lying and from asking others to pay off debts that were not owed. (5) This is the public fame in Marseille, especially among acquaintances and neighbors. (fols. 264v–265r)

On points one, four, and five, Johan brought forward three male witnesses, all of whom gave glowing reports on the good repute of Esteve and

---

[79] ADBR 3B 37, fols. 264r–269r, case opened in June 1339.

Johan, and little else.[80] In response, Jacma assembled her guns. In a tidy two points she argued simply: (1) She paid off the debt fifteen days ago at the doorway of her house; (2) she is a lawful and honest woman, of good life and praiseworthy standing, and judged to be so by acquaintances and neighbors. On her behalf she brought in three female witnesses, all of whom vigorously confirmed that the debt had been paid off in their presence. Judging by their testimony, Jacma, as a tavern-keeper, was in a particularly good position to recruit witnesses to small transactions, for at least two of the three witnesses had been queuing up to purchase wine from Jacma when the quittance occurred. The judge inquired carefully of each witness how much she was worth and, of two of them, whether they were servants of Jacma's, sharing bread and wine with her. The two said no. One of them, the fourteen-year-old Ugueta Segueria, said that she did not know how much she was worth because she had a mother and a brother. A second, Bertomieua Aonna, when asked her worth, explained that she was content with her situation and owned a house, although she did not know its value.

Given that there was no written quittance of the debt, it was a question of Jacma's word against that of the Girmans. Both had witnesses to testify to their good standing. The marked difference in the testimony, namely the fact that Jacma was able to assemble witnesses who saw the transaction, arises from the fact that the transaction took place in her space, at her tavern door. And given that Jacma's clients seem to have been mostly women, that space was a female space.

This last case shows that an all-female group of witnesses could carry considerable authority. Other cases reveal that it was apparently a good strategy for litigants to include both women and men in the witness groups they were recruiting, and Esteve and Johan Girman's inability to prove that knowledge of the debt circulated among neighborhood women was clearly a serious obstacle to their cases. Like geography and status, then, biological sex was one of the factors that litigants considered in drawing up witnesses. It is, of course, hard to assess how conscious litigants were of this need. The highly self-conscious nature of publicity, as argued above, suggests in general that litigants had considerable legal expertise. The evidence surveyed above, moreover, shows how normal it was for witness groups to be diverse; this alone suggests a degree of conscious adaptation. Diversity in witness groups was appealing to judges and ordinary citizens alike. Perhaps the most revealing evidence for this claim comes from a witness called to testify

---

[80] Jacma did not contest the second and third points, although she observed that Ugueta was in fact her husband's niece and not her own.

about a noble feud. The witness reported that a certain fact—that the viguier was corrupt, having been bought off by one of the factions involved—
was so widely known that it was believed as much by Jews as it was by Christians (*tam per judeos quam per christianos*).[81]

The arguments proposed here suggest that we must take fama seriously.
In presenting their cases, litigants ended a list of points to be proven with
some variant of the phrase "That all the above is the public talk and fame"
(*Quod de predictis est publica vox et fama*). As a taverner named Bertomieua de
Gordavilla claims, the facts of her case are public talk and fame "among acquaintances and neighbors of the said Bertomieua and those who have
known her for a long time."[82] A merchant named Peire de Brandis claims
that his facts are known not only in Marseille but in diverse places throughout Provence.[83] Judges could and did quiz witnesses on this point. We have
heard Johan Senequier's response: fama is "that which is publicly spoken
among people." Another witness reported that fama "is that which is spoken
about by many and never has he heard anyone say the contrary."[84] The fama
clause was intended to state specifically just what litigants tried to demon-
strate implicitly by recruiting socially diverse witness groups.

⥿

Witness testimony is notoriously unreliable and it goes without saying
that the witnesses recruited by opposing litigants routinely told very different stories. Sometimes the stories collapsed under the weight of their own
inconsistencies, thereby giving victory in the case to the opposing party. In
other cases, judges, in their effort to sort out the truth, could not rely on internal evidence. Circumstantial evidence, lie detector tests, expert witnesses,
DNA evidence—there are a variety of strategies nowadays that courts can
use to authenticate or delegitimate claims made by prosecutors and litigants.
These strategies have the dual virtues of being, or seeming, neutral and expert. They were not available in late medieval Marseille. Courts of law, accordingly, found independent means of corroboration through examining
the nature of the knowledge-bearing group. At the very least, many litigants
*assumed* that judges would be scrutinizing the social profile of their witnesses
and, to accommodate this fact, consciously recruited diverse witness groups.

Knowledge-bearing groups persuaded judges when they bore the imprint of diversity. This is a stance that emerged from the expectation, in me-

81  ADBR 3B 820, fol. 70v, case opened 7 July 1356 on fol. 8r.
82  ADBR 3B 34, fol. 19r, case opened 24 Apr. 1338 on fol. 19r.
83  ADBR 3B 811, fol. 159r, case opened 11 Feb. 1352 on fol. 136r.
84  ADBR 3B 37, fol. 265v., case opened in June 1339 on fol. 264r.

dieval Marseille, that knowledge itself was a matter of public record, known everywhere, always, and by all. It should be known by close acquaintances and distant strangers, by commoners and nobles, by fellow artisans and legal professionals, by men and women. Knowledge acquired this quality whenever deeds were performed openly, whenever notaries made contracts in public, whenever neighbors observed keys in the hands of fellow householders, whenever men and women announced the deaths of their kinfolk. Above all, knowledge derived its authority, its ability to be true and legally binding, from its public nature.

In conclusion, it is worthwhile commenting on the nature of the knowledge inscribed, by public deeds, in the memories of the general public. We have seen examples of facts related to birth, death, marital status, parentage, title, and ownership. Notarial archives in the fourteenth century, although enormous and growing by leaps and bounds every decade, were primarily concerned with debts; they typically did not record these other kinds of information, and so did not create a written archive of knowledge concerning facts that were frequently the subject of dispute. These facts were stored in the archives of memory, and it was public behavior that put them there. Arguably, the demands made by Roman-canon law courts for these kinds of facts increased the pressure on the archives of knowledge and encouraged the very behaviors discussed in this chapter.

Over the next few centuries, however, these facts would become written data and would pass into state archives and parochial registers. The process was complete in many European states by the nineteenth century. This transformation in the archives of knowledge hardly eliminated quarrels, of course, since one can quarrel just as easily about written facts, and the demands of honor and precedence have scarcely declined in the modern world. But these transformations in archival practice had profound effects on society, for they eliminated one of the rationales for the medieval culture of publicity, namely the legal requirement to create memories. One need not be needlessly romantic about a world we have lost to observe that, with this change, it was no longer legally incumbent on a person to publicize a birth or death to a neighbor. No longer was it necessary to marry in the public eye. One could buy and sell property in the privacy of a lawyer's office without regard to the neighbors and *their* desire to know. In short, this archival shift made possible the sequestration of knowledge, allowing many forms of knowledge to become things manipulatable by a state and by a caste of bureaucrats and legal experts, not by the common opinion of ordinary men and women.

# CONCLUSION

To adopt the perspective of the user of the courts of law in late medieval Europe is to see aspects of the medieval practice of law that one normally does not see. The role of emotions in records of civil litigation and criminal prosecution from late medieval Marseille is a case in point. On the whole, procedural manuals and other normative legal sources such as law codes and statutes have little to say about the emotions, and the normal bureaucratic practice of eliding emotions from all types of records more or less ensures that emotions can be recovered only with considerable effort. Many of the arguments made in this book have been based on an attempt to recover the emotional states or scripts of men and women who took legal action. Records of criminal trials and especially civil suits reveal how late medieval European society was characterized by enracinated structures of love and hatred that played a large role in motivating both denunciations and lawsuits. Not all civil suits were motivated by strong emotions, obviously, but certainly most suits of any length show signs of emotional complexity. Love and hatred, referred to often in the surviving records, are prominently visible, as are their pendants, such as anger, rage, malevolence, affection, and friendship. Other emotions or moral sentiments, such as envy and the desire to aggravate or humiliate, are not referred to explicitly in the records but reveal themselves indirectly. It is easy to object to a history that tries to say something about states of mind, and those who work in the history of the emotions are aware of the methodological problems. But I would say that most historians of law invariably, though implicitly, make assumptions about human psychology or human states of mind. It is better to bring such theories and assumptions out into the open.

It is hardly novel to argue that law engages the emotions. Contemporary lawyers could tell plenty of stories about the role of emotions in suits and trials, and a considerable amount of work is being done these days on law from the perspective of evolutionary biology and neurophysiology. The arguments made in this book go beyond the trivial observation that there are emotions to be found in the records of the law courts of late medieval Marseille. First, growing use of the courts using professional law was a product of consumer desire, not just the desire of princes and states. Second, what consumers wanted was to achieve and to publicize some form of emotional satisfaction, regardless of the outcome of their suits. Caseloads grew because state-sponsored courts of law proved to be a reasonably effective device for fulfilling the desire of some to achieve vengeance and to aggravate their adversaries on a public stage. Most histories of law assume that the decline of self-help and customary vengeance in medieval and early modern Europe was a function of the growing power of states and their law courts. Consideration of the emotions shows that the practice of customary vengeance declined as consumers, largely uncoerced by the state, found law courts increasingly attractive as venues for the pursuit of emotional satisfaction.

Emotions can have few legal, political, or social consequences if they remain unexpressed. The law courts were successful as a marketplace for the transaction of emotions, I have argued, because they provided a public stage on which to advertise and publicize hatreds, humiliations, and social sanctions. Litigation was a performance designed to convey a message to an audience. The court was a theater. A latent argument here is that the growing demographic size and complexity of medieval cities hampered the circulation of news, thus pushing consumers to develop new ways to shape the public talk. Courts served this role admirably. Put differently, the public stage of legal proceedings served to advertise and perform emotional transactions quite efficiently—in some cases more efficiently and certainly more safely than acts of customary vengeance and retaliation.

The major source of evidence used in this book has been the proceedings of secular courts of civil law using Roman-canon trial procedure. Proceedings of this sort are abundant in Mediterranean jurisdictions but have received comparatively little attention from legal and social historians. No source is better suited for studying the role of emotions in the evolution of law. States invested heavily in criminal courts and profited from this investment both financially and symbolically. Civil courts were a different matter, for although the state's symbolic profits were significant the investment was largely a consumer investment. The financial profits, at least in Marseille, largely eluded the state's treasury, flowing instead into the pockets of local officials and legal professionals. Consumer investment in civil suits, moreover, was largely voluntary and relatively uncoerced, at least compared to the criminal cases that did attract some measure of state coercive force in the form of policing agents, jails, and corporal punishments. Records of civil courts, in short, provide the best yardstick for measuring consumer investment in legal evolution.

The arguments I have made here hold the need for emotional satisfaction as a historical constant and treat the human institutions used to express and transact emotion as the variable that changes over time. Older histories of law and civilization used to make a different assumption: the progress of civilization brings with it an interiorization of sentiment and consequent growth in civility. These histories suggest that the institutional changes promoted by wise and farseeing rulers can reengineer human emotions and moral sentiments. In this book, I have assumed that changes in human institutions can have no such influence on the brain, or at least that a simple cause-and-effect explanation does not work well. In developing the essentialist or universalist stance that informs this book I do not deny that the expression of emotions can and does vary from one culture to the next and across time. It is possible that modern citizens of the industrialized nations experience feelings of anger and hatred that are different from the feelings experienced by the men and women of fourteenth-century Marseille, though in my view it is unlikely that the experience of emotions is significantly different. Naturally there are some differences. Many people in medieval Europe chose not to repress their emotions. To use the language of neurophysiology, members of the free Christian population of Marseille did not find it especially useful to exert voluntary, neocortical control over the emotional body states generated by the subcortices of the brain.[1] As Stephen D. White and others have argued, emotional scripts or states of mind such as anger and hatred served important legal and political ends. Suppressing them would have been counterproductive, indeed damaging to one's social status and legal rights. As a result, men and women in Marseille and elsewhere in medieval Europe found it useful to have or autosuggest states of anger and hatred and, perhaps, learned how to perform fictive emotional states if the subcortex refused to cooperate. But there is nothing particularly modern about this ability to exert some degree of voluntary

[1] A useful guide is Antonio Damasio, *Descartes' Error: Emotion, Reason, and the Human Brain* (New York, 1994), esp. 127–64. Damasio shows that emotions do not simply well up from the parts of the brain in which they are generated. Instead, there is a complex feedback mechanism that relates perception and sensation to emotion, or body to brain, and vice versa. Following Damasio, it is easy to see that many people, placed in a situation in which cultural expectations demanded an angry response, would in fact become physiologically angry.

THE CONSUMPTION OF JUSTICE

control over the emotions generated by the limbic and autonomic nervous systems in the brain. I assume that members of the unfree, marginalized, subaltern groups in medieval Europe, including domestic servants, serfs, Muslims, and Jews, exerted such voluntary control, at least in public, as a matter of course. Life would have been too dangerous if the members of such groups routinely allowed themselves to get angry in public. Only free, autonomous individuals were normally allowed to have and perform legitimate emotions of anger and hatred in public. This is still true today. Civilizing one's emotions, therefore, is no great skill, no testament to the progress of modernity. It is simply a question of learning how to do something known to every subaltern. The progress of modernity, in this respect, is simply the progress of subalternity.

Though this book has focused on emotions and the performance of those emotions in courts, I have developed a number of related themes that open up different questions. The process and practice of construing facts, addressed at length in chapter 5, is one such issue, for it flows from the performative nature of social practice but addresses issues only indirectly related to emotions. The history of Roman-canon law is often written as the history of the development of a science of hard-to-know facts. Facts, however, did not play a major role in legal proceedings in late medieval Marseille; this is in keeping with my argument that outcomes were not as important as the inimical gestures made available through procedural law. The nature of procedural challenges, moreover, often turned arguments over facts into arguments about emotional states. The culture of publicity ensured the transparency of most facts of any importance, especially in criminal cases. The difference between the facts known by men and women and the considerable authority given to certain forms of women's knowledge, in turn, is part of another thread running through this book, namely the role of women as users and consumers of the law. Though women's legal capacity is now fairly well known by medieval historians, it remains important to insist that women were fully visible to the law in medieval Europe.

These and other issues should be aired on a broader stage, and the implications of this study, as a case study of a single late medieval city, are necessarily limited. But I defend the relevance of an extended case study on several grounds. First, emotions and intentions cannot be studied unless one has access to multiple and overlapping sources. I have populated this study with real people on the principle that their psychologies will be better understood if they themselves are better known. Such an approach demands the intimate knowledge made available only through a case study. Second, emotions as sets of neurophysiological patterns are one of the truly universal features of all human cultures. It is undeniable that the expression and public use of emotions can vary widely from one human culture to the next. In building the arguments of this book, however, I have accepted the arguments of many researchers in the medical and scientific community to the effect that the neural and chemical underpinnings of emotions are essentially identical in all human brains and, moreover, serve important social ends. If this is true, then it is reasonable to suggest that emotions play a role in legal transformations wherever and whenever such transformations have taken place. The specific patterns found in late Marseille may not duplicate those found in late medieval England, ancient Rome, Han China, or the Incan empire. Even so, it may be justifiable to assume that in all cases, legal and judicial evolution was shaped by the changing emotional ecology of societies undergoing population growth and political centralization.

I have not tried to write this larger comparative study here. By seeing medieval Europe in this comparative world context, however, I hope to suggest that medieval European history as a whole could benefit by eschewing its tendency to engage in relentless medieval-modern comparisons. Most histories of medieval European law have emphasized many of the unique features of European legal systems in part because it is a useful way to justify the study of medieval Europe. Brian Tierney's magisterial studies of human rights are a case in point. All legal systems have sui generis features, and it is certainly not my purpose here to deny any of the unique and arguably beneficent features of European legal systems. But all legal transformations, indeed all human cultural transformations wherever they are found, share some common features that are interesting for what they say about the general rather than the particular. In this regard, medieval Europe is worthy of study not only because its developing legal systems eventually laid the groundwork for future developments such as the language of human rights, limitations on sovereign authority, safeguards for the rights of the accused, and dispassionate forensic devices for proving guilt or innocence. Medieval Europe is also worthy of study because, as a densely documented society, it can provide useful insights into a process that has taken place in many parts of the globe over the last five thousand years or so, a process during which legal institutions emerged to mediate between a relatively unchanging human brain and a rapidly changing social, political, and legal ecology. This, not modernization, not industrialization, is the greatest transformation of all, and one whose lineaments we may see more clearly if we set medieval Europe within its global historical context.

# APPENDIX
## THE NATURE AND FORMAT OF THE RECORD

The archives of the city of Marseille hold a remarkable series of judicial registers from the city's secular courts during the later middle ages. Though most of the original registers have perished, enough have survived for us to be able to extrapolate the original size of court caseloads. Over the course of the fourteenth century, between thirteen and twenty thousand suits were formally initiated in the local civil courts, and a great number of simpler requests involving minor debts, disputed successions, and related issues, possibly as many as eighty thousand over the course of the century, were brought to the attention of the judges. The criminal court undertook as many as fifty thousand inquests and the appellate courts of Marseille heard around a thousand appeals. Notaries of the court kept transcripts of all these proceedings bound in large registers, and required a steady supply of ink, quill pens, parchment, string for binding, and above all paper.

The quantity of paper consumed by the courts, as a measure of judicial activity in fourteenth-century Marseille, was immense. Around the middle of the fourteenth century, notaries of the secular courts were generating around forty-five hundred pages of documentation per year. All judicial orders, summons, and proclamations existed in duplicate, since messengers had to carry them to their destination, and most suits and inquests required or generated enormous quantities of loose paper—notarial instruments, citations, summons, judicial orders, proclamations, juristic advice, witness depositions, and other acts, all of which had to be delivered, on request, to litigants and defendants. All this autonomously generated paper must be reckoned into the total and it is reasonable to suggest that it added as much

[ 247 ]

again to the registered material, bringing the total to nine thousand pages per year. The quantity of documentation produced for the law courts of late medieval Marseille may have been inferior, on a per capita basis, to that of comparable modern bureaucracies, let alone to late medieval Florence or England and other precociously centralized European jurisdictions. Still, close to a million pages of documentation was generated over the space of one hundred years by the judicial bureaucracy of just one late medieval political jurisdiction, and a tiny one at that, about one three-thousandth of the population of western Europe in 1300.

Even so speculative an estimate as this raises many questions, not the least of which is the symbiotic relationship between the paper revolution of the later middle ages on the one hand and judicial and archival habits on the other. As rule of thumb, the desire to archive is as much a function of the cost and convenience of storage media as it is one of perceived administrative needs. The rapidly decreasing costs of paper freed notaries to record the minutiae of court cases in a way that would have been fiscally irresponsible in earlier medieval Europe, thereby adding a whole new layer to the rapidly evolving legal environment of late medieval Europe. The massive quantities of court records from medieval Marseille and other jurisdictions result from this change.

Little of this original richness, of course, has survived. With several important exceptions, England and Florence foremost among them, the European capacity to generate records generally outstripped the techniques, the will, or the luck to preserve them from the ravages of time and political and natural disasters. The vast losses from the period suggest that the ability to preserve an archive in later centuries—and the investment necessary to do so—is an aspect of governmentality that does not necessarily come easily to states or societies. In Marseille, for example, various clues show that elements of the public record were stored in private hands or semipublic institutions rather than in a secure municipal archive. Most notarial casebooks from medieval Marseille remained in the possession of notarial offices until the early twentieth century. Marseille's judicial registers, remarkably, did not find their way into the archives until the 1950s.[1] The losses, accordingly, have been enormous. The modern archives of the city of Marseille retain the more-or-less complete records of about three thousand civil cases from the years between 1264 and 1423, and synopses of another two or three thousand criminal cases have also survived. Survival of particular series has been sporadic at best. Eight registers recording fines collected from criminal sentences have survived, and all but one of these registers are from the fifteenth

[1] Gérard Giordanengo, personal communication, Dec. 2001.

century. Only one register of criminal prosecutions from this period is still extant, and no register of sentences of any of the courts of first instance has survived. Records of judicial orders and rulings survive sporadically and many are in a poor state of conservation. Few registers kept by the notaries of the second appellate court exist. Best preserved are the several hundred registers of lawsuits initiated before the three courts of first instance and the first appellate court, although even here there are large gaps and many have been damaged by worms and humidity. The quantity of extant documentation drops off markedly after 1410 for reasons that may be partially related to the sack and burning of Marseille in 1423 by the Aragonese.

Late medieval court records from southern France and elsewhere are extraordinarily rich in detail and constitute a valuable resource for studying not only law but many other subjects as well. This richness stems from the fact that judges in the Roman-canon legal tradition were accustomed to basing their sentences on a reading of the evidence given in a case, not on the basis of their memory of what had transpired at court. In medieval England, the epistemological demands of a system based on case law contributed to the formation of a judicial record-keeping system; plea rolls and law reports, in turn, have become a staple of later medieval English legal history.[2] In this regard, historians of those areas of continental Europe that relied on the norms of Roman-canon procedural law are even luckier, since the records of proceedings (where they survive) tend to be far richer than the often terse English rolls and yearbooks. Judges, who were not necessarily present at the interrogation of witnesses, always based their rulings and sentences on the transcript compiled by the notary who was responsible for the interrogation. In addition, the yearly rotation of judges meant that they sometimes had to rule on cases argued before another judge. The case of Johanet Salvayre discussed in the first chapter stretched over the tenure of three different judges.

As discussed in chapter 1, it is probable that court caseloads were growing over the course of the fourteenth century. Growing use of the courts had a very visible effect on the record-keeping practices of court notaries, as the somewhat haphazard nature of thirteenth-century record-keeping gave way to the defined bureaucratic templates of the fourteenth century. Among other things, the keepers of judicial records began to think in terms of categories of judicial activity. By the 1350s, for example, lawsuits were usually kept distinct from judicial orders to repay debts and other judicial activities,

---

[2] See John H. Baker, "Records, Reports, and the Origins of Case-Law in England," in *Judicial Records, Law Reports, and the Growth of Case Law*, ed. John H. Baker, vol. 5 of Comparative Studies in Continental and Anglo-American Legal History (Berlin, 1989), 15–46.

and recorded in separate registers. This change in record-keeping reveals a growing conceptual distinction, on the part of court notaries, between the various activities of judges. Since bureaucratic categories typically evolve naturally, as a product of use rather than planning, this growing conceptual distinction suggests that the practice of recording lawsuits in all their minutiae was still something of a novelty in the early fourteenth century. Even so, the somewhat haphazard nature of judicial registers in the fourteenth and fifteenth centuries stands in sharp contrast to the clearly defined structure of royal fiscal accounts, suggesting how judicial bureaucrats lagged behind their fiscal counterparts.

The record of a given suit consisted of a medley of libels, cedulae, instruments, and other documents produced by the judge, the litigants and their lawyers, and the notaries of the court, as well as all the brief notes recording orders, summons, and so on. All these notices, written more or less in sequential order, made up the transcript of the proceedings of a given case. The format of the record itself changed in certain ways over the course of the century, revealing progressive refinements in the nature of the record-keeping template.

Given the annual changeover of judges, notaries of the palace court and the two lesser courts very early on developed the habit of starting a new register of suits each fall, when the judge took office. Notaries did not like their registers to exceed three hundred folios in length and would start binding quires into a new register whenever the existing one threatened to become inconveniently thick. Since this could happen partway through a judge's tenure new registers could open at any time of year, although late in the summer was uncommon. By way of illustration, the judge of the palace court in 1329–30, Bulgarinus de Tiboldis, generated two registers of cases during his tenure. The first, 268 pages in length, begins with a case that opened on 11 December 1329 and closes with a case that opened on 21 April 1330. The second, 330 pages in length, begins three days later, on 24 April 1330, and ends on 21 November 1330.[3] Bulgarinus's registers were close to the average size of palace court records, which was about 350 pages. The length of palace court registers could vary considerably, from 130 to 1,000 pages. Records of the lesser courts were typically shorter and, as a result, often covered a judge's entire tenure, usually a period of about eleven months. With the smaller registers it is sometimes difficult to know whether one is consulting an entire register or a large fragment of an original register.

Within each register the cases generally proceed in chronological order.

[3] ADBR 3B 24 and 25.

Cases range in length from a single page to dozens of pages or even, especially as time went on, more than a hundred pages, and could last anywhere from a single day to several years. Given the reluctance of notaries to date each intervention calendrically—most notaries preferred to date stages in a trial by means of expressions like "the next day" or "the following Monday"—it would be time consuming to tabulate the duration of cases. One case only twenty-two folios in length lasted more than a year, from March of 1323 to April of 1324; important stages of the trial took place in July, October, and November of 1323 and then in March and April of 1324.[4] A particularly contentious case twenty-five folios in length lasted more than two years, from June 1404 to August 1406. The plaintiff, a widow named Nicolaua Nicolaue, was seeking to recover her dowry from her father-in-law, who was called, improbably enough, Nicolau Nicolai. Failing that, she was at least hoping for yearly alimony payments. Shortly after the case had gone into its third year her procurator made an impassioned and highly unusual speech deploring the frustrating series of obstacles thrown up against the poor widow (*paupera vidua*) who was rapidly running out of money.[5] The case fizzled out sadly a month or two later and one expects she gave up. Other cases of comparable length, though, only lasted a month. Legitimate delays arose whenever a litigant, lawyer, procurator, or even judge was absent from the city, in which case judges could grant a delay, though no more than three ten-day waiting periods were allowed. Some litigants were reluctant to respond to a summons at any price and, having exhausted their grace period, would be fined for contumacy. Whatever the situation, at any given moment a judge might have ten or fifteen simultaneously active cases. The notaries of the court had to be careful to record an intervention in the appropriate location, and sometimes made mistakes.

The notaries had no idea how long a given case would last. Most recorded the preliminaries of a given case, allowed for four or more blank folios, and then recorded the preliminaries of the next case. If a given case lasted longer than the space allotted, as many did, then the notaries would sew in an additional signature, guessing at the number of required folios. Court registers, for this reason, were infinitely expandable. This is perhaps the most fundamental point needed for understanding the process of record-construction. One result of this system is that most registers contain a fair number of empty pages both between cases and within cases. On occasion these blank pages were neatly cut out and the paper, presumably, recy-

[4] ADBR 3B 16, fols. 60r–82v, case opened 16 Mar. 1323.
[5] ADBR 3B 143, fols. 124r–144r (foliated in the original), case opened 14 June 1404 and ended in August of 1406. The speech of the procurator, Guilhem de Mellomonte, can be found on fol. 143a recto-verso and is dated 19 July 1406.

cled. More often the pages were left in the register. Thrifty notaries tried to use blank paper when possible, and here too they sometimes made mistakes. To give one example, in 1335 the palace court notary accidentally started to record a new case in the midst of a short and otherwise insignificant dowry suit, only to realize that the dowry suit continued several folios later. To cover his error, he marked a sign on folio 16v, noted "the rest follows at this sign," and marked the sign again on folio 17v, where the case picked up anew. He then crossed out the mistaken case heading on folio 17r.[6]

A few registers do not follow a strict chronological rule.[7] In some cases a notary may have made a mistake when binding together the records of a given year. In one particularly nasty dispute pitting a father against his son, a parchment-bound quire of paper containing the witness testimony, which at one hundred and eight pages in length constituted more than half of the entire record of the trial, was sewn in at the end of the record rather than in chronological order, no doubt because it was too large to fit conveniently where it belonged.[8] A system of symbols, in common use by the early fifteenth century, showed the reader, presumably the judge, where to find the relevant material. More commonly, cases that do not follow strict chronological ordering reflect an attempt by some notaries to use up otherwise wasted paper. Once a register was nearing completion, a notary might selectively enter new cases on the blank folios earlier in the register that were left over from a case that had in the meantime drawn to a definitive conclusion. Earlier in the century, notaries sometimes entered miscellaneous orders and summons in otherwise empty space, and the notary of the palace court in 1407 also took to this practice.[9]

Registers were not consistently indexed or paginated. A beautifully preserved register from 1329 contains a table of contents of the twenty-three cases that make up the register, each identified by the name of the principal plaintiff and the folio on which the case begins.[10] Nine additional cases, with folios, were listed at the end of the table of contents but subsequently crossed out with the notation "Moved to . . ." The notary was making decisions, and changing his mind, about how to build the register. But this index was unusual, and the general absence of indexes is a little surprising. The

[6] ADBR 3B 30, case opened 5 Apr. 1335 on fol. 14r.

[7] ADBR 3B 31 is an example.

[8] ADBR 3B 27, fols. 143r–240r, case opened 28 Jan. 1332. The quire containing the witness testimony begins on fol. 185.

[9] ADBR 3B 26 includes several examples of these recycling practices; see fols. 90–98 (lists of seizures and other orders) and fols. 110–117 (fragments of unrelated court cases). For the 1407 register, see ADBR 3B 147.

[10] ADBR 3B 24. Another indexed court record is AM FF 537 (1360–62), which was indexed by folio number and title of case.

concept was available and relatively common, for some notaries in fourteenth-century Marseille routinely indexed their casebooks and seigneurial records were commonly indexed. What this suggests is that court records, though read by judges in the few cases that required a sentence, were not otherwise consulted at later dates. Appellants needed transcripts of their cases to present to the first appellate court but these would have been compiled immediately after sentencing. In the early fifteenth century, it is true, a number of registers contain parchment tabs sewn onto the first recto folio of a new case, but these were probably designed to help the notary find a given case in the medley of concurrent suits rather than to guide future readers. Court registers, in short, were living records designed for immediate consumption, not for archival use. The fact that many are in good condition and show little signs of subsequent reading before the twentieth century helps to confirm this hypothesis.

The cases found in these registers, for the most part, are not verbatim transcripts of cases as they developed before the viguier and the judge. In Roman-canon law courts a certain amount of activity, including the taking of witness testimony, did not have to be transacted in the presence of the judge, who based his sentence not on his memory of the hearings before him so much as on the written record that was eventually assembled for him to read. As a result, most cases were assembled in stages from notes, transcripts, and other documents, and the records reveal this piecemeal composition. The attestations or depositions of witnesses, as described above, is the most obvious example. Once accepted, the depositions were opened, read, and publicized (*aperiri, legi, et publicari fecit*): in other words, registered in the official record of the proceedings. The separation of witness testimony from the other elements of the record is often clearly marked in the handwriting and even the size and type of paper used, or even, as in the case mentioned, by a parchment cover.

Since all notaries of the court also had private practices, it is not uncommon to find original records of witness depositions and even whole suits in a notarial casebook. Many examples of entire suits date from the late 1340s and early 1350s, shortly after the Black Death.[11] Interrogations of witnesses show up from time to time in notarial registers, such as in cases in which the witness was a member of the clergy, a resident of another city or town, or too infirm to travel to the court, as could happen when a victim of violent crime had to testify to the inquisition about the loss of his hand or ear. A notary who traveled to the witness would keep the original record of the inter-

---

[11] ADBR 355E 1, a casebook kept by the notary Jacme Aycart from 10 Jan. 1348 (a week or two shy of the arrival of plague) to 23 Mar. 1349 contains eleven court cases.

rogation in his casebooks and would then transcribe the interrogations into the master register when asked to do so. In 1393, for example, a notary of the ecclesiastical court of inquest named Guilhem Barban used his casebook to record the interrogation of a monk of St. Victor who had killed another man in the course of the factional warfare of the decade.[12]

Other elements of a case were also recorded on other bits of paper and sometimes did not find their way into the master record. The libel itself is a case in point, since it consisted of a sheet of paper, usually in the handwriting of the consulting lawyer or his personal *scriptor*, that was handed to the judge to initiate the case and then passed on to the notary to be copied—or not copied, as was often the case—into the master record. A case heard in 1331 provides a spectacular example of a suit that generated a lot of paperwork that was never entered into the register. The extant record consists of a single recto folio that identifies the time, the judge, the actors, the nature of the dispute (an unpaid commenda of forty florins) but nothing else, not even the libel. Five blank folios follow, tempting one to conclude that nothing further happened. But tucked into the binding is a loose piece of paper listing the expenses incurred by the plaintiff, a squire named Guilhem Imbert, and a request that the plaintiff's charges be assessed to the defendant. A full list of Guilhem's expenses, paraphrased and slightly abbreviated, is provided in chapter 1. In and among all the salaries or fees and pourboires there is quite a lot of paperwork, virtually none of which found its way into the record. The payments that give most pause for thought are those made to notaries for writing out several libels and titles into the cartulary, because they patently never did so, at least here. Perhaps they never did so because the defendant never paid and Guilhem was unwilling to pay the expenses necessary for recording a hollow victory. This is quite apart from the citations, precepts, orders, and the two instruments (commenda and wardship) that were written on pieces of paper, carried about the city, and, in the case of the citations, read out loud in public squares, without ever finding their way into the master record. This is, perhaps, a somewhat extreme example, but it does show how a suit was composed of many bits and pieces. In most cases, of course, a good percentage of these documents were successfully assembled by notaries into an actual record.

As soon as the record of the case began to materialize in the cartulary it could be subject to a number of annotations and corrections. Entries were commonly made in different hands and hence by different notaries, and judges sometimes annotated the record in the margin. In certain situations,

12 ADBR 351E 92, fols. 35v–36r, 49r, and 160r–166v. This last was entitled "Information given by the arrested party" (*informatio delati*).

we can see the notary returning to previous elements of the record and making notations. For example, when one party submitted a list of points to be proven by means of witnesses, documents, or public fame, the other party was not required to identify immediately the points it would contest. Once the responses were determined days or weeks later, notaries usually flipped back to the original list and interlined the responses (conscientious notaries left line spaces in the original list). That these interlineations or additions were made later is clear from the case itself, and this is corroborated, in many cases, by a slightly different color of ink or a wobbly line of text that was clearly written without the aid of a rule.

The basic rule of chronological ordering is one piece of evidence showing that the judicial bureaucracy of Marseille was working with at least an elementary kind of record-keeping template. The template was being refined over the course of the fourteenth century, although the process was slow enough to remind us that the development of bureaucratic templates, at least in the fourteenth century, was not the product of ratiocination but instead usually evolved naturally, in the culture and practice of the keepers of records. To take one example, the notaries who recorded thirteenth-century appellate sentences had no sense that these cases were conceptually distinct from judicial orders of any type. As a result, the two thirteenth-century records of the court of first appeals indiscriminately mingle judicial orders, cases, and even private notarial contracts. This practice persisted into the fourteenth century. A conceptual distinction between the various aspects of judicial activity—namely cases, judicial orders, estate inventories, wardships, and so on—began to develop by the 1340s or 1350s and after this period the registers of cases were usually kept independently of other court business, although there are enough exceptions to show that this was not a hard and fast rule.

Another element of the emerging template was the case heading. Cases almost always began on a recto folio with a heading that identified the principal party or parties to the case. Early in the fourteenth century these headings were fairly simple: a brief note located at the top of the folio mentioning the name of the instigating party. Over the course of the fourteenth century, the headings moved slowly down the page and were increasingly indented from each margin. The identities of both principal parties, moreover, were established with greater care. The effect was to make the first folio of the case stand out more conspicuously.

A conspicuous and useful refinement that emerged over the course of the fourteenth century was the care taken to copy out libels, letters, and other acts in full into the register. Even short cases generated a large number of loose pieces of paper or parchment (often generically called *cedulae*) that were exchanged between the principal parties and between the principals and the judge in the case. Some cedulae were thin strips of paper with a brief note; others were full folios or even parchments containing important acts. Earlier in the fourteenth century, notaries characteristically folded the sheet in question and slipped it into the binding, sometimes actually sewing it in to ensure that it could not slip out again. They would leave a blank space in the record that corresponded to the length of the text in question, as if intending to copy it out at a later date, but the decision to copy or not to copy was determined, at least in part, by the industriousness of the notary, not by record-keeping rules. A comment made in one register from 1335 suggests that notaries were not required to complete the record of cases that ended without a sentence or a decision by a judge. The case involved an unpaid sale credit of twenty pounds, and the notary noted on the first page that "the said parties came to an agreement and for that reason the said cedula was not placed in the cartulary" (partes predicte inter se convenerunt et ideo cedula predicta posita in cartulario non fuit).[13] Later in the century it became more normal for notaries to copy out the text in full, and there are fewer loose cedulae. Similarly, appellate court cases from earlier in the century did not always include transcripts of the case as recorded by the court of first instance, whereas later in the century these transcripts were recorded more conscientiously.

Foliation is a different matter. Many, even most notaries in private practice routinely foliated their casebooks and in the early fourteenth century some notaries of the court were also choosing to foliate judicial registers. One might expect to find that the practice of foliation was becoming increasingly common. Early fifteenth-century notaries, however, were not conspicuously more careful about foliating a register once it was complete. The foliation of judicial registers was not all that practical, as an example will illustrate. Late in the year 1404, the palace court notary, Laurens Aycart, a scion of the great Aycart dynasty of notaries, decided to foliate the register of cases he had produced during his year of service. His work was somewhat spoiled by the fact that four of the cases in the register were still incomplete. Several lasted more than a year and three of them required additional signatures, none of which could be included in Laurens's foliation.[14] One of these was the two-year-long case of the poor widow Nicolaua Nicolaue. Thus, although other elements of the record show that notaries were

[13] ADBR 3B 30, fol. 26r, case opened 7 June 1335.
[14] ADBR 3B 143, after folio 70 (twelve added folios), 109 (one added folio), 141 (two added folios), and 143 (two added folios).

gradually refining their record-keeping practices, the practice of foliation did not make much headway over the course of the fourteenth century.

It seems natural to us that court notaries even in the fourteenth century put energy into the making and keeping of records. Modern states keep records not only for their utility but also for their symbolic value, because the power to archive is the power to know, to decide, and to classify. Some late medieval states like England and Florence behaved this way. Fourteenth-century Marseille, however, was not embedded in this sort of state, and the making of court records is not something that one should take for granted. That many of the resulting registers were preserved for over six hundred years is likewise a fact that deserves some reflection. Notarial casebooks have a fundamental utility and the contracts found in them can be consulted years, decades, even centuries after they were made. This is not the case with fourteenth-century judicial records from Marseille, virtually none of which are ever referred to again in any surviving contemporary record I have seen. Transcripts used in appellate cases are the exception, but these were taken immediately after the conclusion of the trial of first instance and were delivered by the appellant to the court of first appeals at the booth next door. In pursuing an appeal, one did not need to return to a court record years after the fact. Some of the acts and judgments of the court were exceedingly important to victorious litigants. These, however, were copied out as instruments and archived for future use by the interested parties themselves. The court itself was not an archival or memorial agent in its own right.

Court records are extremely inefficient ways to archive the truly significant acts and decisions generated by the court. The most remarkable feature of the extant court cases is that the bulk of the record consists of wholly unremarkable procedural notices. These are dull and have little or no bearing on anything that we might want to call the facts of a case. Notaries used these notices to record litigants in the act of offering cedulae, summoning absent opponents, making accusations of contumacy, requesting delays or extensions, protesting expenses, hiring procurators, challenging their adversaries' procurators, and proposing any number of exceptions or objections to the arguments and jural standing of their adversaries. Even the notaries found these dry and tedious and their sloppy handwriting betrays their haste to get through the job.

The needs of the judges go some way toward explaining why these procedural notices were written out in the first place. Although judges did not often conclude a case with a sentence or a ruling there was always that possibility, and since a litigant might seek to undermine an adversary's case by means of procedural objections rather than facts it was well to have a complete record of all the stages of a given trial. But the needs of judges is insufficient as an explanation. Many of the shorter cases, after all, are wholly lacking in any procedural elements. One must assume that notaries recorded certain procedures in memory or on loose notes and entered them in a given trial only when it seemed likely that a given case was going to last any length of time. Even the longer cases show gaps. Evidently there was no hard and fast rule declaring that all elements of a case must be systematically recorded.

In asking why such a minute record of procedural notices was often made and kept it is well to bear in mind that notaries of the court were not members of a disinterested and impersonal state bureaucracy. Their job was a sinecure. All received a nominal salary from the council and to some extent can be thought of as officials of the crown, but their livelihood derived from the fees they charged the litigants for writing out libels, articles, cedulae, summons, and so forth. Put differently, it was the litigants themselves who, through the medium of the notaries, invested in the material record of the case.

What did litigants get out of the very large and growing investment they made in a set of records that, in all likelihood, was never read again? The power to sue one's enemy is the power to place that person at one's beck and call and thus to dictate the rhythm of the adversary's life. Every time an adversary was summoned or challenged in any way a messenger was sent to his or her house—an event presumably remarked by all the neighbors—and the adversary would have to make arrangements either to appear at court or to delegate the task to a procurator. Procedural notices record this process. The stages of the process unfolded outdoors, at the booths where the courts met, and it was here that the notaries entered the notice directly into the court cartulary. Each intervention was punctuated at some point in time by the exchange of coins or other forms of credit—a highly visible exchange, meaningful to onlookers, who would know that an adversary's name was once again recorded in the cartulary. In a sense, it can be said that users of the courts were aware of the symbolism of court cartularies even before states were, and cartularies grew as the real and symbolic investment in them grew.

# BIBLIOGRAPHY

Althoff, Gerd. "*Ira Regis*: Prolegomena to a History of Royal Anger." In *Anger's Past: The Social Uses of an Emotion in the Middle Ages*, edited by Barbara H. Rosenwein, 59–74. Ithaca: Cornell University Press, 1998.

Andrews, Richard Mowery. *Law, Magistracy, and Crime in Old Regime Paris, 1735–1789*. Vol. 1, *The System of Criminal Justice*. Cambridge: Cambridge University Press, 1994.

Appadurai, Arjun, ed. *The Social Life of Things: Commodities in Cultural Perspective*. Cambridge: Cambridge University Press, 1986.

Auslander, Leora. *Taste and Power: Furnishing Modern France*. Berkeley: University of California Press, 1996.

Axelrod, Robert M. *The Evolution of Cooperation*. New York: Basic Books, 1984.

Baker, John H. "Records, Reports, and the Origins of Case-Law in England." In *Judicial Records, Law Reports, and the Growth of Case Law*, edited by John H. Baker, 15–46. Vol. 5 of Comparative Studies in Continental and Anglo-American Legal History. Berlin: Duncker and Humblot, 1989.

Baratier, Édouard. *Enquêtes sur les droits et revenus de Charles Ier d'Anjou en Provence, 1252 et 1278*. Paris: Bibliothèque Nationale, 1969.

——. *Histoire de Marseille*. Toulouse: Privat, 1973.

Baratier, Édouard, and Félix Reynaud. *De 1291 à 1480*. Vol. 2 of *Histoire du commerce de Marseille*. Chambre de Commerce de Marseille, edited by Gaston Rambert. Paris: Plon, 1951.

Bartlett, Robert. "'Mortal Enmities': The Legal Aspect of Hostility in the Middle Ages." T. Jones Pierce Lecture, University of Wales. Aberystwyth, 1998.

de Beaumanoir, Philippe de Remi. *The* Coutumes de Beauvaisis *of Philippe de Beaumanoir*. Translated by F. R. P. Akehurst. Philadelphia: University of Pennsylvania Press, 1992.

Becker, Marvin B. *Civility and Society in Western Europe, 1300–1600*. Bloomington: Indiana University Press, 1988.

Bednarski, Steven. "Crime, justice et régulation sociale à Manosque, 1340–1403." Thèse (Ph.D.), Université de Montréal, 2002.

Bellomo, Manlio. *The Common Legal Past of Europe, 1000–1800*. Translated by Lydia G. Cochrane. Washington, D.C.: Catholic University of America Press, 1995.

Berman, Harold Joseph. *Law and Revolution: The Formation of the Western Legal Tradition*. Cambridge, Mass.: Harvard University Press, 1983.

Blanshei, Sarah Rubin. "Crime and Law Enforcement in Medieval Bologna." *Journal of Social History* 16 (1982): 121–38.

Bloch, Marc. *Feudal Society*. 2 vols. Translated by L. A. Manyon. Chicago: University of Chicago Press, 1961.

Bonnaud, Jean-Luc. "Les agents locaux de l'administration royale en Provence au XIVe siècle: catalogue et étude des carrières." Thèse (Ph.D.), Université de Montréal, 1999.

Bossy, John. *Peace in the Post-Reformation*. Cambridge: Cambridge University Press, 1998.

———, ed. *Disputes and Settlements: Law and Human Relations in the West*. Cambridge: Cambridge University Press, 1983.

Bougard, François. *La justice dans le royaume d'Italie: de la fin du VIIIe siècle au début du XIe siècle*. Rome: École française de Rome, 1995.

Bourdieu, Pierre. *Distinction: A Social Critique of the Judgement of Taste*. Translated by Richard Nice. Cambridge, Mass.: Harvard University Press, 1984.

Bourrilly, Victor-L. *Essai sur l'histoire politique de Marseille des origines à 1264*. Aix-en-Provence: A. Dragon, 1925.

Bowman, Jeffrey A. "Infamy and Proof in Medieval Spain." In *Fama: The Politics of Talk and Reputation in Medieval Europe*, edited by Thelma Fenster and Daniel Lord Smail, 95–117. Ithaca: Cornell University Press, 2003.

Brackett, John K. *Criminal Justice and Crime in Late Renaissance Florence, 1537–1609*. Cambridge: Cambridge University Press, 1992.

Brand, Paul. "Inside the Courtroom: Lawyers, Litigants, and Justices in England in the Later Middle Ages." In *The Moral World of the Law*, edited by Peter Coss, 91–112. Cambridge: Cambridge University Press, 2000.

Brewer, John, and Roy Porter, eds. *Consumption and the World of Goods*. London: Routledge, 1993.

Britnell, R. H. *Growth and Decline in Colchester, 1300–1525*. Cambridge: Cambridge University Press, 1986.

Brooks, Peter, and Paul Gewirtz, eds. *Law's Stories: Narrative and Rhetoric in the Law*. New Haven: Yale University Press, 1996.

Brown, Howard G. "From Organic Society to Security State: The War on Brigandage in France, 1797–1802." *Journal of Modern History* 69 (1997): 661–95.

Brown, Keith M. *Bloodfeud in Scotland, 1573–1625: Violence, Justice, and Politics in an Early Modern Society*. Edinburgh: J. Donald, 1986.

Brundage, James A. *Medieval Canon Law*. London: Longman, 1995.

Brunner, Otto. *Land and Lordship: Structures of Governance in Medieval Austria*. Translated by Howard Kaminsky and James Van Horn Melton from the 4th rev. ed. (1959). Philadelphia: University of Pennsylvania Press, 1992.

Busquet, Raoul. *Histoire de Marseille*. Edited by Pierre Guiral. Paris: R. Laffont, 1977 [1945].

———. "L'organisation de la justice à Marseille au Moyen-Âge." *Provincia* 2 (1922): 1–15.

Campbell, Colin. "Understanding Traditional and Modern Patterns of Consumption in Eighteenth-Century England: A Character-Action Approach." In *Consumption and the World of Goods*, edited by John Brewer and Roy Porter, 40–57. London: Routledge, 1993.

Carbasse, Jean-Marie. *Introduction historique au droit pénal*. Paris: Presses Universitaires de France, 1990.

Castan, Nicole. *Justice et répression en Languedoc à l'époque des Lumières*. Paris: Flammarion, 1980.

Castellani, G. "Le rôle économique de la communauté juive de Carpentras au début du XVe siècle." *Annales E.S.C.* 27 (1972): 583–611.

Chambers, David S., and Trevor Dean. *Clean Hands and Rough Justice: An Investigating Magistrate in Renaissance Italy*. Ann Arbor: University of Michigan Press, 1997.

Chapman, Terry S. "Crime in Eighteenth-Century England: E. P. Thompson and the Conflict Theory of Crime." *Criminal Justice History: An International Annual* 1 (1980): 139–55.

Chiffoleau, Jacques. *Les justices du pape: délinquance et criminalité dans la region d'Avignon au quatorzième siècle*. Paris: Publications de la Sorbonne, 1984.

Chittolini, Giorgio. "Il 'privato,' il 'pubblico,' lo stato." In *Origini dello stato: processi di formazione statale in Italia fra medioevo ed età moderna*, edited by Giorgio Chittolini, Anthony Molho, and P. Schiera, 554–64. Bologna: Il Mulino, 1994. Translated by Daniel Bornstein in *The Origins of the State in Italy, 1300–1600*, edited by Julius Kirshner, 34–61. Chicago: University of Chicago Press, 1995.

Christ, Matthew R. *The Litigious Athenian*. Baltimore: Johns Hopkins University Press, 1998.

Clanchy, Michael T. *From Memory to Written Record: England 1066–1307*. 2nd ed. London: Blackwell, 1993 [1979].

———. "Law and Love in the Middle Ages." In *Disputes and Settlements: Law and Human Relations in the West*, edited by John Bossy, 47–67. Cambridge: Cambridge University Press, 1983.

———. "Remembering the Past and the Good Old Law." *History* 55 (1970): 165–76.

Clark, Elaine. "Debt Litigation in a Late Medieval English Vill." In *Pathways to Medieval Peasants*, edited by J. A. Raftis, 247–79. Toronto: Pontifical Institute of Medieval Studies, 1981.

Clover, Carol. "Regardless of Sex: Men, Women, and Power in Early Northern Europe." In *Studying Medieval Women*, edited by Nancy F. Partner, 61–85. Cambridge, Mass.: Medieval Academy of America, 1993.

Cohen, David. *Law, Violence, and Community in Classical Athens*. Cambridge: Cambridge University Press, 1995.

Cohen, Esther. *The Crossroads of Justice: Law and Culture in Late Medieval France*. Leiden: E. J. Brill, 1993.

———. "To Die a Criminal for the Public Good: The Execution Ritual in Late Medieval Paris." In *Law, Custom, and the Social Fabric in Medieval Europe: Essays in Honor of Bryce Lyon*, edited by Bernard S. Bachrach and David Nicholas, 280–304. Kalamazoo, Mich.: Medieval Institute Publications, 1990.

Cohen, Thomas V., and Elizabeth S. Cohen. *Words and Deeds in Renaissance Rome: Trials before the Papal Magistrates*. Toronto: University of Toronto Press, 1993.

Comaroff, John L., and Simon Roberts. *Rules and Processes: The Cultural Logic of Dispute in an African Context*. Chicago: University of Chicago Press, 1981.

Conley, John M., and William M. O'Barr. *Rules versus Relationships: The Ethnography of Legal Discourse*. Chicago: University of Chicago Press, 1990.

Coulet, Noël. *Aix-en-Provence: espace et relations d'une capitale (milieu XIVe s.–milieu XVe s.)*. 2 vols. Aix-en-Provence: Université de Provence, 1988.

Courtemanche, Andrée. "The Judge, the Doctor, and the Poisoner: Medieval Expertise in Manosquin Judicial Rituals at the End of the Fourteenth Century." In *Medieval and Early Modern Ritual: Formalized Behavior in Europe, China, and Japan*, edited by Joëlle Rollo-Koster, 105–23. Leiden: E. J. Brill, 2002.

———. *La richesse des femmes: patrimoines et gestion à Manosque au XIVe siècle*. Montréal: Bellarmin, 1993.

Curtis, Timothy. "Explaining Crime in Early Modern England." *Criminal Justice History: An International Annual* 1 (1980): 117–37.

Daly, Martin and Margo Wilson. *Homicide*. Hawthorne, New York: Aldine de Gruyter, 1988.

Damasio, Antonio. *Descartes' Error: Emotion, Reason, and the Human Brain*. New York: G. P. Putnam, 1994.

Davies, Wendy, and Paul Fouracre, eds. *The Settlement of Disputes in Early Medieval Europe*. Cambridge: Cambridge University Press, 1986.

Davis, Natalie Zemon. *Fiction in the Archives: Pardon Tales and Their Tellers in Sixteenth-Century France*. Stanford: Stanford University Press, 1987.

——. *The Gift in Sixteenth-Century France*. Madison: University of Wisconsin Press, 2000.

Dean, Trevor. "Marriage and Mutilation: Vendetta in Late Medieval Italy." *Past and Present* 157 (1997): 3–36.

de Roover, Raymond. *Money, Banking, and Credit in Mediaeval Bruges: Italian Merchant-Bankers, Lombards, and Money-Changers, a Study in the Origins of Banking*. Cambridge, Mass.: Mediaeval Academy of America, 1948.

Département des Bouches-du-Rhône. Ville de Marseille. *Inventaire Sommaire des Archives Communales Antérieures à 1790*. Série BB. Vol. 1. Marseille, 1909.

Dolezalek, Gero. "Une nouvelle source pour l'étude de la pratique judiciaire au XIII siècle: les livres d'imbreviatures des notaires de cour." In *Confluence des droits savants et des pratiques juridiques: actes du colloque de Montpellier*, 225–41. Milan: A. Giuffrè, 1979.

Donahue, Charles. "Proof by Witnesses in the Church Courts of Medieval England: An Imperfect Reception of the Learned Law." In *On the Laws and Customs of England: Essays in Honor of Samuel E. Thorne*, edited by Morris S. Arnold et al., 127–58. Chapel Hill: University of North Carolina Press, 1981.

Dorini, Umberto. *Il diritto penale e la delinquenza in Firenze nel sec. XIV*. Lucca: D. Corsi, 1923.

Douglas, Mary, and Baron Isherwood. *The World of Goods: Towards an Anthropology of Consumption*. 2nd ed. London: Routledge, 1996 [1979].

Droguet, Alain. *Administration financière et système fiscal à Marseille dans la seconde moitié du XIVe siècle*. Aix-en-Provence: Université de Provence, 1983.

Duby, Georges. *William Marshal: The Flower of Chivalry*. Translated by Richard Howard. New York: Pantheon Books, 1984.

Duggan, Charles. "Papal Judges Delegate and the 'New Law'." In *Cultures of Power: Lordship, Status, and Process in Twelfth-Century Europe*, edited by Thomas N. Bisson, 172–99. Philadelphia: University of Pennsylvania Press, 1995.

Dunbabin, Jean. *Charles I of Anjou: Power, Kingship, and State-Making in Thirteenth-Century Europe*. London: Longman, 1998.

Dunbar, Robin. *Grooming, Gossip, and the Evolution of Language*. Cambridge, Mass.: Harvard University Press, 1996.

Dunning, Eric. *Sport Matters: Sociological Studies of Sport, Violence, and Civilization*. London: Routledge, 1999.

Durand, Guillaume. *Speculum iudicale*. 2 vols. Basel, 1574; reprint ed., Aalen, Germany: Scientia Verlag, 1975.

Eckstein, Nicholas A. *The District of the Green Dragon: Neighbourhood Life and Social Change in Renaissance Florence*. Florence: L. S. Olschki, 1995.

Elias, Norbert. *The Civilizing Process: The History of Manners and State Formation and Civilization*. 2 vols. Translated by Edmund Jephcott. Oxford: Blackwell, 1994 [1939].

Emery, Richard W. *The Jews of Perpignan in the Thirteenth Century: An Economic Study Based on Notarial Records*. New York: Columbia University Press, 1959.

——. "Le prêt d'argent juif en Languedoc et Roussillon." In *Juifs et judaïsme de Languedoc*. Vol. 12 of Cahiers de Fanjeaux, 85–96. Toulouse: Privat, 1977.

Engelmann, Arthur et al. *A History of Continental Civil Procedure*. Vol. 7 of The Continental Legal History Series. Boston: Little, Brown, 1927.

Esmein, Adhémar. *A History of Continental Criminal Procedure with Special Reference to France*. Vol. 5 of The Continental Legal History Series. Translated by John Simpson. Boston: Little, Brown, 1913.

Fenster, Thelma, and Daniel Lord Smail, eds. *Fama: The Politics of Talk and Reputation in Medieval Europe*. Ithaca: Cornell University Press, 2003.

Fontaine, Laurence. "Espaces, usages et dynamiques de la dette dans les hautes vallées dauphinoises (XVIIe–XVIIIe)." *Annales: histoire, sciences sociales* 49 (1994): 1375–91.

Foucault, Michel. *Discipline and Punish: The Birth of the Prison*. Translated by Alan Sheridan. New York: Pantheon Books, 1977.

Fraher, Richard M. "Conviction according to Conscience: The Medieval Jurists' Debate concerning Judicial Discretion and the Law of Proof." *Law and History Review* 7 (1989): 23–88.

Freedman, Paul. "Peasant Anger in the Late Middle Ages." In *Anger's Past: The Social Uses of an Emotion in the Middle Ages*, edited by Barbara H. Rosenwein, 171–88. Ithaca: Cornell University Press, 1998.

Frier, Bruce W. *The Rise of the Roman Jurists: Studies in Cicero's* Pro Caecina. Princeton: Princeton University Press, 1985.

Gauvard, Claude. *"De grace especial": crime, état, et société à la fin du Moyen Âge*. 2 vols. Paris: Publications de la Sorbonne, 1991.

——. "La declinazione d'identità negli archivi giudiziari del regno di Carlo VI." In *La parola all'accusato*, edited by Jean-Claude Maire Vigueur and Agostino Paravicini Bagliani, 170–89. Palermo: Sellerio, 1991.

——. "Les juges jugent-ils? Les peines prononcées par le Parlement criminel, vers 1380–vers 1425." In *Penser le pouvoir au Moyen Âge: VIIIe–XVe siècle*, edited by Dominique Boutet and Jacques Verger, 69–87. Paris: Éditions Rue d'Ulm: Presses de L'ENS, 2000.

——. "L'honneur du roi: peines et rituels judiciaires au Parlement de Paris à la fin du Moyen Âge." In *Les rites de la justice: gestes et rituels judiciaires au Moyen Âge occidental*, edited by Claude Gauvard and Robert Jacob, vol. 9 of Cahiers du Léopard d'Or, 99–123. Paris: Léopard d'Or, 2000.

Geertz, Clifford. "The Rotating Credit Association: A 'Middle Rung' in Development." In *Economic Development and Cultural Change* 10 (1962): 241–63.

Given, James. *Society and Homicide in Thirteenth-Century England*. Stanford: Stanford University Press, 1977.

Goffman, Erving. *Presentation of Self in Everyday Life*. New York: Doubleday, 1959.

Gonthier, Nicole. *Délinquance, justice et société dans le Lyonnais médiéval de la fin du XIIIe siècle au début du XVIe siècle*. Paris: Éditions Arguments, 1993.

Górecki, Piotr. "Communities of Legal Memory in Medieval Poland, c. 1200–1240." *Journal of Medieval History* 24 (1998): 127–54.

Green, Thomas A. *Verdict according to Conscience: Perspectives on the English Criminal Trial Jury, 1200–1800*. Chicago: University of Chicago Press, 1985.

Guenée, Bernard. *Tribunaux et gens de justice dans le bailliage de Senlis à la fin du Moyen Âge*. Paris: Les Belles Lettres, 1963.

Guimbard, Catherine. "Exil et institution du *comune* à Florence dans la seconde moitié du XIIIe siècle." In *Exil et civilisation en Italie (XIIe–XVIe siècles)*, edited by Jacques Heers and Christian Bec, 21–31. Nancy: Presses Universitaires de Nancy, 1990.

Hanawalt, Barbara A. *Crime and Conflict in English Communities, 1300–1348*. Cambridge, Mass.: Harvard University Press, 1979.

Hébert, Michel. "*Voce Preconia*: note sur les criées publiques en Provence à la fin du Moyen Âge." In *Milieux naturels, espaces sociaux: études offertes à Robert Delort*, edited by Élisabeth Mornet and Franco Morenzoni, 689–701. Paris: Publications de la Sorbonne, 1997.

Heers, Jacques. *Family Clans in the Middle Ages: A Study of Political and Social Structures in Urban Areas*. Translated by Barry Herbert. Amsterdam: North-Holland Publishing, 1977.

Helmholz, Richard H. *Select Cases on Defamation to 1600*. London: Selden Society, 1985.

Holderness, B. A. "Credit in English Rural Society before the Nineteenth Century, with Special Reference to the Period 1650–1720." *Agricultural History Review* 24 (1976): 97–109.

Hudson, John. *The Formation of the English Common Law: Law and Society in England from the Norman Conquest to Magna Carta*. London: Longman, 1996.

Hughes, Diane Owen. "Il matrimonio nell'Italia medievale." In *Storia del matrimonio*, edited by Michela de Giorgio and Christiane Klapisch-Zuber, 5–61. Rome: Laterza, 1996.

——. "Regulating Women's Fashion." In *Silences of the Middle Ages*, edited by Christiane Klapisch-Zuber, 136–58. Vol. 2 of *A History of Women in the West*, edited by Georges Duby and Michelle Perrot. Cambridge, Mass.: Harvard University Press, 1992.

Huizinga, Johan. *The Autumn of the Middle Ages*. Translated by Rodney J. Payton and Ulrich Mammitzsch. Chicago: University of Chicago Press, 1996 [1919].

Humphreys, Sally. "Social Relations on Stage: Witnesses in Classical Athens." *History and Anthropology* 1 (1985): 313–69.

Hurnard, Naomi D. *The King's Pardon for Homicide before A.D. 1307*. Oxford: Clarendon Press, 1969.

Hyams, Paul R. "Due Process versus the Maintenance of Order in European Law: The Contribution of the *Ius Commune*." In *The Moral World of the Law*, edited by Peter Coss, 62–90. Cambridge: Cambridge University Press, 2000.

——. "Feud in Medieval England." *Haskins Society Journal: Studies in Medieval History* 3 (1991): 1–21.

——. "What Did Henry III of England Think in Bed and in French about Kingship and Anger?" In *Anger's Past: The Social Uses of an Emotion in the Middle Ages*, edited by Barbara H. Rosenwein, 92–124. Ithaca: Cornell University Press, 1998.

Ingram, Martin. "Law, Litigants, and the Construction of 'Honour': Slander Suits in Early Modern England." In *The Moral World of the Law*, edited by Peter Coss, 134–60. Cambridge: Cambridge University Press, 2000.

Jaeger, C. Stephen. *The Origins of Courtliness: Civilizing Trends and the Formation of Courtly Ideals, 939–1210*. Philadelphia: University of Pennsylvania Press, 1985.

Jordan, William Chester. *The French Monarchy and the Jews: From Philip Augustus to the Last Capetians*. Philadelphia: University of Pennsylvania Press, 1989.

——. *Women and Credit in Pre-Industrial and Developing Societies*. Philadelphia: University of Pennsylvania Press, 1993.

Kagan, Richard L. *Lawsuits and Litigants in Castile, 1500–1700*. Chapel Hill: University of North Carolina Press, 1981.

Kent, D. V., and F. W. Kent. *Neighbours and Neighbourhood in Renaissance Florence: The District of the Red Lion in the Fifteenth Century*. Locust Valley, N.Y.: J. J. Augustin, 1982.

Kent, F. W. *Household and Lineage in Renaissance Florence: The Family Life of the Capponi, Ginori, and Rucellai*. Princeton: Princeton University Press, 1977.

Kirschenbaum, Aaron. "Jewish and Christian Theories of Usury in the Middle Ages. *Jewish Quarterly Review* 75 (1985): 270–89.

Kirshner, Julius, ed. *The Origins of the State in Italy, 1300–1600*. Chicago: University of Chicago Press, 1995.

Klapisch-Zuber, Christiane. *La maison et le nom: stratégies et rituels dans l'Italie de la Renaissance*. Paris: École des hautes études en sciences sociales, 1990.

Klapisch-Zuber, Christiane, and Michel Demonet. "*A uno pane et uno vino*: The Rural Tuscan Family at the Beginning of the Fifteenth Century." In Christiane Klapisch-Zuber, *Women, Family, and Ritual in Renaissance Italy*. Translated by Lydia G. Cochrane. Chicago: University of Chicago Press, 1985.

Kollmann, Nancy Shields. *By Honor Bound: State and Society in Early Modern Russia*. Ithaca: Cornell University Press, 1999.

Kowaleski, Maryanne. *Local Markets and Regional Trade in Medieval Exeter*. Cambridge: Cambridge University Press, 1995.

Kuehn, Thomas. *Emancipation in Late Medieval Florence*. New Brunswick, N.J.: Rutgers University Press, 1982.

——. "Fama as a Legal Status in Renaissance Florence." In *Fama: The Politics of Talk and Reputation in Medieval Europe*, edited by Thelma Fenster and Daniel Lord Smail, 27–46. Ithaca: Cornell University Press, 2003.

——. *Law, Family, and Women: Toward a Legal Anthropology of Renaissance Italy*. Chicago: University of Chicago Press, 1991.

Kuttner, Stephen. "The Revival of Jurisprudence." In *Renaissance and Renewal in the Twelfth Century*, edited by R. L. Benson and Giles Constable, 299–323. Cambridge, Mass.: Harvard University Press, 1982.

Langbein, John H. *Prosecuting Crime in the Renaissance: England, Germany, France*. Cambridge, Mass.: Harvard University Press, 1974.

———. *Torture and the Law of Proof: Europe and England in the Ancien Régime*. Chicago: University of Chicago Press, 1977.

Lansing, Carol. *The Florentine Magnates: Lineage and Faction in a Medieval Commune*. Princeton: Princeton University Press, 1991.

Lavoie, Rodrigue. "Endettement et pauvreté en Provence d'aprés les listes de la justice comtale, XIVe et XVe siècles." *Provence historique* 23 (1973): 201–16.

———. "Les statistiques criminelles et le visage du justicier: justice royale et justice seigneuriale en Provence au Moyen Âge." *Provence historique* 115 (1979): 3–20.

Leon Battista Alberti. *De iciarchia*, in Opere volgari. Edited by Cecil Grayson, 2 vols. Bari: G. Laterza, 1966.

Lesage, Georges. *Marseille angevine: recherches sur son évolution administrative, économique et urbaine de la victoire de Charles d'Anjou àl'arrivée de Jeanne 1re (1264–1348)*. Paris: Boccard, 1950.

Lesnick, Daniel. "Insults and Threats in Medieval Todi." *Journal of Medieval History* 17 (1991): 71–89.

Lewis, Andrew D. E. "The Autonomy of Roman Law." In *The Moral World of the Law*, edited by Peter Coss, 37–47. Cambridge: Cambridge University Press, 2000.

*The Liber Augustalis; or, Constitutions of Melfi, Promulgated by the Emperor Frederick II for the Kingdom of Sicily in 1231*. Translated by James M. Powell. Syracuse, N.Y.: Syracuse University Press, 1971.

Lupoi, Maurizio. *The Origins of the European Legal Order*. Translated by Adrian Belton. Cambridge: Cambridge University Press, 2000.

Luria, Keith P. *Territories of Grace: Cultural Change in the Seventeenth-Century Diocese of Grenoble*. Berkeley: University of California Press, 1991.

MacCaughan, Patricia. "La procédure judiciare à Manosque au milieu du XIIIe siècle." *Revue historique de droit français et étranger* 76 (1998): 583–95.

Maire Vigueur, Jean-Claude. "Justice et politique dans l'Italie communale de la second moitié du XIIIe siècle: l'exemple de Pérouse." *Comptes rendus de l'Académie des inscriptions et belles-lettres* 2 (1986): 312–28.

Martines, Lauro. *Lawyers and Statecraft in Renaissance Florence*. Princeton: Princeton University Press, 1968.

———, ed. *Violence and Civil Disorder in Italian Cities, 1200–1500*. Berkeley: University of California Press, 1972.

Maugain, Gabriel. *Moeurs italiennes de la Renaissance: la vengeance*. Paris: Les Belles Lettres, 1935.

Meredith, Kenneth Frederick. "The Penalty of Banishment in Medieval France and England." Ph.D. diss., University of Virginia, 1979.

Merry, Sally Engle. *Getting Justice and Getting Even: Legal Consciousness among Working-Class Americans*. Chicago: University of Chicago Press, 1990.

Michaud, Francine. *Un signe des temps: accroissement des crises familiales autour du patrimoine à Marseille à la fin du XIIIe siècle*. Toronto: Pontifical Institute of Medieval Studies, 1994.

Migliorino, Francesco. *Fama e infamia: problemi della società medievale nel pensiero giuridico nei secoli xii e xiii*. Catania: Giannotta, 1985.

Miller, William Ian. *Bloodtaking and Peacemaking: Feud, Law, and Society in Saga Iceland*. Chicago: University of Chicago Press, 1990.

———. "In Defense of Revenge." In *Medieval Crime and Social Control*, edited by Barbara A. Hanawalt and David Wallace, 70–89. Minneapolis: University of Minnesota Press, 1999.

Millett, Paul. *Lending and Borrowing in Ancient Athens*. Cambridge: Cambridge University Press, 1991.

Miskimin, Harry A., David Herlihy, and A. L. Udovitch, eds. *The Medieval City*. New Haven: Yale University Press, 1977.

Moore, Sally Falk. *Law as Process: An Anthropological Approach*. London: Routledge and Kegan Paul, 1978.

Muir, Edward. *Mad Blood Stirring: Vendetta and Factions in Friuli during the Renaissance*. Baltimore: Johns Hopkins University Press, 1993.

Mukerji, Chandra. *From Graven Images: Patterns of Modern Materialism*. New York: Columbia University Press, 1983.

Muldrew, Craig. *The Economy of Obligation: The Culture of Credit and Social Relations in Early Modern England*. New York: St. Martin's Press, 1998.

——. "Interpreting the Market: The Ethics of Credit and Community Relations in Early Modern England." *Social History* 18 (1993): 163–83.

Nicholas, Barry. *An Introduction to Roman Law*. Oxford: Clarendon Press, 1962.

Nicholas, David. *The Domestic Life of a Medieval City: Women, Children, and the Family in Fourteenth-Century Ghent*. Lincoln: University of Nebraska Press, 1985.

——. *The Van Arteveldes of Ghent: The Varieties of Vendetta and the Hero in History*. Ithaca: Cornell University Press, 1988.

Odegaard, Charles E. "Legalis Homo." *Speculum* 15 (1940): 186–93.

Otis-Cour, Leah. "'Terreur et exemple, compassion et miséricorde': la repression pénale à Pamiers à la fin du Moyen Âge." In *Justice et justiciables. Mélanges Henri Vidal*, edited by Henri Vidal, vol. 16 of Recueil de mémoires et travaux, 139–64. Montpellier: Faculté de droit, d'économie et de gestion de Montpellier, 1994.

Palmer, Robert C. *English Law in the Age of the Black Death, 1348–1381: A Transformation of Governance and Law*. Chapel Hill: University of North Carolina Press, 1993.

Pazzaglini, Peter Raymond. *The Criminal Ban of the Sienese Commune, 1225–1310*. Milan: A. Giuffrè, 1979.

Pennington, Kenneth. *The Prince and the Law, 1200–1600: Sovereignty and Rights in the Western Legal Tradition*. Berkeley: University of California Press, 1993.

Pernoud, Régine. *Essai sur l'histoire du port de Marseille des origines à la fin du XIIIeme siècle*. Marseille: A. Ged, 1935.

——, ed. *Les statuts municipaux de Marseille*. Monaco: Imprimerie de Monaco, 1949.

Peters, Edward. *Torture*. New York: Blackwell, 1985.

——. "Wounded Names: The Medieval Doctrine of Infamy." In *Law in Medieval Life and Thought*, edited by Edward B. King and Susan J. Ridyard, 43–89. Sewanee, Tenn.: Press of the University of the South, 1990.

Petit-Dutaillis, Charles. *Documents nouveaux sur les moeurs populaires et le droit de vengeance dans les Pays-Bas au XVe siècle*. Paris: H. Champion, 1908.

Pinker, Steven. *How the Mind Works*. New York: Norton, 1997.

Pohl, Susanne. "Negotiating Honor and State Authority: The Prosecution and Punishment of Manslaughter in Zurich and Southwest Germany, 1350–1600." Ph.D. diss., University of Michigan, 1997.

Poos, Lawrence R. "Sex, Lies, and the Church Courts of Pre-Reformation England." *Journal of Interdisciplinary History* 25 (1995): 585–607.

Postan, Michael. "Credit in Medieval Trade." *Economic History Review* 1 (1928): 234–61.

Radding, Charles M. *The Origins of Medieval Jurisprudence: Pavia and Bologna, 850–1150*. New Haven: Yale University Press, 1988.

Raggio, Osvaldo. *Faide e parentele: lo stato genovese visto dalla Fontanabuona*. Turin: Giulio Einaudi, 1990.

Rawcliffe, Carole. "'That Kindliness Should Be Cherished More, and Discord Driven Out': The Settlement of Commercial Disputes by Arbitration in Later Medieval England." In *Enterprise and Individuals in Fifteenth-Century England*, edited by Jennifer Kermode, 99–117. Stroud, U.K.: Alan Sutton, 1991.

Reader, John. *Africa: A Biography of the Continent*. New York: Knopf, 1998.

Reyerson, Kathryn L. *Business, Banking, and Finance in Medieval Montpellier*. Toronto: Pontifical Institute of Medieval Studies, 1985.

——. "Flight from Prosecution: The Search for Religious Asylum in Medieval Montpellier." *French Historical Studies* 17 (1992): 603–26.

Reynolds, Susan. "The Emergence of Professional Law in the Long Twelfth Century." Unpublished paper delivered at the American Society for Legal History conference, Chicago, 2001.

Riemer, Eleanor S. "Women, Dowries, and Capital Investment in Thirteenth-Century Siena." In *The Marriage Bargain: Women and Dowries in European History*, edited by Marion A. Kaplan, 59–79. New York: Institute for Research in History: Haworth Press, 1985.

Roberts, Simon. "Introduction." In *Disputes and Settlements: Law and Human Relations in the West*, edited by John Bossy, 1–24. Cambridge: Cambridge University Press, 1983.

Rolland, Henri. *Monnaies des comtes de Provence, XIIe–XVe s.: histoire monétaire, économique, corporative, description raisonnée*. Paris: A. J. Picard, 1956.

Rosenwein, Barbara H., ed. *Anger's Past: The Social Uses of an Emotion in the Middle Ages*. Ithaca: Cornell University Press, 1998.

——. "Worrying about Emotions in History." *American Historical Review* 107 (2002): 821–45.

Ruggiero, Guido. *Violence in Early Renaissance Venice*. New Brunswick, N.J.: Rutgers University Press, 1980.

Scaglione, Aldo. *Knights at Court: Courtliness, Chivalry, and Courtesy from Ottonian Germany to the Italian Renaissance*. Berkeley: University of California Press, 1991.

Scheppele, Kim Lane. "Foreword: Telling Stories." *Michigan Law Review* 87 (1989): 2073–98.

Schnapper, Bernard. "*Testes inhabiles*, les témoins reprochables dans l'ancien droit pénal." *Tijdschrift voor Rechtsgeschiedenis/Revue d'histoire du droit* 33 (1965): 575–616.

Schneider, Peter. "Honor and Conflict in a Sicilian Town." *Anthropological Quarterly* 42 (1969): 130–54.

Shatzmiller, Joseph. *Médecine et justice en Provence médiévale: documents de Manosque, 1262–1348*. Aix-en-Provence: Université de Provence, 1989.

——. *Shylock Reconsidered: Jews, Moneylending, and Medieval Society*. Berkeley: University of California Press, 1990.

Smail, Daniel Lord. "Accommodating Plague in Medieval Marseille." *Continuity and Change* 11 (1996): 11–41.

——. "Common Violence: Vengeance and Inquisition in Fourteenth-Century Marseille." *Past and Present* 151 (May 1996): 28–59.

——. "Démanteler le patrimoine: les femmes et les biens dans la Marseille médievale." *Annales: histoire, sciences sociales* 52 (1997): 343–68.

——. "The General Taille of Marseille, 1360–1361: A Social and Demographic Study." *Provence historique* 49 (1999): 473–85.

——. "Notaries, Courts, and the Legal Culture of Late Medieval Marseille." In *Urban and Rural Communities in Medieval France: Provence and Languedoc, 1000–1500*, edited by Kathryn L. Reyerson and John Drendel, 23–50. Leiden: E. J. Brill, 1998.

——. "Telling Tales in Angevin Courts." *French Historical Studies* 20 (1997): 183–215.

Soman, Alfred. "Deviance and Criminal Justice in Western Europe, 1300–1800: An Essay in Structure," *Criminal Justice History* 1 (1980): 3–28. Reprinted in idem, *Sorcellerie et justice criminelle (16e–18e siècles)*. Hampshire, Great Britain: Variorum, 1992.

Sombart, Werner. *Luxury and Capitalism*. Translated by W. R. Dittmar. Ann Arbor: University of Michigan Press, 1967 [1913].

Spierenburg, Pieter, ed., *Men and Violence: Gender, Honor, and Rituals in Modern Europe and America*. Columbus: Ohio State University Press, 1998.

Spufford, Peter. "Les liens du crédit au village dans l'Angleterre du XVIIe siècle." *Annales: histoire, sciences sociales* 49 (1994): 1359–73.

Starn, Randolph. *Contrary Commonwealth: The Theme of Exile in Medieval and Renaissance Italy*. Berkeley: University of California Press, 1982.

Stern, Laura Ikins. *The Criminal Law System of Medieval and Renaissance Florence*. Baltimore: Johns Hopkins University Press, 1994.

Stouff, Louis. "Les registres de notaires d'Arles (début XIVe siècle-1460): quelques problèmes posés par l'utilisation des archives notariales." *Provence historique* 25 (1975): 305–24.

Strauss, Gerald. *Law, Resistance, and the State: The Opposition to Roman Law in Reformation Germany*. Princeton: Princeton University Press, 1986.

Strayer, Joseph R. *Les gens de justice du Languedoc sous Philippe le Bel*. Toulouse: Association Marc Bloch, 1970.

Tancred. *Ordo iudiciarius*. In *Pilii, Tancredi, Gratiae, Libri de iudiciorum ordine*, edited by Friedrich Christian Bergmann. Gottingen, 1842.

Teisseire, Raymond. *Histoire des juridictions et des palais de justice de Marseille depuis leur origine jusqu'à nos jours*. Paris: Recueil Sirey, 1931.

Tierney, Brian. "Medieval Canon Law and Western Constitutionalism." *Catholic Historical Review* 52 (1966): 1–17.

Todd, S. C. "The Language of Law in Classical Athens." In *The Moral World of the Law*, edited by Peter Coss, 17–36. Cambridge: Cambridge University Press, 2000.

Vallerani, Massimo. "Pace et processo nel sistema giudiziario del comune di Perugia." *Quaderni Storici* 101 (1999): 315–53.

——. *Il sistema giudiziario del comune di Perugia: conflitti, reati e processi nella seconda metà del XIII secolo*. Perugia: Deputazione di storia patria per l'Umbria, 1991.

Van Caenegem, R. C. "La preuve dans le droit du Moyen Âge Occidental." In *La preuve*, part 2, *Moyen Âge et temps modernes*, vol. 17 of Recueils de la société Jean Bodin pour l'histoire comparative des institutions, 691–753. Brussels: Éditions de la Librairie Encyclopédique, 1965. Translated in idem, *Legal History: A European Perspective*. London: Hambledon Press, 1991.

——. "Law and Power in Twelfth-Century Flanders." In *Cultures of Power: Lordship, Status, and Process in Twelfth-Century Europe*, edited by Thomas N. Bisson, 149–71. Philadelphia: University of Pennsylvania Press, 1995.

Veblen, Thorstein. *The Theory of the Leisure Class: An Economic Study in the Evolution of Institutions*. New York: Macmillan, 1899.

Vincent of Lérins. *Vincentii Lerinensis commonitorium excerpta*. Edited by R. Demeulenaere. Vol. 64 of *Corpus Christianorum*, Series Latina. Turnholt: Brepols, 1985.

Wakin, Jeannette A., ed. *The Function of Documents in Islamic Law*. Albany: State University of New York Press, 1972.

Waley, Daniel. *The Italian City-Republics*. 3rd ed. London: Longman, 1988 [1969].

Watson, Alan. *The Evolution of Law*. Baltimore: Johns Hopkins University Press, 1985.

Weissman, Ronald F. E. *Ritual Brotherhood in Renaissance Florence*. New York: Academic Press, 1982.

Wernham, Monique. *La communauté juive de Salon-de-Provence d'après les actes notariés, 1391–1435*. Toronto: Pontifical Institute of Medieval Studies, 1987.

White, Stephen D. "'Pactum . . . Legem Vincit et Amor Judicium': The Settlement of Disputes by Compromise in Eleventh-Century Western France." *American Journal of Legal History* 22 (1978): 281–308.

——. "The Politics of Anger." In *Anger's Past: The Social Uses of an Emotion in the Middle Ages*, edited by Barbara H. Rosenwein, 127–52. Ithaca: Cornell University Press, 1998.

——. "Proposing the Ordeal and Avoiding It: Strategy and Power in Western French Litigation, 1050–1110." In *Cultures of Power: Lordship, Status, and Process in Twelfth-Century Europe*, edited by Thomas N. Bisson, 89–123. Philadelphia: University of Pennsylvania Press, 1995.

Wickham, Chris. "Land Disputes and Their Social Framework in Lombard-Carolingian Italy, 700–900." In *The Settlement of Disputes in Early Medieval Europe*, edited by Wendy Davies and Paul Fouracre, 105–24. Cambridge: Cambridge University Press, 1986.

——. *Legge, pratiche e conflitti: tribunali e risoluzione delle dispute nella Toscana del XII secolo.* Rome: Viella, 2000.

Wilson, Stephen. *Feuding, Conflict, and Banditry in Nineteenth-Century Corsica.* Cambridge: Cambridge University Press, 1988.

Wormald, Jenny. "Bloodfeud, Kindred, and Government in Early Modern Scotland." *Past and Present* 87 (1980): 54–97.

Wormald, Patrick. *The Making of English Law: King Alfred to the Twelfth Century.* Vol. 1, *Legislation and Its Limits.* Oxford: Blackwell, 1999.

Wrightson, Keith, and David Levine. *Poverty and Piety in an English Village: Terling, 1525–1700.* New York: Academic Press, 1979.

Zarb, Mireille. *Histoire d'une autonomie communale: les privilèges de la ville de Marseille du Xe siècle à la Révolution.* Paris: Picard, 1961.

Zorzi, Andrea. "The Florentines and Their Public Offices in the Early Fifteenth Century: Competition, Abuses of Power, and Unlawful Acts." Translated by Corrada Biazzo Curry. In *History from Crime*, edited by Edward Muir and Guido Ruggiero, 110–34. Baltimore: Johns Hopkins University Press, 1994.

——. "The Judicial System in Florence in the Fourteenth and Fifteenth Centuries." In *Crime, Society, and the Law in Renaissance Italy*, edited by Trevor Dean and K. J. P. Lowe, 40–58. Cambridge: Cambridge University Press, 1994.

# INDEX

243; used for transacting emotion, 64, 243–45. *See also* procedural law *entries*

courts, secular, 39

credit: circumstantial, 144–46, 150, 153 (*see also* dowry *entries*); extension of, 135, 137–38, 144, 148, 184; impersonal, 136–37, 139–40; medieval history of, 136; networks of, 136, 138–39, 148, 180; as security, 147–48; voluntary, 145–46; withdrawal of, 135, 158

credit relationships, 134–35, 138, 141, 147–48, 154–56

creditors: evasion of, 196–97, 201; priority of, 193; and pursuit of litigation, 138, 149, 190

criers, public, 193

criminal law, 131

customary law: in northern French courts, 98; and seizure of property, 189

Dalmas, Antoni, 60–61, 108, 112, 114, 118–20

Dalmas, Peire, 2, 38, 112, 191

Davis, Natalie Zemon, 51, 174

d'Ays, Antoni, 1–5, 10–11, 14–16, 19–20, 23–25, 33, 41, 61, 64, 70, 87, 104, 113, 229; and commensality, 109–11

*De grace especial* (Gauvard), 173

Dean, Trevor, 39, 205

death: attesting time of, 216, 218–19, 236; publicity of, 215–16, 228

debt, 120, 133, 142–43, 145; creation of, 142; forgiveness of, 147; incarceration for, 193; networks of, 148

debt litigation, 27, 33, 142–43, 148, 150–59; and dishonor, 137–38; and fama, 137, 180; impersonal, 157; Jewish, 151; motivation for, 90, 156; as percentage of civil court caseloads, 39; to pursue hatred, 139, 152; rise of, 158–59. *See also* civil litigation

debt recovery, 37, 66, 148–52, 163; costs of, 192; mechanism for, 190, 192–94

defamation, 95, 124–25, 150, 185, 232; and exceptions, 122–23, 130

delays, procedural, 26, 47–48, 61, 251; and case length, 64–66, 66

denunciation, 16, 18, 80–81, 120, 131; in criminal court, 72–73, 76; as inimical gesture, 92, 94, 112–16

d'Esparon, Dousa, 1–5, 10–11, 229; fama of, 23–25. *See also* d'Ays, Antoni

*Discipline and Punish* (Foucault), 161

disfigurement, 160–61. *See also* corporal punishment

disputes: among merchants, 154–56; in civil courts, 41–42; disguised as debt litigation, 39, 86, 154–56; outcome of, 63;

distraint, forcible, 66, 162–63, 190–93; bound by law, 203; private, 148–49

dotal law, 201–3

Douglas, Mary, 20

dowry indebtedness, 201–2

dowry litigation, 39, *40*, 126, 156–57, 184, 202; cases of, 50–51, 144, 237–38

Draguignan, Bondavin de, 140, 150–51, 192

Drendel, John, 36

Duggan, Charles, 17

economic development, 19

economic failure, 124–25

economics, 133–34, 158

*eculeum* (horse), 75–76, 181

Elias, Norbert, 130

Emery, R. W., 150

emotional relationships, 92–94, 106, 133

emotional satisfaction, 11–12, 81, 131–32, 136, 150, 243–44

emotions: and appellate court, 85–86; in civil suits, 27; in evolution of law, 243–46; gendered, 94, 117–20; language of, 90–91, 94, 105; neural and chemical underpinnings for, 246; in procedural law, 92, 242; performance of, 28, 64, 100–101, 243–45; social epistemology of, 90–94; structures of, 89–95, 100; transformed through litigation, 13, 64–65

enemies, 93, 105

enemies, capital, 10–11, 76, 105, 115, 155; in case of Guilhem de Belavila, 76–77, 103, 107, 171

enmity, 3, 12, 15, 17, 167; in case of Antoni d'Ays, 8, 10–11, 25; in case of Guilhem de Belavila, 101, 135; factional, 8, 153–55; performance of, 131, 167; transaction of, 20, 27, 88, 205; and witness exceptions, 97

envy, 14–16, 242; in case of Antoni d'Ays, 10; and obligation, 133

Euzeria, Dousa, 105–6, 135, 141, 158

evasion, 6, 163; through procedures, 71, 87, 196–99; through shelters, 204–5. *See also* flight; shelters, legal

evidence, 48–52

*exceptio* (exception), 60

excommunication, 60–61, 119; for debt, 194; of judges, 84–85; and procedural error, 96; public aspect of, 215

executions, 173, 177–79; in effigy, 170. *See also* evasion; flight

exile, 160; for bankruptcy, 193; conditions of, 188–89; in lieu of corporal punishment, 185–86; self-imposed, 168–76

*extimatio* (assessment of goods), 191–92

factional violence, 8, 90, 99, 141, 152, 165–68, 183, 187. *See also* factions; feud

factions: and capitalization, 140–41; and commerce, 154–55. *See also* factional violence; Vivaut and de Jerusalem parties

facts: construction of, 245; public, 211–12; in Roman-canon law, 65, 96, 207–10. *See also* publicity

fama, 20, 51–52, 185, 209–12, 224, 240; bona part of, 161–62; networks for, 179–80. *See also* public knowledge

fama clause, 58, 226, 240

familial relations: networks of, 111; retaliation by, 171

Ferier, Peire, 107–8, 114, 119

feud, 21, 90, 116–17, 152, 183; Icelandic, 95. *See also* bloodfeud; factional violence; vengeance

fights, 164–67. *See also* assault; street battles

filiation, 218–19

fines. *See* Angevin judicial revenues; contumacy

flight (*fuga*), 103, 160, 163, 168–71, 173–75, 182, 187; for bankruptcy, 193, 201, 203, 207. *See also* banishment; evasion; exile

Florence, 39; archival record of, 210, 248, 257; banishment in, 189; contumacy in, 170; credit metaphors in, 134; peace procedure in, 115

force, coercive, 9, 89, 160–64, 193; in Marseille, 27; state-sponsored, 66, 183

force, private, 162–64, 167, 183, 190

Foucault, Michel, 161

Fraher, Richard, 182, 185

fraud: accusations of, 81; judicial, 84; notarial, 225

friendship, 90–93, 242; exceptions due to, 97, 103–4; language of, 105–6, 108–11; networks of, 90, 106

Frier, Bruce W., 12, 21–22

fugitives. *See* flight

Gamella, Pellegrina, 215–16, 220, 235–36

Gauvard, Claude, 36, 51, 167, 170, 173

Geertz, Clifford, 134

gender ideology, medieval, 117

gifts: counter-, 133, 158; exchange, 108, 133; as metaphor for credit, 133–34, 158; in Marseillais culture, 101; negative, 108, 132–33; and obligation, 133. *See also* injury

Giraut, Alexander, 184, 188, 227

Girman, Esteve, 151–52, 238–39

Girman, Johan, 99, 151–52, 238–39

Goffman, Erving, 107

good name, 20. *See also* fama

goods: assessed, 191; management of, 124–26; ownership of, and public knowledge, 219; transaction of, 20. *See also* bona

gossip: as form of retaliation, 86; and moral character, 128–29; as public activity, 23, 95; as public archive, 184, 210–14; in witness interrogations, 58. *See also* fama; public knowledge

groups, sociology of, 90–91

Guenée, Bernard, 169, 204

Guibert, Peire, 153–54, 168, 207–8

hatred, 14–16, 27, 64, 77, 90–91, 100–101, 117–20, 131–35, 156, 171, 179, 189, 242, 244; as motivation, 112, 115, 119–20, 156; pursued in court, 112, 131, 150, 162; state of, 61, 93, 167, 174 (*see also* enmity); and status, 93–94, 118, 127–28, 141; structures of, 89–92, 242; tracking of, 93–94, 133; witness exceptions for, 59, 61, 84, 97–98

hand loans, *143*, 143–44, 146–47

history: commercial, 136; of criminal justice, 173–74; of law, 13–14

Holderness, B. A., 142

homicide, 8–9, 168, 186–89, 198–99, 207–8; appeals for condemnation, 178; in criminal court, 76, 172, 174, 185; and women, 103

honor, 23

household account book (cartulary), 53

humiliation, 12, 15–16, 45, 120; and criminal litigation, 81, 87, 173

Hyams, Paul, 17

Iceland, medieval, 214; sagas of, 79; procedural law of, 95

ill fame, 123

ill-will, 90, 93, 105, 113, 133. *See also* malevolence

Imbert, Guilhem, 67–69, 228, 254

incarceration, 66, 81, 114, 160, 164, 171, 173–76, 193–94

*indicia* (articles in criminal cases), 76–77

Ingram, Martin, 12, 130

inheritance, 237–38

inimical gesture, 26–27, 57, 64–65, 77, 87, 112, 116. *See also* civil litigation; debt litigation; denunciation; dowry litigation; testimony: hostile

initiations, abandoned, 87

injury, 133; and litigation, 92

instruments, notarial, 53, 55, 210

insults, 89–90, 118–20, 130–33; prosecuted, 92, 95, *186*

intervention, private, 6, 165–68

Isabella, queen of Anjou, 113

Isherwood, Baron, 20

Italy: compared to Marseille, 53–54; factions in, 183

jail, 176. *See* incarceration
Jeanne, queen of Anjou, 194, 196
Jerusalem, Marques de, 141, 168, 174–75
Jerusalem, Peire de, 40, 78, 100, 168, 172, 175, 187
Jewish lending, 136–37, 139–40, 144, 150–52, 245
Jews: excluded as witnesses, 56; participation in courts, 33, 43, 45, 84, 177, 181
Jordan, William Chester, 136
Judeo-Christian moral philosophy, 133
jurisdiction: and coercive force, 169–70, 181; of upper and lower cities, 196–99
justice, public, 33. *See also* courts of law *entries*

Kagan, Richard, 11, 159n
killers, 173, 186; and contumacy, 189–90, 207. *See also* homicide
kinship, 91; networks of, 136; witness exceptions due to, 95, 97–99, 107; in witness groups, 213, 219, 238; women's knowledge of, 236–37
knowledge. *See* public knowledge; social knowledge
knowledge-bearing group, 226–27, 230, 233, 240
Kuehn, Thomas, 13, 100

La Major, cathedral of, 29, 75, 164, 171
Latin, xi-xii, 57
Lavoie, Rodrigue, 39
law: assumptions on history of, 5–10, 13–14; as product, 18–20; professionalization of, 21, 66 (*see also* lawyers; procurators)
law, statutory, 83–84, 97
lawsuits. *See* civil litigation; debt litigation; dowry litigation
lawyers, 7, 21–22, 45–46, 66–68, 71–72
lenders, Christian, 140
lending cycles, 142
Levine, David, 139–40, 148
libel (*libellum*), 43, 46–47, 82
*libri de ricordanze*, 39, 53, 134
litigants. *See* witness groups
litigation. *See* specific types
loans: commercial, 139–40; cyclical pattern of, 142
Louis I, king of Naples, 140
Louis II, king of Naples, 193–95
love, 27, 90–93, 117, 133, 242; as exception, 97–101. *See also* affection; enmity; friendship; hatred

Maine, Henry Sumner, 65
"make part" with court, 76, 114–15
malevolence (*malivolentia*), 27, 90, 105, 242. *See also* ill-will
Manduel, Johan de, 29–30
Marseille, late medieval: archives for, 25–26, 247–48; city council of, 41–42; culture of vengeance in, 8 (*see also* factions); currency used in, xii; history of, 3–4, 25–26, 29–31, 36–37; literacy rate for, 54; merchant families of, 141; municipal taxes of, 86; payments to crown, 195; policing of (*see* sub-viguier); property investment in, 192; syndics, 195–96; vernacular language, xi; wages in, 69–70. *See also* Angevin royal administration; courts of law, in Marseille
Martin family, 8, 141, 153, 187–89. *See also* factions
Martin, Raolin, 164, 217, 223
Mellomonte, Guilhem de, 46–48, 54, 71, 191
memory: archives of, 226–27, 241; and gossip, 210–14. *See also* public knowledge
Meredith, Kenneth, 189
Merry, Sally Engle, 17
messengers of the courts (*nuncii*), 22, 32, 71; as enforcers, 190–92, 194; rate charged by, 67–68
Michaud, Francine, 36
Miller, William Ian, 95
Mirapeis, Primar, 45–46, 114
Montanee, Bertran, 107, 119, 121–22
Montels, Guilhem de, 111, 115, 152–54, 231–33
Moore, Sally Falk, 18, 89–90
moral condemnation, 120–32. *See also* defamation
moral sentiment, 16, 133, 209, 242
moral turpitude, 123–24, 127–29
Morlans, Marin de, 49–50, 57, 99, 112
Muldrew, Craig, 137–38
mutilation. *See* corporal punishment

narratives, 49–51, 102, 207–8
Negrel, 2–4, 33, 101, 106–7, 110; and Antoni d'Ays, 10, 23–24, 111
neighbors, 91, 104–5, 118, 213; and public knowledge, 219–20; in street battles, 165–67
Nercio, Vivauda de, 107, 118–23, 152
networks, social, 90, 136
Niel, Jacme, 47–49, 61, 66, 71, 87, 112, 118
notaries, 32, 71, 83, 247; as interpretive witnesses, 126; rate charged by, 67–68; record-keeping practices of, 249–58; reputation of, 53

Notre Dame des Accoules, church of, 33–34, 55, 74, 93

obligation, 39, 58–59, 133, 144
ordeal, 13, 182, 189–90, 208–9
*Ordo iudiciarius*, 96–97

palace court. *See* courts of law, civil
*palam et publice*, 49, 214–15. *See also* publicity
Palmer, Robert, 137
paper, 247–48
pardon, royal, 173. *See also* amnesty, general
parlement, Angevin, 32, 80–81, 90
paternity, 230–32, 236
*patria potestas*, 47, 184, 209
Pazzaglini, Peter Raymond, 173–74
peace treaties, 115–16, 135, 203
peace, making of: for debt, 135; and fines, 9, 143, 160; required by statutes, 172–75
penalties. *See* corporal punishment; sanctions
Pennington, Kenneth, 6, 7n
performance, 27, 158, 213, 243; of assault, 175, 207, 211; of emotions, 28, 64, 100–101, 243–45; of enmity, 131, 167; of hatred, 93–94; of kinship, 100; and public knowledge, 214–17. *See also* publicity
Peters, Edward, 181
plague, 37, 216, 222, 224, 236–37, 253. *See also* Black Death
Podio, Guilhem de, 2–5, 8, 10–16, 19–20, 23–24, 33, 61, 70, 87, 110, 229
Postan, Michael, 136–37
poverty: and dependency, 112; and moral failing, 122–25, 128; as result of ill-will, 114
Praepositura, 29, 197
prescription, 220
procedural law, form of: 6–7, 28, 35, 42–43, 174; developed through usage, 65–66; exceptions in, 56, 60, 92–96 (*see also* witness exception procedures); fact-based, 210–11, 253; and narrative, 51
procedural law, exploited by users: through delay, 35, 47, 71–72; through denunciation, 113, 210–11; as hostile gesture, 65, 87, 106; as template for emotions, 88, 92, 131. *See also* defamation
procurators, 21–22, 32, 45–46; professionalization of, 71
proof: articles of, 48–50; law of, 25, 182
property, ownership of: and publicity, 220–21; transfer of, 191–92. *See also* bona; goods
public knowledge, 212–13; circulation of, 227–30, 241; differing by sex, 233–34, 238. *See also* fama; gossip; memory

public talk and fame, 51–52. *See also* fama clause
publicity, 22, 34, 52; legal culture of, 211–13, 224, 226, 241, 245
punishment. *See specific types*

quittances, 139, 144–45, *145*, 148

Raynaut, Jacme, 107–9, 114, 119, 125
Raynaut, Peire, 93–94, 189
reciprocity, 158
recusal of witnesses (*reprobatio testium*), 96. *See* procedural law *entries*; witness exception procedure
registers, notarial, 248, 250–57
René, king of Anjou, 195
repatriation, 9, 174–75
*reprobatio testium*, 96. *See* procedural law *entries*; witness exception procedure
reputation, 53, 150–52. *See* fama
restraint, emotional, 245
retaliation, 18, 135, 162, 243. *See also* vengeance
Reynolds, Susan, 21
Ricau, Laurens, 54, 56, 98, 152–53, 231–32
*rixa* (fight), 108, 164–65. *See also* street battles
Robauda, Johana, 102–5, 112, 118, 120, 129
Robaut, Fulco, 77, 79, 102–5, 112, 115, 118, 171, 188
Roberts, Simon, 39
Rogeta, Alazays, 104, 106, 118–19, 128
*rumor* (fight), 164–65, 192. *See also* street battles

Sadaroni, Mathea, 170, 189, 207
Saint Antoine, church of, 75, 103, 171
Saint Victor, monastery of, 75, 121
Saint Augustine, burg of, 107, 114
sale credits, 141–42
Salvayre, Johanet, 47–49, 51–52, 54, 59, 61, 64, 66, 68, 71, 92, 108, 112, 118, 249
sanctions: blood (*see* corporal punishment); bona-based, 27, 142, 160–63, 185, 204; social, 138, 148, 150, 243
sanctuary, 6, 75, 103, 160, 168, 170–72, 175–76, 178, 186, 193, 207; procedural conditions of, 79, 164, 188–89
Schnapper, Bernard, 96
Scoffier, Andrieu, 108–9, 125, 127
secrecy, 53, 213–15
Segueria, Ugueta, 99, 238–39
seizure of goods: by the court, 190–91; resistance to, 81, 194–95. *See also* distraint, forcible
self-help, 19, 86, 131

Senequier, Johan, 212, 226, 240
shame, 23, 81, 120. *See also* humiliation
Shatzmiller, Joseph, 140, 147–48, 150
shelters, legal: clerical, 163, 197–99; dotal, 163, 201–3; for goods and assets, 201–4
Siena, Leonardo da, 75, 103, 188
social knowledge, 238
sociology, performative, 107
*socius*, 109. *See* associates
Soman, Alfred, 18
*Speculum iudicale*, 97
Spur, 101, 107, 167
stalls (*tabulae*), 33
stories. *See* narratives
street battles, 107, 132, 164–67, 189; vocabulary for, 164. *See also* factions
sub-viguier, 153, 164–65; duties of, 74–75, 80, 167–68, 190; efficacity of, 171–72; perceptions of, 183
summons, 47, 79, 131, 186, 190, 258; public nature of, 22
support, networks of, 160, 180
surgeons, 78–79, 103

Tancred, 96–97
testimony: evaluation of, 240; hostile, 57, 107, 112–14, 116; procedural rules governing, 56–62. *See also* defamation; witness exception procedure
Thomasia, Jacma, 99, 112, 129–30, 151–52, 238–39
threats, 101, 107, 116
Tierney, Brian, 246
Tomas, Guilhem, 75–78, 99, 101, 103–7, 113–15, 118, 129, 165–67, 171, 187, 208, 217
Tomasia, Johaneta, 101–2, 166
torture: extrajudicial, 116, 182–83; judicial, 72, 75–79, 160–61, 180–83, 199, 226
two-witness rule, 174

users of courts. *See* courts of law *entries*

Van Caenegem, Raoul, 6–7, 17
*vanamentum* (debt transfer), 147, 149
Veblen, Thorstein, 20
vendetta, 20, 39, 133
vengeance, 16, 27, 35, 89, 95, 162–63, 171, 175, 190; as alternative to litigation, 72, 80; and coercion, 167, 182–83; expressed through court action, 115–16, 131, 243; illegal, 114; in Marseille, 8–9 (*see also* faction,

street battles); paired with justice, 13; women exempt from, 103. *See also* blood-feud; feud; retaliation
vices, moral, 127–28, 130
viguier, 31–32, 168, 171–72; abuse of office of, 182–83; as faction participant, 72; at the parlement, 73, 80–81
Vinsens, Antoni, 58, 119, 140
violence: family-based, 190; legitimized through court use, 16; not controlled by state, 167–68; prosecuted, 89; by women, 117–20
virtues, moral, 127–30
Vital, Bertran, 68–69, 87, 126–27
Vivaut and de Jerusalem parties: and enmity through litigation, 111, 114, 143, 152–55; and extra-judicial torture, 181–83; and judicial system, 45–46, 53, 113; members, 101–3, 118, 140–41; street battles of, 8, 165, 171–72

Watson, Alan, 21
weapons, 81, 120, 129
White, Stephen D., 13, 244
witness depositions, 4, 74–75; Latin transcript of, 61
witness exception procedure, 92–100, 105, 111–12, 118, 130, 174; in case of Antoni d'Ays, 108, 111; in case of Guilhem de Belavila, 103–4; in criminal appeals, 84. *See also* procedural law *entries*
witness groups: construction of, 57, 226–33; diversity of, 213, 227–28, 233, 239–40; and litigants, 213, 227–33; and women's knowledge, 233–39
witness interrogation: procedures for, 57–58, 60, 92; formula used, 97–98
witness testimony, 7, 25; in civil cases, 52, 55, 57, 102, 210–11, 240; public aspect of, 59–60; restrictions on, 56–57
witnesses, 25, 95, 120–31. *See also* defamation
women: authoritative knowledge of, 56–57, 236–39, 245; as creditors, 144; defamed, 128; dotal rights of, 201–3; hatred by, 104, 107, 117–18; legal capacity of, 245; in litigation, 44; networks of, 104; property ownership by, 44; and violence, 8, 103, 117–20, 165–67
worth, personal, 184. *See also* bona; fama
Wrightson, Keith, 139–40, 148

Zorzi, Andrea, 11